MAR 2 0 2018

D0222301

The Bizarre World of
Reality Television

The Bizarre World of Reality Television

STUART LENIG

GREENWOOD™

An Imprint of ABC-CLIO, LLC
Santa Barbara, California • Denver, Colorado

Copyright © 2017 by ABC-CLIO, LLC

All rights reserved. No part of this publication may be reproduced, stored in a retrieval system, or transmitted, in any form or by any means, electronic, mechanical, photocopying, recording, or otherwise, except for the inclusion of brief quotations in a review, without prior permission in writing from the publisher.

Library of Congress Cataloging-in-Publication Data

Names: Lenig, Stuart, author.
Title: The bizarre world of reality television / Stuart Lenig.
Description: Santa Barbara, California : Greenwood, 2017. | Includes
    bibliographical references and index.
Identifiers: LCCN 2017018286 (print) | LCCN 2017033383 (ebook) | ISBN
    9781440838552 (eBook) | ISBN 9781440838545 (hardcopy : alk. paper)
Subjects: LCSH: Reality television programs—United States—History and
    criticism.
Classification: LCC PN1992.8.R43 (ebook) | LCC PN1992.8.R43 L47 2017 (print)
    | DDC 791.45/6—dc23
LC record available at https://lccn.loc.gov/2017018286

ISBN: 978-1-4408-3854-5
EISBN: 978-1-4408-3855-2

21 20 19 18 17   1 2 3 4 5

This book is also available as an eBook.

Greenwood
An Imprint of ABC-CLIO, LLC

ABC-CLIO, LLC
130 Cremona Drive, P.O. Box 1911
Santa Barbara, California 93116-1911
www.abc-clio.com

This book is printed on acid-free paper (∞)

Manufactured in the United States of America

Contents

Introduction

Life itself is a quotation.
—Jorge Luis Borges

When the great Argentinian writer Jorge Luis Borges said, "Life itself is a quotation," he was prophetic. What does it mean that "life is a quotation"? The communal grief that rocked American society when Carrie Fisher passed away had to do with Fisher's life representing a profound aspect of our popular culture. Fisher's performance as the plucky Princess Leia galvanized a society that was disturbed by the horrors of the Vietnam War. Two years after the United States ended its involvement with the war, Fisher became a heroine who was willing to fight armies and empires for her personal freedom and the freedom of her citizens. This was an America we could recognize and support. Fisher was the United States that supported freedom. When Borges says life is a quotation, I think he means this: Fisher was Leia, and Leia epitomized an aspect of American freedom and democracy that unified and ennobled us—her life became a quotation. The loss of Ms. Fisher, the actress, reminded us of our ideals and their fragility.

When we say life is a quotation, we mean that life offers things that are simulations, repeatedly fractured pieces, and dislocated aspects of an event. Not only did we have Carrie Fisher as a living embodiment of the ethos of *Star Wars,* we have had countless spin-offs and references to *Star Wars.* People quote dialogue from the films. Characters are turned into toys, and repurposed for a youthful generation. New shows and formats of *Star Wars* erupt (*Clone Wars, Star Wars Rebels, The Force Awakens, Rogue One*), and many other messages—textual and subtextual—emerge from the original ideas in *Star Wars.* Culturally, these items, these "quotations" are now regarded as memes, information that is replicable, carrying central information like DNA, repeated and reused in the creation of powerful new images and messages based on the original quotation but transformed and adjusted in innumerable ways. These memes become new again with every reiteration. What a person has done in the past can reappear as a living ghost that haunts us at every corner. *Rogue One* did this trick very effectively by having a cybergenerated version of Grand Moff Tarkin in the preceedings, even though the actor who played this character, Peter Cushing, had been gone for many years. Memory interacts with the meme and helps it to penetrate our consciousness.

Life as a quotation does not only take place in movies. We can journey to TV Land and see an episode of *Leave It to Beaver.* Beaver and Wally are typical kids making lots of bad moves. Their mother puts them right, and their father wanders into the house, mostly befuddled. Fast forward fifty years, and the *Beaver* meme is actively replayed in contemporary reality television. In MTV's pastiche of family sit-coms *The Osbournes*, Kelly and Jack Osbourne are also headstrong and wayward children. They have a strong mother in Sharon Osbourne, and they even possess the requisite befuddled father in patriarch Ozzy Osbourne. Reality television is one form of a meme, a quotation from our haunted television past.

Reality television exists as a quotation of our life experience (dating shows), our avocational activities (the Food Network and HGTV), our competitive capitalist culture (*Survivor, Big Brother, Real World*), or our experience of television itself (*The Hills, Hell's Kitchen*). Reality programming replicates something from the past, something we have seen, done, or experienced in the past, only now it is being projected back at us through television, the ultimate doppelgänger.

More than just a revival of past ideas, reality television is a pungent device for reflecting current images of the media specifically how the media depicts people and society. Reality can be thought of as a dark mirror of our behavior and attitudes toward the world around us. In this way, reality programming is not unlike the British speculative fiction anthology series *Black Mirror*. This dark show produced by Charlie Brooker debuted on Britain's Channel Four in 2011 and offered stories each week that discussed some unintended consequence of our heavily saturated media environment. Images of people over-connected to media stimulus presented a horrific world of doom and gloom. While reality TV does not necessarily present the darkest aspects of humanity, such shows offer multiple perspectives on ways of operating and navigating a highly technological and surveillance-driven society. MTV's *Pimp My Ride* offers a loving discussion of urban Americans and their love affair with cars. HGTV's *Love It or List It* pits a real estate agent against a renovation expert to see whether a house can be remodeled or must be abandoned to accommodate the needs of a growing family. *Shark Tank* explores the manner in which businesses are born and grow and gain adherents and win investors. *The Bachelor* explores our complex relationship to coupling and fairy-tale romances that are, more often than not, matters of compromise and hard work. Each program is a reflection of some aspect of individual or collective psyches, and how those reflections indicate our relationship to the society at large.

Perhaps you do not believe that this transformation of our personal lives, this psychological channeling of our experiences through a television medium is happening. Media critic Mark Andrejevic argues it is happening, and it is a main strategy of reality television. He writes that one of the more popular recent permutations of the reality genre is "the rehabilitation of faded stars who agree to turn their lives into reality shows" (Andrejevic, *Reality TV: The Work of Being Watched* 2004, 10). Most famously, MTV struck gold by purging Ozzy Osbourne of his dark demons and restaging his life as a reality show about a buzzed, zombified celebrity dad (the Ozzman) crawling around the house in a stupor while his kids, Jack and Kelly, and his wife, Sharon, proceeded to rule the house and settle arcane family disputes and lackluster domestic squabbles. Here, life was a quotation of Osbourne's more famous and flamboyant career as a professional hard rocker. The show revealed the most satanic things about Osbourne to be the bratty nature of his kids and the goofy medical regime he employed to maintain his hectic touring and performance schedule. What evolved from the program was a fairly consistent and friendly portrayal of upper-class, privileged lifestyles. Osbourne arrived as a postmodern *Father Knows Best*, complete with wise fatherly sayings, polite and often unintelligible ramblings, and a penchant for being guided down the hallway by his stalwart and trusty wife, Sharon.

The Fall and Rise of Reality Programming

Several texts are beginning to situate reality programming in some sort of aesthetic space. Susan Murray and Laurie Ouellette's *Reality TV: Remaking Television Culture* is one of the anthologies that seeks to make sense of this large, growing, and often unwieldy genre. Murray and Ouellette, along with others, point toward its emerging raison d'être. There are many competing theories and ideas about reality programming, why it appeared, and why it has flowered in recent years.

An obvious reason for its appearance was an attempt to reduce operating costs for programming. Reality television responded to pressure on publically held corporations to produce more profit for the stations and stockholders. Performance mediums, by their nature, are expensive, labor-intensive businesses, and the use of real subjects, real people, and quasi-documentary events reduced the costs of gathering and producing programming by diminishing the use of professional writers and performers. Further, producers like *Survivor*'s Mark Burnett could further underwrite shows and production costs by making subcontractor deals with performers, sponsoring companies, and direct tie-ins (vacation companies, airlines, tourist bureaus, food vendors, and the like) to further reduce network and station costs.

Another factor was space. Not only was production expensive for television producers, the necessity of having tracts of land, sound stages, and other costly units of operation could be reduced by using outside studios and facilities for filming. For example, HGTV extends its programming and reduces costs by allowing many of its programs to be commissioned to subcontracting studios in the United States and Canada.

Another factor was the way Hollywood has long been perceived of as an elite bastion of star actors. People complained that Hollywood and its institutions were remote and insular from most Americans. This prompted a form of programming that was perceived as more democratic. If shows featured wealthy and remote Hollywood personalities, audiences throughout the nation sensed a strong disconnect between their image and those found in the nation's less-celebrated regions. By utilizing real people from across the national panorama, people felt more empowered and more likely to relate to the programming. Auditions for shows like *Dancing with the Stars*, *The Voice*, and *American Idol* were held nationally and enfranchised a generation that felt they would never appear on television. Further, as television production spread throughout the nation, particularly through means such as YouTube—which allowed the broadcast and publishing of programming from anywhere to anywhere—the democratizing power, if not the actual monetary clout of the major networks, proliferated throughout the country.

Democratization worked in another way. Previously, the control of television production exercised by networks began to break down through cable (although most of the major networks owned much of the major cable programming) and changed the structure of television. If network programming depended on several sharply defined genres, the new television model featured more diverse programming and allowed more crossovers of genres and style. The advent of Adult Swim, FX, Fox, and Comedy Central proliferated cartoons that appeared to be kid stuff but worked in a more cerebral and insightful fashion to craft sharp and vengeful adult parodies of the commercial world. This process of diversification not only changed the places where television was made but also changed content; means of distribution; ways of receiving and spreading television; and notions about what constituted a program, a series, and a release schedule. Diversification unchained a mass of production energy. Ben Travers, writing for the *Indiewire,* quoted a network executive as saying, "For 50 years there were 60 or 70 scripted original series in America. There will be about 350 this year, and probably 400 next year" (Travers 2014). Industry leaders are worried that there is a glut of programming. What ·the new, unchained, and diversified market of television is creating is the sort of niche marketing that inspired the indie music scene. This now takes music from the hands of a few production companies to the thousands of independent artists and companies that produce music, artists, bands, records, and music media in a dizzying array and assortment of formats from vinyl, to retro mix tapes, to CDs, and Internet downloads. Certainly the television market (if it still can be called just television) has changed and evolved, but there is a vibrancy and diversity unfathomable a mere 20 years ago, and reality television has been a part of that explosion.

On one end of the scale, the spread of this new diverse televisual landscape has led to a willingness for many Americans to endure, and in fact enjoy, extreme levels of scrutiny and often derision in their quest for fame and to be a televisual star. Many featured performers on *American Idol* have opened themselves up to vile critiques, and stars like Honey Boo Boo and Kim Kardashian are joked about and become subjects for ridicule. For Honey Boo Boo, it is her family's poverty, ill-bred manners, and relentless upholding of Southern, rural American culture that much of the nation vilifies. For Kardashian, it is the conspicuous consumption of fame and the vacuousness of the personas that quest for and claim fame in our culture. For whatever reason, Americans have embraced errant visibility and notoriety even when, as in the case of *Kate and Jon Plus 8*, that fame leads to the family and their pursuits being subjects for late-night jokes.

In a society so beset by *1984* paranoia, reality programming has restored a spirit of DIY optimism. This optimism is widely seen in HGTV shows such as the *Rehab Addict,* which portrays a plucky woman buying and refurbishing homes through intensive self-effort to rebuild, remodel, and restore living environments. For the *Rehab Addict*, the show is not only a challenge, but also a life's work to make places better and to make a profit in the process. Other shows produce a feel-good effect for viewers by watching someone improve their capabilities and skills. Martha Stewart and Rachael Ray sell the mantra of DIY crafting, decorating, and cooking as a form of personal empowerment. Perhaps a show that is a double-edged sword of happy family values but also seems extremely bizarre in its normalizing of odd behaviors is *19 Kids and Counting*. The Duggar family has 19 kids, and their kids are courting and having kids very publicly. Yet simultaneously, the household appears to be a serial circus in which the family is loaned out to make enough money to keep the family stable. While the program promotes insular, fundamentalist, family values, it also functions as a gateway for the most permissive, intrusive, media-dominated household in the United States. In a sense, it is a disruption of the very family structure it purports to uphold. Sharing values of the freak show, the Duggars delight in showing viewers how they will feed and clothe such a broad range of family members.

How does anyone live in a state of constant surveillance? Imagine incorporating surveillance and eliminating any last vestiges of privacy left in the United States. Is there a need for a new right in the Bill of Rights: the right to maintaining one's privacy, the right to avoid or deflect surveillance, and the right to reclaims one's anonymity? In recent years, families like the Duggars have all but lost their privacy through the need to film so frequently to cover family expenses. Further, when *MTV* was producing *The Osbournes,* one of the children refused to be filmed and was nearly completely left out of the show. In *Jon and Kate Plus 8*, the family pressures of filming and being on display perhaps helped to ruin the couple's marriage. The scrutiny of reality television has undone many couples who see themselves and their spouses in a different way under the bright lights. The role of privacy in emerging reality television ethics has yet to be determined, and the question remains whether one can have wide-ranging reality programming and still maintain any sense of privacy for participants in reality television.

Consider the factor of globalization. Though for some the idea of globalization is a fearful prospect of taking jobs from one culture and moving them to a lower-paying culture, the true effects of globalization are far broader and more enabling than disabling. For one thing, there are international producers who now produce brands of reality shows across borders and countries. There are versions of *Survivor, Big Brother*, and *American Idol* across the globe. Programming such as the slow television phenomenon from Norway and other parts of Europe has begun to translate to the United States in shows that are often quieter, more reflective, and more of a meditation than an entertainment. Clever comedy-based programming such as *Whose Line Is It Anyway?* illustrates that improv travels easily from one market to another. Programs like *Most Haunted* and *Ghost Hunters* illustrate the concept that paranormal experience is popular around the globe. Finally, competition and game shows seem to be a worldwide phenomenon from Japan to the United States, although the American version of *Survivor* and *The Amazing Race* demand some sort of grand payoff in the end for months of torturous effort. In Japan, sometimes a journey of love or the chance to compete are reasons enough to participate. Many of the contestants on Japanese game competitions do not win anything and suffer excruciating and insulting tortures for the trouble and the effort of being featured on television. They often end up ridiculed nationally and penniless as well.

While we think television itself is changing, it could be that a component of our media use is simply undergoing a metamorphosis. Something that serves the new generation and emerging reality shows equally is an addiction to the Web. Audiences today expect to communicate with their peers through the Net. Further, they make the assumption that, since the people on the Web are like them, simply real people, they feel a desire, in fact almost a compulsion, to meet, greet, and carry on Web dialogues about the characters, situation, and shows and the way the program might end. This change not only has served reality programming well but also has been adapted by *The Walking Dead* with its talk show *The Talking Dead*, which discusses the show after the fictional program ends. Fictional and partially scripted television merge in this hybrid of fanboy gushing and zombie-apocalypse drama. AMC has been successful in a two-screen experience: while viewers watch the show, there is also a popular Web adjunct to the video programming. Many viewers have reported that they now work on a computer, a phone, or a laptop during their viewing of programming on television, and reality programming has put the Web into play as a central mechanism to communicate with shows, producers, and cast members. On game shows like *American Idol*, people can vote for their favorite artist. On shows like *Survivor*, audience members can communicate to producers who they would like to see win the show and who they do not support. Interactivity also extends to suggestions and ideas the show can feed to viewers. HGTV makes resources and techniques available to people trying to fix their homes after watching a show that features players remaking a residence.

Perhaps a less-discussed phenomenon but another along with surveillance that presents a darker side of reality programming is the idea of voyeurism. In other words, by watching a reality show, aren't we, like Hitchcock's viewers, watching women threatened by maniacs, participating in a lurid and unseemly act of voyeurism? Aren't we, by watching, leading to a nation of surveillance, of obsession, and of stalking? Think of shows like the humorously named *Naked and Afraid*, clearly aptly titled because the participants are often naked and afraid. Though the genitals are fogged, we watch two terrified and naked people, one man and one woman, try to exist for 21 days, three weeks, without anything but a fire starter and a canvas bag. It is a nasty voyeur's party to watch the episodes. Are we doing something wrong and pernicious by watching such shows, and are we helping the framers and producers change us into a group of watchers who feast on the anxieties and efforts of players who are active and making a conscious effort? Is the lesson of watching reality television that we as Americans aren't up to doing ourselves but must watch others do for us? Isn't this the same sadistic pleasure we achieve through watching others in competitive sports? We don't play football, but we watch other, younger men play for us, and take the hits that we don't want to risk taking.

The final issue of reality television is the issue of reality itself. How real is it? How real do we want it to be, and can we distinguish the real from the fake? Over 100 years ago, when the Lumière brothers showed their first cinematograph production in November of 1895, people were frightened when the train approached from a distance on screen. They thought it was a real train headed for them. Are we returning to a time when television has become so smart that we don't really know reality from illusion? Certainly people see programming like HGTV and think people are buying house while we watch. Yet, despite the fact that people may be buying, it would be impossible for the camera crew to sit waiting for families to sift through weeks or months of house hunting. Yes, many homes on HGTV are pre-bought and then others, often not-for-sale models, are presented as potential rivals to craft a real, and obviously a more-dramatic, situation. Many have noticed that couples rarely pick the best house at the end of a program like *House Hunters*. That is because they must select the house they already own, and the dream house that audience members drool over is probably not on the market. MTV and other stations rely on professional young actors for many of their "reality" programs to play the charming and attractive young people on the show. They may already be what the show calls for, but the acting skills needed to make their contestants believable comes in handy on such shows. For instance, Zac Efron appeared on an MTV dating show prior to his Disney fame in *High School Musical*.

What Has Inspired the Recent Resurgence of Reality?

An interesting aspect of the reinvention of reality programs arose through the philosophical lens of postmodernism. Postmodern philosophy was linked to media studies, cultural studies, global perspectives, and the sense of contemporary society having exhausted itself. After years of stations and networks following prescribed formats, audiences began to drift away from traditional programming due to its staleness. With profits stagnant and audiences disaffected, reality programming reduced costs (no scripts, no stars, and prepaid programs underwritten by advertisers) and invited new content that audiences found more like their own lives. Shows, programming, and media began to collapse in on themselves. Old genres such as cop shows or sitcoms seemed to have run their course. Many have argued that it was the sameness and repetition of these shows that remained uniformly procedural from *Dragnet* to *Law and Order* that condemned them to declining audience shares. An example of the repetition was the transformation of the vigorous *Star Trek* franchise, which had been a vibrant aspect of televised space opera for 40 years. Following the original series, the franchise was reborn with a new captain and crew in *Star Trek: The Next Generation*. Then an offshoot, *Deep Space Nine*, was created on a stationary space outpost where people gathered. The show featured an intercultural mix of races, ethnic groups, and political views. This was followed by the most far-out and strange version of the show, *Star Trek Voyager*, an adventurous series that cast *Star Trek* 75,000 light years from home and placed the program in the bizarre, otherworldly, strange, dark, and mysterious territory of the Delta Quadrant. This arrived as a sort of space noir series. But the millennial *Star Trek: Enterprise* suffered from prequel problems in which everything that was to be rendered in the future was already known. Just as the modern era seemed to have encapsulated all time through television and other media, so television condemned its fictional formats to unending repetition. Similarly, *Star Wars* condemned its prequels to dull story lines in films like *Phantom Menace, Attack of the Clones,* and *Revenge of the Sith,* all critiqued as markedly inferior repetitions of the first three films in the cycle. In essence, *Enterprise* and *Star Wars* both asked the question: if the next installment is known, what surprises can make prequels new? In the end, they simply retold the same fables, only now the shows produced an ennui and weariness. Reality television responded to the fatigue by revamping traditional forms of programming, and working to make tired television structures vibrant once more.

In this sense reality programming provided an antidote for programming that had become habitual, tired, exhausted, enervated. Unlike formulaic heroes who did the same things, *Survivor* players innovated, responded to ground conditions, and introduced situational ethics into solutions to intractable team problems. If individual heroes were untenable in an age in which presidents, stars, and athletes were flawed role models, then reality television brought teams to life's issues. Perhaps teams working as social engineers might resolve life's intractable problems. So reality television may have found a way out of an endless loop of recycling.

In the postmodern age, (a term that means "following the modern era"), there is a belief expressed by French media philosopher Jean Baudrillard that reality may be laden with simulations. Baudrillard saw that real things were in opposition with simulations. Some simulations are harmless. A robot is a pale comparison to a real human. As our ability to make simulations grows better, a stage-two simulation is harder to detect and often resembles the real version more completely. At the third stage, the real and the unreal merge, and the viewer can't tell the difference. Baudrillard describes Los Angeles as this sort of unreal place, saying, "Los Angeles is encircled by these 'imaginary stations' which feed reality, reality-energy, to a town whose mystery is precisely that it is nothing more than a network of endless unreal circulation: a town of fabulous proportions, but without space or dimensions" (Baudrillard 1992, 154). For Baudrillard, Los Angeles is a simulation. In such a world, a reality show proposes to show us real life but may only show us a simulation of that life. If Baudrillard was right about Los Angeles as a simulation of a city, why not a whole genre of television that simulates that idea of reality?

For example, MTV's *Real World* acts as a simulation of adulthood. Teens are placed in an apartment to act out. Usually, their dreams, their vision of themselves, and their love lives implode, but that is their reality. *Real World*, or Un-*Real World's* longevity attests to the show's ability to present a working model of reality that teens can view from the safety of their parents' basement. It is a real life—at least in their minds.

In the movie *Dark City*, the victims of this Philip K. Dick–style postapocalyptic world live in a reality that is recreated every night by a group of mysterious aliens, the Strangers, who go about "tuning" and revising their construction of the city. Nothing stays the same, but the residents accept the changed city as their new reality. So reality television reconfigures our new world. and, despite the varieties of reality presented, most people accept reality television as, at least, a version of reality. While Baudrillard sees simulations of reality as a problem for society, other authors use other lenses. Italian author Umberto Eco, philosopher and novelist, describes our era as a new middle age in which the monastic life is recreated to help us accept change and lock it out. Reality television helps to engineer this hermetic, cloistered, and alone world but joined via phones, screens, and personal media. Little is shared and communal, while at the same time, everything is global. Eco writes, "The middle ages preserved in its way the heritage of the past but not through hibernation, rather through a constant retranslation and reuse; it was an immense work of bricolage, balanced amongst nostalgia, hope, and despair" (Eco 1986, 84). Eco thinks we reuse the past in reorganized reality programs. *The Bachelor* reconfigures romance for our Internet age, only now we get to vote on who the player should marry.

Finally, historiographic reimaginings re-create our culture through reality television. Linda Hutcheon writes that postmodern fiction is "historigraphic metafiction (and) is written today in the context of a serious contemporary interrogating of the nature of representation in historiography" (Hutcheon 2002, 232). In other words, today's writing questions history and claims of the real. Is the past simply a fiction that we told ourselves? Reality television is a part of the questioning that Hutcheon argues is in literature. Is *Real World* really questioning what it means to be young today? Are shows like *The Voice* and *American Idol* contesting the idea of stardom? Do programs like *Duck Dynasty*, *Storage Wars*, and *American Restoration* dissect maleness? Are such questions overreaching the import of reality programming, or are we avoiding the subtext of a popular genre? Superheroes were once thought superficial, but there are now books on Batman and the Hulk. These subtextual implications are implicit in society. In 1992, *Buffy the Vampire Slayer* took a teen vampire show and explored teen relationships and visions of the grunge generation. So, like the Strangers in *Dark City,* our society is constantly reconfiguring and retuning our society and how it views itself, and reality television is a large part of that interrogation process.

MTV's groundbreaking *Real World*, while setting up parameters for interaction that involved contrivance and staging, mixed the real and acted segments until the audience could not determine what was real or a constructed meme of reality. In such a matrix, the subterfuge and the real cease to be separate things and merge. Baudrillard explains, "The automaton has no other destiny than to be ceaselessly compared to living man—so as to be more natural than him, of which he is the ideal figure" ("Automation of the Robot" 1991,178). Here Baudrillard is discussing robots, but the figures on *Real World* are as fictional as the house they inhabit. The house is borrowed, the students are reality "actors," auditionees who play students. The audience watching isn't living its youth, but imagining it projected on MTV. An example occurred on *The Osbournes,* in which Jack Osbourne, son of Black

Sabbath singer Ozzy Osbourne, accompanied his family to his father's performance in Las Vegas. However, upon arrival, Osbourne and his friends sat avoiding the concert, in their rooms watching episodes of *Teletubbies,* the charming and surreal British television show aimed at preschool children and filled with cooing, ahs, oohs, and yahs. Osbourne and his friends preferred a lethargic period of languid television viewing to watching his father's concert, and the audience witnessed their dissociative behavior. Veronica Hollinger meditated on this generational fascination with technology, often passive technology, in her article, "Cybernetic Deconstructions: Cyberpunk and Postmodernism." She writes, "Common to most of the texts which have become associated with cyberpunk is an overwhelming fascination, at once celebratory and anxious, with technology, and its immediate— that is, unmediated—effects upon human being-in-the-world, a fascination which sometimes spills over into the problematizing of 'reality' itself" (Hollinger 1991, 205). Young Osbourne represented a complete collapse of the power of the real in favor of a devotion to media. The crew filmed the disconnect: Ozzy performing to thousands; Jack watching *Teletubbies.* The audience saw that things were twice removed. Jack preferred TV to his dad, and MTV, representing youth culture, rather than filming Ozzy's concert preferred to focus on Jack's viewing habits. It was doubly ironic since, ostensibly, MTV is (or was) a music television station. The reality show *The Osbournes* showed the network has opted away from the baby boomer generation (circa 1970) that watched Black Sabbath and hard rock acts of the 1970s for the aesthetics of Jack Osbourne and his friends, who disregard Ozzy Osbourne's music in favor of the somnambulistic pleasures of the esoteric, preverbal, cooing, and cuddling expressed by the world of *Teletubbies.*

For many, the growth of reality programming explores the complex economics of television. Many consumers believe that television is related to quality or skill in programming. While these considerations are important to programming, programming is merely a content mechanism designed to make people watch in order to sell them things. In Victoria O'Donnell's *Television Criticism* she explains, "The common wisdom of television is that its primary goal is to deliver consumers to advertisers" (O'Donnell 2007, 24). Television, radio, the Internet, newspapers, magazines, and most mass media require advertising or underwriting revenue to stay in business and to continue to deliver product. While public good would be great, television has no obligation to perform a public service. Government regulation strives to (1) make television accountable to the public and (2) to provide reliable public information, but largely television is a media business, which discourses with federal and local government, but mostly is a business. If it does not remain profitable, it does not survive. As O'Donnell puts it, "In other words, television sells audiences to advertisers for billions of dollars" (2012, 24).

On Halloween of 1938, director/actor/auteur Orson Welles dramatized a version of H. G. Wells's *War of the Worlds,* panicking the United States and creating a public outcry that this child (Welles was 22 at the time) was playing with the media for manipulative purposes and disregarded the public trust. The show sent terrified people leaping from buildings and prompted visions of the apocalypse. Welles was called to Washington to explain his actions and account for the public panic and furor. Welles feigned a lack of awareness of his impact. He knew radio replicated a convincing reality. He apologized to Congress, and the government became more involved in watchdogging the public airwaves. The Federal Communications Commission became instrumental in handing out licenses to stations, and, following World War II, there was a wild frenzy of newly commissioned stations. However, Welles's experiment in terror pointed out that our free airwaves could be used to excite, stimulate, and (most importantly) manipulate the gullible public into believing something. Welles and others proved that the media could be very powerful in directing what people would think and how they saw and interpreted reality. The 2016 election of Donald Trump as president surprised many pundits, but President Trump clearly understood the dynamics of being a reality-program star and how his real, authentic voice spoke to millions of disenfranchised and disaffected American voters. By spouting common themes (America first, American jobs, closing borders, and making America great again) Trump was able to speak directly to a populace that had largely been ignored by more sophisticated media. The impact was that Trump's campaign had grassroots support from people who felt that they had no voice, but that Trump the populist did actually speak to them and care about their conditions and their daily struggles. Trump was a powerful reminder that reality television can be a significant way to bind viewers to a new form of DIY media.

So stations fight for ratings not because they wish to present programs to more people but because they want to deliver more viewers to advertisers. There are subtle means of advertising. Sometimes an entire program is an infomercial for a sponsored product. In early broadcasting, hosts acted as advertisers. The host and the program added their credibility to the product. In recent years, television has moved to direct promotions. Racecar drivers wear clothing embroidered with sponsor names. Many act as living ads for Nike or other sports products. Programs like *Survivor* have found ways to embed ads and products in the program itself. A camera may come to rest on a player drinking a Coca-Cola or Pepsi, and the audience is never sure whether that product was a personal choice of the player or a subtle advertisement.

The power of delivering customers to advertisers is undeniable. CBS, which has often been often designated as the quality leader in network television, was once the ratings leader in the late 1960s due to the success of *Andy Griffith, Beverly Hillbillies*, and *Gomer Pyle, USMC*. All of these popular shows featured poor (at least initially), rural, and mostly Southern characters. An advertising consultant informed CBS that, despite the popularity of their programs, they were not bringing a quality demographic to the market. That is, advertisers did not want poor, Southern customers coming to their stores. They wanted urban, big-city, young professionals to attend their new malls. Within five years, all the agrarian comedies were replaced by cop shows (*Mannix, Kojak,* and *Cannon*) and urban, professional comedies like *Newhart* and *Mary Tyler Moore*. Similarly, demographic markets have played a role in the rise of reality television faire. Programmers have noted that reality programming like *The Bachelor, Real World,* or *Next* can connect with a younger demographic of people who are experiencing such life issues as living on their own, choosing a mate, and dating. While these issues may be on the minds of older viewers, marketing departments have targeted younger demographics as desiring the centrality of these issues.

The emphasis on demographics is an outgrowth of a highly pressurized environment that generates profit. While profit has always been an important aspect of television, the emphasis is greater today. Years ago, individuals and small groups owned media companies and were content with modest profits and high costs. Today, the companies that run media are large, global, publicly held, and answer to stockholders, and they expect huge profits, high revenues, big ratings, and, most importantly, low costs. Jennifer Pozner described the situation succinctly in *Reality Bites Back* saying, "Today, the driving factor for all corporate media production is to turn tidy profits for the tiny handful of mega-corporations that own the vast majority of media outlets and control the bulk of what we are given to watch, see, and hear on TV and radio, in movies, video games and more" (2010, 274).

Pozner points out that demographics, ratings, and another key factor—the cost to produce a program—determine which shows will be shown and what audiences will be urged to view. Thus, reality television has become the love child of the networks and television, in general, because, compared with fictional television, costs can be far lower and profits much higher. Pozner explains that the game changer here was the advent of *Survivor,* a program that paid for itself before it aired. She remarked that few at CBS had any faith in the premise that was "like *Gilligan's Island* with the Skipper and Mary Ann eating bugs" (2010, 281). What sold the show was the cost factor. Pozner writes, "Producer Mark Burnett explained that instead of paying high-priced actors and a team of union writers, advertisers would pay the network for a starring role" (2010, 282). Even in 2000, Burnett's innovation was not that new. Back in 1980, MTV pioneered showing free promotional videos of groups and their albums 24-hours-a-day only interrupted by low-cost and eminently replaceable VJs and endless commercials. The videos were free because the record companies wanted to sell albums and later CDs, pimple creams, video games, clothing, and cars to a youthful 12–34-year-old white male demographic, a group that had the most money (either theirs or their parents) in the United States. MTV's model was quickly replicated by MTV stations across the globe. Burnett's scheme with *Survivor* was something quite similar: let the players work for free, hire a film crew, and pocket revenue. Burnett had all the production costs for his traumatic travelogue covered by companies who had placed products in the program. Soft drinks and snack companies speculated that product placements in the show would take off when reality stars ate their products to fortify themselves for the extreme challenges of *Survivor.* In the end, Burnett sold the show, provided low-cost programming for CBS, and allowed himself and the station to enjoy massive profits. It may not have been quality programming, but it was profitable.

The goal of linking audiences to the fate of program characters has been growing even in non-reality television. On the fourth and fifth seasons of *Walking Dead,* the program added the technique of what the producers called a *story sync,* in which the segments of the program would be connected to audience-participation questions and insights. The idea of making shows interactive through the Net created new ways to build relationships with program fans. Aside from connecting the audience directly to the program, responses to questions brought in marketing data concerning which segments of the program retained viewers. If more people responded to questions in segment three, then that segment was more pleasing to viewers. There were graphic novel images and flashbacks to remind the audience of previous episodes and storylines. The idea was that the viewers would be more connected to the program if they connected to it via two screens. In fact, two-screen viewing of video programming is now common and routine. Many busy families watch video while connected to phones, tablets, and laptops.

Such transformations provide the viewer with a semblance of control, or at least interaction with the program. Shows such as *The Bachelor, Survivor,* and *Dancing with the Stars* offer, at a minimum, interactive Web sites in which additional information about the program, the characters, the week's events, and in some instances whole episodes can be rebroadcast and reviewed. Like David Letterman's long-running joke, "I'm David Letterman, your television friend," the producers of reality television are clearly wanting to make television and its programming the viewer's friend. Binding audiences to the lives of show performers provides a sense of unity. For a society of alienated people, popular television shows may constitute the only sort of friendship some possess.

Henry Jenkins, in his analysis of *American Idol,* entitled "Buying into American Idol," argues, "*American Idol* was from the start not simply a television program but a transmedia franchise" (2006, 344). Jenkins argues that the advertisers, producers, and markets that produce and push reality television host Web sites, viewer voting sites, and fan Facebook pages only for economic reasons and rarely look more deeply into the motivations or longings of their audiences held captive by reality stars, reality dilemmas, and projected reality lives. Jenkins fears that some corporations do not carefully guard the public trust in their marketing or brands, music, and people, and the audience can feel betrayed by the program and walk away from its contents and smooth packaging.

Mark Andrejevic argues that we are learning a new "Visceral Literacy," as he refers to the new televisual model ("Visual Literacy" 2009, 321). He argues that television teaches a new level of voyeurism. If the programs present images that presumably may be faked or manipulated, he suggests that reality television's interactive mechanisms may allow audiences to see behind the curtain. Thus, audience members believe they are seeing a new, truthful portrayal composed of screen image and facts/details mined from the Net, a companion Web site, or a phone app. An interactive call/response mechanism linking programming and the Net leash the viewer. These show disciples become inseparable from the show and live it continuously.

Amber Watts, in her article "Melancholy, Merit and Merchandise," discussed the audience-participation shows of the 1940s and 1950s. Watts's analysis determined that audiences 60 years ago were as interactive as audiences today and that they built close relationships with the subjects of reality- and documentary-format game shows. The most spectacular aspect of *Queen for a Day* was its reliance on melancholy to allure its fan base. Watts writes that "instead of being rewarded for skill or knowledge, women won for having the saddest life story, expressing the greatest need, and generating the most audience applause and sympathy" (2008, 304). We might think that a character on *Survivor* or *Big Brother* is a sad person and deserves to be voted off the show, but rarely do they tug at our emotions. Rarely do we feel their pain. In the 1950s, *Queen for a Day* brought onstage players and the viewers to tears.

Reality television stimulates emotions about characters often manufactured by producers. On *The Voice*, the producers have cast Blake Shelton as the hero; Christina Aguilera as the nice star; Pharrell Williams as the fun, wacky, odd ball; and Adam Levine as the villain, complete with slick hair, snarky retorts, and obvious tattooing. In the show itself, the judges are nominally kind and fair to all players, but, in routines that appear to be scripted moments, Levine snarls at Shelton, who blithely ignores the sour pop star. Their disagreements are ill motivated and arrive from no context. They serve to create some mild tension in a show that is a nominal hug fest of performers, coaches, and novices working to mutual betterment. The audiences are attracted to the supportive culture of the show, and the most difficult scenes for the viewing audience are those turbulent moments when a singer is sent home after a long bout of competition. The audience identifies with the singer, the judge, the competition, and especially the struggle. Clearly *The Voice*, with its epic audition cycle, its lengthy competition format, and its eventual dismissal of most singers parallels the life experiences of many Americans who have lived through the long and difficult Middle Eastern wars (2003–2013), have endured the great recession of 2008, and have empathy with the contestants. Many Americans have experienced batteries of interviews, harsh competition, and derogatory critiques from employers in an era when employment is difficult to obtain and competition is keen for each available job. Like the survivors on *The Voice*, many Americans identify with years of struggle and anxiety, and the program taps into the audience's angst at issues of acceptance, validation, and social scolding. *The Voice* explores the complexities of public criticism, life coaching, participation in a society that often marginalizes and abandons the most vulnerable, and issues of self-esteem, self-criticism, and even self-loathing. Leaving a player behind on the show is tantamount to abandonment or divorcing a family.

Watts addressed an even darker form of audience participation in the 1950s. According to Watts, 1950s television networks devoted an hour of afternoon programming per day to programs with a heavy audience-participation component. Targeted audiences were women. It has been suggested that television for women may have been engineered to re-enslave women who had nominally escaped captivity during the war years. Feminist stirrings were met with resistance by the paternalistic television networks, which presented alluring and engaging day programs for women. The intent was bondage, not pleasure.

One of the most disturbing programs was CBS's *Stand up and Be Counted*. Guests on the show faced a life-changing dilemma, and the audience voted on the top forms of action to advise. The player would go home and consider the audience's advice. Watts explains that the guests "received prizes based on their choices" (2008, 304). People even sent letters in describing their personal and intimate problems, hoping they could win time being a contestant on the show. The set of the show was a porch with chairs, a friendly space for the forum, like people walking through the neighborhood and receiving assistance on the front porch. Wayne Munson, in his book, *All Talk: The Talk Show in Media Culture,* discusses the political dimensions of the interaction of the audience with the guests. Munson wrote that the host, Robert Russell, would speak from the porch, "Saying that 'the American way of life' involves dropping in on a troubled neighbor and helping her make a decision" (1993, 54). The show fearlessly told people what to do with their lives. Munson argued that the show's ideologies "are linked not only with patriotism but with promotion, consumption, and an implicit cure for the 1950s housewife's domestic isolation"(55). While the audiences of *Stand Up and Be Counted* were swayed by helping others, offering advice, participating in the community, and a sense of patriotism, modern audiences share a different set of values. Today audiences look to reality to increase a sense of self worth or perhaps to reduce a sense of isolation felt by many modern people. Some may have a sense of identification with the character or see themselves in the struggling players of *Iron Chef, The Bachelor,* or *Survivor*. Some may suffer from poor body image and see themselves transformed from a goose to a swan. Others might see themselves as decision makers and watch *19 Kids and Counting* to see how big families manage. They might scoff at *Honey Boo Boo* as a dark reminder of the perils of bad parenting.

The globalization of world media is having profound, subtle, and dramatic effects on programming visions of reality. A family in Tibet may be exposed to the same programming as a family in Chicago, Illinois, or Cape Town, South Africa. How the shows are produced and, more importantly, how the shows are decoded through the lenses of different cultures, languages, and ideologies can make a show that appears comic, inconsequential, and family faire into something controversial, serious, and adult. Media theorist Stuart Hall diagnosed the complication of transglobal and intercultural programming in his article "Encoding/Decoding." Hall argues that the messages can offer at least three different meanings without applying any complex theory mechanisms. The first meaning is the dominant hegemonic meaning, or what most people would be expected to read in a message. A second meaning is a negotiated version of the message. Hall defines this as it "contains a mixture of adaptive and oppositional elements: it acknowledges the legitimacy of the hegemonic definitions to make the grand significations (abstract), while at a more restricted, situational (situated) level, it makes its own ground rules—it operates with exceptions to the rule" (2000, 60). The final way that someone can interpret a message, according to Hall is in "a globally contrary way" (61). That is, the listener reorients the message to give it a totally oppositional slant. Background, ideologies, and conditioning rewrite meaning.

Hall grew up in the Caribbean under British rule and authority, and he saw oppositional readings of messages daily. An example might be the various and contrary positions about Obamacare. The hegemonic and standard vision is that a federalized health-care system would reduce costs and improve access to service. The negotiated decoding would be a more cautious reception suggesting that the program could cause problems, debilitate service, and make wealthy health-care providers monopolies. A third and contrary opinion would be the Fox News version, in which deep mistrust of the president and his policies leads to charges of lying, obliterating free choice, and interfering with capitalist processes. Hall's theory makes no judgment on truth value. The oppositional meaning might be just as true for its audience as the conventional meaning. Think of the era of apartheid in South Africa. The government argued that policies of apartheid were instituted to create order and support the well-being of the people. It was obvious to most in the native African tribal communities that apartheid was a repressive regime that subjugated the native people. So oppositional meanings can hold as much power as conventional meanings.

There are varied views of foreign programming, including Europe's slow television of rail journeys and boat trips filmed in real time. Such programming might engender anger in the United States, where pacing and speed are highly valued aspects of television programming. Another example might be Japanese game shows, which are long on embarrassment, schadenfreude, and voyeurism and short on rewards, might be construed as mean, torturous, and deriding the players. A cultural lens often inscribes meaning for potential audiences.

Philosophically, issues of globalism arrive from theories in Robert Hassan's *The Information Society*. He argues that the world is shrinking and becoming smaller, and this manifests itself through a number of media effects. Hassan sites Frances Cairncross's *The Death of Distance*. Cairncross argues the new global media environment will translate messages through different cultures quickly, leading to more opportunity, sharing of information, and chances to share wealth, capital, and information, all key to improving global life, at least we hope.

Historical Reality and Its Corruption

The concept of reality is one that is often conjectural and different for a variety of viewers. My view of reality is quite different from a person sitting near me. Famously, in the earliest narratives of history from the Greek historian Herodotus, incidents of real events and mythic events are mixed with little discernment of the nature of either event. Herodotus is considered the father of history because he sought a more systematic way of viewing people and events around him. Herodotus traveled widely in his time, but Adam Hart-Davis reminds us that "the work of Herodotus cannot, however, be relied upon as fact. His writing still depended to some extent on oral history and was colored by folklore and tradition" (2012, 102).

Myth has often had a hand in influencing our sense of reality. Ancient people saw bad weather as a reflection of anthropomorphic gods' anger with men.

Christianity and Judaism anthropomorphize interactions of God and man in various Biblical stories. Drama arrived to fictionalize real life and create greater interest for audiences. Greeks spent days watching drama festivals that combined religion, history, and myth into complicated messages. In the Middle Ages, church authorities manipulated truth and persecuted scientists like Galileo and Copernicus to retain control over the populace. As with the Greeks, a curious mixture of faith, fact, and history was manufactured.

In the Renaissance, writers like Shakespeare became self-aware of a literary artist's ability to spin a good tale that might deviate from literal truth but gain power from the implementation of metaphorical logic. Whether Marc Antony really denounced Brutus so effectively in his funeral oration for Julius Caesar is not known, but Shakespeare recognized the value of crafting Antony as a man of principle to discuss ambition and politics in the tempestuous reign of Queen Elizabeth I.

Our philosophical sense of reality was reinforced by the French neoclassical vision of drama required to reflect real life, verisimilitude, and the concept of decorum or respect for conventional authority. Henrik Ibsen and Anton Chekov reinforced the modern vision of realism by demanding that dialogue must conform to real action and that people must play real people. Chekov even had to put up with Konstantin Stanislavski's demands that a real outdoor scene must be complete with real imported crickets to make the nighttime and summer seem entirely real. The inexorable movement toward realism was reinforced by new media, such as photography, that could render the real world clearly and capably. But simultaneously, the forces of yellow journalism in the late 19th century and early 20th century wished to paint the facts with colorful suppositions, gossip, and hearsay and tainted our vision of what is actually real and what is a fantastic vision of reality. Today's reality program is a blend of the fanciful, the traditional sense of what we might assume to be real, staged reality, and even coached and scripted performances. Our reality today can be manipulated by many factors, not limited to photography, including computer processing, such as Photoshop; audio processing, such as Auto-Tune; and a skillful editing of reality performed by a show's producers.

The Fall and Rise of Reality

The millennium brought a sweeping change toward reality programming over conventional fictional television. Allison Slade, in her *Reality Television: Oddities of Culture,* argued that the form had been dormant but was rediscovered in the last 10 years. Slade writes, "From *Queen for a Day* to *I'd Like to See* or [Allen] Funt's *Candid Camera,* viewers have long been interested in watching the real, the normal, pictures of everyday life displayed on the small screen" (2014, vii). For Slade, the importance and popularity of reality television isn't new at all. David Escoffery in *How Real Is Reality TV?* argued that the success of the genre lay in its ability to produce a real-seeming representation of the world. He writes, "In the case of a reality show, we are given a representation (a TV program created for entertainment purposes) which purports to present the 'truth' (the unscripted real activities of real people)" (2006, 2). Richard Huff's *Reality Television* argues for different reasons for the emergence of a new reality programming. He writes that "some reality television draws loads of family viewing and a majority of the genre appeals to younger, more elusive viewers" (2006, 5).

However, whether watching real people, a representation of apparent reality, or a programming for a specific demographic, the genre that was popular in the 1950 faded but has returned. Why did it disappear and reappear so abruptly? Consider finances. In the 1950s, television was sparsely financed, and sponsors controlled a show's continuance. Stations needed to sell advertising or replace programming. Today's reality programming responded to rising costs and diminishing profits at networks. Free television carried by networks still depended on advertising dollars. With production costs and talent costs (actors, writers, producers, directors, and studio time) costing more, making income was increasingly difficult. Shows like *Survivor* offered handsome programming at a bargain price. Money saved could underwrite expensive shows like *CSI*, which offered attractive lighting, design, stars, music, writing, and editing. Otherwise, more profits could be pocketed for stockholders.

Another factor may be that television evolved from a one-directional media flow dictated by stations, producers, and sponsors to a format utilizing interactivity and democratic choice. Programming on DVDs, video stores, Redbox, and emerging online services like Hulu, Amazon Prime, Comcast, and Netflix were displacing the networks' centrality as arbiters of viewing. When interactive models were emerging, reality programming—featuring audience voting, two-screen viewing, special Web content, and fan sites—could produce a perfect platform for a more democratized viewing experience. Programmers saw real people in reality programs as a vehicle to get private audiences connected to programming. These shows lacked alienating, untouchable stars, programming that was prescribed by scripts, or edgy formats that were self-contained. Here viewers interrupted the flow of programming and interjected themselves into the programming matrix.

Another factor in reality programming's success was the specter of globalization. If the world was becoming smaller, television was growing larger. Many reality shows had spawned overseas forms, and many large corporations were marketing shows like *Survivor* and *American Idol* as international franchises. Citizens, contestants, and individuals thought of reality programming as a quick and fluid means to penetrate the media. Few saw that reality programming was as tightly controlled, screened, monitored, and supervised as network programming. Surviving the screening for reality was as rigorous as network acting auditions.

The History of Reality

It might seem obvious that reality is what it is, but the more one looks at the levels, the contrivances, the schemes to make a semblance of reality on television, it becomes apparent that reality is a construction that has many meanings and interpretations depending on producers and decoders. Different versions of reality confront us daily: Fox News versus CNN. *Law and Order* versus *Criminal Minds*. Which is more realistic? In truth, there are nearly as many realities as there are people. The road from the obviously real to the obviously fake has never been clear. History, cultures, philosophies, technologies, and tastes have dictated what constitutes a real experience and what determines the chimera. The tale of reality is a complicated story of perceptions, psychology, media, commerce, and ideologies. In the end, reality is neither simple nor direct.

To understand the reemergence of reality television is to presume it disappeared. Reality television preexisted television itself. The impulse to watch people and their existence was the initial theatrical impulse that inspired theater. *Oedipus* was in a sense reality, in that it was a metaphor for all people who carry mistaken beliefs and allow those beliefs to misguide them in their relationship to society. Oedipus could be a resident in any season of *Real World*.

However, there have been periods when reality or nonfiction entertainment has surmounted the fictional creations of writers and storytellers. The Romans were fascinated by real people and wrote biographies, histories, and gossip texts that satirized and ridiculed the popular figures of their time. Shakespeare embedded commentary about contemporary religion and politics in his plays through carefully inscribed metaphors. Molière wrote plays that ridiculed the privileged classes and the power of the Church. In fact, *Tartuffe* could be considered an early reality work. Though a staged play with actors and a script, the audience saw very clearly that the play was only a thinly veiled commentary on the real foibles of deeply flawed aristocratic classes and the hypocritical churchmen of the era.

American culture improvised and wrote famous stage spectacles in the 19th century that again relied on aspects of documenting real life. Minstrel shows were supposedly a depiction of the languid and romanticized plantation lifestyle popularized by white performers like the Christy Minstrels in the 1850s. The use of blackface to portray the happy slaves singing, dancing, telling jokes, and providing entertainment reflected an image of Southern, African American life that simply didn't exist. The programs dwelled on stereotypes and wish fulfillment rather than portraying life as it was, and they failed to portray the brutal regimes of slavery.

In the world of drama, the doctrines of realism were being concocted by Ibsen and others who wanted to portray the actual workings of human relationships behind the fourth wall. In Russia, Chekhov and Stanislavsky rehearsed for months to achieve plays that had the normalcy of real life. There's an ironic quality to creating a fiction that pretends to reality so thoroughly that the two become indistinguishable.

In the 20th century, the notion of film gave rise to special effects that seemed so real audiences feared them. When the Lumière brothers in France produced the first films of trains arriving at the station, people leapt out of the way, thinking the filmed train was really coming at them. Filmed reality had a great power over people. Editing convinced people that a dog could think and reason in Cecil

Hepworth's 1905 production of *Rescued by Rover*. In 1964, audiences unfamiliar with the cinema vérité style of the French New Wave were stunned at the seeming naturalness and reality of a rock band in The Beatles' *A Hard Day's Night*, something audiences saw as a realistic portrayal of pop groups.

Contributing to the evolving sense of the real that audiences see in reality television is the evolving way that reality has been treated in literature. Time, space, and the fantastic have been progressively merged in the literature and films of the South American–based magical realism movement. In stories by Jorge Luis Borges, Isabel Allende, and Gabriel García Márquez, the difference between the real and unreal unravel as the fantastic intrudes on everyday reality.

More recently, in Alejandro Iñárritu's *Birdman*, a failed, fallen film star, Riggan Thomson, invests in performing in a Broadway play. At one point in his attempt to achieve his goal, the Birdman character he plays, flies. In the reality of the film and in the mind of the character, flying is possible, and he succeeds at flying despite its real impossibility.

The Reality of History (on the Tube)

Reality programming was an important part of radio programming in which real folks would talk about what mattered to them. In the province of radio, it was all about sound, and the producers of radio were keen to have sound tell the whole story. Having someone live in the studio was a way to give an audience a sense of immediacy and the impression they were participating in the event. Live performances by Bob Hope, George Burns, and others gave the audience the sense that they were becoming friends with real people who were like them. If the actors were good, the scripts would not be heard and the performance would sound spontaneous. In radio, and later on television, regular phrases and memorized bits would minimize the amount of material that was committed to memory. Susan Currell, in *American Culture in the 1920s*, reports that radio grew very rapidly: "From an amateur hobby and a single broadcasting station in 1920, the number of stations quickly expanded to over 700, broadcasting to 'fifteen million sets, capable of reaching an audience of forty million' that were listened to by the average family for 850 hours each year" (2009, 128). Early listeners thrilled to live fights described by announcers, the World Series, and world events. The technology of radio seemed to bring the world closer.

An important program in creating the rapport between audience and radio was *The Grand Ole Opry* radio program out of Nashville. The program featured country, folk, and bluegrass musicians live from the Ryman Auditorium and gave local Southern audiences a sense of home in the same way New Yorkers could listen to a broadcast in New York and think they were on Broadway.

Bruce Lenthall tells the tale of a little girl who wanted a Christmas present for her father, and she used radio to gain enough money to make her dreams come true. People used radio to build personal relationships through the media. Lenthall writes, "Using radio, Janet and others discovered, they could remake their new public relationships to resemble their private ones and, in so doing, they could personalize and function in their impersonal mass culture" (2007, 54). Radio, like all mass media, existed to either push programming that included advertising to generate revenue or to push a product of some kind through the broadcast.

In 1934, *Major Bowes Amateur Hour* was a big hit and ran through 1945. After Bowes left the show, it was revived by Ted Mack as a television program in 1948 and survived in one form or another through 1970. Mack's show was ideal, home entertainment that charmed audiences with its simple use of a spinning wheel to determine which talent candidate would go first. The show benefited from the fact that the amateurs auditioning seemed real and genuine.

The concept of real-life poverty and social injustice invaded the context of the game show in the sad and often teary *Queen for a Day*. A variety of women from all walks of life would bemoan their fates, and the woman with the saddest story, as voted from an audience applause meter, would be voted "queen for a day." A woman's woes of sick children, lost husbands, foreclosed mortgages, and other problems of industrial life would be swept away by gifts of washing machines and sofas, along with a dusty crown and a tattered sequined robe.

Sports entered the fray, and an early form of superhero enfranchisement debuted with local and national wrestling competitions. Playing the roles of heroes and villains, wrestling became the United States' dialogue on good versus evil. Weekly, sequined musclemen representing the values of honor, fair play, and competitive fitness would joust with fiendish, black-robed demons. The dark-masked wrestler predated the ultimate evil hidden by Darth Vader's mask. Every Saturday afternoon, the struggle of good versus evil would erupt for hours. Every week the evil wrestlers would play dirty tricks to undercut the hero, but eventually the hero would triumph. It was all a game, all staged, and all predictable, but, in a strong sense, it reassured an American sense of fair play and the triumph of good over evil.

Candid Camera worked in another way by portraying an American sense of absurdism. As a theatrical genre, absurdism paralleled existentialism, Existentialism arrived around the carnage of World War II. If God could allow such bloodshed, violence, and injustice, then perhaps God did not exist, or if she did, she simply didn't care about people or their fates. Existentialism presumed that in such a dark universe, man was alone in a nightmarish world that made little sense and stood for little. The absurdist playwrights Ionesco, Genet, and Beckett all decided to dramatize a world in which the nonsense of man's existence could make vibrant, if disturbing, theater. On stage, in *Waiting for Godot*, this turned into an hour of two bedraggled comedians waiting for a mysterious figure, Godot, who never arrives. The two bums play around, joke, frolic, and almost forget for whom they are awaiting and what they are supposed to do, but they wait all the same. In television, the vision of the absurd was carried by shows like *Candid Camera*. Allen Funt's fun romp was less of a game show or reality program and more of an existential investigation of people's search for the absurd. Stunts included planted actors, moving money, rude behavior, and illogical expressions. People became shrill, ill-tempered, confused, and uncooperative. Some had complete behavior breakdowns. Most were explained away by Funt, who comforted the deceived and explained that the illogical events were a gag. In reality, nothing was wrong. But for the sharp-eyed, something was wrong. Modern society was out of sync, and the problems of feeling dislocated, losing sense of the whole, and wondering what was going on came to light in the series. If the game on the show was benign, the underlying logic of a world gone mad was not. If *Candid Camera* wasn't the modern world, it was symptomatic of the increasing deranged-ness of the speedy, hyperbolic, unhinged, irrational, technological modern life. Whether it expressed it or not, the problems discovered in *Candid Camera* emulated the meltdown of postmodern life.

In 1973, *An American Family* reached inside the perfection of American life: a family living in the rich suburban splendor of opulent Santa Barbara comes apart at the seams. The husband is found to be unfaithful, one son leads an eccentric lifestyle, and the mother is on the verge of divorce and a nervous breakdown. The Louds are not the perfect American family but a family on the edge of oblivion. The series on PBS opened a Pandora's box of the United States' declining internal family infrastructure. Reality television began to reflect the strangeness of modern life, and programs like *Real People* and *That's Incredible* began to draw television to the stranger side of modern life.

By 1992, MTV had debuted *Real World,* and the program, inspired by the 12–34-year-old demographic that MTV desired (youthful, well financed, and effortlessly purchasing), showed a preview of adult life. The viewers had a taste of life observing participants arguing with roommates. It wasn't a pretty picture, but to some it was a fascinating, entertaining, and addictive one.

By the end of the 1990s, the world plunged into a new era of real events prompted by the 9/11 attacks. A sense of surrealism and fear predominated the United States, and there was a consequential turn to fantasy (*Harry Potter, Monsters, Inc.,* superhero films, and *Lord of Rings*), while at the same time a rejection of fantasy and an embrace of new reality programming. This bifurcation of audiences was complicated by CGI effects that made fantasy films seem more realistic (*Jurassic Park, Phantom Menace, Matrix, Lord of the Rings, Avatar, Titanic*) and fictional shows (*CSI, NCIS, Criminal Minds, Law and Order*) that borrowed from reality programming in a gruesome dissection of real crime and real (seeming) actors. Further, cable programming embraced a new realism in shows like *Oz, Girls, Breaking Bad,* and *The Wire.*

Anita Biressi and Heather Nunn, in *Reality TV: Realism and Revelation,* discuss the problematic philosophical implications of showing the "real" on television. An underlying problem is that the definition of reality or what appears to be real is not so direct and specific but is somewhat more conjectural, which we might take for granted. For example, when a college class meets, the students have an entirely different definition of college than instructors, administrators, and workers at the institution. In a very real sense, the employees of the college see their daily jobs as work, a useful endeavor that arrives at financial and social rewards for the employee, the institution, and its students. Students, however, bombarded with MTV's vision of reality: *Real World, The Hills, Ridiculousness, Spring Break,* or *Teen Mom* might have a highly different and social definition of college that includes the notion of parties, dating, forming friendships, acting out, participating in pranks and stunts, and largely using the institutional mechanisms of college as an incubator for personal growth, experimentation, and maturation. While there are some intersections between the teenage conception of college fostered by MTV and the perception generated by professionals, in many ways the constitution of reality afforded by these two perspectives is quite dissimilar and consequentially often in conflict. This accounts for discipline problems, failing grades, maladjustment, fraternity and sorority misbehavior, and other mis-adaptations to the college experience. Our society, whether intentionally or unintentionally, presents two very different and inconsistent visions of the same experience. They coexist and participate in our lives regularly with no sense of cognitive dissonance until we, either as students or as workers, must deal with that dissonance in real life and time. Our society and other societies deal with such distinctive and varied visions of the real consistently. Terms like *police, government, war, male,* and *female* are differently defined by various subgroups, resulting in a confusing semantic, philosophical, and often social disconnect. For example, the idea of policing seems straightforward enough, but in reality it is complicated. The notion of police or policing arrived when people created sufficient laws, and there were significant infractions that required a force to enforce and protect such laws from abuse. Despite growing populations and congested urban centers, Americans were by and large highly law abiding and industrious people with little need for law enforcement. The Prohibition legislation of the 1920s, which denied the populace the right to drink alcohol, produced an explosion of lawlessness and the repercussions of that mistaken law are still being felt in the creation of the FBI and other domestic policing agencies. More problematic has been the reports of policing in which seemingly innocent people without weapons have been the victims of seemingly unprovoked police violence. Does commissioning the power of a police force automatically lead to abuses of power and authority, or is this merely the media's interpretation of how the police are or should be viewed? When we add programming like *Cops* or *Dog the Bounty Hunter* to the mix, the real image of real policing becomes more clouded. Add popular fiction shows such as *Law and Order, CSI,* and *Criminal Minds* to the mix, and viewers begin to think all cases are plea bargains, all criminal scene investigators wear chic clothes and work in pristine blue-colored labs, and all police psychologists track deviant, mastermind villains. Obtaining a clear and unfettered vision of the reality of what *policing* is and does becomes infinitely more problematic. Reality television plays a clear role in unpacking the idea of reality expressed by such programming. Biressi and Nunn argue that the current state of reality TV is what they refer to as *post-documentary* culture. In essence, they argue that it is a "radically altered cultural and economic setting which includes an imperative for playfulness and diversion and the erosion of the distinctions between the public and the private sphere, between the private citizen and the celebrity, and between media and the social space" (2005, 2). According to the authors, these conditions of media have altered the sense of reality. This new televisual vocabulary promotes redefined visions of privacy that allow the public and private to merge and incorporates exposure and a new level of exhibitionism. These emerging teledocumentary styles have helped redefine our sense of the real, a world in which scrutiny, invasiveness, surveillance, gamification, and performance of the common are accepted methods of life and behavior.

These may appear as subtle or minor differences in defining the real, but they may have unfortunate broad effects. First, if societies accept surveillance as a normal aspect of life, then the art of being watched begins to condition all experience. So shopping mall cameras, police surveillance, and government snooping into our e-mails and phone records becomes standard operating procedure, if not a particularly agreeable condition. This consequence of documentation culture may have the undesirable impact of eroding a secure sense of privacy.

A second issue is how the culture of watching transforms reality television. Biressi and Nunn argue that "the impetus to depict ordinary people has been linked to by practitioners and critics, both implicitly and explicitly, to often-politicized debates about the real, reality, and about the relative value of realist, naturalist, or anti-realist representational strategies deployed to convey real life" (2005, 4). That is, what used to be called *real life* with real people used to be relegated to working-class people bound by layers of social and class-oriented debate. Fifty years ago, *the real* depicted life on the streets and people mostly hard-pressed by economic disadvantage. Today, *the real* deals with a plethora of social classes. *The Real Housewives of Beverly Hills* is conjecturally as real as the family in *19 Kids and Counting*. However, they both also exist as examples of new, strange, "hyper-real" freak shows. Their oddity and deviance from the norm demands the probing of reality film crews, and their tales seem as strange as anything produced by a fiction writer.

John Corner, in "Performing the Real," speculates that reality might be configured in another way, since the real is ostensibly performed by a group of people who are not acting real at all. Corner notes that the real as we know it, or our conception of everyday life, is negotiated. He writes, "This generic system is not, as we know, a neat and stable set of discrete categories of work" (2002, 44). Corner refers to it as a changing and shifting set of forms that compete with each other for primacy. Corner talks about the program *Big Brother,* in which people are under continual surveillance, and he argues that the show is at once part game show and part documentary and confessional in which the inner stories of players emerge, and the performance space of the program becomes a place for the actors (who are non-actors, supposedly) to act out their docu-soap. The people in *Big Brother* have placed themselves on display like artifacts in a museum to be studied, viewed, and discussed. They become curios. This is a very different metaphysic of the human. If Descartes reasoned, "I think, therefore I am," reality television postulates, "I pose, therefore I am available to be seen and regarded." In our world, without that public display, Corner and an audience might doubt that the people on the program do exist.

Chapter 1: Transformation— Self-Improvement, Home Improvement, and Makeovers

The Makeover and the Modern Narcissus

The problem with introspection is that it has no end.
—Philip K. Dick

In the Greek myth of Narcissus, a nymph, Echo, falls in love with Narcissus, and he ignores her. She prays to the god Nemesis, and he curses Narcissus to be so enamored of his own visage that he stares into a pool of water until he dies. This suggests the Greeks had a very negative view of narcissism and of self-love. But the American version of self-improvement has more to do with a positive set of values and perceptions that come from our Puritan background and European heritage. The Puritans believed in self-improvement and self-fulfillment through good works and hard labor. They believed that the divine plan was to test mankind through adversity and working with difficult problems. In the Puritans' view, hard work could create a modern Eden. Ning Kang (2009), writing for *The Review of European Studies,* said that "moreover, 'predestination' in Puritanism strengthened Puritans' self-awareness to perfect oneself. Puritans believed that their religious purity and salvation could be achieved through self-discipline, self-improvement and their hard work" (149).

So Americans have never really found narcissism all that harmful so long as one's self-involvement results in the general improvement and well being of all people. In other words, there is nothing wrong with being Donald Trump so long as your wealth making makes for a better society. In this sense, the long history of transformative, makeover, and self-improvement shows is wedded to American notions of a better society, a continually refurbished American landscape, and an idealized vision of ourselves. These goals have been championed in the 20th century by magazines such as *Better Homes and Gardens* and *Glamour,* which have popularized a more beautiful home décor and appeal to women to glorify their physical presence through beauty regimes, fitness programs, healthy eating, and correct clothing and make-up. Feminists have argued that such publications have confined and restricted women and subjugated them to men. However, the evidence is mixed. If women can adapt such messages for their own liberation and self-enjoyment, such vehicles do not have to enslave women but can be a means to liberation.

But there is wide cultural evidence that historically Americans see self-improvement as a part of our heritage. The culture has generated movie media that preaches self-help, self-realization, and self-aggrandizement as positive values. *Citizen Kane, Mildred Pierce, Mr. Smith Goes to Washington, Now Voyager, Young Mr. Lincoln, Thelma and Louise, Office Space, How to Succeed in Business, Jerry McGuire, 9 to 5,* and *The Devil Wears Prada* are all tales of young, opportunistic people finding their way in society and making a stand through their own hard work, devotion to self-promotion, and a motto of "never quit until one gets to the top." It has been ingrained in us to try to be the best we can be. Being ambitious and being American are almost synonymous, so there is nothing so odd about self-help, transformation, or home improvement shows being popular. If anything, they show us reflections of a positive, modern Narcissus carving our reflection on the American landscape.

The concept of transformation was further promoted by events in the later 20th century. A decade of economic depression, the 1930s, followed by a decade of war, the 1940s, caused the American people to retreat inside their private lives in the 1950s. Freed from years of low incomes, deprivation for the war effort, and sacrifice, Americans embraced the 1950s as a time to grow infrastructure, rebuild the country through freeways and fast food franchises, embrace exercise and fitness, take up hobbies, and spend more time in pursuits to improve their individual private lives. The 1950s were secretly the first era of an American "me" generation. Television shows of the 1950s and 1960s always showed teens on *Leave It to Beaver, My Three Sons,* and *Father Knows Best* scheming to make money or engaging in some comical school-related competition.

Television reflected the national fascination with remaking ourselves. The radio program, and later television program, *Queen for a Day* featured women competing to see who had the biggest sob story. If they won, they were given a roomful of furniture. Their job was to fabulate stories about their struggle. Disabled children, disease, and unemployed husbands were all woven into their dreary, troubled, and depressing narratives. Another favorite was *Ted Mack and the Original Amateur Hour.* Contestants from across the country would compete to be the most popular performer of the night. Audiences were encouraged to participate and vote for their favorite. While not total makeover shows, little hometown singers like Anne Margaret moved from small-town America to major Hollywood stardom in a few seasons. *The Huffington Post's* Sandy Malone (2014) wrote an article saying that the impetus for transformation and makeover shows was already around at the dawn of television, and the spirit of transformation shows was common in the 1950s. Malone writes, "In the 1950s, women competed to win appliances on television's *Queen for a Day* (also first a radio show). The prizes have improved over the years, but the concept is the same." The idea was to remake and refashion the self to create an improved end product. Television in the 1950s reflected the national fascination with self-transformation.

The 1960s accelerated the trend in self-improvement as self-help books became popular and business manuals preached the power of positive thinking and psycho-cybernetics. The 1960s transplanted the wild fashions of Carnaby Street to the United States, and the Beatles grafted London cool onto the sedate and tranquil shores of the United States. But the concept of makeover wasn't limited to hairstyles and clothing: it extended into all parts of American life. Texas Democrat Lyndon Baines Johnson had a strong-willed and environmentally active wife, Claudia Alta Taylor Johnson, nicknamed, Lady Bird. She was behind nearly 200 environmentally centered bills that went through Congress to protect the environment during Johnson's administration. Lady Bird was involved in the Beautify America program, believed in the renovation of the national landscape, and helped Johnson create his campaign slogan of a "great society." In the 1960s, literally the entire country was making itself over in cars, houses, style, and clothing.

Another factor was the United States continuing diversity. If Irish, Jewish, and German immigrants had reshuffled the culture in the 19th century, the 20th century owed change to new Hispanic, Asian, and Middle Eastern immigrants. A more diverse United States became more acclimated to change as a constant. A mostly conservative Christian nation evolved into a mixed culture of Christian, Jewish, Asian, and Middle Eastern faiths.

Cable and media developments also participated in a culture that championed change. Home improvement shows became a staple of American television programming in the 1970s when *This Old House* debuted. The program featured common people finding ways to renovate their abodes. Over the years, Americans watched master craftspeople re-stamp aging homes with new glory built on hard work, sweat, and expert skills.

At the start of the new millennium, Americans had become quite pleased with their dominant position in world politics and consumption. After 9/11, the actions of angry terrorists made Americans revisit the need for change and transformation. The result was a new self-questioning that encouraged people to reevaluate themselves. A new generation questioned American security and self-confidence. *Queer Eye for the Straight Guy* put together a team of gay men to teach straight men what they did not know about dress, decorum, and behavior. *Extreme Makeover: Home Edition* illustrated the nation's concerns about inadequate housing for the poor and championed volunteerism as a means to redress such issues. Such programming advanced the era's new self-consciousness of society's need to improve. Americans were suddenly dissatisfied with themselves, their government, their bodies, their mood, their food, their environment, their position in the world, their economy, and their dimming prospects for the future. All of these factors propelled the self-help and self-criticism industry to new heights.

The *New Yorker* ran a strong story explaining why reality television altered the makeup of television itself. Reality television, according to the *New Yorker,* became a means for society to review itself. Sometimes this process was critical and analytical. They raised the case of one of the first popular reality programs of the 1970s. The series was *An American Family*, a highly critical and dark view of a family that was supposed to be a typical American family. The idea was that the show would chronicle the day-to-day workings of a family in California living the

American dream. Within weeks, the filmmakers began to realize that something was amiss. The husband and wife were separating, there was infidelity, the oldest son was atypical and openly gay, and the family was in shambles. The program was highly unusual in a world of shows like *The Brady Bunch* and *The Partridge Family*, the mainstream television of the era. The filmmakers determined that despite the fact that the family was probably highly atypical, they should continue to simply chronicle what they had found. The program was a revolutionary ratings hit and a hard-hitting vision of the flaws in American domestic culture. Viewers didn't know how to assess the gay son, Lance Loud. Many found him preferable to the family's philandering husband and father. The program chronicled transformation as it was happening. It redefined the notion of reality programming because it was such a shockingly graphic depiction of what was really happening in the culture at large. Despite the fact the program wasn't planned to be a self-help or transformative program, it had an impact and laid the groundwork for continuing transformative reality programming. In the *New Yorker*, Kelefa Sanneh (2011) discussed Jennifer Pozner's book on the power of reality television, *Reality Bites Back: The Troubling Truth about Guilty Pleasure TV*, stating, "this idea—that pernicious images and ideas are more powerful than benign ones—shapes Pozner's analysis in every case, and explains how she manages to extract clear messages from messy exchanges." The *New Yorker* compared reality television to the ideas of Theodor Adorno and Max Horkheimer, two sociologists who argued we are victims of a "culture industry" that tells us what to do or think. Whether we buy the view that reality TV makes us over like a modern Narcissus or whether we subscribe to the *New Yorker's* darker view of reality television as a culture industry that tries to shape us, the medium makes us keenly aware of ourselves, our society, and especially, our flaws.

Further Reading

Ning Kang, "Puritanism and Its Impact on American Values," *Review of European Studies* 1, no. 2 (December 2009): 148–151; Sandy Malone, "The Real Business of Reality TV and What Determines a New Show's Fate," *Huffington Post*, April 23, 2014; Kelefa Sanneh, "The Reality Principle," *New Yorker*, May 9, 2011.

AMERICAN RESTORATION

American Restoration is a History Channel program that follows the reengineering adventures of Rick Dale, his crew, and family as they tackle complicated and ambitious restoration projects on classic items from old Coca Cola machines and jukeboxes from the 1950s to vehicles, stereos, and appliances from the early part of the 20th century. With the access to new items and the availability of new technologies, many might ask, "Why is there a need for such a program or function?" However, the enjoyment arises from watching Dale and his crew restore life to moribund technologies. Their work is part archeology, part nostalgia, and part magic. These technicians often have to restore products for which schematics and plans no longer exist. Their task is to re-create products using facsimiles and parts that are fabricated from scratch.

The program originated in 2010 and has run six seasons and is currently in production. The program is filmed in Las Vegas, Nevada, the site of Rick's Restorations, where Rick, his crew, and his teenage son tackle complex restorations. The team is a spin-off from the popular *Pawn Stars* program, in which people bring choice items to pawn shops to trade, pawn, or sell. Dale had appeared as an expert on *Pawn Stars* restoring and repairing damaged items. *American Restoration* has featured guests from the *Pawn Stars* series, as well as musicians and celebrities looking to have devices restored.

Dale and his staff take work from pawn shops, restore items brought in by individuals, and tackle projects they find from pickers. Dale's work has physical limitations regarding what he can restore. He has limited staff, must call in experts, and often has trouble keeping the crew in line. Like all craftspeople, they are a very individualistic and idiosyncratic bunch. There is no one manual or training program that covers what Dale's customizers accomplish. Dale's business has been prosperous for 30 years, and he is an area guru for people who want metal and machine work restored. Due to space and size limitations, Dale might only take on six to eight projects at a time. Often Dale has to consult experts in the field of metalwork or electronics to complete a repair.

One interesting aspect of the program is when a celebrity guest stops by Dale's Las Vegas shop for a consult. In a 2013 episode, singer/pianist Billy Joel visited to ask advice on a British Royal Star motorcycle that had a frozen engine. Joel wanted Dale to take on the project, fix the bike, renew the engine, and restore the finish to new. The episode, filmed in an unusually chilly Vegas, had Joel wearing a warm jacket while Dale walked about in a sleeveless shirt inspecting the bike. Joel explained his connection to the bike and spoke knowledgably about restoration, exploring Dale's property. Writer Ben Hurston described the scene saying, "He also share(d) some musical knowledge with Dale, convincing him to refurbish an ol' Steinway piano in the restoration expert's 'boneyard'" (Hurston 2013). Dale's show is always an interesting place to encounter derelict equipment, and Dale and his crew often rise to the challenge when given an old item to restore. Charges have been leveled at the show, and at *Pawn Stars*, that the items aren't real, that the restorations are not accurate, and that the reengineering is done by other, off-camera artisans, but on the program Dale and his crew perform complicated acts of transformation on old items, and audiences have been impressed by their abilities to restore the past and revive dead products, cars, and furniture.

The main focus of the show is Rick Dale and his projects. His son, Tyler, appears to be less productive and, though intelligent, tends to revere Rick's brother, Ron, who is a low-productivity, picker and restorer. "Kowboy" is an expert metal polisher. Brettly is Dale's stepson from his recent wife, Kelly. Ted is a lettering artist. Kyle is a reassembling and finishing artist for the shop. Together, they can accomplish a lot, but getting the maximum out of the crew is a struggle for Dale.

See also: Pawn Stars; Reality Television: Oddities of Culture.

Further Reading

David S. Escoffery, *How Real Is Reality TV?*; Benjamin Hurston, "Billy Joel Featured on Upcoming Episode of History's American Restoration," *Paste*, May 20, 2013.

ASK THIS OLD HOUSE

Ask This Old House is a spin-off and companion series to the popular home improvement show *This Old House* (*TOH*). Like its predecessor, it is hosted by Kevin O'Connor. The show has been active since its 2002 premiere. The show reflects a team orientation with O'Connor joined by craftsmen Tom Silva, Richard Trethewey, and Roger Cook. Longtime resident repair guru and carpenter Norm Abrams was too busy with his other *TOH* commitments to do this show as well. The segments are coupled with *TOH* and usually run side by side. The program grew out of questions sent in to the *TOH* magazine. Producers decided it would be an appropriate separate series. Like *TOH*, the emphasis is on deliberative quality information rather than flashy hosts or excessive production values, and the goal is to answer real problems about building, construction, home improvement, and renovation issues. Like *TOH*, the program has been nominated for multiple Emmys (five at last count). Other experts appear if the question requires someone outside the hosts' areas of knowledge to answer more specialized questions. The show begins with the team loading into a van and heading into a loft in a barn in some rural part of Massachusetts. Segments include answering questions in the loft/workshop and visiting guests' homes to answer specialized questions about their specific properties. The craftspeople usually solve these problems with the help of the resident. A feature called "What Is It?" explains puzzling tools that the hosts and many viewers have never seen before. There is also a feature called "Useful Questions" in which a viewer sends in a tip that the hosts explain to the audience.

See also: HGTV; *This Old House*

Further Reading

T. W. Adorno, "Television and the Patterns of Mass Culture"; David S. Escoffery, *How Real Is Reality TV?*

CLEAN HOUSE

Clean House's methodology was to focus on the fun of revamping a living area. The program aired from 2003 to 2011on the Style Network and ended due to low ratings. The cast included Niecy Nash, Matt Iseman, Trish Suhr, and Mark Brunetz as the team. Nash made the initial contact with the family, provided comedic reactions to their clutter and clarified the need for a cleaned and renovated home. This prompted a call to the program's team of expert cleaners and decluttering experts.

The team grappled with a family's cleaning problems by trying to nudge them toward a better, more attractive household. Matt Iseman (a trained surgeon turned comedian and handyman) served as the go-to-guy and would help with issues of domestic organization and technology. Trish Suhr, the yard sale diva, would cajole the family members into relinquishing family heirlooms and large, costly items that were causing clutter. Suhr's hope was to pry people loose from costly items, so the family could gain enough money in the yard sale to cover some of the basic renovations to the property, thus making it more livable. Mark Brunetz was a design consultant who would also seek to negotiate people away from clutter and toward a house that was more flowing and offered more feng shui appeal. Often Brunetz's aesthetic clashed with the owners, and he exercised real negotiating skill to achieve his goals of happier and healthier design.

Each show began with an introduction and set-up of the family and their cleaning problems. Some problems were related to addictions to possessions, but others were a consequence of a recent move, a lazy family, a single person who was clinging to things, or children who dominated the households with toys and junk.

The yard sale was a pivotal event, and part of the fun was watching the cast negotiate the family out of items that could raise cash to buy new items. The main goal was to help the family live a junk-free lifestyle. In one episode, a father had his drums and a goat head in the living room, and the cast couldn't imagine why he wanted it. In the end, it was revealed that the goat was a symbol of his current wife, and he wanted the goat head to keep some strange totemistic reminder of his wife about him at all times. Eventually, he agreed to part with the disturbing memento.

Some controversies arose when some cast members were not retained, and this erupted into lawsuits against the producers. In one incident, a guest host was not retained when she was accused of bullying a hosting family into giving up items.

The show generated several spin-offs, including *Clean House Comes Clean,* in which the hosts revisited old homes they had cleaned and which included show outtakes and bloopers. *The Messiest House in the Country* showed really messy homes. Proceeds from the cleanup paid for redecorating, and extra money was donated to charity.

The unnerving degree of mess the hosts found in the 2009 finale to *Messiest House in the Country* brought host Niecy Nash to tears. She told the family she didn't want them to suffer like they were suffering by living in trash. The family was living in heaps of trash. The mother of the family shrugged it off, but the cast was appalled by the debris. Nancy Selden, writing for *The Times Union,* referred to it as "three decades in which new things came into the house, but nothing, it appeared, went out." The horror story was finally solved when the family was talked into a massive yard sale, the biggest in the series' history. According to Selden, the crew had to rent a 7,000-square-foot facility to host the sale. The proceeds of the sale netted the family enough to refurbish the house, repair holes in walls, buy new appliances, and start fresh. The show preached that hoarding was a real psychological problem and not simply an oversight or a mistake.

Despite the occasionally serious messages, *Clean House* mostly prospered as a comedy reality program in which the issues of the crew and the homes were not treated as serious. Most of the home changes were practical solutions to obvious problems. Much of the humor derived from headstrong and insistent homeowners who refused to abandon a broken pool table, a child's long-abandoned crib, or a precious set of toy soldiers.

However, over time, ratings for the show waned. Despite the program's use of humor and occasionally serious discussions of hoarding and psychologically unhealthy behaviors, *Clean House* routinely gave tips to modern families and homeowners about how to better their living conditions. Producers may one day revive such a bright, useful, and ingenuous program that promoted, healthy, clean houses and the happy families who lived in them.

See also: Extreme Makeover: Home Edition; 60 Minute Makeover

Further Reading
David S. Escoffery, *How Real Is Reality TV?*; Naomi Seldin, "Threats, Tears, and Vermin," *Timesunion.com*, July 2, 2009.

DR. 90210

Dr. 90210 details the life and career of a wealthy and successful Beverly Hills plastic surgeon. Dr. Robert Rey is chronicled both as an active medical practitioner and as a subject of the show himself. One episode focuses on his haircut and his own personal makeover. The program believes such insights into the doctor and his personal life and health regime are germane to a professional who makes his income by making others look attractive. The series has several subjects, including Doctor Robert Rey, a Brazilian physician, and Doctor Jason Diamond. The program was produced by the E Network but also showed up on other stations such as the Style Network and ran from 2004 to 2008 with six seasons and over 60 episodes.

The program's title, *Dr. 90210,* referred to the zip code in Beverly Hills that was made famous by the Fox drama *Beverly Hills, 90210,* a program which featured the trials and tribulations of a group of wealthy teens and their families. *Dr. 90210* ran an hour, covered the consultations of several patients requesting plastic surgery, and showed the doctor's progress on these various cases.

In one episode, a female Hollywood photographer from Sweden who worked with lots of large-breasted women wanted to have her own breasts augmented. She was small chested and lived in a culture in which augmentation was common, and she felt it would help her socially. Another, more serious case was a young woman who was from a poor, working-class family who had a malformed nose and cleft palette from birth. She had had several complex, successful operations to correct the condition. She was about to be married, and she wanted to complete the treatment. The program wished to address concerns that plastic surgeons were motivated by wealth and served no serious social needs. The program dealt with the issue of doctor's fees (which were often high), but they also dealt with medical ethics issues when doctors were confronted with requests from patients. Often the doctors could see no reasonable need for the requested cosmetic elective surgery, and often they were left in a dilemma. The program also confronted issues such as the marketing of plastic surgery services to teens and a nationwide attraction to altering the body for aesthetic reasons. Many of the doctors featured on the show did surgeries that actually improved the appearance of people who had had unfortunate accidents or deformities since birth. The view of the show was that plastic surgeons do real and incredible work in transforming people. The program illustrated that for some, such operations are frivolous, for others, they can be life-altering.

Since the program dealt with surgical issues, there were many scenes of near nudity. Aside from the blurring of a couple of significant body areas, the audience viewed a variety of nude scenes during the cosmetic procedure. Audiences were treated to traumatic operation scenes in which fierce, invasive practices like liposuction and other daunting procedures were performed. The vibrant filming reminded the audience that there is nothing plastic in plastic surgery, and that the process requires ripping, tearing, cutting, and reshaping of flesh. There is discomfort, pain, and partial, if temporary, disfigurement. The doctors allowed the cameras very close to the surgical procedure for these disturbing moments. Of course, despite the risks associated with all surgery, things turned out fine for most of these patients, and, despite the emphasis on the exterior, the doctors acquitted themselves as caring and studious professionals. For a woman who sought a nose restoration, the doctor told her, "I can make your nose better, but it will always be a bit asymmetrical." Generally, the patients had reasonable expectations, and for the most part they received fantastic results. As one would imagine, the plastic surgeons of this region are brilliantly trained, and they do provide some occasional magic to their charges.

As the program progressed, more doctors were featured, and again the audience was invited to commiserate with the doctors' personal issues and problems. There was a continued focus on the problems and issues confronting wealthy and privileged people, which few of us would call problems. For example, Dr. Linda Li was seven months pregnant, and her husband—also her partner and an anesthesiologist—wished she would stay home more often. Such scenes seemed to be inserted to undercut the otherwise fine and laudable work of surgeons in a profession that is often derided.

Interestingly, the program was partially inspired by the FX drama *Nip/Tuck*, which featured two dubious plastic surgeons who were questionable characters outside the operating room, if not in it. Dr. Rey has come under scrutiny since the show ended, appearing shirtless in *The Daily Mirror*, and Jade Watkins commented that "The 50-year-old showed off his incredibly toned torso and youthful appearance as he went shirtless in Hawaii today." The paper suggested that the doctor had had a little nip and tuck himself to create his toned physique.

See also: Extreme Makeover; 60 Minute Makeover; The Swan

Further Reading
David S. Escoffery, *How Real Is Reality TV?*; Jade Watkins, "Has He Had a Nip/Tuck? Plastic Surgeon and Dr. 90210 Star, Robert Rey, 50, Displays Toned Torso as He Hits the Beach," *The Daily Mirror*, July 31, 2012.

EXTREME MAKEOVER

ABC's *Extreme Makeover* ran from 2002 to 2007 for four seasons and over 50 episodes. As a major network reality show, the program had a strong fan base and a strong premise. Using the format of other makeover shows (*A Makeover Story*, *What Not to Wear*), the program offered volunteers an extreme makeover that involved a quick turnaround, wardrobe help, makeup design, workouts, plastic surgery, and dentistry. The goal was to transform the person, while also increasing their confidence and functionality. Ironically, *Extreme Makeover: Home Edition* debuted in 2003 and quickly eclipsed the plastic surgery show, replacing it. Another spin-off was a weight-loss show.

The concept of *Extreme Makeover* was to transform people through surgery. Richard Huff writes in *Reality Television* that the producer, Howard Schultz, said, "We wanted people for whom surgery would change their life and those who couldn't afford it otherwise" (2006). The show found people in need of repair who were blocked by financial difficulties. They were screened for psychological problems, and they had to have problems that a surgeon thought could be fixed in a fairly straightforward set of operations during the show's run.

Several writers have suggested that the show occurred after 9/11 because the welfare state of the middle 20th century was being retired in a new antiregulatory, low-tax, anti-government setting. In other words, the era was one in which the country was returning to a regime of self-reliance and self-help. The *Extreme Makeover* show was theorized as a way of giving people hope in an era in which it was unlikely they would receive much help from the government.

So television became a preferable way to finance costly and expensive operations that could produce life-changing results. Yet the show, while claiming a self-help objective, seemed to pour extreme resources for high-drama and maximum-effect surgeries. A former surgeon from the program discussed his experiences on the show to *The Huffington Post*. Dr. Robert Tornambe explained that when the show's producers courted him, they "failed to explain . . . that the consultations would be attended by the show's associate producers who tried to influence me in the selection process to choose candidates with the most dramatic storyline or most dynamic transformation possibility" (Tornambe 2011).

A major critique of the show was that it focused on physical appearance. Instead of learning to cope with flaws and shortcomings, the program preached that personal physical flaws can and should be addressed by surgical options. Misha Kavka, in *Reality TV*, said, "The normalization of cosmetic surgery through programmes like *Extreme Makeover*—followed by post-op beauty pageant *The Swan* (Fox, 2004), celebrity-worshipping *I Want a Famous Face* (MTV, 2004), and surgeon-focused *Dr. 90210* (E! 2004–08) led to marked increase in the number of plastic surgery procedures performed in the U.S." (2012, 129). The show was accused of being a two-hour personal ad for the work of plastic surgeons. Further, the show denied that physical appearance could be enhanced by nonsurgical interventions. Transformations unfairly targeted people dissatisfied by their physical appearance. Critics lamented that women have enough body issues and that the show made those women even more dissatisfied with their bodies.

The extreme team from the show included a hairstylist, three different plastic surgeons, a dermatologist, a LASIK eye surgeon, a nutritionist, a personal trainer, and three cosmetic dentists. Again, the emphasis was on interventions to improve appearance. The show tended to neglect less drastic measures to improve appearance. Nutrition and styling solutions were not valued on the show, which emphasized surgical interventions. Amber Watts wrote about *Extreme Makeover* that "forcing subjects to ask for help, diverting potential sympathy into consumerist fantasy, and illustrating the effects of self-sufficiency all work together to create viewers who want to consume because they do not want to ask for help."

See also: Extreme Makeover; 60 Minute Makeover; The Swan

Further Reading

David S. Escoffery, *How Real Is Reality TV?*; Misha Kavka, *Reality TV*, 2012; Robert Tornambe, "Confessions of an Extreme Makeover Plastic Surgeon," *Huffington Post*, November 6, 2011; Amber Watts, "Melancholy, Merit, and Merchandise: The Postwar Audience Participation Show," 2008.

EXTREME MAKEOVER: HOME EDITION (EMHE)

After exploring the world of transforming people's lives via plastic surgery, ABC turned to the more lucrative and less litigious realm of home repair and remodeling. *EMHE* was a product of ABC and explored the lives of people who had

had some extreme life tragedy and needed help. The emphasis was on pathos as host Ty Pennington (previously a personality on *Trading Spaces*) and the crew brought in a group of goodwill pro bono consultants to fix, repair, rebuild, or give a worthy family a new home. The program ran from 2003 to 2012 and filmed 200 episodes.

As the show progressed, it became grander, and, rather than simply renovating unworkable or cramped quarters, the crew ended up building McMansions for some families. The program asked the question as to whether the gifted homes would help the families or burden them with gruesome and exorbitant operating costs. Many of the later homes would need enormous sums to maintain their full functioning.

The emphasis on poor families and schools appeared to be a laudable objective, and the show was filled with optimistic and motivated people, mostly seeking to overcome some aspect of adversity. Usually a family member was ill, or the family had faced some sort of disaster. The producers coordinated the reconditioning activities with local contractors, who brought together a local crew with volunteers and experts to help the unfortunates. The emphasis was on charity and giving. The family was sent on vacation for seven days while the construction team worked their magic on the interior and exterior of the house to make an inviting space for the family to live and work.

ABC acted as a broker, bringing the family and the contractors together. The family paid nothing for the redo, and ABC paid nothing. All the contractors and workers volunteered their services in return for screen time as contributors to the effort. Professionals donated materials and labor, and workers were normally people in the area. So in essence, ABC hosted a free show that trumpeted acts of kindness and goodwill; the needy family received a free dwelling, and the only costs were born by laborers and local suppliers. This form of reality broadcasting was extremely cost-effective and promoted the sense that the network was supporting the public interest. An impressive aspect of the program was the speed at which the home was built or rebuilt. If the family dwelling was thought to be unreclaimable, the crew built a new dwelling on the site. Regardless of whether people received free advertising, the end result was that a family received a huge benefit and kindness. The positive outcomes outweighed issues of free advertising for builders and supply companies. Much about the show's economics can be forgiven by the fact that it promoted goodwill.

One notable high point for the show was that following Hurricane Katrina the series visited New Orleans and spent some time and energy rebuilding homes for people in that devastated area. Several critics have suggested the principle designers on the show did little or no work on the houses being constructed. Allegations were made that the show was simply a means to gain promotion and a cheap vehicle for ratings under the guise of good deeds. Writing for the *Los Angeles Times*, Kim Christensen and Meg James reported in 2007 that "in the last two years, 'Extreme Makeover: Home Edition' has reaped more than $500 million in advertising revenue, according to research firm Nielsen Monitor-Plus."

To its credit, the show stressed social activism, mostly choosing families who were themselves advocates for social action and picking people who had been victimized by natural disasters, violence, accidents, illnesses, and other family tragedies. Michelle Obama appeared and christened a house on the show in support of its direct activism. Many times a family would advocate for a cause, such as Mothers Against Drunk Driving, or against gang violence or bullying, or some other responsible social cause. The show often featured the family's nomination video to give some insight into the family and their issues.

The series began in 2003 as a series of specials and ended the season struggling for ratings. However, in the second through sixth seasons, the show ranked in the top 30 programs and was a favorite on Sunday and later Friday nights. In its later seasons, the audience dropped off, and after eight seasons the show was cancelled. Perhaps the harshest criticism of the show was that families of modest means sometimes received extravagant houses that did not reflect the family's income or mission. Such a house, though a welcome respite from poverty, seemed unlikely to be affordable in the long term.

See also: Extreme Makeover; 60 Minute Makeover; The Swan

Further Reading

Kim Christensen and Meg James, "And Then the Roof Caved In," *Los Angeles Times*, May 13, 2007; David S. Escoffery, *How Real Is Reality TV?*

HELL'S KITCHEN

Gordon Ramsay, known in *Hell's Kitchen* as Chef Ramsay, is firmly in command in this popular but conventional competition show: a team game in which two squads compete to be Ramsay's favorite. The contest is usually a demographic contrast: men versus women, youth versus age, or something along those lines.

Chef Ramsay barks orders to each group in each round of the competition. If the teams are ordered to do something, they must do it with abandon. The suggestion of the show and the structure of the kitchen are organized around highly authoritarian models. This fits with Gordon Ramsay's hyperbolic personality, but it may not be indicative of how well-run kitchens actually work.

The setup is two teams that compete to win prizes and a coveted position in one of Ramsay's establishments. The challenges are precise, and, unlike the rebellious kitchens that Ramsay sometimes investigates and tries to revive in another show in which he stars, *Kitchen Nightmares*, the situation is tightly controlled. The apprentice chefs are given detailed briefs on meal preps, and they are given tasks for each round. Usually the menu is prescribed, but in Ramsay's fully stocked test kitchen, the contestants are free to use other materials. Upon the completion of each meal course, Ramsay tastes the results and provides stern criticism if the chefs bungle an easy part of the assignment. In one round, a chef was asked to prepare a rare steak, and instead it was medium well-done. Ramsay was appalled that the team had botched such a simple order. Garnishes, gravies, and sauces are important items, and Ramsay's palette carefully assesses the team's ability to comply with orders, yet at the same time to add originality.

The show has interesting dynamics involving the virtues of individual chefs and the contributions of whole teams. While the teams are judged as a whole, individual contributors often come under fire for failing to live up to team standards. Often the team will lose when individual members make blunders that result in a loss of points and prestige for the whole team. Thus, the teams are keen to police themselves.

After a challenge, the team that succeeds is usually given a small reward. With a playoff of male versus female chefs in one episode, Ramsay rewarded the winning female team with a spa afternoon. However, by that evening there was a new challenge. All the contestants live in fear of being dumped from the team, and, despite Ramsay's outbursts and fits of pique, the chefs seem eager to claim a job in one of his restaurants.

See also: Extreme Makeover; 60 Minute Makeover; The Swan

Further Reading

David S. Escoffery, *How Real Is Reality TV?*; Amber Watts, "Melancholy, Merit, and Merchandise: The Postwar Audience Participation Show."

HGTV

HGTV, or Home and Garden Television, is a network devoted to exploring programming related to repairing, improving, and buying real estate. All of HGTV's extensive and popular programming celebrates either buying or adding to the home. Of course, cynics argue that such a channel just encourages rampant consumption of home-care products. The need to be up-to-date on home and garden products reflects Americans' commitment and support of their own local economy. The Home and Garden Channel first aired in 1994 from the Scripps Network Interactive division. The motto of the station is "share what home means to you." The headquarters for the station is in Knoxville, Tennessee. The focus of the station is home remodeling, gardening, home buying, crafts, and restorations. By 2013, nearly 100 million homes received HGTV, which is 86 percent of the households with cable television, making it one of the best-known cable stations.

Kenneth W. Lowe came up with the idea for a home and garden channel in 1992. He became CEO, and, with support from the Scripps board, he bought Cinetel, a small video-production facility in Knoxville as the base of operations. The challenge for the station was to produce a network's full programming in a small production house. The station brought in CBS's Ed Spray, who suggested farming the productions out to smaller companies around the nation, where programming could be conducted in a less-congested manner. Thus, HGTV set itself the mission of acquiring a nationwide look and sought varied programs from all over the country. Initially, around 90 percent of the programming was original, with 10 percent being fill-ins of recycled Canadian, PBS, and independent syndicated programs.

Burton Jablin, the vice president for programming, set the style and format for many of the initial shows. The focus has remained relatively unchanged in 20 years. Themes include home buying, remodeling, makeover and repair, gardening, exotic home environments (domestic and international), and decorating and designing. There have been some programs devoted to design competitions and games, but they don't seem to be a central focus of the station.

The station logo is a Gotham bold set of letters with a roof over the H. Initially, the station was a low-budget affair with a skeletal staff. Few believed that Americans would take to a gardening, home-repair channel, but, to the surprise of many, the network won a wide audience of do-it-yourselfers, family viewers, and people who enjoyed the video method of touring sumptuous homes across the nation.

In 2008, Scripps created the Scripps Networks Interactive (SNI) division, which contained their cable and Web properties as a separate company. Scripps TV and newspapers were a separate company. The station moved to a letterboxing format and began to broadcast all programs in the letterbox edition with black bars below and above the content in 2011. In newer horizontal TVs, the format fits perfectly.

Most of the shows deal with some form of home renovation or home flipping project. Popular shows include *Rehab Addict,* in which a young female renovator takes on tough renovation projects. *Fixer Upper* is a Texas-based show that challenges a couple to redesign and renovate homes in a few weeks. *Ellen's Design Challenge* challenges people to make a good furniture design. *House Hunters Renovation* allows people an allowance to fix up a home on the market. *Flip or Flop* follows the adventures of two Realtors and home buyers who take limited cash, buy a home, fix it up, and resell it before the payment is due. If they sell it, they flip it. If they don't sell it in time, they flop. *Island Life* deals with finding the perfect home in the islands. *Buying and Selling* is about the process of buying homes at the right price and, with a little remodeling, selling with a strong profit. *House Hunters International* is an upscale program. Mostly well-off, international families look to buy properties in other nations. There are renovation issues and the problem of finding the right place for people from different cultures. The key is matching families and cultures. *Renovation* is, as it sounds, a show about home renovations and the planning that goes into them. *Income Property* is about people investing in income-creating rental properties. *Love It or List It* is a challenge in which a designer and a Realtor help a family to modify an existing house they have outgrown and to find a new home. The Realtor and the designer are in competition to either make the family "love it (the old, redesigned home)", or move to the new house and "list it." The trick is, there is only so much that can be done with the old houses, and the Realtor, also with a limited budget, has to find a place that will accommodate the family. *Property Brothers* is a show in which twin brothers buy properties and renovate them for families. They are a package deal, and they often take a problematic home and make it much more inviting. *Property Virgins* is for first-time home buyers who are just getting into a condo, a small home, or a renovation. The goal here is to help a young person become a property owner. *Tiny House Hunters* deals with families looking to downsize to very small (sometimes under 100 square feet) homes.

The station has not been without controversies. Some cable carriers have had disputes with Scripps, but most have been ironed out quickly. More significant are the dramatic conflicts on camera. Scripps has had to admit that some of the drama has been created. Many of the homes featured on *House Hunters* had already been sold, and the actual sales were reenacted after the fact. In some cases, it has been discovered that certain homes weren't really on the market. Apparently, some Realtors held different belief systems than the inclusive messages of a diverse United States signaled by HGTV's programming. HGTV presents a racially, ethnically, and religiously inclusive series of shows. They want to make everyone an owner and a buyer. They ran into trouble with the Benham Brothers' show *Flip It Forward* because of their extreme pro-life and anti-gay beliefs. The station had started development of the show with the two Christian graduates of Liberty University, but, when they looked deeper, more than being merely devout people of faith, they found a long record of anti-gay beliefs. Cavan Sieczkowski, writing for the *Huffington Post,* stated, "HGTV has axed an upcoming series due to the hosts' extreme anti-gay views" (2016). The series never debuted, because Scripps was committed to selling homes and products to everyone and didn't want to exclude any audiences.

Scripps is committed to the home business and partners with many people in the home-renovation industry. The company also owns the Food Network.

See also: Extreme Makeover: Home Edition; 60 Minute Makeover

Further Reading

David S. Escoffery, *How Real Is Reality TV?*

HOW DO I LOOK?

How Do I Look? was a makeover and reality television program sponsored by the Style Network and hosted by sprightly host, Jeannie Mai, that ran for a whopping 12 seasons with over 100 programs from 2004 to 2012. Originally, the program was hosted by soap star Finola Hughes, but stylist Mai took it over. The program borrows many elements from *What Not to Wear* but in many ways makes its own innovations in the makeover regime. The program follows classic makeover standard operating procedure, in which friends, family, and coworkers turn in the offending fashion victim and demand he or she receives a makeover. While there are some individual differences, the show tends to follow a standard format. In most cases, two or more family members or friends turn the victim/guest in to the show because they think the guest is making disastrous fashion choices. Usually, there is a life-changing event, a new job, a new location, or a new life condition that merits a change in wardrobe as well, so the guest is put in a situation in which new makeup, new clothes, a new hairstyle, and a new body are required. Fortunately, unlike shows like *The Swan,* which argue that only a surgical solution can transform a person, this show opts for fashion and less-drastic methods of reshaping a person's appearance. In the opening montage, we see the guest in the most hideous and ill-fitting wear, and it is comforting to know that they will soon change.

Armed with a stylist, the two friends invade the guest's closet and start to toss the most offending wearables. Then, there is a showdown in which the guest is confronted by the host and a friend, and they complain loudly and vocally about the flaws in the wardrobe. Sometimes the guest is upset and dislikes the level of criticism, but other times the guest is willing to make big changes.

The ambushed guest confides in the host about his or her true feelings and fears and anxieties about a makeover. The friends and a stylist go shopping for the guest, and sometimes, while the shopping is happening, the guest goes to the spa, dentist, therapist, or on a brief vacation. More often than not, the guest has to recover from the blow to the ego that the ambush has created.

The shoppers return with a collection of three outfits that are tied to the guest's lifestyle. Each shopper has been given $1,200 to start a collection. A doctor's wardrobe might be titled "Doctor's Check-up" or a businesswoman's clothes might be called "Interview Wear." Two of the outfits are tied directly to the professional role of the person; a third outfit is a wildcard outfit that could work and may possess a piece from the guest's previous wardrobe. The guest is given makeup and hairstyle assistance. The guest must select one complete collection for the basis of a future wardrobe.

The next day, the host and guest watch footage of the shopping trip to see how it went. Sometimes the footage is used to provoke the guest, with the friend and consultant choosing pieces like those that were tossed. Then the guest is presented with a makeup and hairstyle plan. Usually, the attempt is to make the guest look like a celebrity.

Then the guest goes through a fashion shoot wearing the newly designed wardrobe, and the host and friends get to hear the guest's reaction to their picks. Finally, the hairstyle and makeup are applied, and the guest does a runway walk asking, "How do I look?" If the contestants can guess the creator of their look (or perhaps as a bonus for all the trauma of change), the guest is given an additional reward, such as a $1,000 gift card to continue purchasing quality clothing and grooming products.

Occasionally, there would be a celebrity makeover (usually making over someone in that celeb's family). Rapper Yo-Yo and musicians in the group Aria appeared in 2010. *The New York Times* ripped the show for being nasty and pushing people with distinctive lifestyles toward the middle. *The Times* was amazed that anyone close to a guest could savagely and vilely tell them how to dress. The examples that *The Times* cited from the show didn't show bad taste, as much as they showed a distinctive personality. *The Times* seemed to believe that if we didn't accept difference, then we were anti-American. If we intolerantly demanded people change to be more like us, then we stood the risk of becoming more intolerant ourselves. *The Times's* Jon Caramanica wrote that, following a typical show makeover, "What's lurking beneath that shaggy exterior is a revelation, but not as big as the realization of how hard it is to stand alone when your closest friends are pulling you inexorably toward the middle" (2005).

See also: Extreme Makeover; 60 Minute Makeover; The Swan; What Not to Wear

Further Reading

Jon Caramanica, "Beyond the Desperate Housewife," *New York Times*, June 12, 2005; David S. Escoffery, *How Real Is Reality TV?*

I WANT A FAMOUS FACE (IWAFF)

I Want a Famous Face described the goals of people who desired to look like living or dead celebrities. In MTV's reality documentary series, we were treated to an Elvis impersonator who wanted to torture his lip into Elvis's characteristic snarl because he thought it would improve his profitability. The reality was that a surgeon could not provide him with the level of perfection he wanted. In several cases, the guests had fairly unrealistic expectations, and the doctors, ingenuous though they were, could only make the subjects more like their ideal visions and could not totally transform them into new people. Imagine the discomfort of being in a room with a person whom you could never please. You could never make them into who they wanted to be.

The pursuit of a new face appears related to issues of identity. These people wanted to be different people, specifically, a famous person. Heather Hendershot writes in "Belabored Reality" that "though participants' goals may be stated loftily as 'finding true love,' or 'resolving emotion issues," the vast majority of reality TV focuses in some way on work" (2009, 245). The goals of the transformations on *I Want a Famous Face* were often work goals combined with the guest's vision of his or her identity.

MTV's *IWAFF* was a program popular in the early millennium, in 2004, when the fear of post-9/11 attacks drove Americans to want to change everything about themselves, including the way they looked. The program ran one season for 12 episodes and was abruptly cancelled. It is possible that audiences didn't identify with people who were so distressed by their own identities and appearance that they would want to change them. As the United States slowly came away from self-analysis after 9/11, the hunger for self-improvement and self-change may have dissipated. Matthew Gilbert, writing for *The Boston Globe,* said, "*Famous Face* is not a pretty sight." Gilbert wrote that the show elevates "star worship to a disturbing level" (2004).

The idea of transforming oneself and going for a complete change was here transformed into an indulgence in harsh plastic surgery techniques that produced painful and agonizing recovery periods for small end rewards. Audiences seemed to forget that surgery was rough enough when it was needed, but making surgery into a necessity seemed extreme. While the guests seemed completely sincere and determined, one must ask whether perhaps the money spent on plastic surgery could not be more cost-effectively spent on therapy. Underlying all these transformations was an overwhelming purpose to outsmart, outwit, and fool one's DNA. Further, the subjects of the MTV show wanted to look like stars who mostly were very temporary commodities. Suppose the subjects did achieve goals to appear to mirror Brittany Spears, or Ricky Martin, or Jessica Simpson. Would the show's guests wish to retain that appearance after the star's popularity faded?

One contestant, Gia, was a transsexual woman, and, though she had made a successful gender switch, she wished to emulate the look of Pamela Anderson. Gia believed that looking like the celeb would increase her earning power and that by looking more like her idol she would feel better. These issues suggested there were some ethical issues to be discussed with the contestants' plastic surgeons. Should surgeons take money from people who have an infatuation with a celebrity, and are such fixations a sign of potential mental health issues?

In one episode, Gia went to her doctor, and he told her he could make her look more like the figure she admired but that nothing was going to transform her. She had her lips plumped with collagen; she had breast implants to make her bosoms even larger; and she had liposuction to remove fat around the belly. For all intents and purposes, it appeared makeup might have produced a similar effect.

Like *The Swan* and other extreme makeover programs, the palpable discontent with one's own appearance was as disturbing as the guests' goals. The cult of celebrity was part of a larger cultural obsession with the entertainment industry. In fact, the issue of wanting to look like a star had something to do with the entire cult of fandom. Anne Helen Petersen commented that "from the start, ET's tone (*Entertainment Tonight*) had mirrored that of a traditional fan magazine, offering fawning, flattering portraits of the stars and Hollywood delivered by Hart and her various co-anchors in a bright cheery fashion" (2013, 238). So in a way, *I Want a Famous Face* was in part a fan show, like an episode of *Entertainment Tonight* praising Michael Jackson or another celebrity.

Sadly, most of the people emulated were merely visual images. Faces such as Brad Pitt, Jennifer Lopez, or Britney Spears might be beguiling on screen, but a physical transformation didn't make individuals into those people. Perhaps the final word on the show is Matthew Gilbert's when he wrote, "Watching 'I Want a Famous Face,' I wanted aspirin, and later as I thought more and more about MTV's Makeover documentary series, cyanide" (2004).

See also: How Do I Look?; The Swan

Further Reading

David S. Escoffery, *How Real Is Reality TV?*; Matthew Gilbert, "Famous Face Is Not a Pretty Sight," *The Boston Globe*, March 29, 2004; Anne Helen Petersen, "Entertainment Tonight/Tabloid News," 2013.

LA INK

LA Ink chronicled the adventures of a group of tattoo artists in Los Angeles. Partly a show about creating and maintaining businesses and partly a show about the close-knit fraternity of tattoo artists who live in the area, the program did a very credible job of documenting the profession of tattoo artists and their relationships with their clients. Tattooing—by its definition, inscribing a person's skin with images, pictures, mementos, color, and changes to their appearance that can last forever—is an unusual profession, like doctors and stylists. Tattoo artists can have great personal and emotional rapport with their customers, like therapists or priests. There is a need for a level of trust, and a need to allow the artist to become familiar with their skin and body. In a way, the person being tattooed has allowed a person access to the body that can be difficult to grant. The artist has to be sensitive to a subject's vulnerable areas, such as the back or stomach, and the client can be self-conscious of those and other body issues.

The show benefited from a wide range of celebrity guests coming to the tattoo shop, including Lady Gaga, Dave Navarro (Jane's Addiction), Jenna Jameson (porn star), Scott Ian (Anthrax), Nick Barnett (Green Bay Packers), Stephen Baldwin (actor), Eve (rapper), and Margaret Cho (comedian). You never knew who would come in for a quick tattoo.

The program featured a variety of LA's top tattoo talent, including Kat Von D, Corey Miller, and Hannah Aitchison. The program ran four seasons from 2007 to 2011 and offered over 80 episodes in the lives of tattoo artists. The series started with a personal narrative of Kat Von D, who was relocating from Florida (and the program *Miami Ink,* from which this show spun off) back to her native California, and she was working to integrate herself into the LA tattoo scene again and to open her own shop in the overheated economy of the LA basin.

The program focused on the customers coming to the shop every week to be tattooed and why they wanted specific images attached to their bodies. The artists, again acting as mediums or surrogates for the design process, would try to fulfill their design image and provide the customers with the closure they were seeking. Some wanted to remember a loved one, some wanted to remember a time, and some were responding to their own personal cultural heritage.

The program illustrated the high volatility in the tattoo trade with Kat and her crew changing regularly. Many people move on to careers as stylists or makeup artists, while others have personal squabbles and end up working for other shops. The program followed Kat's journey, opening with her attempts to find work and her struggle to find and retain artists in her own shop. Von D was involved in several competitions, including breaking world records for the most tattoos of a single image during a 24-hour period. Von D tattooed the *LA Ink* logo onto over 400 recipients in a 24-hour marathon.

The show was a ratings hit for TLC and dragged in the important 18–49 buying age group to watch the channel. Kat Von D had troubles during and following the show. In 2010, her Hollywood Hills home was damaged in a fire that also killed her cat, Valentine. She tweeted, according to the *Daily Mail,* "In order to gain everything, you must lose everything. RIP My little Valentine." It was suggested that Von D started the blaze by leaving candles burning unattended in the home. Then in October of 2014, she had a fire at her shop, High Voltage Tattoos, that included smoke and water damage.

See also: How Do I Look?

Further Reading

David S. Escoffery, *How Real Is Reality TV?*; Todd Van Lulling, "Here's What Really Happened to the Cars from *Pimp My Ride*," *Huffington Post*, February 25, 2015; Heather Waugh, "*LA Ink* Star Gets Angry outside Her Famed Tattoo Shop after Assessing Damage from Early Morning Blaze," *Daily Mirror*, October 23, 2014.

A MAKEOVER STORY

A Makeover Story takes friends who have drab wardrobes and places them in striking clothes with the help of a fashion consultant. Usually, the guests are already attractive and possess good wardrobes, but they need a little expert advice and some prodding to enhance and maximize their appearance.

A Makeover Story was one of the first makeover shows in the new generation of reality shows that began their existence on TLC starting in 2000. The program ran as a daytime series, produced the highest ratings of any TLC daytime show, and encouraged TLC to add other daytime reality programming. It ran for five seasons and produced effective shows that depended on solid, simple design and good grooming ideas. The show was straightforward and free of gimmicks, snarky commentary, or hyped, puffed, and coercive techniques that dominated later makeover programming in this genre. Later programs often employed bullying, contrivances, and overbearing hosts who dominated the proceedings. As practiced here, the makeover concept is devoted exclusively to bringing out the best in the guest, who was in need of sartorial assistance, while along the way sponsoring clothing, products, and services. Sadly, modern makeover programs often devolve to bashing, diminishing, and browbeating guests to achieve stronger ratings.

The program worked in a 30-minute format, and during this time two people would receive the makeover experience. This contrasts with contemporary programs that distend the experience, produce cliffhanger dramas, and focus less on the subject of transformation. The half-hour format demands compression and efficient work to transform the fashion subject. In later seasons, the show added experts in the roles of fashion consultant, Dan Brickley; costumer, Alison Freer; hairstylist, Moses Jones; and salon owner, Gretchen Monahan.

A Makeover Story was quite a popular program in its era. Courteney Stuart, writing for *The Hook* commented that "the makeover show that receives 1,000 applications every week" chose two Afghani women living in Charlottesville for the opportunity for a makeover. The show liked the women's story. Their family had moved to the United States in the 1980s to escape the strife in Afghanistan. Stuart wrote, "'They're extremely attractive,' says Sullivan. Still, the show felt they'd be able to transform each of them. Adding to the sisters' appeal . . . was the opportunity to do both a makeover and a make-*under*." (Stuart 2003) As was typical of the program, they didn't start with subjects with grave fashion issues. The show begins with careful, smart, attractive, well-groomed people and provides extra help to allow them to be even more attractive. Victoria Muradi was an assistant admissions person at UVA and already dressed like a professional. The producers wanted to "de-drab" her wardrobe and bring out more color in her style. Her younger sister, Sahara Muradi, was still in high school but worked hard to produce a good make up regime and spent hours preparing a complicated makeup and clothing ritual each day. The producers wanted to simplify, modernize, and decomplicate her prep routine. The show presented the women at the end of the makeover, still beautiful, still modest, and still attractive, but with added color and sparkle in their wardrobes. The results were subtle but transformative, and the show provided inspiration to common viewers to remake their own lives and attractiveness by using careful makeup preps and a non-fussy and sensible wardrobe. The program set the stage for countless makeover programs and raised the standard for what such a show could accomplish.

See also: Extreme Makeover: Home Edition; 60 Minute Makeover

Further Reading

David S. Escoffery, *How Real Is Reality TV?*; Courteney Stuart, "TLC in Town: *A Makeover Story* Visits Charlottesville," *The Hook*, July 31, 2003.

PIMP MY RIDE

MTV's *Pimp My Ride* was a fun, car enthusiast show in which the guests who owned feeble and failing vehicles presented their faltering cars to a mechanical and custom repair shop, and the shop renovated their rides to their former glory—and often beyond. The program hit the target demographic of 12–24-year-old boys that MTV widely courts. The fantasy of having your broken car repaired and revitalized is apparently in the back of many young men's minds, so the program had a loyal fan base and featured a wide assortment of cars.

Host Xzibit checked out the owner's car before taking it to the remodel shop and usually passed a negative judgment on it. In the opening episode, the proud owner of a Daihatsu minivan asked for help. Xzibit exclaimed that if he kicked the car's tires, the car might fall over. The car was a hideous wreck with doors removed, little seating, few comforts, and lacking any interior carpet or proper body work. Xzibit took the car to a local remodeling shop. Like a fashion makeover, the team of auto-detailing specialists suggested an intensive course of surgery, changing out everything but the engine. The doors were rehung, the hardware replaced, a stereo system installed, seats refurbished, carpeting layered across the van, and painting providing a beautiful, glossy glow. The amount of attention and detail showered on the car reminded viewers of MTV dating shows like *Next* and *Dismissed*. If the boys on those shows were as attentive as these auto detailers, they would have never been dismissed.

However, there has been general controversy over how much on MTV is real, particularly in its reality TV programming. Todd Van Luling, writing for *The Huffington Post*, exposed some of the show's secrets: "From cars that would break down in a matter of weeks to fat-shaming a contestant to one MTV employee apparently trying to convince another car owner to break up with his girlfriend, there was a lot more to the creation of this show than Xzibit simply saying, 'Yo dawg'" (2015). Sometimes the program would show additions to cars that were just for show for the program and were taken out of the car immediately after the program. Some products placed in the vehicles did not perform properly or never worked at all, like several cars that had television screens placed in the back seat. Many of the cars were simply so irredeemable that, despite the crew's best efforts, they could not be reconditioned satisfactorily.

The program was a popular MTV entry, running from 2004 to 2007, creating over 70 episodes, and detailing a broad cross section of different types of vehicles. In the half-hour series, owners would bring in wreckers and have them transformed into cherry vehicles in a brief span. CMT ran a competing series called *Trick My Truck*, emphasizing trucks over cars.

The show used different customization shops, including West Coast Customs and Galpin Auto Sports. The rebuilds of the cars were extensive. Xzibit had a great time making fun of the low quality of the cars, but the owners were adamant that their vehicles not only needed restoration but were priceless, worthy of saving. The impact of the makeover was a custom pimp that was tied to the owner and their interests. If the owner was a surfer, the detail work exaggerated a nautical theme. If the owner was a banker or financial person, then money might have been the dominant motif.

Unlike other MTV reality shows in which the players were faceless, nameless, and quickly forgotten, the identities of cars and owners on this show are remembered and widely reported. Many remember individual cars and makeovers. Each is unique, and it makes one wonder how unique people are when the car grabs more attention than the people. Everything from Daihatsus to Cadillac limos to Dodge Caravans to Chevy Bel Airs to Toyota Wonderwagons were reconditioned on the show.

Some of the reinventions of the cars were truly creative. One guest had a shoe rack put into the trunk so he could grab new shoes when he desired. Another guest had an aquarium installed between the front seat and back seat. A big part of the drama and dynamics of the show was the crew at West Coast Custom. The engineers, technicians, and restoration team each had their own look and style. Each had a unique take on how to bring out the best in old cars. Some of the crew specialized in building unique gear into the car. Others tried to add new or novel equipment that had not been featured in a car previously. Every once in a while, the cars being restored were too far gone, and, in such instances, MTV replaced the old vehicle with a new edition and pimped it instead.

See also: Top Gear; The X Factor

Further Reading

David S. Escoffery, *How Real Is Reality TV?*; Todd Van Luling, "Here's What Really Happened to the Cars from *Pimp My Ride*," *Huffington Post*, February 25, 2015.

QUEER EYE FOR THE STRAIGHT GUY

Queer Eye for the Straight Guy promoted the concept that not only was it okay for straight guys to hang with gay guys, it could be downright beneficial. Wives, girlfriends, and even children offered up heterosexual hunks-in-the-rough to be transformed by the Fab Five, men with expertise in perceived gay fortes. Fashionable Carson Kressley dressed the makeovers. Kyan Douglas groomed them. Thom Filicia redecorated bachelor pads, while Ted Allen honed the wining and dining expertise of the "make-betters." Jai Rodriguez kept straight men abreast of popular culture while adding youth and racial diversity to the cast. The series ran on Bravo from 2003 to 2007, providing animated water cooler conversation in the days before Tweeting. The cast was among Barbara Walters's most fascinating people of 2003. The show also garnered critical acclaim, winning Best Reality Show in 2004.

For a show based on stereotypes, it also broke them down. Only two of the Fab Five presented as obviously gay: Kressley and Rodriguez. By dropping *for the Straight Guy* from its title in season three, the show broadened its range, suggesting that there could be dorky gay people in need of do-overs, as well as flannel-shirted lesbians. As the team worked on special projects, such as planning the perfect evening for a marriage proposal, it became obvious that what gay people thought romantic worked for heterosexuals as well.

The show began with the Fab Five in a vehicle on the way to meet that week's "Cinderfella." Their discussion provided background about the candidate for change. Transformation candidates included husbands whose wardrobes consisted of jogging pants and concert T-shirts; boyfriends whose apartments scared live-apart girlfriends; and fathers whose look had not evolved since 1963. Candidates for change included a zookeeper, a widower, and a policeman. The Cinderfella spent time with each expert.

Carson would prance into the makeover's closet and decimate his wardrobe, borrowing a cue from *What Not to Wear*. Sometimes outfits were in such disarray that clothes needed to be sniffed to determine whether they were clean or dirty. Kyan would introduce the makeover male to skincare, fragrance, and hair products. Sometimes manscaping was involved, as beards, mustaches, and ponytails disappeared along with nose and ear hair. Thom would style the living area, providing organization and consistency at the very least. Some featured bedrooms originally consisted of a mattress on the floor. Ted would head for the kitchen and teach the chosen one how to make a simple yet delicious meal served with appropriate liquid refreshment. Sometimes Ted's perusal of the refrigerator and cupboards turned into an archeological dig, uncovering foods years past their expiration dates. Jai would usually involve the "make-better" in an activity. Initially, Jai's area of expertise was unclear even to him. The other cast members were specialists in their fields. "I was the only actor" (Nededog, 2013). Eventually he became the "culture vulture."

Although team members did not know one another before casting, viewers sensed camaraderie between them. This friendship extended to the Cinderfella who spent time with them during the makeover. Occasionally one of the cast, usually Carson, appeared to fall in love with the man he had created, a la Henry Higgins.

The transformation would culminate in an event—a first date, a reunion, an art show opening. Cinderfella was left to practice lessons learned while the team watched his efforts via video. Relaxing, drinks in hand, the team critiqued his efforts. Often proud papas seeing their instructions followed to a T, at times they also cringed—"I never told him to do that." Carson's and Kyan's improvements were obvious as soon as the nominator saw the remade man. But Thom's decorating often elicited the most "ahs" from female nominators. Unless the rookie cook's efforts went terribly wrong, the couple enjoyed a romantic dinner. Jai may have had Cinderfella create a one-of-a-kind piece of jewelry for his date, or he may have taught him salsa if the lady liked to dance.

The show would end with a general acclamation of "we done good." And the straight guy offered appreciation and comfortable hugs to his teachers. In 2013 Bravo aired *Queer Eye Reunion: 10 Years Later*. During the media hype preceding the special, the Fab Five shared their impressions of that time. Kressley remembered, "All I wanted to do was get rid of mullets and pleated khakis." Douglas, clearly the shyest of group, worried that he'd never done television before. Filicia felt the series "allowed a lot of people to make really bold decisions about feeling comfortable with themselves." In fact, Allen confessed that the show precipitated his outing to his family. "I don't really understand to this day why I tried so hard to get that job. I almost wonder if that's part of it. It forced me to tell them." Rodriguez, as well as other cast members, initially objected to the *queer* in the title. In fact, his family, though totally accepting of him, refused to use the name when discussing the show.

All cast members were agreed on the legacy of the show. To this day people come up and thank the cast for helping them deal with identity issues. Troy DeVolld, a reality producer, says, "*Queer Eye* did for reality television what *Will and Grace* did for scripted television"(Arellano, 2013). Viewers, some for the first time, knowingly invited gay people into their homes and decided they liked them.

Liz Hufford

See also: Real World; Teen Mom

Further Reading

T. W. Adorno, "Television and the Patterns of Mass Culture"; David S. Escoffery, *How Real Is Reality TV?*

RAMSAY'S KITCHEN NIGHTMARES

Gordon Ramsay, the confrontational, screaming English cook, chef, and star of multiple reality shows is some people's nightmare, but, oddly enough, some people's hero. Ramsay does not shirk from a fight. He is forthright, practices tough love, and doesn't tolerate any nonsense. Ramsay works to make the restaurants he encounters the best he can. He struggles mightily to help people who can't see the obvious mistakes they are making in cooking, managing, and marketing their private restaurants.

First, Ramsay may be a mogul, but he supports the endeavor of individuals who wish to achieve something. That is, at his utmost, he is strongly a supporter of the little guy, wielding maximum control through acts of personal creativity, entrepreneurial zeal, and a spirit of enterprise. Ramsay's restaurants don't fail for lack of trying. The tireless entrepreneur is out there hustling, pushing, bullying, and supporting his clients. If he doesn't care, it doesn't show. He looks absolutely, 100-percent committed to making each restaurant the best it can be. Further, he doesn't advocate some cookie-cutter Gordon Ramsay plan. He sides with each restaurant, forming its own unique and individual identity and style. Not everyone would want to be Ramsay, the pugilistic, pushy, obnoxious, aggressive, cursing, furious, angry, and often berating coach. However, the moment Ramsay knows the team is on board, trying, and rightly positioned for success, he changes into a careful, articulate, audacious, and charming coach and supporter.

Kitchen Nightmares started with Ramsay visiting a kitchen that was known to have serious problems. In one episode he visited a friendly little country restaurant in Wales. From the word *go*, he hated the place and its ugly, loud blue décor. When he entered, the place was in interior disarray. The husband/wife team who owned and ran the establishment quarreled and bickered, the young and competent waitresses snickered and waited for the fighting to subside so they could serve up some food. Sometimes they had to wait awhile.

Ramsay's show was half therapy session and half business advice. Ramsay would see the owner fussing over loads of cookbooks and tell him to jettison the baggage and develop his own identity. The brutal Ramsay told him he was imitating a chef and spending far too much time with intricate recipes when he should just go back to his Italian family roots and produce vintage, rustic, provincial Italian food. The owner took Ramsay's word and started to develop a smaller and more efficient batch of food that could be served faster, prepared in advance, and required less complex preparation. Ramsay discovered the wife had been ducking out for a smoke, berating the guests, acting surly in front of customers, and getting combative when the kitchen was running slow.

Ramsay indulged in a bit of marriage counseling, telling them they couldn't have fights in the restaurant and they are killing the place with the bad atmosphere created from their quarrels. Then the star put together a nice cuisine, ordered some assistance for a relaunch, and paraded through the town in a grass-covered coach spreading leaflets and asking people who had avoided the place to step back in and try the food again.

The magic wasn't instant, and there were some rough nights getting the timing down. Ramsay had his doubts about the place's survival, but a month later when he returned, they had repainted, and they had adhered to his regime and now had happy customers. The owners had stopped fighting and had their self-esteem back. Things were transformed, but this was not the miracle transformation brought about by magic plastic surgery doctors. It was a tough victory won by Ramsay's vitriolic love.

An article in *The New Yorker* by Bill Buford referred to Ramsay's famous temper tantrums and failure to control that inflammatory anger. Buford writes, "Once Ramsay allowed himself to get angry, he seemed to look around for other things to stay angry about, as though something had been switched on that he couldn't control." This seemed to be a big problem for him. The volcanic temperament might make for interesting TV, but it seemed like it could make life in his restaurants as one of his workers highly disagreeable. While it might taste good, his food seemed made from his employees' blood.

See also: Extreme Makeover; Restaurant: Impossible

Further Reading

Bill Buford, "The Taming of the Chef," *The New Yorker*, April 2, 2007; David S. Escoffery, *How Real Is Reality TV?*

RESTAURANT: IMPOSSIBLE

Restaurant: Impossible and its cast of retoolers, entrepreneurs, and distressed restaurant owners has all the drama and anxiety of Gordon Ramsay's *Kitchen Nightmares*, without the hyperbolic Gordon Ramsay screaming at everyone. What we see in *Restaurant: Impossible* are suicide rescue missions for kitchens that look ready to perish. In one episode, a family of Florida restaurateurs has sunk all their money into the restaurant, and in recent years the fortunes of the business have been declining.

Food Network's *Restaurant: Impossible* has been popular, featuring celebrity chef Robert Irvine. The show starts with the premise that the host has two days and $10,000 to transform a failing kitchen into a successful one. The show debuted in 2011, and in 2015 had scored nine eventful seasons and shows no signs of quitting. The ambitious chef and crew rise to the challenge of taking a tough-luck environment and turning it around.

Resident rescue magician Irvine comes into the environment to investigate. He has a few invited families order up, and he samples what the kitchen is putting out. The food is soggy, dull, and often gross. Preparation is slovenly, and the chef/cook/owner is doing a lackluster job of leading his crew. Add to this a deflated economy and a poor return-business ratio, and the restaurant is in dire trouble. The owner mutters that he makes less than $300 a week from the investment.

Irvine studies the situation and discovers an unclean roach infestation. He closes the establishment as an unsafe health hazard. He stops people from eating. He closes the shop. He bug bombs the place and hires pest-control experts to analyze where bugs are entering. He throws away old fridges and bad storage, tosses an old grill, buys new equipment, and brings in designers and builders to give the place a top-to-bottom cleaning and redesign.

A key part of Irvine's ministry is menu trimming. Irvine advises the owner that he is making 32 types of protein in the menu, and this huge and varied inventory is bleeding him dry. Irvine recommends only a few meat dishes and a smaller menu to contain waste and rotate his stock of meats and other perishables more quickly. Both are cost-cutting and convenience measures. Irvine's tips not only save money but time, and Irvine's subjects find themselves completing dishes much faster under his regime.

When the place reopens, the husband and wife team are greeted by a cheerful façade that reflects the intense cleaning and makeover that Irvine and his crew have engineered. The facility is spotless, reportedly smells better, has a restricted but more efficient menu, and has a reenergized and better-purposed crew, with the husband leading the kitchen with more energy and will to lead. There is less time spent on complicated recipes, fighting bugs, and worrying about finances. The new structure looks capable of bringing in more customers and sustaining interest in the restaurant.

The New York Times summarized the show's appeal as "salvation arrives in the form of Robert Irvine, a brawny British chef in a snug black polo shirt, who, through a mix of tough love, expertise, and shouting (and with an assist from an interior decorator and crew of carpenters), transforms the place." The *Times* investigated Irvine's miracle cure by talking to restaurants that had received Irvine's treatment, and, to their surprise, Irvine's work was successful in most cases. Some restaurants recanted on parts of Irvine's prescription and actually restored some popular products to the menu, but the *Times* found that Irvine's advice was generally solid. The *Times* did say that the show promotes the myth of the management consultant and the notion in American minds of hiring some guru who knows more than we do to fix a person's problems. The *Times* suggested that believing that myth is dangerous. Several restaurants that followed the show's advice closed. Also, The *Times* mentioned (no surprise) that everything you see on reality TV isn't completely real. The *Times* explained that a decorator showed up a month before the 48-hour makeover and made plans a month in advance. Materials for the makeover arrive in advance of Irvine and his crew, and the surprise redecoration is preplanned and only assembled in the 48-hour window.

What makes the show so successful and popular is complicated. Irvine is demanding and can be brutal, but he is far more concerned in keeping the morale of his crew high than Gordon Ramsay, whose advice is tinged with invective, and constant, outbursts of pique. Further, Irvine steers but doesn't seize control. He extends a hand to the drowning, and he asks them to climb on board while expecting them to lend a steady hand while the rescue is in progress.

See also: Extreme Makeover; Ramsay's Kitchen Nightmares

Further Reading

Bill Buford, "The Taming of the Chef," *New Yorker*, April 2, 2007; David Segal, "After the Cameras Leave the Kitchen," *New York Times*, July 9, 2012.

THE SIMPLE LIFE

The Simple Life is a reality show from 2003 that championed the exploits of multi-millionaire heiress Paris Hilton, living the simple life in bucolic Arkansas after her wild and feted existence in Beverly Hills. This program ran on reality TV for five seasons from 2003 to 2007 and chalked up over 50 episodes. First appearing on the Fox Network, the program completed its run on E! Many were fans of Hilton's life lessons after living in the rural South.

The show mirrored the plot of *Green Acres* with pampered city slickers having to adjust to the rigors of country rural life. Despite its humor and often unintentional vision of the rich and the farm community, the show was revealing in that it illustrated firsthand the massive income, lifestyle, and intellectual gap between sectors of American culture. Make no mistake, Americans do live in entirely separate countries with entirely different cultures. In this sense, the show was a sociological reverse *Wizard of Oz* parable about the idea that "there's no home in that place." By the end of the program, one questioned the reality of the Arkansas agrarian community, who came across as far more knowledgeable, tolerant, and viable than one would expect, and Paris Hilton and her friend Nicole Richie, whose cartoonish behavior seemed to exist in an animated world in which magical creatures and make-believe props would appear to solve the protagonist's wildest problems.

The program debuted with Hilton and Richie safely ensconced in their Beverly Hills cribs as spoiled and idyllic young people living the life of richness and little care. Then there was an attractive party before their adventure, similar to some sort of initiation rite. It was as if the girls must face living with dangerous primitives for a few weeks, until they could return to the clan, pound their chests, throw their spears in the air, and claim victory. The girls boarded a private luxury jet and were whisked away to rural Arkansas. At the airport there was a car to meet them. It was an old truck with no driver. They must figure out how to drive a stick shift, plot a course for the farm, and arrive without running down any goats or mules. They navigated through the rural splendor and were greeted by the family on the farm that would be their home for a month. They were given porch outdoor accommodations for the visit. They were sent to town to buy delicacies like pigs' feet and tobacco. Upon their return, they were given a list of chores and other duties, like plucking dead chickens. The girls declined their duties with the suggestion that their temperament was too delicate for preparing meat dishes.

The genesis of the show was at Fox productions. The studio wished to produce a new comedy outside the confines of a sitcom. The executives wanted something that was a reality program but would strike a chord with viewers. They proposed taking some high-concept CBS sitcoms from the 1960s, like *Green Acres,* and transforming them into reality fodder. Just as MTV retooled the drama *90210* as a reality drama in *Laguna Beach* and *The Hills*, so Fox would re-create *Green Acres* using real-life, wealthy celebrities. Simultaneously, Fox was talking to Paris Hilton about doing a show, and the producers felt her charming, rich-girl innocence would blend well with the idea of taking a city slicker into the woods.

After a couple of successful seasons, Hilton and Richie had a falling out, and the show was cancelled at Fox but picked up by E!, the Entertainment Network. Richie and Hilton patched things up, but they had DUI charges and health issues plaguing them that dogged their last seasons. Finally the show was cancelled, and 20th Century Fox fought hard to resurrect the show in some guise with Kimberly Stewart and Kelly Osbourne. Osbourne quit after a few days, suggesting the show and the idea of showing wealthy people stuck on a farm was juvenile.

Nicole Richie, now married and with two children was asked if she would ever reunite with Paris to return to *The Simple Life,* and she replied, "'I don't know that I could think of doing it again and with anybody else," Nicole admitted during a Twitter Q&A while visiting *E! News*. 'It was fun to do in my 20s. I was 20 or 21 when I started it and it was like the best time ever'" (Blackwelder 2015). However, with midlife creeping in, Richie will likely find other challenges, like her 2015 VH1 series *Candidly Nicole*.

See also: Real World; Teen Mom

Further Reading

T. W. Adorno, "Television and the Patterns of Mass Culture"; Carson Blackwelder, "Would Nicole Richie Do a Simple Life Reunion with Paris Hilton?" *Wet Paint,* July 21, 2015; David S. Escoffery, *How Real Is Reality TV?*

60 MINUTE MAKEOVER

60 Minute Makeover is a British show with the remarkable premise that the program's crew can re-create a dwelling in 60 minutes. The claim is supported by the fact that the show offers a lengthy reconnaissance and a full consultation with the principles. They map out a plan and bring a team of approximately 20 craftspeople to lay flooring, cut carpet, paint and wallpaper walls, move in new furniture, and spruce up the window treatments. The show works on low-cost procedures, unlike American programs that detail the high-end buying experience, and the principles in *60 Minute Makeover* seek to find items on a budget. The show's premise includes a pre-refit cleaning, and all old furnishings and materials are trashed before the 60 minutes commences. Filming details the work of each crew member. Usually, each person has a specific job, such as flooring, furnishing, or wall treatments. The team leader directs those projects throughout the house. Each room also has a team manager with the plans, the layout, and the items preassembled in a tent outside the dwelling. The result is that the crew moves with the speed and precision of an army, tearing out the old, recovering the space in new materials, and giving the place a nice sprucing up.

A feature is that during the 60-minute refit, there is an obligatory tea breaks after 30 minutes for checkups. The crews have reorientation talks and then head back in for the second half. The key person is the designer who creates the plan for the house and each room. It helps that many of the dwellings are British council houses of the 1950s and 1960s, so the crew are aided by already knowing the layout and design of most of the dwellings. The council houses were a socialized housing experiment to make sure after the bombing of Britain that every British citizen could have a home of his or her own. Admittedly, some of these homes are small, cramped, and not opulent, but for the most part, Britons did become home owners, and the social experiment largely worked and created a nation of homeowners. Today, these houses are succumbing to age, and the council house experiment, long over, requires a lot of additional retrofitting to keep such homes in good working order.

The *60 Minute* crew performs in the guise of public servants making families, and life in general, more agreeable. Usually the repairs are done in an afternoon or weekend when the family is away for an outing, and the families selected are often in some drastic need—a family surgery, an employment situation, a disability, a layoff that has hampered repair efforts. The crew is keen to make someone's life better, similar to the 19th-century American institution of a barn raising, a group of modern church volunteers, or Habitat for Humanity craftspeople. The speed and budget differ from the American model, in which the emphasis is not on economizing but on spending, spending, and spending. The results are transformative. Some houses have inadequate flooring, improper bedding, tired decor, or simply dated, used, furniture. The crew places a little shine and luster back in the family life. It may not be a perfect fix, but it makes the day-to-day reality of life a bit easier for families under stress. When compared to the costly *Extreme Makeover: Home Edition* and other high-end programs on American television, these programs reflect enormous practicality, DIY spirit, and entrepreneurial zeal.

See also: Clean House; Extreme Makeover: Home Edition

Further Reading

David S. Escoffery, *How Real Is Reality TV?*

STYLE BY JURY (SBJ)

While some reality television can seem dull or like an infomercial between infomercials, *Style by Jury* is insightful and revelatory. The show hails from Canada as a makeover show, ran on the W Network, and appeared from 2004 to 2010. A show with the same name debuted in 2015 on TLC, reviving the concept of the original show: that you cannot undo a bad first impression. In the original program, hosts exhibit good sense and offer solid advice to their hapless respondents. The jig is that people come into the show thinking they are being interviewed for a potential makeover, but in reality the producers have already chosen these fashion-challenged types for the ultimate redo.

When the guests step in, there is a room with one-way glass where a team of nine jurors and some experts in fashion and design look these anti-fashionistas over. The results of these first impressions are often devastating and debilitating. People cry, scream, and walk out. For the most part, they stay, and take their lickings. The host, Bruce Turner, talks to the contestant and often asks how they came to adopt such ugly garb. Sometimes the guests are coy and offhand, and at other times they indulge in lengthy self-justifications. Some look made up to be clowns. Some question that the contestants could really look so hideous. Perhaps the program was staged with makeup help. However, many of the guests appear clueless about their debilitated appearance.

The most enticing part of the show is the seven-day transformation and makeover segment. As reality shows have a desire to see drastic results these days, the host and team are anxious to push the contestant into a battery of self-improvement procedures that, while reinvigorating, can seem draconian, harsh, and simply dangerous. One woman needed a new chin, and the plastic surgeon recommended liposuctioning fat out of her face and rebuilding her cheekbones. It was not an attractive sight, and further it looked painful and risky. Watching the procedure on the program was gruesome. The semiconscious, rebuilt contestant seemed to come around quickly and loved the changes to her facial structure. She went through the violent alterations to better herself, and the doctors, the host, and her boyfriend were filled with compliments. Considering that when she entered, the jury joked about her purple outfit (calling her Barney's little sister), shivered when they saw her wardrobe closet, and guffawed at some of her reasoning for not changing her appearance, the change created by the show was quite revolutionary.

While the show is fun, gets results, and truly seems to improve people's lives, there is an intrusiveness that can be discomforting at times. Theodor Adorno's mid-20th-century critique of the culture industry argued that the rulers of culture expect our conformity. Adorno writes that "the more the system of 'merchandising' culture is expanded, the more it tends also to assimilate the 'serious' art of the past adapting this art to the system's own requirements" (160, 2005). According to Adorno, people lose the right to look different in a society in which conformity is the norm. He writes, "The ideals of conformity and conventionalism were inherent in popular novels from the very beginning. Now however, these ideals have been translated into rather clear-cut prescriptions of what to do and what not to do" (163, 2005).

Conformity isn't new, and it is not new to reality shows, but the trend toward making everyone the same is worrisome. *Style by Jury* ran on the W Network in Canada, and a new series of the show was picked up by American channel TLC in 2015.

The main element of the show is the way people make first impressions. Usually when contestants enter *SBJ*, the jury box behind the smoked glass cry, "Oh!"— like seeing this wretched person has brought them physical pain. The assumption is, anything imperfect must be corrected. Conformity to some unwritten code of dress becomes the norm. After the candidate hears these harsh judgments, they are mortified, visibly shaken, and often emotionally fragile. Host Turner turns on the charm, pushing the contestant to go for the full makeover. This makes for an interesting antagonism, because sometimes the guest does not desire nor wish for the oppressive makeover the cast, crew, producers, and Cinderella-hopefuls in the audience wish to see.

One episode featured a resister named Steve. While he dressed rather cartoonishly in oversized baggy pants, silly hats, John Lennon glasses, yellow patterned shirts, and so on, ultimately he was emotionally happy. The jury raked him, referring to him as a Weird Al Yankovic clone, or a guy who just didn't care about his appearance. While the commentary was especially vile and mean-spirited, Steve kept a pleasant level of composure. The show "sold" Steve as a loser: a 40-year-old guy who lived with his parents, worked part-time jobs, got up late, played guitar, dressed like a slob, and was a little overweight and unkempt. No problem. Steve had a good attitude about himself. He didn't opt for the veneers on all of his teeth or a procedure to whiten them to crystal perfection. He didn't want the LASIK surgery to perfect his vision. He traded his clunky Beatle glasses for contact lenses. He didn't want to take off his hat, but the barber clipped him to a shorter, controlled hairstyle, and they even integrated a partial hairpiece into his hairline to make him more attractive. His motto that he repeated when people asked him why he didn't go further was simply, "I don't want to fix what isn't broken." In the end, he looked great in slimmed-down fashions, new jeans, and an attractive topcoat. Maybe it wasn't the total makeover, but it was a makeover made on Steve's own terms, a democratizing effect of the whole program that the producers accepted.

The best moment was when the lifestyle counselor tried to get Steve to change, and Steve told him nicely that he was happy where he was. So often in reality shows, people allow themselves to be manipulated and railroaded by coaches, producers, or other provocateurs, but here the individual showed a modicum of sanity and self-respect and didn't allow the media to mediate him.

Usually, the week ends with the candidate before the jury again, only it is a new jury. In the case of Steve, they brought back the original jury, and they were suitably impressed. It was even more impressive that Steve had a hand in remaking his own makeover. A kicker to the experience is the inclusion of an added guest. Usually, this partner knows the guest and has prior knowledge. In this episode, that person was Steve's mum, and she wished him well. On the whole, *Style by Jury* is fun, creative, and a real tug-of-war between transformers and transformed. It raises important questions about self and society, self and appearance, and the desire for a homogeneous society and what that means.

The candidates undergo a top-to-toe overhaul that includes extensive cosmetic dentistry, dermatology, hair, makeup, and fashion. But the cornerstone of the makeover is with the internal transformation and coaching that enables the candidates to view themselves in a whole new light.

See also: Real World; Teen Mom

Further Reading
T. W. Adorno, "Television and the Patterns of Mass Culture"; David S. Escoffery, *How Real Is Reality TV?*

THE SWAN

The Swan holds certain distinctions as a reality show. Jennifer Pozner, in her book *Reality Bites Back*, referred to it as "the most sadistic reality series of the decade" (2010, 93). *The Swan* featured women who saw themselves as ugly ducklings. The show encouraged extreme bouts of multiple plastic surgeries to compete against other women to win the title of "the Swan" for that episode. *The Swan* was a 2004 reality makeover program that existed for two seasons. Though the show was previewed as having a potential third season, it was canceled after the second season for low ratings. In all, there were 18 episodes.

The Swan attempted to make women subject to an abstract and conformist vision of beauty ordained by others. Sociologist Theodor Adorno said that "the ideals of conformity conventionalism were inherent in popular novels . . . now, however, these ideals have been translated into rather clear-cut prescriptions of what to do and what not to do" (163, 2005).

The Swan was indicative of Anita Biressi and Heather Nunn's idea that many therapeutic shows were about self-revelation, and the idea that "our 'real' selves are only ever the performance of a role" (2005, 101). Few of the contestants on *The Swan* could be seen as ugly or even unattractive, but the coaches appeared to appeal to these women's vulnerabilities about appearance and enticed them into having more done to cosmetically alter themselves. In the beauty competition, women were routinely mortified, fat-shamed, taunted, cajoled, coerced, and mind-gamed into playing in the contest. Unlike shows like *The Biggest Loser* that seek to transform people (not always by ethical means) by changing eating habits, altering dietary regimes, increasing exercise, and instilling values of self-confidence and self-worth, *The Swan* baited and demoralized its charges, making them susceptible to suggestions of copious surgeries to procure an elusive prize at the show's end.

The show used forceful rhetoric to draw viewers. The title of *The Swan* suggested something ugly that needed transformation. The show stressed surgical options. In 2014, a former *Swan* contestant, Lorrie Arias, reported to *The Huffington Post:* "A decade later, she is depressed, bipolar, agoraphobic and believes she continues to suffer from body dysmorphic disorder" (2014). The short-term surgeries and beauty makeovers didn't seem to last for many former contestants, suggesting that such reality programming is perhaps manipulative and mostly false.

Each episode chronicled two of the women's progress in operations, body conditioning, mental attitude, and preparation for the final competitions/pageants. After multiple medical procedures, a 1,200-calorie daily diet plan, and endless workouts, two women were judged each week. The one who had shown the least growth from ugly duckling to swan was cut loose and sent home. Dismissal was coupled with negative self-image, causing a double blow to many women's egos. The final pageants were beauty contests. Instead of looking at the whole woman, the competitions were focused on appearances. There was an evening gown competition, a swimsuit competition, a Q and A session (more of a poise competition rather than a knowledge test), and finally, a lingerie competition.

Prizes for the winners included a year's spokesperson contract with Nutrisystem, a modeling contract, a gym membership, a trip, and in the first season a cash prize. Amanda McClain argues that the values represented by reality TV in such shows as *The Swan* may be rigged against everyday women. She writes, "On reality TV, the primary female beauty characteristics are youth, whiteness, thinness, surgical alteration, and hypersexuality" (2013, 51). Women don't conform to all or even most of these qualities in reality, so women watching such shows are virtually destined to feel inadequate.

Still, despite the potential for negative messages about a woman's physical appearance in *The Swan*, not all critics read it as a vile message. Some makeover gurus lauded the show as a program offering women a new chance to change their lives. Richard Huff wrote that "the series took women who are 'stuck in a rut,' and overhauled their lives through surgery and mental health help" (2006, 67). Still others saw shows like *The Swan* as devaluing women in other ways. Shana Heinricy in "The Cutting Room: Gendered American Dreams on Plastic Surgery TV" describes the dialectic of shows like *The Swan*. She writes that "by accepting these constructions of women's labor and bodies, a hegemonic discourse is created which attempts to limit women's access to other versions of the American Dreams, ones which may not require her to have such invasive procedures done upon her body" (2006, 163). Heinricy argues that such shows change beauty from a woman's definition and production to a male doctor's definition and work of beauty. Rather than a woman empowered to make herself beautiful, beauty is defined and controlled by men. However one sees *The Swan*, its surgical vision of beauty seemed to deprive women of the right to determine their own aesthetics and again placed their lives out of their own control. They moved from being a somebody to being an object for others' pleasure and unfortunately, judgment.

See also: Extreme Makeover; A Makeover Story

Further Reading

T. W. Adorno, "Television and the Patterns of Mass Culture"; Anita Biressi and Heather Nunn, *Reality TV, Realism and Revelation*, London: Wallflower Press, 2005; David S. Escoffery, *How Real Is Reality TV?*; Shana Heinricy, "The Cutting Room: Gendered American Dreams on Plastic Surgery TV"; Richard Huff, *Reality Television*; Jennifer Pozner, *Reality Bites Back*. 2010.

THIS OLD HOUSE (TOH)

This Old House is one of the most knowledgeable and venerable reality shows, hailing from PBS and responding to the maker manifesto of the late 20th century that Americans must continue to make and design their own dwellings. Richard Huff, in his book on *Reality Television*, referred to it as "the granddaddy of home makeover shows" (2006, 73). The original host, Bob Vila, became deeply associated with the show and branched off to create his own shows and line of products. However,

Vila was not the creator of the idea of *This Old House*. The idea was the brain child of Russell Morash and came from the notion that American craftspeople needed positive representation in the media. As the growth of professional degrees and professions accelerated in the late 20th century, *This Old House* extolled the virtues of craftsmanship, diligence, individual work in the context of construction teams, and the deeper-held idea that Americans by nature are craftspeople, engineers, builders, and makers. In a consumeristic society, that manifesto has almost gone extinct, but shows like *This Old House* have been powerful in keeping that tradition alive. The present incarnation of the program is hosted by Kevin O'Connor, with long-serving craftsman Norm Abram as carpenter.

The show is distributed by Warner Bros. domestically, but the program has been produced by PBS regularly since 1979 and has produced well over 900 episodes and holds records as one of the oldest reality, craft, and maker shows currently available in television.

Due to its stable home on PBS, its relatively low cost, strong fan base, and common sense, the show has remained a strong, popular favorite of the network despite the arrival of more glamorized and catchy reality shows. *This Old House* has often been lionized as the most authoritative, genuine, and knowledgeable of the home repair and restoration programs in the medium. Unlike other shows that tend to sidestep tough issues of how to re-create and rebuild homes, *TOH* explores the real costs and shows the intense labor needed to make a home repair work and succeed. The experts show great credibility and expertise in their no-nonsense approach to explaining all the crafts engaged in the process of home restoration and rebuilding.

The program is currently owned by Time, Inc., and costs are subsidized by GMC, State Farm Insurance, Lumber Liquidators, and the Home Depot. Previous underwriter Weyerhaeuser donated a million dollars a year to the show's production costs. Sponsors in the past have included reality companies, paint companies, Ace Hardware, and lock companies. Anyone at all involved in building has likely been associated with the show.

Today the show is *TOH* and *Ask TOH*. A third show, *Inside TOH*, features retrospectives of old shows and explores the completion of these old projects. Old shows have been resyndicated as *Classic TOH* on the DIY Network. An initial controversy of the series was the fear that hosts and guests were giving away industry trade secrets. When Bob Vila was hosting in the 1970s and 1980s, there were no other home improvement shows on television. However, the show grew into a cultural icon, and creator, Russell Monash, became known as the "father of how-to."

The cottage industry of *TOH* has literally turned into big business. The show has at least four spin-offs and classic episodes. There is a branch starring Norm Abram called *The New Yankee Workshop*. There is a subscription Web site. There is a magazine. The show has won 17 Emmys and garnered 82 nominations.

The series first began as a 13-part, one-time series out of Boston but picked up legions of fans right from the start. Huff described it as "leading a homeowner through a major renovation" (2006, 73). The Boston PBS station bought two houses to create labs for renovation. Then the station hit on the idea of taking family dwellings with the original residents involved in doing some of the labor and basically becoming cast members and paying for some of the renovation costs through their labor contribution. However, controversies erupted on that score as well. In the famous Weatherbee Farm case, Abram and Vila had heated discussions with the family over how the reconstruction was conducted. By the late 1980s, the series had headed toward restoring more upscale homes using master craftspeople. Huff comments that a major difference in the production of *This Old House* was that "homeowners needed to have the cash for the original remodel, although the show dramatically supplemented the project with donations of major new technology" (74).

Another controversy was Bob Vila, the popular host himself. *TOH* was underwritten by Home Depot, but Vila did commercial ads for another rival company and was fired for starting his own show, *Bob Vila's Home Again*. The crew complained that Vila was a screen hog, and they all felt the show and the people featured were democratized by Vila leaving. New host Steve Thomas took over the show for 15 years, hosting from 1989 to 2003. Recent host Kevin O'Connor has helmed from 2003 until the present.

The show's fan base and infrastructure has continued to grow and spread. As other shows on home improvement began to arrive, *TOH* became the continuing authoritative leader that everyone admired. *Time* came out with a *TOH* magazine in 1995 and bought the show from WGBH in 2001. Current host Kevin O'Connor was actually a homeowner asking questions on *ATOH* before joining as a cast member. Norm Abram's part has been upgraded on the show, and various area craftspeople receive feature time for their contribution to the show's repair schedule.

The program has been involved in community projects, including a restoration of two really decrepit homes in the 2009 season, through a project partnership with Nuestra Comunidad, a community-based organization seeking to build shelter for poor people. Many of the home renovation shows on television appeal to upscale viewers and flatter these viewers with restorations to elite dwellings. *TOH* moved significantly in the opposite direction, since they perceived a greater need among less-affluent viewers.

See also: Extreme Makeover: Home Edition; HGTV

Further Reading

T. W. Adorno, "Television and the Patterns of Mass Culture"; David S. Escoffery, *How Real Is Reality TV?*; Richard M. Huff, *Reality Television*, 2006.

TLC

TLC, formerly, The Learning Channel, is a station that began as a federally sponsored network devoted to learning and originated as the Appalachian Community Service Network in the 1970s, turned into The Learning Channel in the 1980s, and became TLC in the 1990s. Its origins were in providing educational programming to the disadvantaged populations of the Appalachian region, and this foundation gave it a head start in the early expansion of cable. TLC is an example of federal money that later stimulated private economic growth and industry. Today, TLC is a part of the Discovery family of channels, including the Discovery Channel and Animal Planet. The station's programming was originally focused on learning and educational shows, but by the start of the millennium, the focus had evolved toward lifestyle, reality, and personal-enhancement programming. TLC has a strong penetration of the cable market, with over 85 percent of cable-connected homes receiving TLC programming. The channel originated as a governmental project but devolved to private control and has been experimental and striving in its programming formats.

In its early incarnation (in the 1980s), *Captain's Log with Captain Mark Gray*, a boating safety series was a highly rated learning show with an educational focus. However, over time the programming evolved to include shows for daytime audiences, stay-at-home moms, and lifestyle programming far from the original educational focus. As the programming evolved, the channel changed its content from an education-based programming source to the motto of "life unscripted." This indicated programming featuring real-life events and documentary programming. Then, in 2006, the network moved to a new identity, calling itself a station about "living and learning." This programming stage cycled to a moderate use of reality programming, mixing education- and lifestyle-perspective programming. The station created an interesting blending of the two versions of reality. Kristen Acuna, writing for *Business Insider,* commented on the station's transformation from educational programming to unscripted reality shows like *Extreme Cougar Wives*. Acuna explained the station was hung on the twin horns of a dilemma. It was originally mandated to be educational but veered toward reality-formatted shows due to their popularity. Acuna writes, "In an attempt to get back to its roots, the network changed its tagline again to 'Live and learn.' It strayed from home improvement shows with *Little People, Big World* in 2006 and the tattoo/lifestyle show *L.A. Ink* the following year" (17, 2012).

By 2008 the station had moved to the theme "life surprises" and programmed series like *Kate Plus 8*; *Little People, Big World*; *19 Kids and Counting*; *Cake Boss*; *Toddlers and Tiaras*; and the popular *Here Comes Honey Boo Boo*. Despite its popularity, that show was cancelled in 2014 because Boo Boo's mom was seeing an alleged sex offender.

To say the least, the programming has evolved, and it is clear that the station is searching (sometimes successfully) for an identity. Recently, the programming has focused on alternative-lifestyle programs and freakish families (large families, small families, overweight subjects, etc.). Acuna commented that many of TLC's programs "consist of shock value." The show *19 Kids and Counting* dwells primarily on the unusual issue that the Duggars have a large amount of children, 19 at last count, and thus they need to exhibit them and their activities to generate income to maintain their large household. There is little learning and more novelty in such shows than valuable life lessons. Perhaps such programming is interesting to people as a curiosity, a freak show, indicating that this is how people living under extreme conditions exist. *The Inquisitor's* Tiffany Bailey reported that a 2016 return of the Duggars to TLC posted high ratings. She wrote, "There was some worry that people would avoid the program and the ratings would fall, but it appears that even the ones who abandoned the family can't do much damage" (2016).

The programming has taken some odd turns, and in recent years there have been specials like 2015's *My Husband's Not Gay,* a special about Mormon men who admit they are attracted to men but will marry women or are already married. In a way, the show sticks to accepted Mormon theology but opens the door to changes in that theology and in the Mormon community. This may reflect societal trends toward even fundamentalist religions achieving some tolerance of gay people. Longtime religious fundamentalist Pat Robertson announced in 2015 that wives whose husbands had dallied in gay relationships could accept the offending husband back. It is unclear whether such programs support the Mormon faith, critique it, or offer ways for the church to discuss problematic theological issues.

Samantha Allen, writing an article entitled "Your Husband Is Definitely Gay: TLC's Painful Portrait of Mormonism" for *The Daily Beast,* illustrates that TLC has always had a strong commitment to gay characters and to showing gay people in a productive manner in shows such as *What Not to Wear, Trading Spaces,* and *Say Yes to the Dress,* but the new special points out the puzzling treatment of gay people in the Mormon church. The special illustrates how gay men, or gay-leaning men, shelve their need to be with men in order to commit to relationships with women based on friendship, not passion, and these relationships rest on obligation over successful life choices. The church's position through the 1980s was solid that "Church leaders were adamant that homosexuality was not inborn and that heterosexual marriage was its chief cure" (Allen 2015). Science seems to be painting a different image of homosexual and heterosexual sexual orientations in recent years, and perhaps such shows are TLC's way of educating the public about this complicated and evolving issue.

See also: Here Comes Honey Boo Boo

Further Reading
Kristen Acuna, "The 40-Year Transformation of How TLC Went from The Learning Channel to the Home of Honey Boo-Boo," *Business Insider,* November 2012; T. W. Adorno, "Television and the Patterns of Mass Culture"; Samantha Allen, "Your Husband Is Definitely Gay: TLC's Painful Portrait of Mormonism," *The Daily Beast,* January 1, 2015; Tiffany Bailey, "Duggar Family Dominates Ratings for TLC: 'Jill and Jessa Counting On' Brings in Millions of Viewers," *Inquisitor,* March 17, 2016; David S. Escoffery, *How Real Is Reality TV?*

TRADING SPACES

Trading Spaces was a reality program produced by TLC that ran from 2000 to 2008 for eight seasons. The program was based on the British reality series *Changing Rooms,* in which two sets of couples were tasked with making significant upgrades and changes to another family's living space given a weekend and a small budget.

What was splendid about the show was that one did not need large amounts of money, fancy crews, or even large abodes to produce splendid and noticeable transformations of people's living spaces. Richard Huff writes that the show "took two families, had them swap homes for a weekend, and spend no more than $1000" on 'remaking a room'" (2006, 74).

The rules were pretty simple. Each family met with a designer/consultant who spoke with the family and learned what they disliked in the living space and what they would like to see happen to it. Mostly, the best designs were when people had a general idea of the type of change they wanted, and the designer worked hard to fulfill their ambition, not the designer's vision of a perfect room. Results were all over the map. Once the family agreed to the trade, the couples were crisscrossed and installed in the other team's abode. Once in the new location, the family team gave input on the changes made to their competitor's abode, but the team had no say over what happened in their own house. The teams were not allowed back into their dwelling until the repairs and redesign were completed. Some of the work, when first viewed, puzzled the family who found the new design no better than what they previously had. Others found rooms that were more manageable and more conducive to living than what they left and were deeply satisfied. It was a program in which the small things mattered.

See also: Extreme Makeover: Home Edition

Further Reading
T. W. Adorno, "Television and the Patterns of Mass Culture"; David S. Escoffery, *How Real Is Reality TV?*; Richard Huff, *Reality Television*. 2006.

WHAT NOT TO WEAR

One of the joys of *What Not to Wear* was to be treated to the fashion disasters that people didn't notice, and to see those problems remedied by the team. *What Not to Wear* was a popular program that ran on TLC from 2003 to 2013. Hosts Stacy London and Clinton Kelly performed clothing miracles, transforming dull clothing and appearances into clever fashions that maximized the attractiveness of guests on the show.

The hosts on *What Not to Wear* started with an inventory of the guest's closet. They did a grab and toss of all the worst-offending items. Then they let the guest pick something more attractive and concluded with a critique of the guest's taste, suggesting better alternatives. So the hosts had seen the worst, discussed the guest's taste, and made an assessment. At this point, the show was ready for action. The makeover began with a variety of shopping trips to find the best selection for the guest.

Originating in 2003, the decade of the program produced over 300 episodes. A strength of the show was that it often illustrated a remarkable difference in a person purely on the strength of what they chose to wear. Longtime host London would let the guest have it with a frank assessment of their worst looks and why they had chosen their own fashion suicides. London is back with a new show, and *The Huffington Post*'s Michelle Persad has described it as "Similar to 'What Not to Wear,' 'Love, Lust or Run' aims to help build people's self-esteem through the lens of style." There is a bull market for people like London who can help all of us look our best.

What Not to Wear began with someone recommending a contestant for a makeover. These nominations were normally from coworkers, family members, and friends. Sometimes people would self-nominate, saying that they didn't know how to make themselves more attractive. A powerful technical aid to the show was the use of 360-degree mirror setups, in which the mirror's cameras can capture a guest from all angles, and from which the guest can discuss his or her issues.

The hosts of the program for most of its run were London and Kelly. The two would obtain access to the nominee before he or she was on the show. In a surveillance segment, the *What Not to Wear* crew would film the subject going about his or her daily routine for several weeks before the program. Sometimes the nominator had as many problems as the nominee and would be invited on as well.

Somehow, either by a roommate or a family member, the crew obtained access to the guest's closet, and the hosts would deconstruct the subject's wardrobe. Humor was at the heart of this analysis, and many times the hosts would comically assassinate a guest's entire clothing choices. Stacy and Clinton poured through the closet and looked for examples of the most reprehensible fashions haunting the guest. Derogatory terms like "seventies goodwill wear" and "leisure suits" filled their dialogue. They asked caustic questions, such as, "Where would someone find this?" and "Does this person dress entirely from hand-me-down clothes?"

Following this setup period, the nominator and the team discussed the person's wardrobe malfunctions and scheduled a meeting with the nominators and the team. The team revealed their footage and the fact that they had been stalking the nominee for the prior few weeks. Rarely were the guests upset, and they took the good-natured assault on their privacy and wardrobe malfunctions as a challenge. Then it was decision time. The poor victim had to decide to accept wardrobe help. Though this moment was embarrassing, most contestants saw the need for change. They could also choose to refuse help and appear to be a loser. If the person refused, there was no show, and a lot of cajoling and convincing seemed to be needed to bring some potentials into the game.

Once a person accepted an offer of wardrobe help, the show went into an intense makeover segment. The candidate must agree to jettison their wardrobe by turning it over to the hosts (presumably for demolition or burning), and the respondent was given a $5,000 gift card to buy a new wardrobe that fits his or her size, body type, professional status, and activity level.

The later sections of the show were makeover and transformation events in which the contestant was given grooming advice, and the shoppers visited top shops for refined clothing. On the first day, there was a meeting and an hour of reckoning regarding the fashion missteps. More often than not, the nominee presented arguments of resistance, suggesting that his or her current fashions is presentable, he or she is comfortable, and that no fashions are fitting as well. The team reviewed the candidate's personal fashion choices in front of the 360-degree mirror and explained the "rules" of why appropriately fitting and correctly cut clothing would alter, taper, and reflect the proper professional guise the person needed. There was some push and pull and negotiation in these proceedings, and, ultimately, most candidates saw the sense of the style experts and accepted the majority of their reasoned opinions.

Many times the sorting and selecting process reflected other, hidden body-image issues within the candidate. The team had a traditional garbage bag, and, as they discarded items from the candidate's trashed clothing, they explained why it had to go. In actuality, items that vanished into the garbage bag were traditionally shared with others by donating them to a vintage shop of some sort.

Then the candidate was sent shopping with the credit card to high-end shops. The candidate was allowed to discuss with merchants and pick on their own, but a secret camera followed the candidates on the trip to make sure he or she obeyed the rules. Sometimes, their choices conformed, and they made good purchases. Sometimes they veered off track and needed to be corrected.

The third day was another ambush. The hosts would swoop in, usually in the middle of the shopping spree, and spot-check the candidate to make sure he or she was following the established rules. If the candidate didn't conform, clothes were returned, and he or she would be forced to start over. Usually candidates tacitly obeyed the rules. There was nothing more embarrassing than having the hosts spank you on *What Not to Wear*.

The fourth day was normally set aside for fun self-indulgence. The candidate got a grooming, often including a facial, makeup consultation, pedicure, tanning, haircut, and a style. The show had resident stylist Ted Gibson design a cut for the face, shape, and size of the candidate. The show's makeup artist, Carmindy, altered the makeup to give the candidate a stronger profile, facial presence, and appropriate coloring. This procedure was often transformative for many women who simply didn't apply makeup or applied it poorly. Many women went from drab to radiant in this segment.

The fifth and final day in New York was a presentation and rehearsal. The candidate would show three outfits to the critics, and they would remark on how the redesigned person benefited from the enhanced clothing selection. If nothing else, the show was a study in self-deception. Many of the people could not see themselves and their actual style blunders but, highlighted in front of the studio crew and exposed on camera, most of these troubled fashion victims could come to see the truth about how they looked and realized that with some help they could do better.

The final part of the show was the coming-out portion. The candidate returned home to a party environment, and all of the friends and family discuss how his or her appearance has been altered and how the change in clothing and grooming have helped his or her confidence and self-image.

Over the 10 years of the program's existence, the series did some celebrity make-overs, actually re-dressing some people in the entertainment business, including agents, actors, and choreographers. It was interesting that notable people who were viewed for a living could still have fashion issues.

A criticism of the show was that it promoted consumerism among people. Jennifer Pozner, in *Reality Bites Back,* commented that such shows "encourage us to lust after things we might have never thought we wanted or needed, even things we might have previously considered wasteful or distasteful" (2010, 142).

This show was rare in that it actually had a finish, an actual closer, in which the hosts took two hours to reassess what the program had accomplished. They revisited old allies who helped them rewrite people's fashions, and they even took on a new challenge at a Vegas hotel. In the end, the hosts felt they had done a service to people, and all said that the show was less about nasty comments on people's dress and more about transforming people through making them aware of their visual communication to others.

One supposes everyone has dress issues. It deals with how we look, how we are perceived, and how we see and view ourselves in the world. Stacy London's new show, *Love Lust, or Run,* deals with how women are seen and takes the perspective that extreme fashions can work for some women if they know they will have an extreme impact. London comments, "The idea is that the way that they are dressing is so extreme that when we go out into public and ask just a cross-section of people what they think, whether they love the look, or lust after it or want to run, there is a complete disconnect between the way the general public sees these people and the way they see themselves" (2015, Persad). London is now older and wants to make statements about how women dress at all ages. Make no mistake, our visual outfits do make us appear either transformed or diminished, and, during its run, *What Not to Wear* made viewers aware of what they wore, for better or for worse.

See also: Real World; 60 Minute Makeover

Further Reading

David S. Escoffery, *How Real Is Reality TV?*; Michelle Persad, "Stacy London Can Tell You More Than Just What Not to Wear," *Huffington Post,* January 22, 2015; Jennifer Pozner, *Reality Bites Back.* 2010.

Chapter 2: Competition and Talent Programming—Chefs, Singers, Survivors, and Every Man for Himself

The Gamification of American Culture

> *To know whether democracy or aristocracy governs better is a very difficult question to decide. But clearly democracy hinders one man and aristocracy oppresses another.*
>
> —Alexis de Tocqueville

De Tocqueville's classic study of American society illustrated the classic divide in American culture, in which everyone wanted to be equal and simultaneously everyone wanted to get ahead. These polarizing issues of freedom, independence, and competition have stimulated the American interest in capitalism, with its strong interest in material well-being.

No one can deny competition is a strong part of the American cultural scene. Like the Greeks, U.S. culture has long prided itself on healthy living, healthy minds and bodies, and a facile competitive nature that is normal and genuine to the American mind-set, which may have confused the more placid and European-disposed de Tocqueville. However, historically, governmental and social factors contributed to the American sense of competitiveness and play. In the 19th century, states began to pass mandatory education laws, which led to children having not only time for school and work but a new time designation known as free time. Prior to the 19th century, most Americans and people of the world worked as did their children. When the United States adopted compulsory education, child labor laws, and the benefits of industrialization, free time began to appear, and for some it was a problem.

First, free time affected children, since they were the youngest and most vulnerable members of society, and the ones most needing the relief from physical labor and the pernicious ailments that plagued people who had to work hard. Remember, there were no worker's compensation, no leave time, and no unemployment insurance. If you didn't work, you did not receive income, nor did you receive medical benefits if you were injured on the job. You were just unemployed. Hilary Levy Friedman writes about children's sports and competition for the *Atlantic Monthly*:

> In 1903 New York City's Public School Athletic League for Boys was established, and formal contests between children, organized by adults, emerged as a way to keep the

boys coming back to activities, clubs, and school. Formal competition ensured the boys' continued participation since they wanted to defend their team's record and honor. (2013)

So the goals of continuing a child's education and building adult skills of pride and cooperation nurtured the growth of competitive sports among young people. Of course, since adults—who themselves had been forced through years of compulsory work and adult behavior—were often the coaches and supervisors for such activities, the adults became equally addicted to the positive values (and some negative values) of sporting competitions.

By the 1960s, it was not uncommon to see some parents brutally coaching their children through Little League baseball. As the baby boomers grew and entered college, the competition that was once on the baseball diamond and soccer field moved into the academic realm, making parents neurotic, driven guides of students, seeking the best schools to ensure the best lives. Many worried that competitive children's sports might leave out students from poor families and students who lacked social advantage. These parents and social advocates preached that games should be open, that everyone should have a chance to play, and that games should encourage self-image and positive values of cooperation and teamwork. Schools shifted from fiercely competitive, individualistic games like baseball and football to more team-centered games like basketball and soccer, where more could play and more than one student could appear heroic. The self-esteem movement hoped to make everyone a player, a competitor, and a winner. It was tricky stuff. Further, parents and children became obsessed with tests, pre-tests, prep courses, advanced placement classes, summer boot camps, and any other device that might help students in the constantly evolving and complicated game of college admissions. Some schools' massive tuition fees for the status of attending and the price of attending emotionally was taking a toll on families who wanted the best education money could buy for their sons and daughters. Friedman reports that the competitive spirit with kids became trickier and trickier. She writes, "It's thanks to changes in the 20th-century educational system—like compulsory schooling, the self-esteem movement, and higher-stakes college admissions—that this is how American families are spending leisure time today" (2013).

But gamification has affected U.S. and world culture in another specific way. The world has become addicted to video games, and researchers are still trying to determine the long-term effects of video gaming on the population. We now have reached a stage where, due to the gaming industry, the dividing line between adulthood and childhood is strangely blurred. Is an adult gamer an arrested child or an advanced freed adult? James Cote writes in *Arrested Adulthood*, "Consequently, psychological adulthood is increasingly a personal, individualized journey, and as such it has many pitfalls and many misdirected trajectories" (2000, 42). Are video games part of our progress toward adult years or a rejection of adult roles?

Originally, the Atari system dominated video games in the 1970s and early 1980s. Kids who had been going out to video arcades came home to play a rectangular wood grained box that attached to television sets. Atari sold over 30 million devices, and many Americans learned about gaming through the Atari system. An important part of game play in the Atari universe was that mostly game play was conducted with two or more players. Video game play was competitive but also communal. Much as modern reality television is competitive, featuring people playing a game for love, to win money in a competition, or perhaps to upgrade their appearance in a makeover program, so the origins of video gaming were both communal and competitive. *The Boston Globe* talked to an MIT professor who studied the early era of video gaming. Nick Montfort said, "Maybe we forgot some things that were good about play experience. Maybe we want the computer to be a device that is more like a hearth that members of the family come around and use to interact with each other" (Edgars 2009). In fact, many feel that video gaming culture prepared us for group interaction and the competitive function of reality television competition shows.

Despite parents and society sometimes disapproving of the time, money, and energy spent on gaming behavior, there are some reports that gaming can be a productive source of skill building. David Corso at the University of South Carolina wrote that "additional studies by Green and Bavelier (2012; 2006) indicate that spatial skills, executive function, task-switching, multi-tasking, and visual short-term memory are being affected and enhanced by video game play as well as a plethora of other cognitive skills (Boyan & Sherry, 2011)" (2014). Corso and others have been pointing to the benefits of gaming behavior, which includes social functions and strategy skills. It isn't a stretch to imagine that such skills transfer quickly into a love and fascination with competition shows created for reality audiences.

The format of competitive shows in which talent, audacity, skill, or coping mechanisms have long been an under-acknowledged and lowly regarded but popular and profitable form of television has existed long before the notion of reality television emerged. Perhaps such shows became prominent through their negative reception in the 1950s game show scandals. Jason Mittell writes that "media historians have focused on this crucial moment in the genre's history, looking at the big money primetime quizzes, which were revealed to be rigged, to the virtual exclusion of other periods or incarnations of the genre" (2004, 32). Certainly, money and greed helped create the style of competition reality programming, but other elements explain the fascination in watching people compete. Heather Havrilesky writes that "the truth is the best reality shows feature exactly the kinds of fresh, surprising characters that most sitcoms and dramas lack" (2004, 21). Our youth culture has institutionalized sports and competition throughout the 20th century. Young viewers may be viewing reality programming to maintain video's ability to produce a more realistic experience, even if that experience is itself scripted, choreographed, and directed in our surveillance panopticon.

However, the entire idea of winning and competing has taken on a new dimension in the postmodern era as the process of gaming or playing games (video, employment, life, war, marriage, business) has accelerated at a remarkable rate. The role gaming plays in our world has changed, and the passive activity of video gaming may have moved to the more active role of watching people game online and through some form of video entertainment. That is, it isn't enough anymore for us to simply game, but we have to watch others compete as well to reinforce our gaming behavior.

The popular site Twitch is a powerful Web destination for gamers. It isn't enough for many video gamers to play the games. They must know about the games, their creation, their creators, their stars, their various forms of playing and cheat codes, the mythology behind the games, and the drama of people who play the games at the highest levels. The Twitch site actually offers gamers insight into playing various games by watching pro and semi-pro video gamers interact and play the games for an online audience. In a sense, Twitch presents an animated preview of the life of a gamer, or a game player. In a generation, we have moved from kids being active in school-sponsored sports activities; to the act of video gaming, in which individuals game in a virtual environment; to actually watching other gamers do the playing while they simply watch—a strange progression from participant, to cyber-participant, to spectator. For gamers, such activity is rewarding and perhaps serves an educational and coaching function by watching others play the game. Is the act of gaming moving from being a competition to an actual culture with its own worlds, codes of ethics, rules for playing and living in the gaming world, and means of winning and rising in status? If so, Twitch, like reality competition shows, may be providing the viewers with ways and means to model behavior in the real world that can teach them to win in that environment. Nick Wingfield wrote for *The New York Times* that "Twitch did not exist a little over three years ago, and it now has 55 million unique viewers a month globally, helping turn games into a spectator event as much as a participatory activity" (2014). Twitch is part of a phenomenon like reality competition shows, which move competition from an actual battle to a spectator sport. So in a brief time, our competitive urge has moved from sports field to video game to video game spectator back to watching real people compete.

Further Reading

David Corso, "A Review of Video Game Effects and Uses," *Caravel*, Spring 2014. Web; James Cote, *Arrested Adulthood*, 2000; Geoff Edgars, "A Talk with Nick Montfort," *Boston Globe*, March 8, 2009, Web; Hilary Levey Friedman, "When Did Competitive Sports Take over American Childhood?" *Atlantic Monthly*, September 20, 2013. Web; Nick Wingfield, "What's Twitch? Gamers Know and Amazon Is Spending 1 Billion for It," *New York Times*, August 25, 2014.

THE AMAZING RACE

The Amazing Race overcomes a potential for self-parody by strong production values and strong editing to keep the audience engaged and supporting various teams. The show is a juggernaut for quality reality-programming leader CBS, having created over 25 seasons and over 300 episodes. The program is produced by film-spectacular director/producer Jerry Bruckheimer. *The Amazing Race* is, in a word, *amazing*. The plan is 11 teams of two people each journey around the world in a race and face various logical, intellectual, physical, and emotional challenges along the way. If the race were merely an external competition, it would be routine, but the fact that it engages the teams at multiple levels—allowing insights into personalities and motives and coupling personal struggle and biography with outward challenge—gives the program a deeper resonance.

Part competition show and part sports show, the program offers wide-angled vista shots of the terrain that enhances the challenges and gives a strong sense of the geographical terrain of the program. Geography plays a major role in the way the globe-trotting teams are covered. Tears and joy are equally chronicled in rapid-fire style to keep the audience attentive to the challenges, the struggles, and the obstacles the teams face in their globe-trotting escapades.

The beginning of the show features the host announcing the race is on. The 11 couples are assembled to fly across the world in a race from one locale to another. The show carefully finds the perfect contestants who represent what they hope will be the diverse America that they want to include in all programs and that they hope to court as their viewership. The demographics are diverse, and CBS believes that if they feature diversity in the groups represented then diverse groups will watch. There is the aggressive young sports couple, usually with a sports celebrity or a semi-celebrity attached. There is a gay couple. Sometimes there is an older fitness couple. The mix of people and their birthrights are knowingly diverse, and each season assembles a different cast of diverse contestants. There are fathers and sons, identical twin sisters, minority families, mothers and daughters, brothers and sisters, and assorted permutations of these groups. We meet each briefly and get to hear them say how and why they will win. The challengers are assembled. How these bright, engaged, and seemingly fully employed people could obtain an entire month away from work to participate in a grueling worldwide challenge is unknown to us, but somehow they manage it.

An early criticism of the show was that it was strongly imperialistic. In other words, every place they passed on Earth was a sort of a playground for Americans to visit. The view was that such an attitude is not particularly respectful or aware of the cultures these people are visiting. For example, in an episode in which the teams go to Taipei, Taiwan, they get a clue that takes them to a Confucian Temple. There is no talk about the significance of the place or the cultural value of Confucius to Chinese people; rather it is just a stop along the way.

Some of the aspects of the show are crudely rigged like an episode of *Hunger Games*, in which DNA-engineered wild dogs are manufactured just to chase and kill the contestants. Fortunately, the forces of *The Amazing Race* are not quite so deadly. They may be tricky, but not lethal. However, some dirty tricks are employed. Initially, in one season, when the contestants were given some letters to find their first destination, they were required to find more letters in umbrellas that had added letters. These letters were necessary to find out where they were going. The competition wasn't very clear. It became just a mad scramble to find the umbrellas and sort of open them in front of the whole group to find whether the umbrellas contained the letters. The directions didn't specify what they were to do, and it was confusing for the camera to highlight who was first or last. At will, the producers inserted obscure penalties and rewards throughout the contest. So if someone completed a task last, they might add an obnoxious and unexpected penalty to that team's chores. In the first round, two showgirls were singled out for being last. The presumption was that it was proper to pick on the women for being less intelligent and to taunt them, tease them, and humiliate them. Would the program's viewers have remained comfortable with the taunting of black or gay couples? Much in the superficial rules seemed like an unfair slap on the wrist, and such tactics seemed emotionally targeted at younger attractive women.

Further, the mechanism of the penalty seemed awkward. Supposedly, the women were to be punished for being last. So when they went to buy gas before going to the airport, one had their passport dropped, mislaid, stolen, or simply removed from the car. It was unclear whether this was planned or simply an accident. So that was the penalty? The audience never saw someone take the passport, but it wound up on the ground. The girls quickly went back to the station but couldn't find it. Puzzled, they went to the airport, knowing that they didn't have completed passports and could not board a plane. Eventually, a driver found the passport, and someone miraculously ascertained they were going to the airport, followed them, and delivered the passport to them at the terminal. The entire scenario seemed manufactured, contrived, unrealistic, and simply a shallow means to retard the girls' progress. It seemed hard to believe, a weird penalty, and a weird mechanism to remedy it. As a show contrivance, all of this seemed highly unlikely as a means to engineer the show and appeared a crude attempt by the producers to get the couple angry and fighting with each other. It appeared that the rigors of their 12-stop tour of the world would be enough without throwing nasty monkey wrenches at the couple. This sort of intervention seemed to pollute the game and its challenges and to some degree spoiled the purity of the sport.

The program has had an illustrious 16-year history, debuting in 2001 and winning Emmys consistently from 2003 to 2013 for best competition reality program. Personality Phil Keoghan from New Zealand has been the program host since its inception. The rules of the game are that generally the couples competing should have some sort of connection. Oddly, in 2017, the program inexplicably changed formats to pair couples who had no overt connection. The competition is broken into various pit stops. If you are first in each leg, you can get prizes and advantages.

If you are last, there can be various penalties and eliminations. Sometimes, the awards and penalties can seem arbitrary and capricious. Modes of transportation are varied, and sometimes getting around is as hard as the tasks. Some travel is done on foot, and there are many challenges and tests along the way. At each stop there are clues to the next destination, or some sort of challenge, or a task to be overcome before moving on. Like a globe-trotting *Indiana Jones* game, the players circumnavigate the globe, trying to interact with the cultures they visit in some way. Many of the challenges are often related to the nationality of the people the teams are visiting.

Sometimes a challenge can involve a single team player, and sometimes it can involve both members of a team. Sometimes a weaker member is singled out to try to push for an elimination. When all but three teams are eliminated, there is a final round, the last leg of the race. The winning team wins a big prize, usually a million dollars or something equally as grand.

At the heart of the show is watching the couples either bond together or unravel under the pressure. This dynamic is chronicled in interviews before, during, and after legs of the journey. Fans have used terms like *dead teams* or *killer fatigue* to comment on the level of exhaustion the players have during the competition. Like watching *They Shoot Horses, Don't They?* seeing the teams go through excruciating agonies in their pursuit of wealth is a key drawing card of the show. Sadly, a rather sadistic pleasure at watching people suffer comes from some of the challenges that revel in the cruelty of the program. This suggests that a negative type of voyeurism exists in the underbelly of much reality programming. A question remains: should we encourage people to cheer people's success in the midst of an act of suffering? Such programming is highly connected to films like *Hunger Games* or *Battle Royale,* in which we see teams of teens trying to kill each other. Sometimes the stakes are high, and the difference between reality and illusion is low. Michael Goodspeed wrote about "the Sci-Fi channel's *Scare Tactics*, individuals are set up by their friends for extraordinarily ghoulish and realistic pranks. The majority of these victims are actually led to believe their lives are in danger" (Goodspeed 2004). There is real concern that such programs could be teaching people pathological competitiveness. Is this psychological addiction to winning a state of humankind, a redirection of our natural competitive and hostile instincts as animals, or a new type of dark and irrational voyeurism in which watching people self-destruct is the new normal? In any case, the suggestion is disturbing.

On the plus side, puzzle solvers find the show engaging, and gimmicks like the U-turn, where a team can force another team to repeat a trip detour or some other nasty slowdown, can be an amusing distraction. A fun twist is the *interaction requirement,* which forces two teams to travel together and pool resources for a time. Sometimes this instantaneous cooperation is annoying, and sometimes it conditions greater respect and self-confidence.

On several occasions, the show's rampaging world tour has produced insensitivity not only to foreign cultures and governments but also domestically. In 2013, a March episode of *The Amazing Race* showed contestants traveling through Vietnam, arriving to find a clue at a memorial to a downed B-52 bomber. The B-52s were used to drop bombs and napalm on Vietnamese citizens during the long 10-year Vietnam War. The scene was a national monument to a horrible and negative incident in Vietnamese history but was also a highly anti-American memorial that did not show American troops, American purposes, or American accomplishment in a good light. Veterans protested in an open letter to CBS, and the station apologized to the veterans publically on air.

At any rate, *The Amazing Race*, despite its many faults, allows Americans to step away from xenophobic images of other cultures, engage in active cooperation toward a goal, work to solve problems, test their group endurance, and overcome obstacles and difficulties in strange foreign environments.

See also: American Ninja Warrior; Survivor; The X Factor

Further Reading

"*The Amazing Race* Apologizes to Vietnam Veterans for B-52 Wreckage Scenes," *The Huffington Post*, March 3, 2013; David S. Escoffery, *How Real Is Reality TV?*

AMERICAN IDOL

American Idol has been a leading program in the reality-talent competition category since its inception, filled with quarrelsome judges, catty remarks, and varied talent competing in a variety of formats. One of the delights and disturbing aspects of the show is the often odd juxtapositions of soul and R and B acts bumping into heavy metal and dance acts. The program has been a juggernaut of popular reality programming. *Idol* was devised by Simon Fuller, debuted in 2002, has been popular ever since, spawning over 500 episodes. If the search for superstars found by the show often comes up dry, the list of judges is impressive, featuring a variety of the entertainment industry's biggest names. In the show's run, Ellen DeGeneres, Paula Abdul, Keith Urban, Mariah Carey, and Steven Tyler have all been judges. The show was one of the Fox Network's stellar performers, and, for many, watching the finalists on *American Idol* is a national pastime, much like the Super Bowl. The final episode in which the winner is selected has become an anointing/crowning ritual worthy of royalty, scoring a win in the ratings virtually every time a winner is announced. The show, which is moving to ABC in 2018, remains one of the most popular programs of all time. Interesting, this deeply American show featuring singing performers fighting for the top spot isn't really an American idea, but an import from Britain. England's *Pop Idol* pioneered the idea of a new singing competition show before *American Idol* debuted in this country.

Actually, the show had a rocky start in the States. The original show was *Popstars* in New Zealand and was brought to the UK as *Pop Idols*. However, when the program was pitched to American television executives, many were cool to the idea. Rupert Murdoch's daughter, a big fan of the British program, urged her father to gamble on the *Pop Idol* format, and Fox Network selected the show as a summer replacement in 2002.

Under the reign of veteran host Ryan Seacrest, the show seeks to find the best singer in an elimination competition in which a variety of performers sing standards using their own powerful and unique vocal apparatus. While perhaps none of the contestants have become "idols," many of the performers have gone on to significant and notable careers as entertainers. The audience, through text message, phone, and Internet have picked Kelly Clarkson, Carrie Underwood, and Taylor Hicks to become winners, and all have had varied degrees of music-industry success since their work on the program. Probably the greatest difficulty with the *Idol* concept is it places all the emphasis on interpretive singing, not on songwriting, career building, performing live on the road, or developing an individual and distinctive act and approach. It would be asking a lot to develop that in a performer in a few weeks, and the truth is television can only accomplish so much. Making an *Idol* in 10 weeks is probably beyond any entertainment company's ability.

The program brings out the singers, and they perform in competition, receiving coaching, critiques, and advice from the judges. They return to compete until they win or are eliminated. The program seeks to provide enough information about the performers and their struggles to create a bond between the performers and the audience, so that viewers feel a vested interest in the fates of each performer. Even some runners-up, like Clay Aiken, have had significant spin and success from their appearances on the show. It is estimated that over 300 chart-topping songs are associated with performers on the show, and the program has had an influence over recording and musical tastes of American audiences in the 16 years of its dominance. The show received an added zing from the acid criticisms of judge Simon Cowell, who was popular for saying nasty and outrageous things to the performers. Of course, the reaction was that the audience grew to hate him as the bad guy judge and to gravitate more toward the performers. It arrived as pure soap-operatic theater, but the cheesy remarks and the audience backlash of hating Cowell and warming to the performers, though a crude form of manipulation, worked beautifully.

American Idol benefited from a wide range of changes to television programming during its run. Lucy Hood, one of the team of insightful marketing and communication executives at Fox, had the idea that audiences would respond to two screens at once and that television programs could have a continued life through Webisodes. She pioneered that idea by making mobile episodes (mobisodes) of Fox's popular *24* terrorism and espionage series. With *American Idol*, she conceived the idea of text voting so that people could quickly and simply vote for their favorite acts using their cell phones.

The process of eliminations on the program is brutal, grueling, and continuous. Many people want to be pop stars, and the demands placed on performers for this program are among the most intense. Auditions are held in major cities nationwide. Like the *Hunger Games, American Idol* selectors take them young. Performers must be between 15 and 28 years old. The performers must not have competed in later rounds before or have label or artist representation. Three rounds of competition start the contest. First, hopefuls perform in front of selectors in their hometown. The leading candidates then perform for producers. Those selected are then sent on to Hollywood for an additional set of auditions, leading to a final selection of who will appear on the show. During the show appearances, there can be mentoring by guest artists and additional criticism by guest judges. In the semifinal rounds, the performers are judged by the audience who call, text, or vote for their selection on the Internet for a few hours after the broadcast. After the final competition, the audience also selects their personal choices for the ultimate champion. Then after the finale, there is a two-hour results show. Not only is the judging and series of rounds exhausting, it is an endless loop of programming around the *American Idol* concept that often welcomes viewers into the competition later. Through recaps and continually refreshed performances, audiences can be brought up to speed on the proceedings. This multiple entry point strategy allows *Idol* to keep audiences and add new audience members while the competition is ongoing.

The winner of the competition earns $1 million, a recording contract with a major studio, and a deal with an artist management and representation agency. While this is a great reward, in recent years the amount of recordings given to the winning artist has been pared down to a single recording. Not all the *American Idol* performers have fared well in the marketplace.

A criticism of the show has been the phenomenon of "WGWG" or "White Guy With Guitar." At least 10 of *Idol's* first 13 success stories have been Southern white guys who play guitar. This may be because Southern performers are better. Another reason is that Southerners watch the show more, and they vote for their own candidates. Finally, there is a preponderance of cell phone–only households in the South, and these regions may watch the program and call in more frequently than viewers elsewhere.

Other controversies include concerns about the exclusive contracts the performers sign to the *Idol* management group at the end of the program. This management company has extensive rights over the performers for an extended period. Another issue is whether producers have allowed ringers or professionals who they already have a vested interest in promoting to perform. If so, the concern is that the whole competition could be rigged. A final concern is the quality of voting information. Some have argued that the voting process is flawed and does not accurately reflect the real votes of the audience.

However, all series and formats come to an end, and the long dominance of music-oriented reality/competition shows may be declining. Bill Carter writes, "The phenomenon of music-based television shows, which have dominated the ratings for more than a decade, seems by nearly every measure to be over or in steep decline" (2014). It seems even the once-powerful *American Idol* has been hit by middling-to-minor ratings in recent seasons, and the reversal in fortunes has prompted some to suggest that perhaps the interest in reality music competition shows may be waning. Another problem is that the show's average viewer has crept from a 20-something to a middle-aged 52. This is not the audience demographic the producers wished to court. Despite these fears, *Idol* continues to perform well, and its creeping demographic might be related to the fact that it has kept viewers from youth into their middle years, quite an achievement for a reality program.

See also: Survivor; The Voice; The X Factor

Further Reading

Bill Carter, "Overextended, Music TV Shows Fade," *New York Times*, May 11, 2014; David S. Escoffery, *How Real Is Reality TV?*

AMERICAN NINJA WARRIOR

American Ninja Warrior is a competitive sports reality show based on Japanese game shows in which contestants must endure extreme sports challenges, huge obstacle courses, and physical impediments with mechanical battering devices that serve to unbalance, destabilize, and undermine the candidates' equilibrium and prowess.

The show, hosted by Matt Iseman, Akbar Gbaja-Biamila, and Jenn Brown, is a popular competition show that has produced over 100 episodes, served audiences for over eight seasons, thrills with stunt-performing contestants, and features a strange assortment of mechanical war machines in each round.

The program, sponsored by NBC and programmed by NBC's G4 Network, offers a series of competitive obstacle courses of increasing difficulty. At each round, there are eliminations until the finalists must assault Mount Midoriyama. Initially, this competition was held as part of the Sasuke competition in Japan, but the original Mount Midoriyama has now been recreated in Las Vegas. Today competitors in the United States perform their own competition there. A competition between American and Japanese teams was held in 2013, with American players sweeping the competition.

The program debuted in 2009 and after eight seasons shows no signs of declining as a popular competition show. The idea of *American Ninja Warrior* is to toughen people's resolve. The course for the demanding Sasuke challenge in Japan is so difficult that only a handful of players have successfully completed it. It remains so demanding that for several years running there have been no winners.

For the Japanese, and increasingly for the American audience, the notion of a game that is rigged so tightly that no one can win is increasingly becoming a reality. Instead of the American game show philosophy in which there are distinctive winners and losers, the Japanese concept is endurance despite adversity, and that mantra transforms itself into a game that is part competition and part philosophy of life. The complicated and arduous Sasuke competition in Japan has had over 26 competitions since 1997, and each year around 100 challengers assault the trail. Only three have succeeded. In recent years, more Americans have made it to the finalists' spot in the Sasuke competition. Mike Hale, writing for *The New York Times,* questioned, if super-competitive Americans take over this distinctively Japanese idiom, will it change the nihilistic nature of the game's existential bent? In essence, the trail is about playing, not about winning. Hale writes that at present the Sasuke competition is "a semiannual festival of friendly competition and odd-ball theatricality" (2011). The thing that makes such competitions charming is the goofy falls, the tortured screams, the cries of the aspirants, and the deadly complexity and fierceness of the course. Winning is just one aspect: the real game is to teach the lesson of perpetual struggle. Like Rick and his gang of ragtag punch-drunk zombie-killing warriors on AMC's popular *Walking Dead*, the program is about striving, enduring, and surviving, not about defeating. Defeat means there is a winner and a loser, but to struggle nobly, if fatally, is a strong lesson of the program.

James Cote postulates that this brand of identity television is reshaping audiences. He writes, "As Western societies are moving into the era of postmodernity, beliefs in a stable inner character and reason-governed behavior are being abandoned in favor of an externally oriented 'relational self,' shaped by 'socializing technologies' that increasingly mediate our relationships with others" (2000, 102). Cote and others see a world in which television instructs the audience about importance issues, and competitions like *American Ninja Warrior* may represent a better destiny for some viewers than the fragmentary games of modern corporate life. Win or lose, playing *American Ninja Warrior* represents a personal best against feelings of adversity and hopelessness.

The program offers a variety of competitive courses that athletes struggle to complete. There are sideways jumps that throw challengers into the drink if they miss a step. There is a log grip in which challengers have to hold onto a log and roll it to the next station. There is a breakaway floor that collapses as one crosses it. There is a swing that ejects players onto a net that they must then crawl under without touching the ground. There is a ring grip where players have to move rings to successive grips to stay on the overhead beams and move forward. There is a vertical runway that a player must scale to reach the top and grab a hold. There are daunting pull-up bars that the player must thrust up to proceed to the next crawl-across. There are moving monkey bars that the player must jump from to gain the next level. There is a sequence of poles that a player must jump from one pole to the next. Some poles are five feet apart. It is an arduous competition offering part child's monkey-bar play set and part gymnastics challenge.

Hale described the show as "The American embrace of full-contact Japanese game shows . . . has to do with the appeal of bright colors, spectacular crashes and other people's embarrassment and discomfort" (2011). The German term *schadenfreude*, or the fun of watching others in extremely embarrassing situations, is an underlying draw to such programming. Japanese audiences don't seem to be noticeably meaner than American audiences, but they do enjoy watching people have the wind knocked out of them, watching people cry, and even watching people land in disgusting slime and goo. For Japanese cultures, such embarrassments might be self-reflexive. That is, audiences watching extreme sports with extreme and vile endings may be self-reflexively commenting on their own selfhood. A Japanese person watching another's failure is not celebrating the defeat of another but remembering that we stand on the verge of catastrophe at all times, and it is only by being aware and cognizant of the struggles we all endure that we become better, more mature people.

See also: Survivor; The X Factor

Further Reading

James Cote, *Arrested Adulthood: The Changing Nature of Maturity and Identity*, New York: New York UP, 2000; David S. Escoffery, *How Real Is Reality Television?*; Mike Hale, "A 'Ninja Warrior' Upgrade into Network Prime Time," *New York Times*, August 11, 2011.

AMERICA'S GOT TALENT (AGT)

This popular reality show parades a series of people performing variety acts past the judges. The program debuted in 2006, has spawned over 12 seasons, has hosted a wide assortment of celebrity judges, has sponsored many talented performers, and has participated in a global franchise of *Got Talent* (GT) programs that exist throughout the world. In past seasons, people such as Howard Stern and Jennifer Lopez have been celebrity judges. More often than not, the audience and judges are treated to questionable talents that theoretically have been put through a vigorous selection and verification process. Often, however, the talents do not seem to be prescreened, and in fact the term *talent* could be argued to be a qualitative term. Many of the contestants have questionable talents and include bad acrobats, animals acts with odd animals, including an uncooperative pig, and people with quirky skills that, though unusual, would be difficult to define as *talent*. Perhaps a better description would be: Americans perform tricks and oddities that sometimes could be termed talents but often are just quirky oddity acts.

The show has a history as a ratings winner for home network NBC. Since its debut in 2006, it has been home to a variety of celebrities, from initial host Regis Philbin to actor/host Howie Mandel, Sharon Osbourne, Jerry Springer, David Hasselhoff, and model Heidi Klum, among many varied acts and artists. There is a certain irony in the program's title, because few of the hosts themselves are particularly known for any noteworthy talent. Like the guests, most of the hosts are personalities, like popular off-color radio host Howard Stern. The program has produced many seasons, spin-offs, and over 225 episodes and shows no signs of exhausting the audience's desire to see performers do their thing. The program was the brainchild of reality television bad boy Simon Cowell.

AGT is part of a global group of shows that showcase regional talent, including acrobats, singers, actors, magicians, jugglers, and a plethora of performers who used to proliferate in American television but became scarce as the United States moved to conventional narrative drama and comedy in the last 40 years. Variety performers derived from the old variety and vaudeville cabaret acts of the early-20th-century musical networks. This system of performance was largely replaced by an assortment of orthodox forms of entertainment. The reemergence of variety through shows like *America's Got Talent* takes television back to its earliest period in the 1940s, when programming like *Ted Mack and the Original Amateur Hour* was a popular and provincial favorite. One of the allures of the show is the massive prize money at the end of large-scale competition. The winner gains $1 million in prize money, which makes it unlikely that a winner on the show needs to perform frequently after winning. Another added perk is the opportunity to headline a show in Las Vegas, a perfect launching pad for a variety act in the heart of one of the United States' best live performance venues.

The program has been a ratings winner since its first season in 2006. Among the features that make it distinctive is the use of audience votes to determine competition winners. Further, it propels amateurs with little previous exposure to national prominence, which signifies the show as an extremely democratic organization. The program had a rocky start. Cowell had arranged for the program to debut first in England, but the American version debuted before the British series due to changes in hosts. Cowell wanted to judge and have greater involvement, but he was under contract to Fox for *American Idol,* and, after leaving that program, Cowell was a judge on *The X Factor* for Fox. The program has had a range of judges, including Sharon Osborne, Piers Morgan, and Melanie Brown. The judges expanded from three to four judges in season four.

The setup for the program is quite complex. Prior to the actual filming, contestants are picked from producers' auditions held in various cities across the United States. The finalists in these auditions are then submitted to the competition, which is aired on nationwide television through the Fox Network. The live auditions are filmed before a live studio audience, which gives the judges some sense of an act's popularity with the local population.

Voting is by the judges in various cities watching the contestants. The judges can choose to vote *no* on a performance and stop the candidate from moving to the next round. If three judges vote *no* while a performer is performing, the performer stops at once. For a performer to move to the next round, three judges have to approve the performance. There has been an intermediate round called the Vegas or the New York round, in which acts have a chance to perform for the judges to determine pecking order for the live shows or to gain a chance to be a wild card for the "live judges shows," in the event there are places for additional acts. Another entry point since season five has been YouTube auditions. Acts may audition on YouTube. Those selected after a live audition can compete in the live stage shows. The second-place winner for season five was Jackie Evancho, a YouTube auditioner. The eliminations proceed thusly. Usually, judges hear from 20 to 60 performers, eliminating quite a few. Several of these performers seem to be comedy acts that are so bad they are just there to inspire derision and laughter. Wild card acts and YouTube are folded into the live shows in a quarter-final round. The elimination rounds feature the best finalists, usually around 10 contestants. At this point, the judges aren't judging, but audience votes determine the ranking. The winner gets $1 million and a headlining gig in Las Vegas.

Controversies have surrounded the show. First, many of the acts have been poorly talented, suggesting that the show is planning to feature certain acts at the expense of other acts. Some acts are so laughably bad it is hard to imagine they made it past any set of qualifying judges. Further, many of the acts have, at best, minor careers after the show, suggesting that the show's picks are neither substantial nor reflect the real talent pool out there.

Probably one of the funniest reality moments on the show came in 2014 when host Nick Cannon disguised himself as a mime and did a credible job of bad mime routines, including the box, pulling the rope, and the pratfall. Howard Stern bounced the performer with an X, quickly followed by the other three panelists. They scolded him for an unoriginal act. A stagehand gave Cannon a microphone, and Cannon quickly retorted in a thick Southern accent that they were incapable of judging his mime work. After producing some semi-obscene gestures and approaching the judges, the worried panel called for security to protect them. While the entire event may have been staged and choreographed, the panel looked genuinely surprised when Cannon began to strip and revealed himself. He shouted, "Got you!" and laughed at his ability to prank the panel of "experts."

See also: American Idol; Survivor; The X Factor

Further Reading

Anna Chan, "Nick Cannon Pranks, Scares 'America's Got Talent' Judges on the Season Premiere," Today.com, May 28, 2014; David S. Escoffery, How Real Is Reality TV?

AMERICA'S NEXT TOP MODEL (ANTM)

America's Next Top Model is an elimination/reality/game/lifestyle show that has run starting in 2003 on the UPN Network (that became CW when UPN and WB networks merged) and features host and judge Tyra Banks, a media personality and top model.

Banks originated the idea for a competition modeling show because entry to the field is so fiercely competitive. The show involves a series of elimination rounds, judgment by three or four judges per round, and finally a grand competition between the remaining candidates. The winners hope that such a show will launch their modeling careers and offer a platform for career growth as America's Next Top Model or ANTM. The show has had a successful 20-season run, taking young girls from across the nation and submitting them to trials and challenges from runway walks, makeup competitions, and selections of strong ensembles for a fashion show. Throughout, the show has been a ratings performer, being UPN's highest-rated show, and has continued receiving high ratings on the CW in recent seasons.

A group of talented, successful, and ambitious young model wannabes audition in regional auditions, are selected for the competition, and are placed in the game hotbox with a group of like-minded young competitors. They learn to walk and face off against other young models in a runway walk trial. Some are naturals, and some have to practice to appear comfortable. Each girl is given a makeover to address attractive features and to downplay faults in their face, hair, and complexion. Some girls don't like the massive attention that appearances receive and become emotional when their hair is cut or their nails are redone in a new way. What might be an exotic and self-indulgent beauty regime for some women becomes a trial for some contestants. Some of the girls naturally become lonely, frustrated, self-conscious, or simply unsure, and cat fights and negative behavior occasionally erupts. The program emphasizes the pressure-cooker effect of placing so much emphasis on external appearances and the fact that models are often solely judged by appearances. There is something innately dehumanizing about a profession where only looks count, and the women are keenly aware of their precarious relationship to the professional world of modeling.

The program aired some of its own dirty linen with an *Exposed* segment that discussed big meltdowns and backstage squabbles during previous seasons. This program showed the rocky road to making some women beautiful and selecting great models. The program included input from some former contestants and winners on the show.

The program has had a lively afterlife in syndication, something unusual in reality programming, with VH1, Bravo, Oxygen, the Style Network, and other stations running marathon repeats of whole cycles of the show.

Not without controversy, the writers (yes, reality shows have writers, and yes, not everything that happens is spontaneous) went on strike in 2006, and, between July and November of that year, the striking writers were removed from the program. Reality television in general has had a tempestuous relationship with writers, staff, and labor relations. If one keeps in mind that a lot of reality television originated to trim costs, one recognizes that stations often have difficult working relations with stars, writers, and others hired under temporary conditions. Writers are often called upon to write for a brief season, and then they are dismissed.

Perhaps the most disturbing thing about the program is that it is indeed a beauty contest, or at least it is about maximizing the models' looks. In the early weeks, all models undergo a makeover to transform them. The 10 to 14 contestants are judged by three criteria: (1) overall appearance, (2) performance in weekly competitions, and (3) appearance in weekly photo sessions. Usually a contestant is eliminated each week, whittling down 10 contestants over 10 weeks to one remaining winner. Sometimes two people are eliminated per week, and sometimes there are no eliminations. About midway through the series, the contestants are shuffled off to an exotic location to see how they do under test-fire conditions. The thinking is if they can look beautiful at some exotic locale on short notice, they can survive the rigors of a model's hectic life.

The show has some product and media connections. Contestants sometimes appear on Tyra Banks's talk show, and a line of *ATNM* fashion products have appeared at Wal-Mart.

Critiques of the show have called it demeaning and another way to subject women to scrutiny merely for their looks. Kelly McLaughlin, writing for the *Daily Mail* commented that "from rehab to felonies, several contestants fell into lives of crime after being dismissed from the show" (2015). McLaughlin suggested the show might be cursed, since, after starring on the show, contestant Mirjana Puhar was shot dead as she opened the door to her apartment. The robbers entered the house and shot two more men in the head killing them (one was Puhar's boyfriend) over what appeared to be a drug-related robbery. There have been suggestive segments, including two contestants mud wrestling, using the runway catwalk as a strip club device, demanding the women wear skimpy bikinis, and makeovers that often transform them into tougher, cruder, harder looking figures without necessarily adding to their overall attractiveness.

Allure magazine accused the show of not producing supermodels or even competent models. This is generally a big problem in reality game shows and the industries they seemingly serve. Chef shows don't seem to create chefs; acting shows don't create actors; singing shows don't create singers; and dancing shows don't create successful dancers. The outcome seems to be that reality show performers appear only to groom people for appearances on more reality shows.

Some of the criticisms of reality programming are generic. One cannot lift semi-talented people out of the mire of masses who wish to become famous and find talented, hardworking professionals in any field. Film stars, models, writers, and singers are the products of years in the public arena, hard knocks, good luck, comprehensive training programs, and prolonged and continual mentorship. These shows cannot provide such support services, so reality performers are likely ill-equipped for the real rigors of these professions. A 10-week appearance on television isn't the same as 20 years of bit parts for minor films and television programs.

Socially, the models have been criticized for their behavior. There have been further criticisms that the loft where the models stay has been damaged by the cast and crew who apparently have partied hard in the facility.

See also: American Ninja Warrior; Survivor; The X Factor

Further Reading:
David S. Escoffery, *How Real Is Reality TV?*; Kelly McLaughlin, "Is ANTM Cursed?" *Daily Mail,* March 1, 2015.

THE APPRENTICE

A group of smart, talented MBAs and JDs who seem to have been hit hard by the reeling economy following 9/11 and especially after the 2008 "great recession," the contestants on *The Apprentice* seem to have made two grave miscalculations. The first is why would anyone want to apprentice to Donald Trump? And the second and perhaps most obvious problem is why would 16 people compete for a single position? While admittedly there are probably longer odds in a lot of industries, it would seem that most people could find better work and less anxiety than by being brutalized by someone who likely re-watches *Whiplash* every morning before stomping on another soul.

Seriously, for all of his gruff commanding and demanding exterior, Donald Trump appears to be mostly a hard-driving businessman who expects only best efforts. Like most bosses, he is rightfully miffed when those best efforts do not produce good results. The series has been quite successful, produced and managed by Mark Burnett, who successfully masterminded much of the reality TV boom back in the 1990s. He prepackaged and presold ads into his groundbreaking *Survivor* program before the show aired, thus giving CBS an almost cost-free and attractive show to run on its stations. The show speaks to Burnett and Trump's own ideas about what makes a reality program successful, and they both seem to understand the trade of show-manship, as well as the business of making money. The program debuted in 2004, has run 14 complete seasons so far, and has continued to receive strong ratings.

Like a lot of season-running reality shows, the program is a continual elimination-round program, in which a group of young recruits are set tasks by Donald Trump and then must fulfill the tasks to heir/hair Trump's approval.

The premise of the show is fairly simple and straightforward. The candidates, a whopping 16 of them, explain the sad circumstances of being brought to beg for a job with 15 other people in front of an audience of gawkers. Each describes how he or she has been downsized, undone, sacrificed, eaten, and spit out by the hungry mouth of American oligarchic industry.

Trump, astride his throne, looks down at his pathetic minions and deigns to entertain one of them as his apprentice, where he or she can have a suitable and worthy task and bask in the glow of the great man as he performs his daily business transactions. Trump and his team have set plans, activities, and challenges before the group of 16 and explain that the challenges will lead to many being eliminated over the coming weeks. Gamely, the challengers prepare for their first day at battle and select team captains they hope will lead them to curry favor with the Donald. The team captain position is at once enviable and precarious. If the team does well, the captain can receive credit, but if the team performs in a subpar manner, the captain may be the first to get chopped.

Trump and his outsized personality is a central part of the show. Trump himself is the voice-over of the program, leading with his own brand of credibility and bravura toughness. Leigh Edwards writes, "*The Apprentice* offers a good example of voiceover narration . . . slamming hapless contestants, hawking products, or intoning business philosophies. Donald Trump narrates the show as cast-members compete to run one of his companies, and his voice-over identifies the show with his celebrity viewpoint" (2013).

A criticism of the show, as a criticism of most business media, is that for a medium and a show that should be concerned with the rank-and-file actions of business in the United States, an obscene amount of time is lavished on Trump. His ravings seem to dominate, while the show is entitled *The Apprentice* and should in some sense be the story of the many working-class people who make business work. Yet it is similar to business news in the newspaper and online, which tends to focus on chief executives and not the many people in the organization who actually make the company successful.

There are some ironic touches. For example, the theme song is "For the Love of Money" by the O'Jays. The end result of having to endure a season of the often-grueling Mr. Trump is a contract worth $250,000 to run one of Trump's companies for at least 12 months. While all shows deserve a moment for a trash wallow, Trumps perhaps exceeds the others in that he gets to be an actor himself on the show, and weekly, when a contestant falls by the wayside, Trump gets to scream with his usual enthusiasm, "You're fired!"

Naturally, wherever you have the flamboyant, hyperbolic, and sometimes-bankrupted Mr. Trump, there will be fireworks, and there have been plenty on the program. In 2005, NBC proposed a spin-off from *The Apprentice* and launched a companion piece with Martha Stewart. The program ended after one season. Trump complained that the confusion between the two shows hurt his show's rating, and Stewart accused Trump of sabotaging her program.

Trump reserves the right to fire people at will, and people have even resigned, although such behavior is discouraged. Near the end of the season, the last two candidates are interviewed and assessed by Trump's executive board, and the finalists are tasked with a big project and have to work with a team of fired former contestants to pull the project together. This is dicey stuff, since the castoffs may not be the most cooperative team to pull together. They then go to a final board meeting and make a final plea before Trump, pleading their case as a superior employee.

Other controversies have plagued the show, most notably problems generated by Trump himself. Women's groups have protested because more men have won than women. Further, Trump made derogatory statements about President Obama before running for and winning the presidency himself, which puts him on television as a character promoting his own agenda and seeking ego gratification by beating up other famous people in public. While Donald Trump may not be a fun and happy man, Trump's demanding personality, and the difficult tasks foisted on the apprentices, *The Apprentice* is often an entertaining romp.

See also: American Ninja Warrior; Survivor; The X Factor

Further Reading
Leigh Edwards, *The Triumph of Reality TV*, 2013; David S. Escoffery, *How Real Is Reality TV?*

THE ASSISTANT

MTV's *The Assistant* was a horrific, deadpan, and sometimes-funny parody of a reality show (mostly *The Apprentice*) in which comedian Andy Dick served as a host, mentor, and demigod to a group of pathetic losers/hangers-on/teens/reality junkies who longed to be Dick's assistant. The show made Dick a cartoonish villain—almost a spitting image of the cartoon character Roger, the demented alien that lives in the attic of the Smith home in Seth McFarland's *American Dad*.

The show was conceived for laughs; played upon all the common reality show tropes: weekly challenges and eliminations; Donald Trump's famous "you're fired" line; a cringing and whiny group of incompetent assistants; a carefully balanced multiracial, youthful, and attractive telegenic cast; a ridiculously opulent central location/staging area; by lengths ugly, squalid, depressing, irrational challenges; hopelessly inept camera work; and, as always, brilliantly realized editing that somehow managed to pull the random pieces of cast-off footage into something resembling a television program.

At center stage was the figure of Andy Dick, who guided the proceedings like a minor, self-absorbed, unattractive, glitchy, angry, former television star. Dick was fairly silly and clearly had fun playing the gruff and unpredictable, taciturn, anxious, whiny, comedic host/mentor to patient slaves.

The poor cast of contract slaves that Dick pulled together to torture could have never guessed that working in Dick's employ could be so annoying and ultimately so much fun. Andy would send the troops out on deadly missions. One poor schmo was sent to dump Andy's girlfriend. The girl demanded the assistant call Andy back, and he repeated the order to dump her. She ran after the poor, beleaguered assistant, still complaining. Another assistant was required to get Andy a limousine, and he obtained a pink limo that resembled a ghetto pimp-mobile. Dick ushered his team of 10 assistants in the car to arrange a spa day.

On another occasion the assistants found Andy in bed with—you guessed it— the ex-girlfriend he had asked an assistant to chase away the day before. When the gang went for a spa day, they found all the quality hotels booked, so they ended up trying to give Dick and his girlfriend a spa experience in a fleabag Sunset Strip hotel. An assistant poured foul-smelling bath salts into the tub and used paint rollers to give Andy and his date a massage. Eventually, a trip to the tub in bathing suits ended in disaster, and Andy's date left in a huff. Episodes ended with a rose ceremony, parodying the odious finish of *The Bachelor* programs. Someone must pay, and Dick would fire the offending servant with a famous, "You're fired!"

The show was one of MTV's better productions. The show was deeply cheesy, but noticeably and clearly cheesy, and it was obvious that all the characters were in on the joke. The scripts zinged a variety of reality shows, including MTV's own dubious products. On occasion, one could see the cast cracking up in the wide-angle shots. The show had the intentional awfulness that shows like *SCTV* pioneered in the 1980s, in which a cast of characters parodied television stereotypes so completely that the difference between reality and parody was slim. Dick was so close to the self-delusion of some reality show characters (Donald Trump, anyone on the *Kardashians, The (Un) Real Housewives of Beverly Hills*) that he was funny and prophetically ridiculous, simultaneously. *People* magazine wrote that "the survivor will be the one who most assiduously sucks up to the squirmy comic, portraying himself here as a capricious, clumsy and insecure pretender to A-list status" (2004). If one despises reality television, *The Assistant* was a great place to revisit the most-despised clichés in the genre. The show is missed for its sharp parody of a genre that often inadvertently parodies itself.

See also: American Ninja Warrior; The Apprentice

Further Reading

David S. Escoffery, *How Real Is Reality TV?; People* Staff, "Picks and Pans Review: *The Assistant*," People.com, July 19, 2004.

THE BIGGEST LOSER

The nicest thing about *The Biggest Loser* is that there is an instant bonding with the contestants, because most people can relate to being overweight and out of control and not having your body the way you like it. The premise of *The Biggest Loser* is that people with weight problems are encouraged to lose weight by inducements, including cash prizes.

The group of 12 players is split into the red team and the blue team, and they struggle with various challenges. An incredibly uplifting aspect of the program is the personal stories of the contestants. Many of them have weight problems for a variety of social, family, psychological, and self-esteem issues, and hearing their stories is often emotional and heartbreaking. When the contestants congregate at the lodge before the competition begins, they are confronted with a scale, where they weigh in. It is embarrassing and distressing, and for some it is a rallying cry to put their lives together. When they are told there is food available and they can eat, there is massive temptation, and many are tempted to use food to comfort themselves. There is lots of talk and lots of bravado, but the viewers can tell the players are genuinely frightened and fear the temptation of the food. The program deals with people suffering from extreme addiction problems, and there is a serious and therapeutic side to the program. Both coaches tend to be hard on the teams and push them to extremes, but both also provide counseling and a supportive shoulder to help the combatants make it from day to day. There is a real sense of triumph when a contestant gets on the scale and loses a single pound. Every step is a victory. Every fitness criteria is a blessing.

The first day's challenge is rough. In one episode, both teams had to drag a car around a racetrack to a finish line. So teams of 8–10 people were pulling the car, and one contestant had to be inside driving it. The doors were sealed, so the overweight player had to be lodged in the car like a slimy sardine. It was an intense challenge, and all the players were sweating and exhausted by the end of the road. All had real concerns about how their weight would impact their health and ability to compete. Several broke down in tears during and following the competition. The entire show is a strongly emotional self-challenge.

The Biggest Loser premiered in 2004 and has been a consistent performer with audiences and has been highly regarded with critics, avoiding the negative stereotypes of reality shows by focusing on the creative growth of individuals. The show chronicles the struggles of contestants to lose weight. For this they are rewarded with cash, and they achieve partial victories by overcoming their cravings and meeting physical challenges to be healthier in the process. Unlike some shows in which the goal is to become thin or beautiful instantly by surgical means, this show succeeds through patience, sensible procedures, willpower, and perseverance. It teaches strong but positive life lessons, endurance, and compassion, and, although both sides want to win money, there is a marked lack of mean-spiritedness that permeates other reality shows.

The program has produced an international following, and *The Biggest Loser* franchise extends across the globe. In Australia, the program found the heaviest contestant in Kevin Moore, who weighed over 500 pounds. Some losers have been able to lose over 50 percent of their weight.

Not all previous contestants are fans. The show has its critics. Some see it as making fat people freaks and accentuating their difference by calling them out as different. Kai Hibbard, who was a contestant in 2006, told *The New York Post*, "The whole f--king show . . . is a fat-shaming disaster that I'm embarrassed to have participated in" (Callahan 2015). According to Hibbard and *The Post*, the program makes contestants sign a release allowing the show to use a player's life story and to agree not to discuss the show in a negative manner. Another contestant said the show confiscated a laptop and phone for 24 hours, presumably to bug the devices. The 50 contestants are cut to 14, who end up going to the fat farm to work out, lose weight, and be continually monitored. The show begins with the contestants checking in, talking, and being given diets to reduce their calorie intake and hopefully reduce their weight and an exercise regime to make them stronger. Unfortunately, Hibbard reported that after a physical the contestants worked out long times—from five to eight hours. Hibbard reported, "My feet were bleeding through my shoes for the first three weeks" (Callahan 2015). Apparently, the physical conditioning coaches were allowed to be quite abusive, and abuse was one way to yoke a defiant player on the show. Hibbard said that a coach sent her a message that read, "'We've picked out your fat-person coffin'" (Callahan 2015).

Opponents have criticized the show for taking too much weight off of people too quickly. Apparently, a safe weight loss is a few pounds a month. Rapid weight loss can cause people to regain weight quickly because their bodies have not adjusted to their new weights. Rachel Frederickson, the show's biggest loser of 2014 went from 260 pounds to 105 pounds, over 155 pounds in a few months. She gained 20 pounds back within a month of the show's end. People ran her picture on magazine covers and asked whether she had lost "too much, too fast." The first biggest loser, Ryan Benson, cut from 330 to 208 pounds but gained it all back over time. The violent weight loss had him excreting blood, a potential sign of organ damage. The show disowned him as a failure because he did not maintain his weight reduction. When Hibbard injured herself on the show, the producers did not admit that high-energy athletics might damage severely overweight people, and "they edited her to make her look lazy and bitchy and combative" (Callahan 2015). Apparently, one of the show's long-term trainers, Jillian Michaels, quit the show over concerns that the players were not receiving proper medical treatment from the trainers.

Whether the optimistic, idealistic program that viewers see or the darker, brooding, mocking, and health-threatening program that *The Post* describes is the truth remains to be seen. Certainly, *The Biggest Loser* depends on rapid weight loss and remarkable transformations to convince people that changing one's life is a great goal. One problem that permeates all of reality television is the need for time to be greatly compressed to achieve results. This is the case for *Extreme Makeover, The Swan, What Not to Wear,* and other programs in which makeovers and transformations are accomplished quickly. What emerges is that the timeline of television and the way humans work may be strongly diverging. We want the quick impression—that everything can be changed in a person rapidly—but maybe what we truly desire is to see rapid changes in ourselves. We know that more than half of Americans have weight problems. Perhaps the impatience we all feel would be better served by realistic self-improvement and realistic self-perception shows, rather than lose-weight-fast programs like *The Biggest Loser*. However, television relies on drama to achieve an audience, and it is doubtful that people would tune in week after week to see a one-pound weight loss on a patient and steady, healthful progression in one's lifestyle. Such a show might be good weight loss and a better workout regime, but it would not provide the massive appeal that *The Biggest Loser* engineers. Still, the remarkable change in people over the weeks of *Loser* is compelling to legions of viewers and keeps eaters glued to the screen, probably munching donuts.

See also: American Ninja Warrior; Survivor; What Not to Wear

Further Reading

Maureen Callahan, "The Brutal Secrets behind *The Biggest Loser,*" *New York Post*, January 18, 2015; David S. Escoffery, *How Real Is Reality TV?*

ANTHONY BOURDAIN

No matter how intriguing the concept and innovative the format, the success of reality shows depends on the personalities involved. Many shows, such as *Big Brother*, *Dancing with the Stars*, and *The Bachelor,* refresh the screen each season, bringing in a new cast. Sometimes a popular former cast member will reappear on a show or jump to another. The late Joan Rivers, a winner on *The Apprentice*, made her last television appearance as a guest on the show. Omarosa, who appeared in the first season of *The Apprentice*, subsequently appeared in 20 other reality shows.

A singular personality, however, is behind four reality shows: *A Cook's Tour, Anthony Bourdain: No Reservations, The Layover,* and *Anthony Bourdain: Parts Unknown*. Additionally, Bourdain has judged both *Top Chef* and *The Taste*, eaten *Bizarre Foods*, and gotten his fourth tattoo on *Miami Ink*. He is an insightful and careful writer of the food scene, exuding massive glee about working with his hands in a craft. What is it about Bourdain's personality that wears well with television audiences?

For female fans, he is the boy your mother warned about—the lanky, tattooed kid slouched in a dark alley. For decades, a cigarette was the sixth appendage on his hand. His prodigious drinking has been chronicled on many episodes. His language can be colorful. In his youth he never met a drug he didn't like, including cocaine and heroin. He confessed to being "high all the time" in the 1980s.

But Bourdain is also a man's man—not the friend who would bail you out of jail, but the one who's in the cell with you. He holds his own against the world's most renowned drinkers, including Russians. He has a ninja fantasy. He'll try anything, including cliff diving and fermented shark. He and his crew were trapped in Beirut during the Israeli-Lebanese conflict. Later, there was the illicit romance of a guy long married, long childless, who fell in love with a younger woman and became a family man.

And Bourdain knows his stuff. A graduate of the Culinary Institute of America, he was a working chef who subsequently became executive chef at Brasserie Les Halles in New York. In 2000 he published *Kitchen Confidential*, an insider's look at the food industry. It was followed by *Medium Rare*, which dished dirt on other chefs. He's subsequently written novels with a food-industry theme, such as *Bone in the Throat*.

Whether in books or on television, Bourdain champions the little people of the food industry who get as much acclaim as the backbone of a healthy 12-year-old. He believes the restaurant business "would collapse overnight without Mexican workers" (Bourdain, "Under the Volcano," 2014). Besides supporting the underlings of the food industry, he's also a proponent of using the "nasty bits" of food sources, such as skin and bones. He himself has sampled eyeballs and testicles.

His first show, *A Cook's Tour*, aired from 2001 to 2002 on the Food Network. Although short-lived, it established the formula for Bourdain's subsequent shows: travel, food, drink, and culture aided by liaisons, who might be drivers, translators, friends, or local chefs. In the Tokyo episode, he described himself as "ignorant but enthusiastic" about Japanese cooking. Other food hosts may be knowledgeable but don't convey their expertise as vividly. He is sometimes bleeped (and you know exactly what he said). He often uses Western analogies in describing regional cuisines. He has said that eel is Japan's "Viagra of the sea." Libations are also important to a culture. In Japan he enjoyed sake at the end of a sushi meal. (The Russian episode of *A Cook's Tour* is entitled "So Much Vodka, So Little Time.") Often, he shows viewers an attraction not readily available to the casual traveler. In Japan, he visited a sumo stable and enjoyed the wrestlers' typical meal.

In 2005 *No Reservations* premiered on the Travel Channel. Bourdain would travel the United States and the world in search of culture and food. No location was too downtrodden or too exotic, from the Rust Belt to Kurdistan. While he did partake of fine dining, he often consumed street food and delighted in home cooking. Ever eat warthog prepared by Bushmen? Bourdain, as host, was nominated three times for an Emmy. The show won for outstanding cinematography for nonfiction programming. The last episode aired in 2012.

The Layover, also on the Travel Channel, appeared in 2011. An additional element was added to the established formula: the stay was limited to 24 to 48 hours. How can a visitor best spend that time? Locations were limited to those cities a business traveler or tourist might be most likely to pass through—Rome, London, and Chicago, for example.

In 2014 Bourdain abruptly changed direction (and channels). In CNN's *Parts Unknown,* he visits places Westerners are less likely to go or out-of-the-way locations in well-traveled areas. Episodes include a trip to Iran and a less-touristy Jamaica. In *Parts Unknown* a more thoughtful Bourdain sometimes addresses serious topics involving economics and politics. He revisits Cambodia after a decade and speculates who changed more—the country or himself. The bad boy of the food industry is older and wiser, and it shows. But he's as much fun as ever.

Bourdain shot to prominence as the bad boy of the cooking world with *Kitchen Confidential* (2000), a text that showed the seamy underbelly of the cooking industry, with love affairs in the kitchen, wild profanity, drug use among chefs, and questionable morals from everyone in the business. In his insider works about the restaurant business, Bourdain always revisits his challenges, including his recovery from heroin addiction, describes how difficult being a chef in first-rate kitchens can be, and reports on his own questionable practices. He warns diners off fish on Monday (probably from last week) and well-done beef (also probably old and tough cuts of meat). Bourdain started the restaurant chain Les Halles, serving working-class French food, and runs a tough schedule of personal appearances, TV programs, and book and commentary writing on food and restaurants.

Most recently, his CNN series *Parts Unknown,* part travelogue, part cooking show, and part perceptive commentary on foreign cultures, has won the Peabody Award for television programming. Bourdain mentioned on NPR's *Fresh Air* that reporters who ask many intrusive questions freeze many locals who fear Western interrogation. Bourdain's jocular approach is to sit down, eat with the locals, and ask them, "What is it that makes you happy?" While he is a world traveler and a hip respondent to local conditions (*Parts Unknown* has visited conflict-ridden states such as the Congo, Beirut, Gaza, and Libya), he is aware that eating what the locals eat means that he can in some way enter the inner lives of his subjects. Eating pig guts, eyeballs, or skin is often a prelude to his wry commentary on the cultures he encounters. He balances his daredevil world-trotting lifestyle with time at home with his nine-year-old daughter, who likes established fare like mac and cheese and burgers. Bourdain started as a dishwasher and rarely forgets the common people who eat at small eateries, but he reports that sometimes when writing he doesn't mention the little treasures and tucked away eateries he encounters. He fears by mentioning them, he might change them.

Liz Hufford

See also: Ramsay's Kitchen Nightmares

Further Reading

Anthony Bourdain, *Medium Raw: A Bloody Valentine to the World of Food and the People Who Cook*; Dave Davies, "In 'Appetites,' Bourdain Pleases the Toughest Food Critic (His 9-Year-Old)," *Fresh Air,* October 27, 2016.

THE CHALLENGE (ROAD RULES VS. REAL WORLD)

The Challenge takes the same teen, slacker, whiner, wannabe characters who populate *Road Rules* and *Real World*—largely clueless, pretty, inoffensive, naïve, southern Californian 20-somethings—and pits them against each other in ersatz *Survivor*-style competitions.

Generally, alumni from *Road Rules* and *Real World* competition shows are turned into two tribes at a remote location. The program was a spin-off from the original *Road Rules/Real World* programs and began as an alum show in 1998. It has produced a remarkable and impressive 26 seasons, showcasing a variety of previous MTV contestants and "new blood" (aka, "fresh meat") to enter the competition. Some of the competitors (since *Real World* has been a staple for 20 years) are edging out of MTV's target demographic, and some competitors are well into their thirties, heading toward their geriatric/VHI forties. When the 20 players introduce themselves, many call attention to their age, saying they've changed, and, that in the future, they will conduct themselves differently and perform in a more professional and competitive fashion. We can only hope.

The show came to be when things clicked into place when the *Real World Boston* season and *Road Rules: The Island* season converged. In a break from filming *Real World,* the cast vacationed in San Juan, Puerto Rico, and the *Islands* cast was in town filming for their series. The producers quickly set up a match between the two teams that became heated and competitive. The two teams played for a cash prize. The ratings on this special event were strong, and people gravitated toward a new challenge for the largely static *Road Rules* and *Real World* programs. A spin-off series was born.

In one of the early challenges, *Inferno*, the competitors met at an attractive hotel in Central America and held an initial enclave in which the host, Dave Mirra, read them the rules of the competition. Here teams/tribes of ten were pitted against each other in a series of encounters. There were cash prizes of $10,000 for each feat won by a team and a grand prize of $150,000 for the final triumphant team. The first challenge was to slide between two multistoried buildings on a guide wire. The players had to slide halfway, then release from their harnesses, grab the wire, and pull themselves to the other side while trying to pull their opponent off the wire. If pulled free, the opponent was left dangling by a bungee cord about six feet below the wire and had to be hauled to the finish. Few of the players had the energy or the aggressiveness to wrestle with an opponent on a wire several stories up in the air, and most were thankful to be across the wire and safe. It was a visually compelling sequence.

The program is better paced and more active than *Road Rules* and *Real World*, shows where viewers are presented with tightly scripted, whiny, privileged, Californian brats. Mostly, these are people whose biggest issues are "BMW versus Audi." Unlike those shows, which focus predominantly on the inert, internal struggles of teens trying to come to grips with themselves and each other, *The Challenge* is a more of an upfront competition/dare show in the mode of *Survivor*, which it strongly resembles. The only difference is the players are all young and pretty in

The Challenge. It is pointless to try to describe the mechanism and format of the series, since MTV has a penchant for changing the rules each season and transforming the show to try a new spin. Each season the show adopts a new subtitle to explain the new orientation.

The makeup of teams changes yearly. Some years it is all "fresh meat," or girls versus boys, or bad guys versus good guys, and so forth. In essence, the kids are sent on missions, and the weakest team or the weakest players are put into an elimination round. This is where things can get dirty, because team members can vote each other off the team or eliminate other team members weekly. As in all MTV reality shows, loose-lipped teens gossiping and undermining each other is the predominant meal of the day. The camera zooms in to hear someone insulting someone, and the caustic outbursts seem acted.

Despite the self-absorbed silliness of the program, there have been real-life issues, including illnesses and deaths. Diem Brown, a *Challenge* strong competitor died at 32 after a long battle with ovarian cancer. Ryan Knight, another MTV *Challenge* competitor, died mysteriously, with initial police implications that he may have been a victim of intense partying.

Still, despite a constant need to keep the competition fresh, *The Challenge* continues to dig for new ways to surprise the audience. In the 2015 season, the theme was *Battle of the Exes,* in which people who previously dated would compete. Lindsey Putnam, writing for *The New York Daily Post,* said, "There's one [challenge] this season where there are two big trucks racing down a highway and the cast mates have to jump back and forth from one to the other. It's just thrilling to watch" (2015). The stunts are bigger and the risks higher for the freewheeling stars.

See also: American Ninja Warrior; Road Rules; Survivor

Further Reading

David S. Escoffery, *How Real Is Reality TV?*; Lindsay Putnam, "MTV's the Challenge Carries on after Two Deaths," *New York Daily News,* January 9, 2015.

CHOPPED

Chopped is a highly entertaining cooking show in which a series of cooks from different restaurants and locales are brought together for a cook-off competition. The end prize for the winning chefs is $10,000, enough to add to their own businesses or help them in their careers. The panel of judges, usually three, set specific challenges for the chefs in each round. Usually there are four contestants during the hour show. First, we are introduced to the contestants and fed a little information about their background and personal/professional challenges. The details include some private information and their budget, but mostly the overall outline of their career, their interests, and their current employment. Then they are in the kitchen. In three progressive rounds, the chefs are "chopped" from the ranks until only one chef is left standing.

In one episode, the chefs were met with a clever series of challenges. The theme was chocolate, and the goal was to prepare an appetizer, a main dish, and a dessert, all with chocolate somehow in the menu. Each chef addresses the challenge in different ways. The chefs are handed a set of ingredients that must be in each course, but they are allowed to make additions and adjustments using materials found in their well-stocked and prepared kitchen.

The series has a 12-hour turnaround for filming the episodes. Players are introduced to the kitchen and basic techniques of using the stoves, ovens, and operations of the kitchen. Segments are filmed, and the judges need around 90 minutes to render their judgments.

The series is quite popular and successful and has run continuously on the Food Network since 2009. By 2015 it had reached its 22nd consecutive season, with many special shows as well. The show is blissfully short on hype; the chefs are serious, hardworking cooks who make few errors; show responsibility, resourcefulness, and impressive skills in the kitchen; and do a great job of describing their strategies and responses to their tasks and materials. The logo shows a meat cleaver cutting the term *Chopped* in half at the program's opening. In each round of the hour-long series, one chef is usually eliminated. The chefs all know the drill on the show and provide excellent commentary on their attempts and their failures. The chocolate show presented four people who all seemed to love chocolate and knew it was a challenge to integrate that material into all segments of the meal. The four gamely tried to make it a part of a pork-based appetizer and tried everything from a chocolate sauce, a mole sauce, and a chocolate-laced taco for starters.

Food Network's *Chopped* has a strong structure, pitting the four chefs against each other in competition, but they are also working against themselves and their normal way of cooking. They must take a group of materials presented to them in boxes, literally mystery ingredients, and integrate them into a recipe that will impress the judges with their visual quality, taste, and flair of presentation.

With each round—appetizer, entrée, and dessert—the chefs are given a chaotic mix of ingredients that do not naturally seem to be aligned with the meal or the course. Their job is to make coherent displays and meals from each packet. In one episode, the cooks had to combine watermelon, zucchini, sardines, and pepper jack cheese into a coherent dish.

One of the steepest challenges of the show is the presentation of the food. Each cook is given limited time for preparation. There is a 20-minute limit on the appetizer round and 30-minutes apiece for the entrée and dessert rounds. The players must produce and set plates for three judges and a display plate within the time period. Naturally, it is expected that the competitors will use all ingredients, but sometimes an ingredient falls out of the mix. When the final judging of the dessert round is considered, there are only two players left, and the judges must weigh not only the quality, look, and taste of the dessert, but also the overall effect of the entire meal.

The Harvard Crimson ran an article on the show praising its brazen simplicity and forthrightness. Writer Thomas Westbrook wrote, "Now, here's where most shows would go so terribly wrong and 'Chopped' goes so terribly right: there is nothing else to the show" (2015). Westbrook's point is the show eschews the absurd fishing for complexity that damages the credibility of much reality programming. The producers play it straight. The show is about preparing quality food, and the focus is on watching cooks make quality food. There are no backbiting, complaining, and whining interviews. There are no personality and quirk insights. There are no hidden, secret, diabolical plots the producers plan to undo or embarrass a competitor. Finally, the accent remains on the cooking. Sure, there is plenty of interest, and, yes, there are some tough bouts and some people win and some lose, but the program keeps the drama on the creativity and originality of the cooks—not some mismanaged game to outwit the players and the home audience. At its core, *Chopped* respects its audience. Westbrook describes the secret ingredient as "The incredible part, for the viewer, is in seeing how differences in culinary background and preferences lead different chefs to take the exact same challenge and spin off in wildly different directions" (2015). Despite the fact that these incredible chefs are given the exact same materials to fashion their works, their variety and capability of making unique choices is itself a thrilling aspect. Unlike a real cooking show in which we are taught and guided through every step, this is a food art show in which, although we see much of the procedure, the final products are sometimes real magic.

A tribute to the no-nonsense popularity of the program was the introduction of the *Chopped Champions* and *All Stars* series. In the *Champion* rounds, 16 former winners returned to the program to compete to retain the title of champion and win an additional $50,000 prize. The *Chopped All Stars* playoff pitted 16 chefs against each other in an elimination tournament in which four chefs competed in four shows. The finalist of that round, the grand-finale winner, received $50,000 to be donated to the charity of his or her choice. The *All-Stars* edition began airing in 2011. In 2012, Food Network added the *Chopped Grill Masters* competition, filmed outdoors in Tucson, Arizona, for the best grill chefs. The series has even spun off an amateur series and a children's cook-off. The show thrives on hard-working chefs, celebrities, and amateurs competing to make creative, attractive, tasty, and distinctive culinary works.

See also: Diners, Drive-ins, and Dives; Ramsay's Kitchen Nightmares

Further Reading
David S. Escoffery, *How Real Is Reality TV?*; Thomas Westbrook, "Why the Food Network's 'Chopped' Is the Most Serious Entertainment on TV Today," *Harvard Crimson*, March 24, 2015.

DANCING WITH THE STARS

ABC's *Dancing with the Stars* has been a strikingly successful American reality series since 2005, presented by ubiquitous reality show host Tom Bergeron and spawning over 20 seasons of unique, dance-studded programming, performed live and featuring winsome couples composed of a celebrity with a professional dancer. The show was derived from the British program *Strictly Come Dancing*. The setup is usually one dancer, either a professional or semiprofessional dancer, paired with a celebrity or athlete, and the couple (sometimes with the help or direction of other choreographers/coaches) must put together a series of two-minute dance routines created to make the best of the couple's skills and physicality.

Often the choreographer has little to work with. Many of the performers are not natural dancers, nor are they athletically trained or fit. The couple can be mismatched, and the chances of creating vehicles that work well for everyone are difficult. Miraculously, the choreographers, the unsung heroes of the show, manage to make the notables and the dancers blend in seamless harmony, and many of the contestants move to the finale.

The sequence of the show is a progressive elimination of players, usually beginning with a field of 10 couples and then in weekly eliminations, narrowing the field to two or three couples who are left to show their stuff in the final dance-off rounds. There is enormous enthusiasm from the home audiences, and watching the final dance-off competition is usually a pastime for millions of Americans, rivaling professional sports. The panel of show judges and audience polls decide who will be eliminated weekly. The judges have been stable and include Len Goodman, Carrie Ann Inaba, Julianne Hough, and Bruno Tonioli. Guest judges have included Ricky Martin, Cher, Kelly Osbourne, and Paula Abdul.

The trick to the program's high audience interest is the pairing of guest/celebrities on the show with professional dancers. That dancer, sometimes in conjunction with other choreographers and trainers, prepares the celebrity to be danceworthy as a contestant. Over 230 celebrities have appeared on the program. Besides the celebrity partners, a dance troupe has appeared as part of the show's Tuesday night results program.

The show is scored by raw ballots from the judges, and scores are combined with audience home scores. Audiences can vote by phone, Facebook, or e-mail. Apparently there has been some controversy about this, since some people have tried (successfully) to vote multiple times and thus sway the score.

Because the show is extremely physical and demanding, many contestants have bowed out during the program, citing injuries or personal crises. There have been some famous collapses during the show. Marie Osmond did an onstage faint following her performance on the show, driving the program to a commercial break. A few performers claimed to have had food poisoning, forcing them to forego some performances. Jennifer Grey overcame tumors, cancers, torn tendons, and other injuries to eventually win season 11. There were many knee injuries, stress fractures, leg fractures, ankle injuries, and broken bones in the knees, legs, or feet. Melissa Gilbert had a head injury, and Billie Dee Williams withdrew for back problems. The obvious conclusion is that taking nondancers and putting them in high-pressure professional dance competitions is risky to the health of the celebrities who may not be trained or fit for careers as dancers. Our society still associates dance with variety acts such as magic. They think it is all done on stage, when, in reality, the effortless shows we see are the conclusion of lifetimes on the dance floor. Muscles must be conditioned, bodies stretched, and memories toned to remember the complex dance routines.

The New York Times ran an article on "Why Don't We Dance Anymore?" Writer Heather Havrilesky quoted Brazilian author Paulo Coelho, saying, "When you dance, you can enjoy the luxury of being you" (2013). The art of dance, as she understands it, is the art of being yourself and having the opportunity to express yourself without inhibition. Part of the joy and wonder of dancing is the act of self-expression. Sure, there is lots of planning, choreography, and professional assistance, but the audience understands the electricity of just having the dancers get out and do their routines.

An interesting statistic of the show is that athletes only represent 20 percent of the actual celebrity competitors, but they have won six competitions and placed second four times. This is a win record of 36 percent. Athletes are better conditioned than other celebrities, and they are trained to win, and win under pressure. It is likely they are also better prepared for winning at dance, a practice they consider another athletic competition.

The program has been a popular venue for stars wishing to recharge their careers, and *Forbes* magazine reported that the show has been a real goldmine for these stars because of the show's audience size, the amount of female audience members who learn about athletes, the amount of media coverage of the event, and the fact that the performances are live.

There were some stirring tributes to Patrick Swayze and Michael Jackson offered by the show. The American program is avowed to be far more polished than the British version. Carrie Dunn wrote for *The Guardian*, "Everything is so much shinier and slicker on the US show than it is in *Strictly*" (2010). Judge Len Goodman is ridiculed in the U.K., and "over the Atlantic, he's booed by the crowd in pantomime fashion for being the nasty judge who offers stinging criticism" (2010). Dunn's final analysis is that the American program is stronger on glitzy performances and that the British show is more tasteful for people who want more angry criticism. In any event, *Dancing with the Stars* is a crowd pleaser, because, unlike so much reality fare, the stars on board actually must do something besides be a celebrity.

See also: So You Think You Can Dance; Survivor; The X Factor

Further Reading

Carrie Dunn, "*Dancing with the Stars* v. *Strictly*: Which Has the Fancier Footwork?" *The Guardian*, September 23, 2010; David S. Escoffery, *How Real Is Reality TV?*; Heather Havrilesky, "Why Don't We Dance Anymore?" *New York Times*, October 11, 2013; David Schwab, "Why *Dancing with the Stars* Is Marketing Gold for Celebrities," *Forbes*, March 17, 2015.

DINERS, DRIVE-INS, AND DIVES (DDD)

Guy Fieri, the ubiquitous host of many Food Network programs, hosts *Triple D* (*Diners, Drive-ins, and Dives*) as an adventure travelogue, wandering across the United States in search of underrated and hidden treasures in food and eating establishments.

The show began in 2006 using selected themes to guide the adventures. Most of the shows are road trips in which Fieri and the crew hop into one of his classic GM cars and head up the road to some unassuming hole-in-the-wall restaurant that on another day, munchers might pass by. The theme might be late-night food, sweets, or comfort food. For each episode, Fieri and his team find restaurants that pertain to the theme. The accent is on regional foods, ethnic foods, cultural foods, or unique blends of styles and forms of cuisine that many Americans may not know about. The only thing that he seeks to avoid is large chains or well-known venues. Even if the theme is something simple like sweets, the restaurants Fieri seeks are likely to treat that food in a new or unique fashion.

Despite the idea of dives, Fieri finds hidden treasures among restaurants that bring in fancy aesthetic designs to their foods, high-art stylings, unique presentations, and clever dining and table arrangements. One aspect that Fieri follows is natural ingredients. Wherever possible, Fieri looks for restaurants that feature local flavors, recipes, ingredients, and fresh things (herbs, fish, wildlife, exotic fruits, etc.). Many of the eating establishments have longtime cooks or unique recipes that have been passed from generation to generation. In Louisiana, New Mexico, and the Northeast, Fieri has found unusual spices and spins on classic dishes. At other venues, he finds people who add a gourmet or chef's touch to common foods, such as a hamburger transformed into a foreign dish and provided with layers of ingredients to make it new.

A typical show has Fieri pop into a bar or stand and order food. He goes back in the kitchen to talk with the cooks and to see how they prepare a meal. They often demonstrate their technique and specialties. Most are happy to share their insights and what works in their area. Then Fieri tries a dish, usually sitting with customers and locals who confirm his opinion on the food or explain why the cuisine at the eatery is a local favorite. At one point, the series was going to focus on visiting all the Hooters locations in the United States as a tie-in to that chain, but the idea was abandoned in favor of more restaurants across the wide stretch of American culture. The program seems like a cost-effective entry. It only entails Fieri, the occasional local guest, and a camera crew. The show, like Fieri's new food finds, operates on a budget.

DDD offers a wide assortment of different types of food. Many nontraditional drive-ins offer their own versions of popular grub, and Fieri bravely dives into buffalo burgers, chili fries, and triple shakes in the pursuit of fast-food sensations that might be somewhat off the beaten track.

A fun part of the show is the guest stars, including Rosie O'Donnell, Dennis Miller, Brad Paisley, and Matthew McConaughey, who pop in for a bite at some eateries in their neck of the woods. Fieri gets around. In the eight years the show has been featured (it debuted in 2007), Fieri has crossed the nation multiple times and found food in some of the strangest places.

Fieri's program debuted in 2006 as a one-off program about visiting dive bars for good food. Audiences liked to find out about good places to eat across the nation. In fact, on the show's Web site, Fieri has an interactive map showing where he has been and what the food was like there. The goal is to give Americans a map to good places to eat across the country without having to stop at dull and colorless chain restaurants.

One of the great things about the program is the classic tie-in to localities and businesses. Fieri's reviews draw business to local eateries, and local media eat him up. The deal is that when Fieri stops in to sample the local cuisine, it places the area on the national map. The more original, unique, and resourceful the restaurant, the more Fieri likes it. His restaurant guide coincides with local journalists all over the country, spouting about how their town and restaurant was featured on Fieri's show. In Arizona, Fieri visited local restaurants, and the event appeared on ABC News. The story read, "Three Valley restaurants will be featured on the popular show *Diners, Drive-Ins and Dives* Friday night" (2015). What a great way to celebrate food and local cultures. Reality TV devotees like Fieri's earnest, real-person approach. Fieri eats the food and talks with locals. Restaurants across the country hope that Fieri and *Triple D* come to their town. I'm sure they will be on the road soon.

See also: American Ninja Warrior; Survivor; The X Factor

Further Reading

"Arizona Restaurants Featured on Food Network's Diners, Drive-ins, and Dives," *ABC News* 15-AZ, February 6, 2015 (Web); David S. Escoffery, *How Real Is Reality TV?*

GUY FIERI

Guy Fieri is a popular host and guide to culinary regions on the Food Network and the popular host of *Diners, Drive-ins, and Dives*, a cooking show that tours some great lowbrow, American eating establishments. In Fieri's regime, price is not as big a factor as taste, and exotic cuisine can be found in bountiful amounts on Fieri's expeditions, where he travels far and wide to find the odd, the unusual, and the often-tasty overlooked cuisines at our own domestic backdoor. Fieri, 48, was born in 1968 and is the owner of five restaurants in California.

The advantage in Fieri's presence is that he brings a plain, male charm to cooking shows, and his impact on the Food Network has been that he has transformed the programming from a mainly female domestic audience into a more-mixed and sometimes male-dominated group of real dudes who either like to cook or enjoy good cooking and yummy eating at dives and places that aren't necessarily healthy eating establishments. He has been a reliable everyday persona on the Food Network, and he is seen in a variety of guises and shows to promote the network and its values of unusual and distinct cuisines, competition shows, varied recipes, and eating places.

Fieri was devoted to food as a kid and actually sold pretzels out of his Awesome Pretzel Cart. He financed a trip to France to study French cuisine by washing dishes in a restaurant. He returned to his home in California and worked for the Red Lion Hotel restaurant. He enrolled in the hotel management BS program at the University of Nevada at Las Vegas and worked for the Stouffer restaurants in California. He then managed restaurants and was a trainer for Louise's Trattoria in California.

Fieri began to open in his own restaurants around 20 years ago, with locations in various cities in California, a location in Vegas, and a grill in New York. The New York grill was the subject of some controversy in 2012, when the *New York Times* wrote a scathing review by author Pete Wells. Wells wrote caustic and wild comments about the establishment, which probably helped the place more than harmed it. Wells quizzed in the review, "Did you notice that the menu was an unreliable predictor of what actually came to the table? Were the 'bourbon butter crunch chips' missing from your Almond Joy cocktail, too? Was your deep-fried 'boulder' of ice cream the size of a standard scoop?" (2012). Wells's assault suggested that lots of what Fieri advertised on the menu didn't appear on the plate, and he suggested that the place specialized in false advertising. Wells was unrelenting in his criticism of the place as second-rate, incompetent, and simply not offering what it claimed to promise. Wells continued, "What exactly about a small salad with four or five miniature croutons makes Guy's Famous Big Bite Caesar (a) big (b) famous or (c) Guy's, in any meaningful sense?" (2012). The question is, did Wells like the food? The review endlessly ridiculed the place, saying the food tasted like formaldehyde and radiator fluid and suggested one sandwich looked as much like its description as Fieri resembled Emily Dickinson.

Fieri is himself the alum of the reality show competition grind and won a contract and a show by winning the *Next Food Network Star* competition in 2006. Appropriately, he did become the next Food Network star. He had a commitment for a six-episode series, *Guy's Big Bite*, a program that is still running. He created the *Diners, Drive-ins, and Dives* program; an ultimate recipe showdown; a live-audience show, *Guy Off the Hook*; and hosted a game show for NBC entitled *Minute to Win It*. He partnered with Carnival Cruises to offer Guy's Burger Joint on board all the Carnival cruise ships. He hosted a reality series with Rachael Ray entitled *Rachael vs. Guy: Celebrity Cook-off* and the chef-challenge show *Guy's Grocery Games*.

Several of his books on diners and American cuisine have sold very well; he has appeared in commercials for AFLAC and TGI Fridays and was given the keys to the city of Ferndale, California, due to his role in putting the city and the state on the map in a positive manner. He has also tirelessly promoted the Food Network, appearing on tours and at regional events. Apparently, Fieri has officiated at a number of gay weddings, uniting many gay couples in matrimony. Fieri, clearly a hard worker, resides in Northern California with his wife, Lori, and their two sons. There he has a classic collection of cars, including some mid-1960s and 1970s GM products.

See also: Diners, Drive-ins, and Dives; Iron Chef America

Further Reading

David S. Escoffery, How Real Is Reality TV?; Pete Wells, "As Not Seen on TV," New York Times, November 13, 2012.

FOOD NETWORK (*FOOD NETWORK CHALLENGE, THE NEXT FOOD NETWORK STAR*)

The Food Network is a joint venture between the Scripps Networks Interactive company and Tribune Cable Ventures. Scripps owns 70 percent, and Tribune owns 30 percent. Both were formerly companies affiliated with the newspaper business, and over time they have acquired holdings in other media. Scripps does the majority of the management of operations. The main offices are in New York City, and the network cable station is available to 83 percent of all household that subscribe to cable. In recent years, the programming has deviated from food-oriented how-to programming to more adventurous reality fare like *Iron Chef America*, and the crowds have responded favorably.

The network was launched in 1993 and was one of the first cable companies to have a female president in Erica Gruen, who saved the network from bankruptcy by changing the focus from "people who love to cook" to "people who love to eat." It was presumed that "people who love to cook" is a pretty small group, but "people who love to eat" is a far larger group.

The station divides broadcast into daytime and nighttime programming. Mostly the daytime shows are how-to, in-the-kitchen shows, and the evening shows are more entertainment-oriented. The station has made major investments in courting celebrity chefs and in birthing its own cooking personalities. One of the biggest early personalities, launched in 1997 and maintained a strong show through 2007, was Emeril Lagasse, who hosted *Emeril Live*. This was a live cooking show with audience participation. Guests would help Emeril cook dishes, and he would often share his productions from the kitchen with the studio audience, walking around and handing out spoonfuls of this or that. He would often spout funny expressions while cooking, like yelling "Bam!" when he tossed a spice or seasoning on a dish. Lots of guests appeared on his show, including Jimmy Buffett, Aretha Franklin, and Charlie Daniels.

From 2002 to 2013 the station had a long-term arrangement with Southern cook Paula Dean, but a lawsuit suggesting that racial slurs were common in her organization turned the station off, and her contract was dropped. Their current most-famous celebrity is Rachael Ray, who is a strong cook, a solid businesswoman, and a winsome television personality. She has programs such as *30 Minute Meals* and *$40 a Day*. The *30 Minute Meals* is the basis of Ray's career. She has made a business of suggesting quick, inexpensive, and healthy dishes that families can enjoy together quickly and easily. Her *$40 a Day* deals with eating well while in a variety of environments. Both are hosted by the funny and easygoing Ray.

The programming came closer to reality television when the station began broadcasting the *Next Food Network Star*. They offered a competition among amateurs to be stars on the Food Network. The idea was to have a culinary competition in New York that would decide who would obtain their own show on the channel. One of the winners was Guy Fieri, who has logged thousands of miles and spawned several shows for the Food Network. Fieri's earnest regular-guy status has enabled the station to capture a much-larger male audience, when 10 years earlier the majority of viewers had been women.

The station has remained popular and appears to be growing with the Cooking Channel, a sister companion channel coming on strong as well. The Fall 2015 season was announced with great fanfare. Mark Joyella, writing for *Adweek*, announced that the channels would offer "a staggering 40 new series, 30 returning shows, and 15 specials" (2015).

Some of the new shows are pure fun, with a touch or humor and reality television show thrown into the mix. There is *Cutthroat Kitchen-Evilicious*. This series brings back evil, maniacal cooks from the *Cutthroat Kitchen* show. Mostly, cooks are team workers, but occasionally wild and unpredictable chefs can be a handful. *Rachael Ray's Kids Cook-Off* features kid cooks fighting each other in a cook-off competition show to be the next child celebrity on the Food Network. The winner of the program gets their own Food Network program. It looks like the future is simmering nicely over at the Food Network.

See also: Iron Chef America; Survivor

Further Reading
David S. Escoffery, *How Real Is Reality TV?*; Mark Joyella, "Food Network Beefs up Its Primetime Menus with 24 New Series," *AdWeek*, April 22, 2015.

GAME SHOWS
Writing about genre and television, Jason Mittell wrote that "the history of any given genre is a subjective articulation of the genre's definition, meaning and cultural value" (2004, 29). Game shows are no different, and they have been a part of television history since before television arrived. A game show is a genre of programming that involves a game, a competition, or a sports activity that challenges players in a physical, intellectual, or emotional manner. The outcome usually produces a reward or benefit for sustained achievement.

Douglas Kellner frames television in the theories and aesthetics that have arrived in the past 100 years, and he includes Herbert Marcuse's idea of how society was structured. Kellner writes, "Marcuse saw television as being part of an apparatus of administration and domination in a one-dimensional society" (2010, 33). For Kellner and Marcuse, television was about controlling the populace through messages—at least as it was conceived as a medium at mid-century. So game shows like *To Tell the Truth* or *What's My Line* were peripheral entertainments to keep the audiences under control. The modern game show as a part of the apparatus of the surveillance society and the state is no different. If the game is changed to *Survivor* and we are watched for months on end to show how well we can play the game, that sort of game still illustrates how we can be controlled. If *What's My Line* placed celebrities in competition to guess a profession to discover how good their questioning could be, today's reality shows pit contestant against contestant to arrive at winning by eliminating each other. The 1950s game show lulled us into a sleepy, false consciousness in which we assumed everything was okay. The brave celebrities would victoriously uncover the guest's line. However, today the lure of money has taught us to betray and undo our opponents for the possibility of cash prizes. The morality of 1950s game shows was mostly absent. The perspective today is abhorrent. Lie, cheat, betray, and win—or as *Survivor* frames it, outwit, outplay, and outlast. If anything, modern reality programming has darkened and deepened the rhetoric of the game show. In the 1960s, *The Dating Game* meant spending a few hours in someone's company for a pleasant evening of entertainment. Today, game shows like *Room Raiders* or *Next* are massive penalty machines. A person has an untidy room, and the date is deleted. Say the wrong thing on an MTV dating show, and you get "nexted." These shows are far harsher, crueler, and unrelenting in their punitive side. The pleasant aspects of *The Dating Game* are replaced by scrutiny and trauma. We have begun to live in Kellner's world of domination and administration in which television exists to teach us very harmful and negative lessons about people and life.

Even more distressing, today in the postmodern era, game shows perform double duty. There isn't just the work on reality TV of playing the game, there is the coding of the game while encoding and performing yourself. Honey Boo Boo had two tasks. First, she must play at being Honey Boo Boo so the audience knows who she is and remembers her. Second, she had to play at winning the beauty pageants to secure her place in that world as well. Misha Kavka expresses it well in her book on Reality TV. She writes, "*Survivor* participants are utterly caught up in their performances as game-players while simultaneously being invested in producing an authentic performance of their self-hood" (2012, 105). What Kavka and most of today's authors understand about the modern game show and its context in reality television is that it is playing a game with society (selfhood, administration, domination, cultural value) while the game show in this new context is always about the self. It isn't a dating show: it is about the player and dating. It isn't about the winning of *Iron Chef*: it is about Rachael Ray or the person winning *Iron Chef*. It isn't about *Ghost Hunters* finding a ghost: it is about the stars' encounter with the ghostly.

While such considerations may not completely change what game shows are or do in today's world, the multiplicity of levels that games shows articulate (selfhood, conversations with society, issues of gender, gaming behavior, matters of geographical origin) makes them more complicated in the frame of reality programming and therefore less simple to discuss. As Mittell said at the start, genres have cultural value, but over time such value may change and morph to different values (2004).

See also: The Dating Game; Here Comes Honey Boo Boo; Survivor

Further Reading

David S. Escoffery, *How Real Is Reality TV?*; Misha Kavka, *Reality TV*, 2012; Douglas Kellner, "Critical Perspectives on Television from the Frankfurt School to Postmodernism"; Jason Mittell, *Genre and Television*, 2004; Janet Wasko, *A Companion to Television*, Wiley-Blackwell, 2009.

GHOST HUNTERS

Ghost Hunters is not your typical reality program because it features paranormal investigators going to locations where strange, spooky experiences have been witnessed or where ghosts have been reported. On the downside, faking ghostly events is standard fare for television, and making something spooky has been television's bread and butter for decades. This sense is not aided by the fact that the investigators on the show turn the lights down low for all investigations, perform most studies at night, and use arcane gear that benefits from spooky lights, ghostly fogs, and all the apparatus of a cheesy, 1950s Hammer horror film. That said, whether real or reality, the program is classic television, and one would expect our ghosts to be primed to keep the project interesting. The program's paranormal team claim to be skeptics and opt to disprove the phenomenon they are investigating. Does this mean they don't become frightened or they don't fancy meeting an occasional real ghost? No, they acknowledge what they believe to be a spiritual phenomenon from time to time, but they keep it real by keeping an eye on the electromechanical manifestations of their poltergeist and working hard to keep their psyches from running away with the dead.

Benjamin Radford, writing for Live Science, suggests that as a culture we should be more skeptical of claims of afterlife phenomenon. It isn't that there is definitive proof against such ghosts, but there is little evidence of real ghost manifestations that can be quantified, objectively collected, and critically accessed. He writes, "The most famous ghost hunters are two plumbers who moonlight as paranormal investigators, seen in the popular SyFy Channel reality show/soap opera series 'Ghost Hunters.' They go to haunted places and find 'evidence' of ghosts such as cold spots, photographic anomalies called, and other such spookiness" (Live Science 2006). But Radford doesn't see any of this as very conclusive and suggests we are just fooling ourselves into believing in the possibility of the supernatural by ingesting such programming.

The program has been a favorite on the struggling SyFy Network, which in recent years has moved to featuring wrestling, horror comedies such as *Sharknado*, and repeats of crime thrillers to maintain a viewing audience. *Ghost Hunters* began in 2004 amid the first wave of revived interest in reality programming and seemed a good bet for SyFy's stock-in-trade in gore, science fiction, and horror. The show has run over 10 seasons, scored over 200 episodes, visited hundreds of specter-infested haunts, and found electrical manifestations at more than a few.

The setup is similar from episode to episode. Usually, a concerned establishment or private individual has experienced or heard of odd manifestations at a dwelling or at a place of business. Generally, these are old or historic buildings with respectably lurid pasts filled with carnage, bloodshed, Indian graveyards, mass murderings, mobster hangouts, or other assorted malicious surroundings. The types of sightings range from sounds to ghosts sauntering around the premises to sounds of weeping and crying disturbing resident guests. The two resident spook hunters are Jason Hawes and Grant Wilson, who come across as two pretty normal average Joes who hunt ghosts for a living. A strength of the series is its lack of claims of authenticity or real pronouncements of the possibility of ghosts. These two bubbas seem just as earnest and as nonchalant in their investigations as can be. In fact, they were both Roto-Rooter plumbers, fixing pipes by day and investigating ghosts in the houses they repaired by night, until the show took precedence over their day jobs.

Hawes and Wilson formed a group, TAPS (The Atlantic Paranormal Society), which champions the investigation of paranormal phenomenon, and the two, plus their various team members, use electronic equipment to pick up sounds, electromagnetic energy, vibrations, spectrographic light signatures, night-vision goggles, and a host of other sound- and video-recording devices to tell them if indeed there are spirits or some other funky energy lurking in their maladjusted locales. There is no scientific evidence that anything they use detects real ghosts, but their investigations catalog case studies of sounds, noises, lights, and random images that they perceive as perhaps having some kinship with the supernatural.

Most shows begin with a stroll around the problematic premises with the owners or caretakers. The intrepid team then ushers everyone out but their investigative team, and they usually spend a night in the dwelling to check out the manifestation personally. They set up the cameras, recorders, electromagnetic field readers, and any device that they hope might capture some entity. They even verbally talk to ghosts and try to coax them into communicating with the team. Sometimes that produces positive results and sometimes summons playful poltergeists that offer whimsy but little positive proof of hauntings. Usually, later-evening visits produce a creepy ambience. After the visit the team goes back to the lab to analyze their results. They have a final meeting to reveal their findings to the owner and draw the conclusions they feel comfortable relating.

Skeptics like Radford point out that the findings of these "experts" are dubious at best. Radford reports that "no one has ever shown that any of this equipment actually detects ghosts." Joe Nickell, a ghost investigator who spoke with NPR volunteered that lots of what ghost hunters think of as evidence may be nothing more than natural radiations and little else. He reports, "They're surprised that they're getting results in an old house, when in fact there are all sorts of non-ghost sources such as faulty wiring, nearby microwave towers, sunspot activity and so on" (Ahmed 2011). Many other things can cause ghost hunters to see the signs of ghosts, but, regardless of whether the ghosts are real or the skeptics are right, *Ghost Hunters* has spooked viewers for 10 years and shows no signs of fading away.

See also: American Ninja Warrior; Survivor; The X Factor

Further Reading

Bennish Ahmed, "Paranormal Technology: Gadgets for Ghost Hunting," *NPR*, October 31, 2011; David S. Escoffery, *How Real Is Reality TV?*; Benjamin Radford, "The Shady Science of Ghost Hunting," *Live Science*, October 27, 2006 (Web).

IRON CHEF AMERICA

Iron Chef America is one of the Food Network's most popular programs, running as a cooking-competition reality program from 2005 to the present continuously. At this time, there have been 11 seasons, over 200 episodes, and many clever challenges. The show has a sense of humor, with a chairman character and real martial artist, Mark Dacascos, jumping and leaping to the center stage position to start the program. The four iron chefs (or master chefs) are shown in dramatic lighting and introduced with great ceremony, and then the challenger is brought in to do battle with one of the master chefs. The series is derived from Fuji TV's Japanese version of *Iron Chef*. *Iron Chef* mimics the imagery of combat in which food warriors battle to the death in the kitchen. The concept of a "kitchen stadium" where the cooks do battle is a fun, cinematic concept, and the exotic and dramatic lighting add to the effect of the program. The show is based on the concept of food preparation as a competitive sport. Though a novelty in American culture, the concept of food competitions has been a staple of some nations' television programming. Each week, a worthy challenger is summoned to do battle with one of the iron chefs in the kitchen stadium. Usually, the basis for the cook-off is a secret ingredient or perhaps a theme. The tone is mock seriousness, but with enough overplay to make the chefs and the audiences partake in the culinary experience. However, there is nothing laughable about the chefs and their incredible preparation skills. The fiction behind the show is that the original iron chef set out to have a cooking stadium where chefs would do battle, and each week, according to the show's mythology, the battle continues to see who will be the remaining iron chef.

All of the four iron chefs on the show have either been Food Network personalities, earned a position as an iron chef in the competition program the *Next Iron Chef*, or were part of the original *Iron Chef* show. The players have high averages against their challengers. That is why they are iron chefs; they are competitive masters who produce extraordinary results with each meal they prepare. The best battle averages are Michael Symon with 82 percent of wins, Mario Batali with 79 percent of wins, and Bobby Flay with 72 percent of wins.

Although all the chefs wore jackets to designate them as master chefs from the beginning, in the sixth season, judge and designer Marc Ecko made new jackets for each chef with distinctive sleeves, patches, and quilted-embroidered names on the jackets. Left shoulder patches give the chef's country of origin, and each chef has an American flag on one arm of their jacket to designate their place of competition now.

The show originated with a special broadcast, *Iron Chef America: Battle of the Masters,* which borrowed several chefs from the Japanese program and provided a sense of continuity with the Japanese program. The format of the show begins with the introduction of the four chefs. The challenger is introduced, and the match ensues when the challenger announces who he/she wishes to battle. Of course, the actual combatants are planned well in advance of the show's airing.

The secret ingredients are revealed, and the cooking begins. Sometimes the secret ingredients are revealed as ground beef, buns, and tomatoes, and the ingredients turns out to be some form of lunch burger or sandwich. In reality, the chefs are given a list of the ingredients in advance, so the secret ingredients are not really secret. Then the cooks are off with the ritual phrase: "So now, America, with an open heart and an empty stomach, I say unto you in the words of my uncle: 'Allez cuisine!'" The phrase is screamed with a blend of menace and excitement. The show has added drama from the excessive amount of ritual provided by the program. The term *allez cuisine!* just means, "go cook" or "start cooking," but it has charm as an amusing battle cry.

Then the cooks get to work. They have 60 minutes to prepare five dishes for the judges using the secret ingredient. Usually, 20 minutes into the show, the chefs present one dish, and the chair throws them a cooking curveball by introducing an all-new condition, presentation, or ingredient into the mix. The chefs scurry about preparing exciting dishes and having brilliant insights and ideas along the way. Finally, at the program's end, the five dishes are rushed to the judges for inspection. The food is scored on a 20-point gradient: 10 points for taste, 5 for appearance, and 5 for originality.

Village Voice writer and guest at an *Iron Chefs America* taping Robert Sietsema said, "We'd been promised moments of brilliant creativity, but what we saw were drones going about their appointed tasks with well-tested recipes, while swooping cameras, flashing lights, smog, and frantic commentary on the part of Alton, the judges, and the floor reporter distracted us from the true nature of the situation" (2008). What Sietsema discovered was that much of the show was canned and staged. While Sietsema seemed stunned and horrified at this, it would seem only natural that there had to be some production, some pre-orchestration and thought put into the creation of the meals before the show began, otherwise, even with trained chefs and sous chefs, there would be massive chaos during the cooking portion. Sietsema called the two hours of judging after the contest a "colossal bore" (2008). Again, the show probably needed a bit of creative license in taping the complex and highly complicated and choreographed wizardry that made the show look like a frantic explosion of energy. Frankly, the miracle of *Iron Chef America* is not only that the chefs can make quality food on the spot, but, thanks to their technical assistance, brilliant lighting, fog effects, and a clever fiction story, they manage to make the whole thing exciting and interesting. Despite the *Village Voice's* reservations, it is still a fun show to watch.

See also: Diners, Drive-ins, and Dives; Ramsay's Kitchen Nightmares; Survivor

Further Reading

David S. Escoffery, *How Real Is Reality TV?*; Robert Sietsema, "Iron Chef Boyardee," *Village Voice,* February 19, 2008.

NAKED AND AFRAID (NAA)

Probably one of the most revealing but alternately excruciating game competition shows is the Discovery Channel's *Naked and Afraid*. Here we take two strong, survivalist individuals, usually a man and a woman, and we transplant them to a desert, the Amazon rainforest, or a barren badlands with no clothing, minimal equipment, bugs, predators, and vile conditions and expect them to hunt, produce shelter, and thrive for three weeks (21 days). This is one competitive show.

While the camera crew is likely fully provisioned and comfortable a few feet out of view, the program does have a palpable sense of grief and anxiety in its composition. The players may not die, but they can be foully stalked by mosquitoes the size of mice, frozen by cold night desert temperatures, feasted on by leeches, who attach to their legs and feet, and starved by a lack of wild game and fish. Although the physical ravages are outrageous and enough to doom many contestants, equally difficult are the psychological pressures. Many of the contestants leave their family and children for the extreme test and are paired with a complete stranger, upon which they are fully dependent for the duration of the trip. Further added to this is the trauma of being naked for 21 days. While some women and men fashion modesty coverings for themselves to make themselves feel more comfortable, many live in a commando state for three weeks. They are attacked by wind, rain, heat, sun, cold weather, and burning draughts.

The problems in the show erupt almost as soon as the survivalists hit the ground. One issue is compatibility between teammates. Unlike game shows, in which the team players do not need close contact, the mates on this awkward program must look at each other naked for 21 days, stay in close proximity, snuggle to stay warm each night, and bond over hardship and adversity. If there is not the slightest bit of emotional and relational camaraderie, the couple is likely doomed to failure. Another issue is the harshness of the terrain. If there is not sufficient shade, cover, heat, food, or raw materials, no matter how well the survival contestants have prepared, their struggle may become almost unendurable. A further complication is the wide range of insects, pests, snakes, leeches, hostile animals, and parasites that can bug the players. Some have found mosquitoes alone to be enough to end the competition.

The show's structure is simple. We are introduced to two strong, skillful, and willful survivalists who have experience in the outdoors and feel they are physically fit enough to tackle the struggles of outdoor life for 21 days. They are profiled, and their survival rating is examined and calculated. We are introduced to the couple at touch-down, and they are shown to us completely naked and vulnerable. The chests and genitals of the women and the genitals of the men are heavily pixilated, but we as an audience understand their nudity and embarrassment. The problem with nudity is that they have little to protect their fragile human bodies. What we see is that as a spe-cies we are quite vulnerable to puncture, invasion, infection, and laceration. Instead of the freedom of nakedness being a blessing, we discover quickly that a few hours of naked interaction with the environment reduces the human body to shreds of ravaged skin. Many contestants resort to covering with leaves, makeshift wraps, or even mud to give their skin a break. Many players succumb to harsh sun and windburn. If noth-ing else, *NAA* sends a strong message about skin care and the dangers of exposure.

The couple usually bond in adversity and buckle down to the tasks of finding and creating shelter, finding and securing water and food, and finding a means to become comfortable at night sleeping in the elements, exposed, and subject to hostile animal and insect attack. The film crew and the lights that must be emitted from the filming procedure seem to secure the couple from predators, but bugs devour the fleshy couple in some locales.

The show suffers from certain problems. For one thing, there isn't much of a prize at the end of the rainbow. Mike Hale, writing for the *New York Times*, comments, "They don't compete for anything, beyond bragging rights—each week's pair of strangers put in the time simply to say they survived (and, presumably, to earn their appearance fees)" (2013). Further, once they set up base camp, they don't go all Indiana Jones on us. Long journeys are problematic and dangerous in the wild. A sort of survivalist inertia sets in, and soon we are watching two people sit around and moan and mope for three weeks as their conditions deteriorate, becoming more unhealthy, unsavory, and starved as the days pass. In many of the locales, water is a big problem, and finding potable water is extremely difficult and nerve-racking. If water isn't found in a few days, the players begin to dehydrate and suffer and become even more morose and unresponsive. Some people revert to whining children, while others become stoic monks or resourceful cheerleaders. The show at least brings out the best in some peo-ple, who are strong and engaged by the challenges the show presents.

Despite what the title implies, there is nothing sexual or sexy about watching these couples struggle for their lives. This show is work, and rather excruciating for the participants as well as the audience. However, critics have cast doubt on the show's authenticity. Mike Hale suggests that it is largely staged, the cast are never in any danger, they don't look so weight-wasted for three weeks with marginal food, and their survival skills don't seem that great. Hale writes, "Overall, the notion that these two could survive without help for more than a few days, even in the relatively gentle jungle where the episode is shot, seems increasingly laughable" (2013). So either *Naked and Afraid* is a laughable farce of survivalist theories, or it is a superior whine fest in which two deeply unhappy survivalists must find ways to cope with the wilds—and mostly, each other—for three weeks. For many it is a ride through a hellish jungle marriage of necessity.

See also: American Ninja Warrior; Survivor; The X Factor

Further Reading
David S. Escoffery, *How Real Is Reality TV?*; Mike Hale, "They Didn't Pack Sunscreen or Anything Else," *New York Times*, June 21, 2013.

OZZY AND JACK'S WORLD DETOUR

If you are looking for a traditional travelogue, you should not start here. *Ozzy and Jack's World Detour* is an engrossing pairing of rock singer Ozzy Osbourne (famous for his own band and notably Black Sabbath, and his popular MTV reality program/send-up *The Osbournes*) and son, Jack Osbourne (famous as a member of the dysfunctional Osbourne tribe). The program, which originated in July of 2016 on the History Channel, explored a wide range of sites in the United States and overseas. Ozzy and Jack visited Washington, D.C., Cuba, England, Japan, Roswell, New Mexico, and Mt. Rushmore. Ozzy and his son crossed exotic places around the globe. Since the program was a popular hit with fans, the father-son team has considered doing another season. Ozzy spoke to the *Houston Press*, saying, "[I'm looking forward to] my bed; my dog, Rocky; and, of course, my family. I will have a few weeks to rest and then there are talks about filming a second season of *Ozzy & Jack's World Detour* with my son, Jack" (Smith 2016). Osbourne and son, Jack, experienced many of the famous tourist attractions on their globe-trotting expedition, but they also experienced places and events that were far from normal tourist destinations and far from conventional tours.

The show began with a surprisingly media smart and literate Jack Osbourne introducing the show and its content. He told viewers they would be seeing the two adventurers on a grand tour of unique sites. He explained that unlike his father's normal retinue of touring managers, musicians, and upscale suites in famous hotels, the team would explore territories, visiting sites that both had always admired. Jack described his father as a rock and roller, a "prince of darkness," and, surprisingly, a history buff. When he told his dad there would be camping involved, the elder Osbourne, looking every bit the rocky, disheveled, long-enduring rock presence of the past 40 years, was less than enthused, but when Jack assured him it would be upscale camping, his father brightened considerably.

The structure of the show was direct, and Jack performed the role of the host and explained the goal of each trip and locale to be examined. In New Mexico, he explained they would visit the Roswell site, look into alien abductions, and visit the National Museum of Nuclear Science and History. Immediately, Ozzy was excited, having studied and read about the history of the creation of the atom bomb and possessing an expert knowledge of the bomb's impact in World War II.

In their tour of the nuclear energy museum, they received fan adulation and a personal guided tour of the early American achievements in nuclear weapons. Ozzy was far more engaged, alert, and vocal than his persona in *The Osbournes*, where he often was a solemn and remote presence. Son Jack was every inch the

American entrepreneurial spirit, and he lovingly ushered his dad from place to place with humor and grace.

Light moments included the loving father questioning his son ("I didn't know you liked camping,") and his dismay at the barebones dullness of their road equipment (a very small truck with a camper on the back). However, the show didn't wish to be simply sensational or exploitive about the two stars, and the focus was clearly on their explorations in their environment. In, episode one, Jamestown, Virginia, the duo had a complex discussion of the possibility of cannibalism in the early English American colony. Jamestown was the first official permanent colony of the British in the 17th century, and the first few years brought war with native Indian tribes and near starvation for most of the residents. While there, the duo visited a museum of military tanks. Ozzy appeared deeply engaged, watching tanks fire and having the opportunity to travel by tank. He wryly commented that the tanks made nearly as much noise as his band, Black Sabbath.

But at a subtextual level, the show was plowing more complicated issues. Taking the pair of luminaries around to American (and foreign) mythic or nearly mythic sites, sent the two on a quest to evaluate the reality of what they see firsthand, with stories and books that have been written from an ancient or remote perspective. Joseph Campbell, in his classic work on mythology *The Hero with a Thousand Faces*, writes, "The dangerous crises of self-development are permitted to come to pass under the protecting eye of an experienced initiate in the lore and language of dreams, who then enacts the role and character of the ancient mystagogue, or guide of souls, the initiating medicine man of the primitive forest sanctuaries of trial and initiation" (2004, 5). Here Jack and Ozzy alternated the role of mystagogue, but both were keen to explain ancient mysteries, and the duo was also deeply impressed by the expert testimony and research done by their various hosts. It appeared that Jack and Ozzy function as units of the audience, assuring the audience that their perceptions are just as keen as the celebrity visitors.

Deeply entertaining and participating in the long history of travel shows and presentations, the program was rewarding not only for the well-informed coverage of topics and places but also for the no-nonsense approaches provided by Jack and Ozzy Osbourne. The program appeared to be a labor of love, and there were few angry words or scenes of dysfunction so common in *The Osbournes'* MTV series. A much healthier and robust Ozzy Osbourne and a career-making, well-informed hosting opportunity by Jack Osbourne made the program a delight for viewers curious about celebrities and also interested in the study of world and regional histories.

See also: Anthony Bourdain

Further Reading
Joseph Campbell, *Hero with a Thousand Faces*, Princeton, NJ: Princeton UP, 2004; Nathan Smith, "Ozzy and Black Sabbath Close the Book on One Hell of a Career," *Houston Press*, November 9, 2016.

PROJECT RUNWAY

Project Runway is a popular reality competition elimination show that has been in continuous production since 2004, has scored 13 seasons at present, and has produced over 180 episodes. The hour-long program began its run on Bravo and moved to the Lifetime Channel in 2009. The structure of the series is derived from competition game shows, but the contestants are fashion designer apprentices. Many have had experience in the clothing trade and either have family members or are themselves the owners of fashion concerns. Several were in associated businesses and decided to make the jump into the harsh and trendy market of apparel.

The high-tech world of fashion is challenging, and the show focuses on the nuts and bolts of being a designer, with a mixture of quirky challenges thrown in to keep the guests guessing as to what the next challenge will be. In the program's opening, we are introduced to the 12 challengers, and they all outline their experience, their dreams, and their desires to be a part of the fashion industry. Most are looking for the opportunities that the show can afford them. *Project Runway* launches the winner's name, his or her brand, and his her craft or signature as a designer. Then, there is prize money to help the winners to hawk their wares. Finally, there is a prestigious chance to be a designer and to design a line for a fashionable clothing firm, such as Gap, Banana Republic, Guess, or some other trendy design company. Because there is high volatility and trends emerge and decline in a season, there is a high premium on creativity, flexibility, and variety in the design visions of the creators, and the group is tested severely by challenges that can seem quixotic and taxing but probably are similar to the real-world experiences of professional designers.

In one season, the designers were fighting for an opportunity to design for Banana Republic. They were housed at the Parsons School of Design in New York, and they were chaperoned by one of the instructors in the design department, who guided them through their paces and tested their mettle in various off-beat design opportunities. The first challenge to eliminate the less plucky was a trip to a middle-class grocery store. The designers had $50 to spend to find fruits, vegetables, grocery bags, butcher paper, ribbon, and anything else that could be used to clothe a woman. Each designer was assigned a model, and then the team of 12 had 12 hours to assemble what they had purchased into something that the models could wear. One designer assaulted the produce aisle and bought only corn husks. They dried after he designed a corn husk evening gown, and he had some fast rethinking to do. The dried husks did not work with the original design. Another designer constructed a coat out of butcher paper that had the unfortunate quality of looking like a coat made out of butcher paper. One designer used decorative plastic grocery wrap festooned with pieces of color, fruits, and fringes of paper. All were made nervous by the exercise in odd materials for clothing. One designer simply took paper and tin foil and wrapped it around the model. After a midnight curfew, the designers were released for eight hours and came back in the morning ready to outfit the arriving models for a noon runway walk/preview. One of the models failed to appear, so her designer ran up and down the street looking for a replacement model. Eventually, the model arrived in tears with some personal tragedy haunting her.

The best thing about *Project Runway* is that it engages the life and the struggle of the designers in the heat of creation. Everyone can be a bit edgy and angry and frustrated, but most of these student apprentices confessed they were happy just to survive a round. Many found the thrilling and exhilarating experience of being in the New York fashion scene reward enough.

Unlike many reality shows that highlight glamour and glitz and prizes and fame, this program shows the realistic grunt work that goes into the profession's challenges and veers toward honest documentary. There is little of the cheesy get-rich-quick reality soaps in which the tear-jerking climb to the top is dotted with picturesque, staged, and scripted emotional epiphanies. *Project Runway* has such moments, but, for the most part, it is a delightful rough-and-tumble through a maze of design conventions that many outsiders would not know or recognize as challenges of the design profession. Like any field, much of the work is people work, and understanding the complex personalities in the field is a big step toward success.

Some seasons are hosted by successful people in the fashion world, such as model/performer Heidi Klum. The progressive elimination rounds are skillfully produced and executed, and, for the most part, the audience can understand the judges' decisions for eliminating certain candidates and certain designs. Not only are some designs not fit for the runway, some designers are also woefully ill-suited to the rigors, tortures, and stresses of fashion life. After most contestants are eliminated, the finalists are prepared to design a runway show for New York's prestigious Fashion Week. The designers who can live through the pressures of working with models, other designers, and companies have to have a mix of creative talent, energy, marketing zeal, and competitiveness to survive in the New York fashion industry. The program has been honored with a 2007 Peabody Award for programming because the series accurately describes the rigors of the industry and attempts to present an accurate portrayal of industry practices and stresses. For an industry suffused with glitter, Lifetime's *Project Runway* is an unvarnished view of the rigorous fashion world and its denizens.

Some of the program's challenges are more difficult than others. Designers have been made to design from the clothes they brought with them to New York. Sometimes, a designer has been asked to create using their personal wardrobe as a basis. Another unique challenge was to manufacture a show using the furnishings used for an office. Other perplexing cases included model shows constructed from materials found at office supply stores, groceries, edibles, living plants, or garbage and things found in the street. A particularly tough assignment was designing clothes for a specific celebrity to wear. This bound the designers to certain sizes, temperaments, and models that may or may not have flowed directly with the designer's mind-set.

Another aspect of the program is the tight and scrupulous monitoring that the team receives. Since the designers have been housed in New York or Los Angeles apartment buildings on various seasons of the show, the producers have exercised great control over their movements. The designers could not leave the building without permission. Further, the designers have been barred from using the Internet or design books to help them create their projects. They have further been barred from contact with friends and family, which potentially could have aided them with their design process.

A further highlight are show trials that have demanded specific materials for a design, a specific person for a wardrobe, a specific company with a formal aesthetic, or a specific purpose, such as a wrestling outfit, superhero garb, an evening dress, or a prom outfit. These specific demands have forced the designers to fit their work to a brand, a person, an audience, or a scientific material.

The rules and judging have been similarly rigorous, making the show a model for design and other competitive reality shows. Further, the designers have been bracketed by limited time and a limited selection of fabrics and materials, and they also have responsibility for fitting, dressing, selection, makeup, and hairstyles to emphasize and support the designed look. Once everything is assembled, the models do a runway walk in which three or four judges make copious notes and grade (on a scale of 1–5) the quality of the design, the fit, the look, the use of materials, the originality, and the composition of the total look. At the final seminar, competitors meet with the judges and are interviewed. The reasoning and the design manifesto of each is considered in placing the designers in context. The six finalists are ranked from one to six, with two groups given a bottom-three and a top-three criteria. The top winner obtains limited immunity for a round, but then is thrust back into the central and merciless competition. Klum "auf Wiedersehens" the losers (literally German for "until we meet again"), and the blow-off kiss she gives the rejected is often classed as being "aufed"—or offed—from the show, a play on words.

See also: American Ninja Warrior; Survivor; The X Factor

Further Reading
David S. Escoffery, *How Real Is Reality TV?*

QUEEN FOR A DAY

Queen for a Day probably had one of the most emotionally conceived concepts in the history of television. It was a strong audience-participation show, and it tugged at people's emotion. Watching it was a ritual experience. It was a forerunner to modern reality programming because it encouraged audience manipulation, and there is no way of knowing how much of the show was fabrication and how much was true. However, during its time, it was the apex of women's reality shows, and it parleyed the experiences of a biblical-style, Job-like character to win audience interest and sympathy. Host Jack Bailey opened the women's program with the question, "Would you like to be queen for a day?" Many women in the studio audience and at home must have answered yes to the call, because the program was a ratings success.

The setup of the program was simply and effective. A series of women were brought by the host to describe the horrible events of their lives. A husband horribly wounded, persistent unemployment, loss of a house, a terminally ill child, and other horrific events haunted these women and their families. No illness was too horrible, no deformity too great, and no tragedy too gruesome to stop them from appearing. The women, with some coaching, told their tales to the studio audience and the home audience. Tissues and smelling salts were always close by, in the event of a fainting spell or an emotional breakdown. Host Bailey could almost orchestrate the crying like a conductor, asking the women more and more leading and probing questions until they could not help but burst into tears. Questions like, "Is your other child blind, too?" or "Is there ever a day you think your husband will stop drinking?" These leading questions seemed to provoke streams of tears from the agonized heroines of the program. Eventually, the story would end, and the host would bring our another poor woman with another vile and graphic story about her bad luck, her diseases, and her life catastrophes. After all of this, the host would turn to the audience and ask, "Who do you want to be queen for a day?" The camera would pan back across the three disheveled women, and the applause meter would show the amount of applause each heart-wrenching story would win. After a thunderous applause for the best sob story, the host would anoint the winner "queen for a day."

The dubious honor would allow this poor victim to be sat on a tacky, glitz throne and adorned with a moth-eaten royal robe and dime-store tiara. The show was highly gimmicky, and the prizes awarded would be things like washing machines or new furniture. All the domestic items that relegated a woman back to domestic slavery were foisted on her like some breathtaking prize. Needless to say, a washing machine could not restore a child's health, nor could a set of furniture put an unemployed husband back to work. Pathetic though it was, it opened the door to other audience-participation and reality programs that tweaked our emotions, involved us with real people, and substituted storybook pathos for the solving of real problems. More importantly, it predated *Phil Donahue* and *Oprah Winfrey* as programs in which women en masse could commune and commiserate.

Bailey, with his slicked-back hair and smooth moustache, was the quintessence of avuncular charm. He was the sort of psychiatrist one could trust with all one's problems. The show was slimy and reprehensible for its use of obvious manipulation, but it sold lots of ads. At one point, it was such a big retail ad seller for the networks that they expanded the running time from 30 to 45 minutes to squeeze a few more minutes of advertising into each episode.

The concept of *Queen for a Day* is still alive and well. The concept today is owned by Michael Wortsman, and the *Queen for a Day* Web site reports that "the show recently aired in Puerto Rico with excellent ratings and is now being developed for U.S. Television. The original format has been revised and the show is now a celebration of women making a difference." Even though its predecessor thrived on maudlin talk of domestic tragedy, it did allow a generation of Americans a voice on television.

See also: American Ninja Warrior; Survivor; The X Factor

Further Reading
David S. Escoffery, *How Real Is Reality TV?*; Michael Wortsman, *Queen for a Day* (Web site). 2015.

RACHAEL RAY

Many would describe Rachael Ray as America's cute, little, girl-next-door cook, but that would diminish much of Ray's substantial achievements as a cook, businesswoman, and entertainment guru. Where the Food Network can come across as perhaps too professional, protracted, and official or where Martha Stewart arrives as elitist, complicated, or class-based, Ray makes direct and effective cuisine approachable.

Ray is mostly known from her cooking shows, and the most prominent platform is the *Rachael Ray Show*. Ray arose under the tutelage of mentor Oprah Winfrey. Her own syndicated show debuted in 2006, and she has become a household staple, carried in markets across the United States. The focus of the *Rachael Ray Show* is Ray and her cooking recipes. She always features a cooking segment on the show and often shares the stage with celebrity guests.

Ray became famous for her early cookbooks, including *30 Minute Meals*, which were enormous hits. Ray's charm was that she was common and down-to-earth in her cooking style, and her idea of preparing quick but healthy meals fit snuggly with the emerging pattern of quicker food preparation for most Americans. Her meals offer quick ways to prepare healthy cuisine for an active family on the go that rarely has a chance to plan or prepare elaborate dinners. Her no-fuss make-it-quick attitude fits the lives of busy moms and businesswomen and has crossed over to men who also wanted better cuisine, but quickly.

Ray was born into a family where her mother managed restaurants in upstate New York. Early in her career, Ray worked at the candy counter at Macy's and was a buyer for the Cowan & Lobel gourmet grocery market. Her experience in food businesses made her keenly aware that people did not like to cook. She wrote about quick meals, appeared on local newscasts, found a spot on PBS, and was featured on the *Today* show, landing her a contract with the Food Network.

She is blissfully free of arrogance and argues that her rapid cooking style developed from her Cajun heritage and Sicilian grandfather. She answers critics who say she is not a chef that she isn't, she's just a cook. She argues she's never been qualified for any job she has had, she just does it. She made friends with Oprah Winfrey and made numerous appearances on her show. Her own show was a spin-off. The arrangement has been great for Ray and Winfrey.

The *Rachael Ray Show* has been called several things, including *Everyday with Rachael Ray* and *Rachael*, but is mostly known as the *Rachael Ray Show*. Her show is extremely positive and has strong Web and marketing tie-ins. She does not speak to women as victims or sufferers of trauma but talks of opportunity, empowerment, and new advantages women can win in work and in their lives. There are continual segments on healthy lifestyles for families, interviews, and segments on celebrities and discussions of their careers and how they remain successful and healthy. There are lifestyle features, musical guests, and film promotions, but Ray always keeps an accent on the culinary.

Ray shoots her show in a New York studio, and her show has won Emmys for its successful blend of talk and entertainment. The show has been popular as daytime fare and was renewed for two-year cycles in 2006, 2008, 2010, 2012, and 2014. The show is currently in its 10th season and continues to draw strong ratings.

Ray performs on a busy schedule and has appeared on *Iron Chef* (winning a competition), late-night television, *Sesame Street, Oprah, The View,* and virtually the whole daytime circuit of shows. Her guests have included President Obama, Jim Parsons, John McCain, Diane Sawyer, Tim Allen, and many others.

One thing that makes Ray a favorite with reality television audiences is her intense sense of self. There is little pretense or artifice about her. In a candid interview with Dan Schawbel for *Forbes* magazine, she volunteered that a view of hers was to "take your work very seriously, but don't take yourself too seriously" (2013). Ray pours herself into work, including her nonprofit organization Yum-o!, which tries to teach people and families to have good relationships with food and nutrition. She credits her mother, who worked in restaurants for 60 years, with having a profound influence on her life. All of her family instilled into her a healthy work ethic. Her grandfather taught her to laugh regardless of how things were going. And when she was asked what her job was, she told *Forbes*, "I cook and I chat." Rachael Ray is what she seems, a nice person who works hard at cooking. For many reality fans, that is enough.

See also: American Ninja Warrior; Survivor; The X Factor

Further Reading
David S. Escoffery, *How Real Is Reality TV?*; Dan Schawbel, "Rachael Ray: What You Can Learn from Her Rise to Fame," *Forbes*, December 3, 2013.

SO YOU THINK YOU CAN DANCE (SYTYCD)

So You Think You Can Dance is a dance competition show that uses the progressive elimination sequence to showcase dancers competing in a variety of styles and in a variety of settings—from solo to duo to group choreography. The program was produced by Simon Fuller, the juggernaut behind television's titanic rating's winner *American Idol*. Premiering in 2005, *SYTYCD* has run 11 consecutive seasons on Fox, pulling strong ratings during its run and offering a wide range of dance styles.

As the progressive eliminations end, the voting is taken over by the audience, who are attracted to the program because of its interactivity. Celebrity judges have included Paula Abdul, Toni Basil, and Christina Applegate, and the program has spawned over 200 episodes. The series has been a top ratings performer, becoming the most popular show in its time slot and day during the summer of its premiere. The show is hosted by British television star Cat Deeley.

The sequence of the show is standard reality competition structure, with official dance auditions staged in select U.S. cities. Nominally, there are about 20 contestants who make it out of the grueling city trials, and these performers compete against each other in the weekly shows held on nationwide television. The scores of judges are blended with audience reaction and scoring, and these combined scores determine which performers will be advanced and which will be cut.

A feature that renders the show fun and varied is the wide range of dance styles that the performers attempt. Everything from calypso and reggae to grand ballroom and classical styles coexist with punk, hip-hop, dance theater, and ballet formats. Usually performers do not get to select their styles; they draw them at random. The format works quite well, and the program has been awarded seven Emmys for choreography among its nine Emmy Awards. The program is popular with foreign audiences as well and has been successfully exported to over 20 nations, making it an international sensation.

The series is strongly formatted with the first few episodes (2–4) focusing on the selection process of the final 20 dancers. The last seven to eight programs are devoted to the competition between the dancers. The first round of cuts appears when the producers in various cities hold auditions. Some people are advanced to the next cut of callbacks, while some may be held for an additional test by professional choreographers.

The callbacks, or Vegas week (because initially these callbacks were held in Vegas), demands that the performers work with choreographers, choreograph themselves, attend rigorous rehearsals, perform unfamiliar choreography, pick up things fast, and generally exhaust themselves to prove they are capable of taking direction in a variety of styles with a variety of teammates. More dancers are screened out in this phase.

Following this event, the dancers move to the showcase round, where they have an opportunity to pick routines and teammates and perform things of their choice, in their style. Then, the dancers are paired off with male and female performers with whom they will work on duet performances during the elimination rounds in the next few weeks. Usually two dancers are eliminated per week. Traditionally, the dancers perform their duets, sometimes solos, and there is a video packet of the dancers revealing their style and some clue to their private discourse and personality. A strong ingredient is, of course, critiques by the judges. The choreographers introduce the pieces, discussing the style, format, content, and storyline of the various dances assigned weekly. The judges draw out the finer points of the performance and call out flaws and highpoints. The end of the show is a recap, with information for call-in and online voting. In the final weeks, couples are reshuffled (dancers can be eliminated from a couple at any time, and couples can be reengineered week to week). Dancers are given new challenges, and judges lose their ability to vote. Eliminations are conducted by audience vote.

The question, in the minds of all viewers, is how good are these judges? Another issue is "Do the home viewers really know what good dance is?" or "Are they bought off by flashy and impressive stunts that perhaps do not constitute good dance steps?" Elaine Stuart, writing for the *New York Times*, checked in with a group of professional New York dancers and choreographers who were watching the show to verify its quality. She found opinion on the show to be varied. She quoted choreographer Bill T. Jones, who said, "'The shows distort dance into a sport'; Mr. Jones recently said he sometimes finds them 'obscene'" (2011). The issue for some is that the shows reduce all of life to a competition and reject the finer details of art, nuance, and individualism in the drive to excel, be spectacular, and place ego above skill. For some, excellent dance is replaced by audience-pleasing bravura.

Following the final judging, after the prize of $250,000 and the honor of being America's favorite dancer (whatever that means) is determined, the top-ten contestants go on tour, performing popular routines from the program.

A fine point that Elaine Stuart discusses in her article is the show's relationship to dance training. Is the show training future dancers, or simply future coaches for contestants on the show? She describes how professional dancers watching the program responded. They said, "The first season the prize was money and a rent-free apartment in New York so you could audition . . . The next year it was like a show with Celine Dion, and now I think they get to be in a commercial for Gatorade" (2011). The point Stuart and her panel of experts was making is that the show is moving further from a professional dance base toward shows that are a middlebrow audience's image of what a dancer is and does. The reality is a far cry from the reality show's perspective.

See also: Dancing with the Stars; The X Factor

Further Reading

David S. Escoffery, *How Real Is Reality TV?*; Elaine Stuart, "So You Think You Can Judge Dance," *New York Times*, August 4, 2011.

STAR SEARCH

Genially hosted by longtime Johnny Carson sidekick Ed McMahon, *Star Search* was a vehicle for amateur performers similar to *Ted Mack and the Original Amateur Hour*. With *Star Search*, however, there was a long-term competition that lasted throughout the season, and contestants from throughout the program would be advanced to a semifinal and final round. The show was a popular staple of syndication programming conducted during the early years of cable broadcasting for stations that wanted quality programming to fill all hours of the day and night. *Star*

Search arrived in 1985 and ran uninterrupted through 1995, all the while hosted by Ed McMahon. In 2003 the show was revived for a season with Arsenio Hall as the host. The show was created by Alfred Masini and was produced by Rysher Entertainment. The show broke down the entertainers into broad entertainment categories such as male and female vocalist, teen and junior vocalist, teen and junior dancers, vocal group, models, comedy, and dance. The goal was to find the best performer in each of the 10 categories.

The *Star Search* methodology would have performers in eight categories per program competing. Usually, there would be a champion versus challenger round. The players on the show auditioned locally, and the best contestants would be chosen to sing or dance nationally. Usually the challenger played first, followed by the champion.

There were four judges, and each cast a vote of between 1 and 4 stars. The player with the highest score became the new champion. Ties were broken by a house audience vote. McMahon revealed the results of that vote at the program's end. Many times, champions would go on winning until defeated by another performer. Eventually, the show changed the rules and cashed out champions after three wins. The biggest winners would return for a semifinal show. There was one semifinal in the spring, and one in the fall. The winners of these rounds would not be revealed until the finale show, where the finalists would compete in all 10 categories. The winners in the vocalist and group category could win $100,000. While no recording contract followed the win, many of the winners did receive contracts. In the junior category, a finalist could win $10,000.

The 2003–2004 revival added an audience-participation aspect to the show. After the judges voted on candidates, the home audience could augment the scores of individuals they championed. Many performers who later became phenomenally popular had their start on *Star Search*. Britney Spears, Christina Aguilera, Beyoncé, Dave Chappelle, and Adam Sandler were all contestants.

Part of the show's appeal was the appeal of host, Ed McMahon, who had assisted Johnny Carson for 30 years, and had found fame on his own through the program. In the 1990s, there was a synergistic move to Orlando to audition and shoot the show at Disney World. The collaboration and the growth of the show proved to be a very successful strategy for Disney's marketing plan to grow and expand as an entertainment corporation. *Star Search* planted Disney one step closer to being involved in major studio television. This occurred a few years later when Disney merged with Capital Broadcasting, purchasing ABC and de facto becoming the ABC Channel. Catherine Hinman, writing for the *Orlando Sentinel* in the 1990s, explained how the new arrangement had benefited the program. She wrote, "Thousands of visitors who make their great escape to Disney each year will have a chance to be in the studio audience and a part of the drama. The enthusiastic audiences at Disney-MGM have been the best in the show's history" (1992). So while *Star Search* passed into history, Disney's entry into reality television helped the studio prepare for its next position as the studio behind television production at ABC.

See also: American Idol; Survivor; The X Factor

Further Reading

David S. Escoffery, *How Real Is Reality TV?*; Catherine Hinman, "McMahon and Mouse Are New Dream Team," *Orlando Sentinel*, September 26, 1992.

STORAGE WARS

Storage Wars is an often cantankerous and gruff reality show that features feisty and eccentric characters. It is a funny competition and reality program from A&E that follows the adventures of a group of pickers and junkers who bid low budget on abandoned storage units in hopes of collecting on great found and rare items. While there are occasional finds that are significant, these freewheeling storage-box gamblers often come up with just enough to cover their costs. The bids for units can sometimes escalate, and the cagey bidders have to know if the contents could be worth the gamble. Part of the process is knowing where the storage is, what the clientele might store there, and what—if anything—could be gained by reclaiming the lost items. Even if the bidders hit pay dirt, they still have to find a buyer for the lost treasures they uncover, but the discovery of the unknown is what it is all about.

The players are sometimes known by their pseudonyms, like the Hustler, the Gambler, and the Mogul. There are a cast of main bidders, and each is a distinctive character with a personal philosophy to assure junk-shopping success. The cast of junk-locker mavens includes Dave Hester, Darrell Sheets, Barry Weiss, Jarrod Schulz and Brandi Passante, and Dan and Laura Dotson. Some cast members enter and exit by season, but the crew of locker shoppers is fairly determined, ambitious, and regular.

A standard charge against the show is that it is all fake. The accusation is that the auctioneers tip the clients/bidders to lockers worth bidding on and that few people bid on real junk lockers. Further, the competition between the junkers looks inflated, if not entirely scripted. Finally, the drama about the wondrous things in the lockers seems designed to encourage people to bid on junk lockers, thus promoting the business and artificially inflating the potential value of such a business to unlucky speculators. A more worrisome cheat of the show is the concept that the United States is becoming a culture of scammers and pickers because there is so little of value left in our culture. In a culture of leftovers, the fear is that there is so little of value that the remaining junkers are fighting each other for society's scraps, while the real items of value remain untouchable. In reality, this leaves dispossessed multitudes who don't have much chance of finding real treasures. In the end, there are only a few dogs left in the lot, fighting over the remaining trash in the yard. Many fear that that disturbing, cynical scenario is what A&E is actually pedaling.

The show opens with a tracking shot of people roaring through storage sheds at high speeds. Locks are broken, and the rolling metal doors are opened. Dan

Dotson and wife Laura preside over the auction and lay out the rules. They crack the locker, break the lock, give the bidders five minutes to look, and take bids. The bidders can't enter and rifle through boxes. Lots of lockers contain people's furniture and personal items and a lot of mess.

There is a genuine sense of excitement generated by the speedy editing and the fast bidding, as Dotson yells and pushes the bidders to up their bids. Dave Hester bids nearly $2,000 for a locker with mostly junk furniture. The reasoning was his brother was bidding against him, and the bids were out of pride and anger, not out of reason. Sometimes the bidders volunteer what they bought and what it was worth. Sometimes we learn little about the purchase. The presumption is, if you want to know what is in the unit, bid yourself.

The program debuted on A&E in 2010 and has run for over six seasons and over 150 episodes. The show has been a ratings hit, attracting people who, like the bidders, want to know what are in those crates. Most of the shows are taped in Southern California, where there is substantial wealth, and the potential discovery of hidden treasures in unopened storage units. State laws allow the owners of storage units to sell the contents of the units if rent has not been paid for three months.

Most of the stars, the bidders on the show, own their own junk stores or are auctioneers in their own right. Despite the claims that the show is rigged, producers say that the show is unstaged, and what is found in the lockers is actually just laying there in the lockers. Spin-offs have included *Storage Wars: Texas* and *Storage Wars: New York*. Neither has been renewed or revived. The key to the show's wondrous finds is in the editing. For the most part, lockers are either empty or fallow, but, when the filming takes place, the crews focus on the lockers that offer the most resalable items, giving audiences the inflated impression that many lockers contain refuse gold.

One of the series' stars, Dave Hester, sued A&E and *Storage Wars* in 2012, claiming that he was wrongfully fired from the show and that the show itself was largely faked and the lockers were "salted." Hester told *Bloomberg Business*, "The truth, however, is that nearly every aspect of the series is faked" (Paskin 2013). Hester said the lockers were salted with good stuff, when, in reality, most contained nothing but trash. Willa Paskin, writing for *Bloomberg,* describes: "A BMW will be buried under a pile of trash, or a stack of newspapers will turn out to be from the day Elvis Presley died—a practice known as salting. The suit also accuses A&E of staging entire storage units and asking Hester to salt lockers with his own memorabilia" (2013). The suit was dropped when Hester came to an agreement with A&E and was reinstated on the show.

See also: Survivor; The X Factor

Further Reading

David S. Escoffery, *How Real Is Reality TV?*; Willa Paskin, "Dave Hester of Storage Wars Sues A&E: The Series Is Faked," *Bloomberg Business*, May 23, 2013.

SURVIVOR

Survivor is one of the oldest and most successful reality competition game shows on television. It was a revelation for CBS, mostly known for being the quality leader of the old network system. *Survivor* was a product of producer Mark Burnett, who presold the show through ads, licensing agreements, and marketing placements within the program. The program's production costs were almost nil when the show was delivered to CBS.

This was a marketing and financing revolution for the television industry, and it set the stage for all reality programming that came after it. It produced an environment in which the stations had very little content and production-cost risk. Thus programming became about delivering low-cost shows to stations premade, and quality became a secondary consideration. This new, bifurcated industry began churning out these lower-cost reality programs. Stations and companies that wanted to produce fictional television would also adopt the outside-producer model to deliver completed fictional series to network and non-network entities, such as Hulu, Netflix, and Amazon Prime. Rather than the station having to sell ads to subsidize the production of the show, the shows were presold and offered the station the chance to run a program that had all production costs covered in advance. All ad revenue became pure profit to the station, making *Survivor* a great deal for the network.

Further, *Survivor* debuted at a time when much of network programming had run its course, and audiences were looking for a new vehicle to experience television. The show was the first popular reality show, was a top-ten viewed show during its first 11 seasons, and transformed how people watched television. The program became a national viewing phenomenon, with individuals rooting for their favorite survivor like sports stars in a competition.

Adding to Mark Burnett's product were great production values in exotic locations and a concept pitting the contestants against each other that had ceaseless, inherent drama. Imagine a colony trapped on a desert island, assigned a variety of dangerous and difficult tasks, having to band together to accomplish those tasks, and forming temporary alliances. The survivors know that only one person will win, and they are constantly watching their backs. There is no loyalty, only self-interest, and playing the game to survive and eventually undo the other players.

Survivor has a motto built into its logo. The words are *outwit, outplay,* and *outlast*. This summarizes the stakes and mind-set at work in *Survivor*. The show has been proclaimed as a reflection of American society and our corporate cut-throat culture. The program has been accused of gamifying all aspects of life, including the use of duplicity to win the $1 million prize at the end of the annual series. The concept is: how low can you go to survive and outlast the other competitors?

The show was conceived by Burnett and produced starting in 2000 and has run over 400 episodes and produced over 30 seasons. The concept of the show was designed by Charlie Parsons and was the basis for a popular Swedish show the *Expedition Robinson* that premiered in Europe in 1997. Presumably, this title reflects the origin of the series in Johann David Wyss's 1812 novel *The Swiss Family*

Robinson, a story about a family stranded on a desert island. The story has been a popular subject for films, including a popular Disney version in 1960.

The setup is that a group of survivors are marooned at an isolated location with no way to get food, shelter, and water. While isolated, the players must solve various challenges. The last two or three survivors are judged by a tribunal of eight or nine players who were voted off the island. They decide the winner of the game and the winner of the million dollars. The program has won Emmys, accolades, and even awards for the recent award category of best presenter. Jeff Probst has won the title of best announcer for a reality show, has been a strong voice for the show, and has proclaimed many of its ritual catch phrases. Probst won a newly instituted Emmy category—presenter of a reality/competition program—four times. In fact, the show was responsible for several Emmys in the new category of reality/competition programming. *Time* magazine listed it among the top 100 greatest television shows of all time.

The game rules of the show are simple but have constantly evolved to throw long-time viewers off and to prevent people from copying a previous strategy to win the competition. A group of about 16 players are removed to a remote, usually temperate location for approximately one month. There they are left with modest housing, food, water, and clothing and a series of challenges. The players are divided into two teams that fend for themselves, create bonds and alliances, and compete in the challenges to acquire additional rights, privileges, food, and immunity to being voted from the island. The program runs for 14 to 16 weeks during the regular television season, chronicling the efforts of the two teams as they struggle to maintain membership on the island. A weekly tribal council meets, and one team must vote a member off the island. When the teams are down to half their original size, they are merged, and the remaining players must continually whittle away at their numbers until there are only two or three survivors left. The previously voted-off members form a team of jurors. They ascertain who the best player is and who deserves to be deemed the sole survivor. They vote for a final survivor who wins the $1 million prize.

Monkey wrenches are thrown at the teams, including new rules, tribe reversals, difficult physical challenges, gross outs, and other methods of foiling individual and group strategies to win.

Usually about two seasons per year are recorded, which means there are several *Survivor* series filmed per year. Each season is given a different name, like *Survivor: Cook Islands* or *Survivor: Redemption Island* based on the location or theme of the season. Over 300 people serve on the show's technical crew, and over 400 people have appeared as contestants. The rising crew and production costs have caused the once relatively inexpensive show to be more costly for the producers to create.

Many have noted that the show has elements of class warfare embedded in it. As the show has progressed, fans have studied the show in preparation for playing as a contestant and the producers have had to make modifications to keep it updated, interesting, and not too easy for fans to master. There has been the added twist of Redemption Island. When players are voted off, they may be given the chance to endure tests and other challenges on Redemption Island, and, if they master their challenges, they may be allowed to return to the main island. In the February 25, 2015, episode of the 30th season of *Survivor*, known as *Survivor: Worlds Apart*, the series was transplanted to San Juan del Sur in Nicaragua to minimize the contamination of the team by modern media. The 30th season introduced some unique challenges. First, the program had 3 tribes and 18 players split into 6 players per tribe. The element of class warfare was emphasized and directly addressed by separating the teams by social class. There was a white-collar group, a blue-collar group, and a no-collar group, seemingly reinforcing class stereotypes that are perhaps mean and malicious into the structure of the show. However, vile and low-moral codes have been synonymous with the program's popularity and players from the start. After all, they are after a million dollars, so the main rule is "take no prisoners." The intention is to see which group fights the meanest, the shrewdest, and the hardest to survive. In interviews with presenter host Jeff Probst, he volunteered that the white-collar group did not like being typed as white collar and tended to see their team as having elements of blue- and no-collar behavior.

As with all high-stakes television enterprises in which big money and headlines are at stake, there can be legal issues. After the first season of *Survivor,* the lawsuits started. Stacey Stillman, a lawyer who was a contestant on the show, sued CBS and producer Mark Burnett for her early removal from the show, telling the *Guardian* she had been removed because the show favored an earlier player, and Burnett encouraged other players to vote Ms. Stillman off. Duncan Campbell of the *Guardian* writes, "She claims that she was voted off third out of 16 contestants because Mr. Boesch was the only remaining survivor aged over 40 and the program did not want to lose older viewers" (2001). Stillman's claim was that the show showed bias against her, and she deserved compensation. The show's popularity has generated catch phrases like "being voted off the island," and it is likely that controversies concerning the program will continue as has its popularity. For the most part, *Survivor* has chronicled the rise and fall of American resilience and failing character following 9/11. After the trauma of a domestic attack, the rise of terrorism, and the decline of the economy, the show seems to reflect American struggles in a world culture after the events of the early millennial period.

See also: American Ninja Warrior; The X Factor

Further Reading
Duncan Campbell, "Survivor Sued," *The Guardian*, February 15, 2001; David S. Escoffery, *How Real Is Reality TV?*

TED MACK AND THE ORIGINAL AMATEUR HOUR
Ted Mack and the Original Amateur Hour was an early *Star Search*–style program that allowed amateur acts to debut on television. This program was popular from the late 1940s through the 1960s and even featured the children and grandchildren

of people who debuted on the show decades earlier. Notable guests included the Reverend Louis Farrakhan, Ann-Margret, a young (seven-year-old) Irene Cara, and singer Jerry Vale.

The program was hosted by genial Ted Mack, who exuded a family, avuncular, quiet, and understated charm. At times it seemed that Mack was not reading cue cards or teleprompters but was actually extemporaneously chatting with the audience and performers. The performers were well-trained and drilled and were uniformly polite and pleasant. There was a high degree of professionalism not illustrated in current reality competition shows. Players were told where to stand, how to respond to the red light indicating the camera was running, and what to do when cued. The performers appeared to have been trained on stage and produce what seemed like picture-perfect versions of their act on cue.

The program was notable for showcasing a variety of roots, folk, and pop music that might have been lost as ephemera without the program. Mack and his crew were an early transplant from radio, and the accent was on singing and vocal performance, which was the only way such a talent show could operate on radio. Occasionally other dance and variety acts were added to the festivities. These were extensions of performance that could not have been possible in radio.

There were some incredible moments that were recorded, including Ann Margaret as a teenager assailing jazz standards. Several notable a cappella doo-wop groups from New York and Chicago predated the advent of Motown but provided stellar insight into the street music of urban America in the 1940s and 1950s. Into the 1960s, Mack's stage band even backed up early Beach Boy/Ventures–style electric guitar combos. The program was homespun, cool, charming, and almost like watching a back porch hootenanny. The sense was the producers desired to provide a warm and inspiring place to bring the family.

A fan Web site devoted to the original program credits the success of the series and its longevity to four people. The first was Major Edward Bowes, the original host of the *Amateur Hour* program. Bowes did not arrive from an entertainment background and knew little of the business. He was a real-estate speculator who bought a theater in Boston, which turned him into a producer. He built the Capitol Theatre in New York, and he became interested in nurturing talent and running the theater as an enterprise. The theater featured an open-mic session on Sunday afternoons, and the program had such a following it was picked up by local radio station WHN and went national in 1934. The program was an instant success. The program was an early example of an audience-participation show. Audiences could phone in their choice for the most popular performer on the air, and, in some big markets, there would be upward of 20,000 calls an hour after a popular performer. The war placed severe restrictions on calling due to the need for military use of phones. The show languished during the war years.

Ted Mack was an assistant to Major Bowes, and he had worked as a talent scout for the show from 1935 on. Mack was a talented big band musician playing saxophone and clarinet. He fortunately also had good radio skills, a strong voice, and a magnetic and pleasant television face. When Bowes retired in 1945, Mack assumed the host position on the show and in 1948 moved the show to television, where he remained host and guide of the show for the next 24 years. Mack's remarkable run was a product of a natural and calm stage presence and a love of the varied musical and vocal acts he presented. During his tenure, over 1 million people auditioned for the show.

A musical show requires a strong music director, and the program was fortunate to have Lloyd Marx, a talented New York music director, a staff conductor at CBS, a music director for the Emmy, Clio, and DGA Awards, and a savvy industry insider who often directed the show and led the orchestra.

Another key factor in a program's success is the strength of the producer behind the scenes. *The Original Amateur Hour* was helmed by producer Lewis Graham (aka Lou Goldberg) who worked in production and promotions for the Paramount, Loews, Criterion, Publix, and Warner Theatres. He knew many people in the industry. It was Graham who suggested the popular and profitable Ted Mack touring troupe, which took winners from the show on the road. Graham also innovated in bringing the program to television. While dated and amateur-looking by today's standards, the Ted Mack show set the stage for later competition and reality programming that featured new blood, small-town Americans with a dream of fame, and continual auditioning and filtering schemes for providing the country with a steady stream of ambitious, talented, and competitive performers. It was also one of the first television programs to give audiences a strong voice.

See also: *American Idol*; *The Voice*; *The X Factor*

Further Reading

David S. Escoffery, *How Real Is Reality TV?*; Albert Fisher, *The Original Amateur Hour* (Web site), Shadoeworks, 2008.

THAT'S INCREDIBLE!

That's Incredible! was hosted by John Davidson, Cathy Lee Crosby, and Fran Tarkenton, and was a popular reality show from 1980 to 1984. Star power came from the guest hosts, who lent the program polish and glamour. In this early example of reality programming, the emphasis was on any aspect of reality that was strange and unusual. Here the accent was on absurd and strange acts, a cast of hosts, and showcasing oddities and strange talents in a popular documentary reality format. The focus was on obscure, strange, and often heartwarming stories of American life. Many of the tales dealt with outliers, folk procedures, and craft skills. Malcolm Gladwell discussed the concept of outliers in his book of the same name, which dealt with positive and creative forms of deviation from normal, everyday practice. The outliers often achieve creative answers to problems that plague the rest of society. In this sense, *That's Incredible!* was permeated with that feel-good form of American optimism that seemed to spread over television in the 1970s and 1980s and inspired programming like *Love Boat, Donny & Marie, The Waltons,* and *Dallas*.

The program began with a wide shot of the audience applauding and yelling, "That's incredible!" to the camera. The focus changed to a sweep-in on host John Davidson, who announced the first segment. One by one, the hosts announced their segments. Davidson announced a group of fast-talkers. Cathy Lee Crosby showed off a man who was dragged behind a race car at 160 miles per hour. Fran Tarkenton discussed a helicopter rescue squad that rescued people from burning buildings.

The program offered impressive and complex introductions to each segment, and the credits featured eight writers, a rarity for most reality programs. However, the program shared more of a documentary spirit than some modern reality fare that constructs stories in the editing. Here, it seemed scripts establish how the hosts were planning to describe the phenomenon, and then footage was inserted to conform to the predetermined storyline. Thus, despite the documentary feel, viewers got the impression they were watching scripted and contrived television.

In one episode, an old woman discussed a young disabled man who could neither talk nor see. The family played him music as a form of therapy, and it turned out that he could hear and recreate the tunes on the piano. Many of the "incredible feats" described on the show had hints of the arcane and the supernatural. In another eventful segment, the hosts introduced a story about a potential ghost seen at a Toys"R"Us store. The idea was that a playful ghost wanted to be in the presence of children and was determined to haunt the kids shop. Cathy Lee Crosby introduced the segment in a faux *60 Minutes*–style with a variety of footage focusing on spooky events at the Toys"R"Us, including bikes that rode themselves, skateboards that rolled across the floor, and stuffed animals that sprang to life in the aisles. Before the audience got too excited, the broadcasters reminded them through titles that the entire sequence was a re-creation staged by producers on the basis of eyewitness reports. Broadcasting standards being what they were in the 1980s, it was not uncommon for broadcasters to tease with footage that would suggest the supernatural and then retract the suspicious claim later with titles that would correct the misperception. The story continued with an interview with a psychic who visited the premise and with supposed still pictures taken of a shadowy figure treading down the aisle of the store. The producers brought in all the hosts to track aspects of the story. They explored the credentials of the psychic, Sylvia Browne, supporting her credibility. They used stills and recreations to discuss the history of the store, the property, the house that used to stand on that lot, and the people who lived there. It turned out that in the 19th century, a man by the name of Johnny Johnson, an itinerant preacher, lived on the plantation and occasionally worked it. While chopping wood one day, he slashed his leg and bled to death before help could arrive. The hosts theorized that the ghost was actually from that era and didn't realize the store had arrived since his demise. The team decided to host their own séance in the store and hired an independent camera crew who had little idea of what to expect. They built a sense of reality by having the medium talk to the ghost and try to convince the spirit to move on. The subtle and evocative "therapy" session seems to suggest a less-ostentatious sense of reality than the brightly lit show palace concoctions of *American Idol*'s flamboyant performances. The cameramen admitted they saw no one on the premises, but they were stunned to see ghostly images on their filmed footage. There were clearly shadows on the prints that gave the impression of ghostly images.

The program had an easy camaraderie. The hosts traded off stories and incredible feats like a group of campers around the fire. There was a mixture of local folklore and legend and the hosts traveled to all parts of the world to find their anomalies. In a sense, this was a buddy form of reality programming, and the sense of reality was easy, documentary-styled, and less obtrusive.

The difference between this rendition of reality and later reality faire is more in how the audience and producers conjecture what reality is. Here, the sense of reality was conjured by the simplicity and directness of means. Tricks, obscure game rules, and vying for fame have little to do with this sincere—if also contrived— version of reality. In the end, reality is evoked through the direct observance of phenomenon. The people on the reality show acted and seemed like real people, so even if it was a performance, like theater, it had the appearance of reality. Jan Westerhoff, in *Reality: A Very Short Introduction*, remarks that philosophically reality is hard to quantify. She writes, "It appears that we are left with the unattractive choice between a continuous self so far removed from everything constituting us that its absence would scarcely be noticeable, and a self that did actually consist of components of our mental life, but contains no constant part that we could identify with" (66, 2012). I think the definition of *reality* in shows such as *That's Incredible!* favors the former definition, in which the version of reality didn't need us to exist much at all for reality to exist. For later reality shows, reality is predicated on us being there, but only in pieces, so the freaky aspects of reality dominate our consciousness.

See also: American Ninja Warrior; Survivor; The X Factor

Further Reading

David S. Escoffery, *How Real Is Reality TV?*; Jan Westerhoff, *Reality, A Very Short Introduction*, Oxford UP, 2012.

TODDLERS AND TIARAS

Toddlers and Tiaras followed the quest of families and their young daughters to compete and win child beauty pageants. The program ran on TLC from 2009 to 2013. The popular *Honey Boo Boo* series was a spin-off of the show. A normal episode follows one or more pageant contestants as they prepare, compete, and respond to judgments in the beauty pageant community. The show ran for seven seasons and fell somewhere between homage and mockery. The mothers and grandmothers dressed these little girls (some as young as three years old) in lavish gowns and trained them to prance, preen, and perform in a coquettish manner. While some of the transformations from little girl into beauty queen were clever and charming, some portrayed vampish figures, and there were disturbing aspects of child exploitation and perhaps inadvertent sexploitation of underage children. The emphasis on physical appearance and making the child into a parody of adult stereotypes is simply odd. The program was a popular entity on TLC and spawned over 100 episodes.

In one entry, the surreal drama had little Elizabeth taken to a pageant by her mother and grandmother. The grandmother admitted to spending thousands on pageant clothing and entry fees, and little Elizabeth seemed genuinely interested in becoming a pageant queen. The family dutifully dressed the little girl in a pink princess outfit, and the little girl confessed to having an outsized personality and admitted to enjoying being the center of attention and the focus of the camera lens. The performance space was filled with like-minded parents and family members who were all fixated on their child winning the competition. The performance took on a more surreal edge when the judges were introduced. They were a series of headlining drag show veterans from a Vegas revue. The performers, dressed as Cher, Britney Spears, and Lady Gaga, quietly reviewed the candidates; made commentary on the kids' styles, dresses, and wigs; and dished on which children seemed out of control and which had real talent. Finally, the judges rendered their decision, and Elizabeth won for brightest personality but not for Grand Pageant Beauty. She seemed a bit depressed at the outcome and tired by the end of the day. The female impersonator judges thought it was all fun to judge the little girls, but the children and their parents seemed too invested in winning the competition to be healthy. One is reminded of the tragic JonBenét Ramsey murder case, in which a young beauty pageant contestant was mysteriously murdered, but the killer was never found or identified. Such disturbing revelations and details about Honey Boo Boo's family and charges that children may have been harmed are further disturbing aspects of this unusual but highly dramatic child pastime.

Many critics attacked the program as appealing to pedophiles. Many objected to the practice of padding little girls' chests to resemble adult women. This behavior suggests sex-based stereotyping and role playing that deprives children of innocence and casts them in the shadow of sexualized icons. Again, like many things on the show, it sent mixed and disturbing messages.

Several spin-offs have arrived from the program. *Eden's World* showed the adventures of Eden Wood, a little girl with dreams of being a pageant queen. *Here Comes Honey Boo Boo* followed the adventures (or misadventures) of the Boo and her goofy family. *Cheer Perfection* was about some of the competitors from the pageant regime and their mothers, who were involved in starting a cheer club for the girls and running a gym.

The exploitation of little girls and their bodies was the program's hot-button issue, and further outrage was generated because often the perpetrators of the said exploitation were the child's own parents, who were either exploiting the child for pleasure, money, or fame. The media also found many things about the pageant shows objectionable. The *Huffington Post* ran a series of articles attacking the show. Laura Hibbard, writing for the *Post*, assaulted the show for a video featuring, "A 3-year-old dressed up as Julia Roberts in the opening scene of the film *Pretty Woman*"

(2011). What makes the criticism more worrisome is that ads attached to the Web feed of the article were clearly targeted to certain audiences. In the images previewing the ads with the phrase "you may like," there were pictures of female child models and a headline: "The Most Beautiful Girl in the World Is Only 9." Is the *Post* commenting, reflecting, or profiting from the exploitation of children in beauty pageants? The disturbing trend of attaching ads that track where the Internet surfer has been (sites about children in beauty pageants) suggests that there is a dark underbelly of Web content that appeals to the prurient interests even of casual viewers.

The *Huffington Post* ran another article by psychologist and PhD Vivian Diller, who argued that the beauty pageant regime and narcissistic parents who compete with their kids may ignore the content of the pageant and just be focused on winning at any cost. She writes, "While the parents of toddlers in tiaras may be hyper focused on enhancing their children's beauty—narrow as that 'talent' may be—is it really that different from the dynamics involved in other children's competitions?" (2011). She suggests that perhaps all types of hypercompetitive games between children (baseball, soccer, spelling bees, go-cart racing) may in the end be detrimental to kids and their parents.

See also: Here Comes Honey Boo Boo

Further Reading

Vivian Diller, "Narcissistic Parents: Will Their Kids Be All Right?" *Huffington Post*, October 12, 2011; David S. Escoffery, *How Real Is Reality TV?*; Laura Hibbard, "Toddlers and Tiaras. Three-Year-Old Dressed in *Pretty Woman* Prostitute Costume," *Huffington Post*, September 4, 2011.

TOP CHEF

Healthy foods, desserts, and outdoor cooking—you are liable to find all that and more on *Top Chef. Top Chef* is a cooking competition show in which top chefs compete for prizes and opportunities. The program has been popular for 12 seasons and over 140 episodes. The show began telecasts on the Bravo network in 2006. The show is produced by Magic Elves Productions, the company that produced *Project Runway*. One example of the show's success has been the varied and productive spin-offs it has spawned. *Top Chefs Masters* has featured master chefs. *Top Chef Healthy Showdown* was inspired by a partnership with Healthy Choice foods that featured recipes that could lead to a lean and healthy diet.

In the program's spin-off *Just Desserts*, the chefs are required to work on pastry dishes. In one episode, the chefs were asked to design and build a wedding cake in one and a half hours. This was a notable feat, since wedding cakes often take days to construct, layer, and perfect. Some came up with creative solutions, including fruit-based icings, while some couldn't create anything.

The show remains resilient, popular, and dramatic. The program delves into the thinking and the strategy of the chefs under time constraints. After 12 seasons and several spin-offs, the show maintains a tight sense of competition, and Bravo has learned that real challenges and real tests of skill outweigh flashy production design. The judging is conducted by working chefs, famous food personalities, and luminaries of the culinary world. The show has had many popular spin-offs in foreign countries as well.

Each season features a different host city, and the selected/auditioned chefs use recipes and ideas derived from the local cuisine. Each episode features the original 12–20 chefs in what are termed "quick-fire" cook-off challenges. Winners are granted immunity or some valued prize, and the loser is booted permanently. When the competition narrows to just four or five candidates, the competition shifts to another subject city. There the final two or three chefs compete, creating an entire meal for the judges. The winner of this competition becomes the top chef for the season.

The elimination round is a great test and very dramatic. In the finale, the remaining chefs are joined in teams against each other. The survivors are joined by former players—and sometimes celebrity chefs—to form teams. Sometimes the remaining chefs team up to produce a dish or series of courses for a meal. Sometimes the teams are drawn at random by having each chef pull different-sized knives from a butcher block. The chefs cook for the judges and often for invited guests. The prize for the winning top chef is usually more than $100,000.

Usually halfway through a season, the contestants are put through a restaurant challenge, in which the players are asked to construct a restaurant complete with name, design, theme, and menu. This is similar to the sort of exacting detail and planning that defines the edgy and complicated *Project Runway*. This is not a glitter show; it is a nuts-and-bolts search-out-the-details show about cooking.

The program has offered special episodes, including *All Star* shows that feature players from the first and second seasons completing against each other to win money for a charity of their choice. There have even been reunion shows.

Top Chef Masters has featured master chefs. The chefs in *Top Chef* competition are comparatively amateurs without distinguished cooking careers. The spin-off has been offered over five seasons. Another spin-off is *Life after Top Chef,* which features the private lives of former contestants and their adventures running restaurants and dealing with staff and management issues. Another spin-off, *Top Chef Duels,* provides new competitions between former contestants.

The program has been nominated for several Emmys and won the Emmy for the best reality competition program. Though mostly professional discourse permeates the show, there are sometimes scrappy challengers. Season six's winner, Michael Voltaggio, was a motorcycle-riding chef who had two young daughters and a secret love life he refused to share with the network. At times, he could be caustic and referred to challenger and competitor Kevin Gillespie's food as "Kevin's food is what I cook on my day off" (Quinlan, *Food & Wine,* 2010).

See also: Iron Chef America; Ramsay's Kitchen Nightmares

Further Reading
David S. Escoffery, *How Real Is Reality TV?;* Christine Quinlan, "The Double Life of Bravo's New Top Chef," *Food & Wine*

THE VOICE

The Voice is often considered the softer side of *American Idol*. Rather than address contestants with cutting remarks, the judges on *The Voice* compete with each other to coach and mentor the best singers. The show is competitive, but the role of embracing and encouraging these singers underlies and underscores the show's mechanism. The program has run 8 seasons, two per year since 2011, and is a top ratings draw for NBC, sometimes offering two hours of sing-offs an evening. The intensity of the show generates a lot of fan response. The judges usually dismiss a contestant a week, and there are multiple ways for retaining players, such as one coach bidding for or stealing another coach's players. The contestants are chosen from auditions across the country, and fighting for a seat on the show is intense. Voting is conducted by the public, who can vote via phone, computer, text message, or even by buying the recordings of the artists on iTunes. Winners obtain a recording arrangement with Universal Music and a cash prize of $100,000. The original *Voice* was a program from the Netherlands known as *The Voice of Holland*. Since then, the program has been franchised to incorporate multiple countries and cultures.

When *The Voice* was introduced in 2011, it was a spring replacement program and proved an immediate hit for NBC. The judges pick their teams through blind auditions. They hear the artists and select on the basis of their performances. Each coach has between two and four performers that they aid. They mastermind the players' song selection and give them tips on ways to perform to captivate the audiences in the studio and the voting home-viewing audience. Clearly, the judges do make changes to the repertory and the style of the performer, but, though they respect these talented, young people, they are careful to avoid turning them into clones of their own artistic style. A drawing factor is the fame and attractiveness of the judges who have coached and mentored the players. Celebrity singers such as Christina Aguilera, Adam Levine, Blake Shelton, Pharrell Williams, and other famous celebrities have worked on the program and have had large fan bases of their own. Sometimes it is clear the performer has chosen a rendition of a song they like, and sometimes their taste betrays them or opens the door to new fans and praise. The coaches try to give advice in their brief and fragmentary time on the air with their mentees, but often little of the players' recording sessions are shown during the program time. The players are groomed for huge, orchestrated, cathartic, emotional set pieces. As with many American programming ideas, the notion that bigger is better underlies the sumptuous mounting and performance of the players on the show. Sometimes this pomp and ceremony supports the performers, and sometimes it simply seems overambitious, dwarfing, and simply daunting. A simple song and a good singer are lost in the mega-production values the show requires. It is presumed that this is what the audience craves: the massive power ballad delivered with long and extended notes and fittingly garish, rock instrumental flourishes. However, some performances are contrastingly small and intimate. Often performers try to incorporate their story, their coach's coaching, and the show's strongly digested sense of intimacy that is developed between players and home audience in their actual musical interludes. NBC seems to want intimacy and vastness simultaneously, which seems a curious and difficult-to-achieve blend. Still, it has not hobbled ratings. Quite the contrary, audiences have warmed to the spritely coaching of Adam Levine, Christina Aguilera, CeeLo Green, Pharrell Williams, Gwen Stefani, and especially Blake Shelton. Audiences warm to Shelton, whose down-home and earnest words of encouragement and enthusiasm ring true and seem to show genuine concern about the players, their talent, and their fates.

The belief is that fans will gravitate toward a show in which the judges and the players are appreciative of each other and offer each other opportunities to build community rather than to indulge in cheap shot teardowns of people and their skills. This philosophy has won the show a strong following of kinder and gentler reality programming fans. *The Voice* proves that reality programming does not have to be aggressive, strange, or brutal to be fetching. On *The Voice*, bettering the candidates and helping people achieve their potential career goals has turned out to be a profitable stance. It suggests that in a society in which there are so few jobs and so few success stories that even a marginal victory on a reality program is considered a mark of achievement. *The Voice* may be a response to our society's reality of diminished expectations for all. Sadly, considering the candidates' lack of success as singers after the show, the show tends to prove that audiences are fickle, and that, in the end, a person who is the winning singer on a reality game show may have only proven that they can be a winner on a reality game show and little else.

A problematic aspect of the show is the tight and binding contract that singers must sign to compete. Don Kaplan, writing for The *New York Daily News,* described the conditions by saying, "The contract, obtained by *The News,* says the NBC show can, Change the rules at any time, eliminate contestants at any time, even if they are 'winning' with the public, ignore the show's voting system, which includes sales figures for contestants' songs on iTunes, in the event of problems, (and) force contestants to undergo medical or psychological testing and, under certain circumstances, release the results on TV" (2014). While these conditions seem fairly draconian, they aren't atypical in the world of reality television, where some networks have found reality stars problematic employees. Annoying as such contractual restrictions are, they are probably becoming a standard in the reality industry.

The show's eight seasons have produced over 180 episodes. The coaches have remained fairly stable. Unlike other reality shows in which points are gained by snarky comments and nasty confrontations, the judges embrace and nurture the program's contestants. Mentors frequently bid on their peers' performers, suggesting that most of the judges/coaches are involved in a pleasant competition with each other. The pointed criticisms after each performance are left in terms of issues that singers can address and improve over time. There are few personal attacks on the show, although Adam Levine and Blake Shelton seem to dig each other in what appear to be scripted barbs that have little to do with contestants or singing quality.

The structure of the show provides a competition among singers who audition in local auditions and then compete in televised elimination rounds. The goal is to find solo singing performers to perform in elimination rounds. The winner is determined by audience votes from television audiences who can vote by phone or Internet means. Winners obtain a $100,000 prize and a recording contract with Universal.

Viewer ratings have risen steadily during the shows tenure, starting at a paltry number 20 ranking in 2011 and rising to a number 7 in the ratings by 2014. The show's mixture of drama and pathos for its struggling singers show no sign of declining.

See also: American Idol

Further Reading

David S. Escoffery, *How Real Is Reality TV?*; Don Kaplan, "Exclusive: Secret *The Voice* Contract Says NBC Can Ignore Votes," *New York Daily News,* March 14, 2014.

WIPEOUT

Wipeout is a fun, physical challenge and punishment racetrack, a triathlon-style physical workout in which guests are mercilessly beaten and punished on a track that has pools, mudslides, punching balloons, ejection levers, bouncing balls, cascading rolling stairs, and any number of challenges to knock, kick, drag, submerge, dunk, upset, and unsettle the player. The machines are all padded with soft material, plastic, and Styrofoam, but, even though the blows are cushioned, the contenders take a lot of punishment. Not all of them are young, but most seem to wear a level of protected padding, so they are not too clobbered by the great punching, squishing, rolling, bouncing, balancing machines that give the contenders a rough time.

Much of the fun comes from watching the players like good-natured goofs shrug off their woes. They bare their frustration and embarrassment like participants in Japanese game shows, who diligently smile as they are being poked, dunked, splashed, kicked, and knocked down. The name of the game here is abuse. Competitors will take a lot of physical punishment, and the purpose of the show seems to be to thrust them pell-mell into the melee so they can catch the greatest amount of slop and disgusting grossness. Men and women alike are rattled, wrinkled, crinkled, and made dirty and messy in the competitive course, and they seem to enjoy the various pounding their bodies are taking. They smile like good soldiers going to the firing squad, and they grin in good spirits. They signed up for it, and they want the prize in the end. The winner is the person who completes the course fastest, but the rule is that everyone will be damaged during this ferocious set of messy games. Adults can imagine it is like the popular Nickelodeon show *You Can't Do That on Television,* in which wrong answers were greeted with the contestants being covered with yucky green slime.

Wipeout originated as a fun comedy/physical game show in 2008 and was hosted by John Anderson and John Henson. It has run for over 7 seasons, been pulled, gone on hiatus, and has been revived. There have been over 130 episodes, and there are innumerable international versions of the show, including South American and European editions. There have been lawsuits triggered by the program's strong resemblance to *Takeshi's Castle*, a Japanese classic sadistic game show, in which a group of Japanese contestants go through slimy hell to reach a castle that holds the prize.

In *Wipeout*, the contestants are briefly introduced, and then viewers get to the real fun of watching them fall and get kicked, punched, slimed, and beaten by a variety of machines on an obstacle course that eventually gets them to their end goal. Viewers don't care who they are, to the audience they are all cannon fodder for amusement. What makes *Wipeout* such a huge winner is the size, scope, and scale of its over-the-top obstacle course.

ABC, the program's producers, knew the show had great potential for sports viewers and for people who want to see sports players go for a dive. The second season pitted a series of sports all-stars against the obstacle course in a show that ran against the Super Bowl. Quickly the show became one of the world's most popular game shows. Indeed, the show has been instrumental in breaking down gender barriers. Girls can be slimed just like guys. The show has featured female athletes, and several have won the competition. There have been specially themed shows cataloging U.S. heroes (firefighters, police officers, rescue workers, National Guard soldiers, people who help people). There have been "tournament of champions" episodes, and one of the enduring pleasures of the show is how boldly the contestants strive to run headlong into the wild and attack the obstacle course full speed, no matter how harshly it batters them.

There have been phone games and video games developed on the concept, and they have been popular on Apple's app store.

The program designers excel at creating crazy machines that knock people about without killing them. Some of the fun devices include the Topple Towers, which knock people into the moat below; the Sucker Punch, which has big fists come out and punch people while they are climbing along; the Big Balls, which look like a stable path to cross a water trap, but they bounce and throw contestants into the water; and the Cookie Cutter Swing that stops the player from hanging on by splitting in half and leaving the player hanging in space.

Japanese companies demanded payment, because they said the ABC concept closely resembled Japanese games shows (especially *Takeshi's Castle*) and that the obstacles in *Wipeout* were merely mild modifications of devices Japanese engineers had made. The case was settled out of court, and it is presumed that the judge ordered ABC to compensate the Japanese originators. No one is talking about the settlement.

A big problem with physically grueling shows like *Wipeout* is that they can cause injuries no matter how well the show attempts to protect its contestants. As the NFL has come under fire for allowing many sports stars to have continual concussions, so wacky physical game shows run the risks of common people being hurt by extraordinary and dangerous stunts. Daniel Frankel, writing for the *Wrap*, reported that injuries highlight "an emerging challenge for the increasingly dominant nonfiction TV business, which relies heavily on everyday individuals, often placed in difficult situations" (2009). Despite the fact that the programmers try to keep people safe, if you put them in a dangerous situation that even occasionally harms stunt people, people can be harmed. Frankel's story was occasioned by the sudden death of 33-year-old USC grad communication student Tom Sparks, who suffered brain injuries and eventually died of a stroke. He had the stroke while performing a stunt on *Wipeout*. Even though Sparks may have had a preexisting condition that may have led to his stroke on the show, it pointed to the fact that stunt shows (*Jackass* or *Rob Dyrdek's Fantasy Factory*) are always dangerous.

See also: American Ninja Warrior; Survivor; The X Factor

Further Reading

David S. Escoffery, *How Real Is Reality TV?*; Daniel Frankel, "Another Reality Show Death," *The Wrap*, November 11, 2009.

THE X FACTOR

If a viewer has seen *The Voice* or *American Idol*, they have seen a program similar to *The X Factor*. Though produced by reality show titan and veteran Simon Cowell and ostensibly conceived before many of the other music competition shows, *X Factor* arrived looking familiar. The program had its genesis in the United Kingdom and was imported to the United States under Cowell's leadership for the 2011–2013 seasons. After starting the show in 2004 for a replacement for the British *Pop Idol* show, the program has been a popular venue for up-and-coming singers to exhibit their skills. The American version debuted far later due to legal wrangling and only appeared in the United States from 2011 to 2013 on the Fox Network.

The program featured the vocal talents of young singers (ages 12 and older), and the talent was culled from public auditions held across the country. Like most of the popular talent competitions, the singers deliver a karaoke performance of a popular and well-known pop song and are judged on their vocal skill and presence. The term *X Factor* refers to the extra quality—or the something different—that renders the performer unique or remarkable. The show has been a consistent ratings performer in England for over 10 years and has had a more fitful relationship with American audiences since it arrived later and met a saturated market from its first airing. The competition is for a recording contract, and ultimately part of the reward is the exposure afforded emerging artists by being featured on the program. This not only benefits the winner, but other performers who are finalists on the program.

The program has been hampered in the United States by legal challenges. Simon Fuller, the producer of *American Idol*, argued that the program violated the copyright of his show and brought suit against Simon Cowell. Fuller wound up receiving a 10 percent share of *X Factor* profits in the UK in a settlement and basically kept Cowell out of the U.S. market until 2010, when Fox scheduled a U.S. version of the show. In 2011, Fuller sued again, because he claimed he was owed a co-producer credit for the new program.

Unlike *American Idol,* where judges only judge, in *The X-Factor* judges also serve as mentors to finalists in four categories. The judges help the contestants in terms of look/style, song selection, vocal coaching, and performance tips. They still participate as judges, which suggests they could have a conflict of interests.

The program has courted a variety of controversies internationally. Reality shows, and particularly reality competition performance shows, are all very similar and share characteristics of game shows and heighten drama by relating personal stories of contestants. In essence, they are television programs ultimately created to provide entertainment and to keep people viewing. Fuller and Cowell in their court battle over the *American Idol* and *The X Factor* franchises finally brought the issue of "Can a format be copyrighted?" to the fore. This was perhaps the most groundbreaking thing about these reality programs, but, instead of the courts providing a definitive answer, the parties settled before a judgment was reached. Further troubles have erupted internationally. The Danish version offers participants a contract so binding they can't appear anywhere else for three months. In New Zealand, a judge insulted a street performer participating in the show and said she had wallflower body language. Worse, the New Zealand version featured convicted murderer Shae Brider as a contestant. The program was chastised for poor editorial control of its content and selection process.

Of course, many contestants on talent shows win and are never heard of again. Such fame rarely lasts, but few understand the hard work needed to sustain an entertainment career, and many of *The X Factor*'s winners have had to learn that lesson the hard way. Mark Lawson, writing for the *Guardian* described the post–*X Factor* career of singer/performer Alexandra Burke, who won the fifth *X Factor* competition in England in 2008. Today she is over *The X Factor* and performing in the West End production of *The Bodyguard,* a musical adaptation of the hit Kevin Costner/Whitney Houston film. Burke explained,

> *The X Factor* is a "Fame Academy" crash-course, that's what it is. So you have to go into it in the right frame of mind. I think the mistake that a lot of people make is that they go in wanting to be famous, rather than wanting to be successful, and those are two different things. *The X Factor* will give you an opportunity, but the hard work starts once you win it. (2014)

Burke, like many candidates for success on such shows, realizes that such shows are stepping stones in a career path and that the ultimate path to success is not reliant on quick or temporal fame but on persistence, hard work, careful planning, and luck.

Peter Fincham, one of the television executives at ITV, was partially responsible for the invasion of reality television shows in England and helped to secure the popularity of that format. He explained that reality television revived Saturday night family programming in England by giving groups a deeply affecting series of programs that personally engaged the audience in the struggles of the individual performers. Fincham points out that, at the time, the shows were novel reinventions of television tropes. He says, "The shows turned out to be a clever way of bringing together various elements, including interactivity and competition. From the beginning, these series weren't a short snack: they were a long and involving entertainment" (Lawson 2014). So for Fincham, the connection of interactivity; on-air, on-the-computer, and audience voting; and long-term audience involvement transformed how the shows were conceived and received.

Another factor that mattered to British audiences was the high-stakes drama of the individual against the machine of the big entertainment corporation. *X Factor* contributes to this by placing supposed outsiders in the midst of the industry. Audiences noticed the reaction shots of family and friends backstage. They were often in tears that their family member had risen to such heights. Further, people seemed to enjoy the drama of the underdog in the competition. Someone with slim chances can rise to become an audience favorite in shows like *The X Factor*. It is the underdog status that makes such shows resonate with the masses. In England, *The Guardian* reports these shows are known as "showoff shows," something that marks them as distinctive, but some offer behavior that is often derided as self-congratulatory and not what good people would do. It reflects a boisterous, self-involved mind-set that is at once pleasing but perhaps not enviable. *The Guardian's* Lawson opines that the reality shows of this generation are regarded more strongly than previous reality shows because many viewers are addicted to interactive programming and the new breed of reality programming, *The X Factor* being a prominent example that has benefited from audience interactivity and audience voting. When *The X Factor* had its last finale in England, the program was the most tweeted show on television.

Criticism of the show includes the fact that harsh judges like Cowell encourage painful audience judgments and they encourage vile and mean-spirited public discourse. Instead of praising performers for their efforts, the emphasis grows to be catty and angry. Realists argue that regardless of one's talent, performers need to be prepared for vile critics and that the criticism received on *The X Factor* is simply part of the work of being an entertainer. Handling such criticism is part of the job.

See also: American Idol; Survivor; The Voice

Further Reading
David S. Escoffery, *How Real Is Reality Television?*; Mark Lawson, "Ten Years of the X-Factor: The Show-Off Show with a Talent for Survival," *The Guardian*, August 29, 2014.

Chapter 3: Friends, Family, and Frenemies—Personal Lives of People

Unfriending Television: Intersecting Reality Programming and the Web

As reality television has grown, the interactive communities surrounding these shows have grown during the same time period. If Web one (1.0) was characterized by people surfing, Web two (2.0) has been more about finding a set of strong destinations and settling in to commune with your brethren, a place where your tribe can meet. Television programs denied this association between television programming and Internet sites at their own peril. Late-night talk show host Jimmy Kimmel described the new reality for television. He said, "Our competition isn't NBC or CBS or Fox. It's everything else. You have so many other places to spend your money now. And that sucks for us. We hate that. Now we have to compete with nipples and dragons" (Thielman 2015).

Nowhere is the acceleration of the nexus of programming and Web accessibility more apparent than in the world of reality programming, where fans get minute-to-minute updates on their favorite reality program characters, and this is profoundly changing how we interact with people on these shows. Kim Kardashian seems to dress to be pursued by fans everywhere she goes. The prominent reality star rocketed to fame through her sex tape with hip-hop artist Ray J that was leaked (released?) in 2004. Kim became a household name, and fans still follow her everywhere.

But reality television has arisen in a new world with new media and quickly changing codes of ethics. Consider the massive changes in the time since the Internet erupted. The Soviet Union declined as a world power, the war on drugs effectively ended, youth culture evolved into a nearly autonomous time period in life, and cell phones became small computers with nearly the same capabilities as laptops. Patricia Hersch, in her *A Tribe Apart,* explains, "In the vacuum where traditional behavioral expectations for young people used to exist, in the silence of empty houses and neighborhoods, young people have built their own community" (1999, 21). This city within a city was created and mostly not acknowledged, but it changed the way young people lived, worked, and related to the rest of society. Many of these new methods of socializing debuted through vehicles such as reality television. These programs showed new ways that people were relating to each other as dates, neighbors, friends, and antagonists. They showed a culture that was separating from the previous mainstream via generational and technological divides.

The reality bug has even bit programs that were staunchly fictional. AMC's popular *The Walking Dead*, a post-apocalyptic, zombie fantasy has many different elements of reality programming built into its apparatus. There's the popular one-hour post-zombie talk show *Talking Dead* with Chris Hardwick, where actors, producers, and special effects people talk about the hour the audience has just watched, say goodbye to beloved-bitten cast members, and sign off the various zombies offed during the week's zombie carnage and bloodbath. Another way fans stay connected is through social media. Facebook has 32,000,000 fans for the official *Walking Dead* page. Another bonus is the dual-screen experience. It is estimated that a large number of television fans now watch television connected to another screen simultaneously. They either have a tablet, phone, or laptop running while they are viewing television. While watching *The Walking Dead,* the dual-screen experience raises questions about the current threat assessment of what is happening on screen, reminds viewers of past episodes and experiences, asks viewers opinions on the character's actions, and previews upcoming events and episodes. In essence, the Web helps to contextually orient current and new viewers to the program as they watch. Television and other media have quietly entered into a partnership, a merger that is largely ignored and woefully unreported.

Dubious programs like VH1's *Basketball Wives*, celebrating the tempestuous and exciting lives of wives and girlfriends of NBA players, has a gossip page connected to the VH1 site that fills fans in on the happenings of reality show stars connected to VH1. A big splashy photo of *Basketball Wives* star Tami Roman lauds the *Basketball Wives* diva on her birthday, and for her audacious performances forehead slapping costar Meeka Claxton, and touts her documented struggle having an abortion on the *Real World*. The reality star has surmounted personal and relationship struggles to become a respected businesswoman and strong-willed media personality.

Different reality shows court the Web and media in different ways. T. V. Reed, in *Digitized Lives,* comments, "While fandom has a long history prior to the rise of the Net, the online world has exponentially increased the amount and depth of fan activity" (16, 2014). The famous (or infamous) Duggar family of TLC's popular oddity program *19 Kids and Counting* courts media in many different and fascinating ways. Of course, because of their strong fundamental belief system, they are the darlings of fundamentalist Christian media. *Christianity Today* even runs stories on the Duggar children's birthing events, including things as trivial as gender-reveal parties. Is nothing private or off-limits to this highly public family? The Duggars have their own family Web site separate from their TLC program site. It is populated with demographic information about the family and even has its own e-newsletter sign-up so that viewers can stay connected to the family and their daily activities. The site is heavily monetized with ads on every page. Bios of the family are included, and father/patriarch Jim Bob's bio describes his pastimes as "spending time with my wife and children." Next to the children's scrapbook pages are favorite Bible verses and favorite Bible characters. There are videos on the site where Michelle and Jim Bob cheer their children having children and anticipate upping their grandchild count from three to six in a single year. Of course, the proud family stuffs the Web site with recipes. The TLC site is even more elaborate, with Michelle's blog chronicling the life of the family. The seemingly three most important topics that arrive in the video blog are recipes, courtship rituals, and ubiquitous births. There is a special section detailing the Duggars' formal views on courtship. Michelle explained her whole take on modest dressing, chaperoned courtship, and how she was transformed by being reborn at 15. All of this is compelling, important data for the Duggars' Christian fan base.

The interest generated by the Duggars isn't all positive, and not everyone loves the Bible-touting family who seem intent on dominating the airwaves, at least by family numbers if not by quality programming. A liberal petition and social justice organization and Web site, Change.org, has initiated a campaign to take the Duggars and their program off the air. They already have 180,000 signers. Such moves are as invidious, divisive, and disturbing as anything the Duggars might have said. Change.org accuses them of anti-gay behavior and argues that their rhetoric preaches hate. Joe Wissick on Change.org writes, "Duggar words reek of ignorance and fear mongering." That sort of rhetoric probably inflames the situation more, and if nothing else maintains public attention on the family. If anything, the Duggars of *19 Kids and Counting* may not be medical freaks, right-wing zealots, or heroes of the Christian right. They may just be the new shape of American wealthy families. *Forbes* magazine reported in their article "Big Families Are Back in Style" that "According to the *Council on Contemporary Families*, there's been a significant increase in three- and four-children families among the 'super rich,' or the top-earning 2% of households, which translates to an annual household income of about $400,000 or more" (Goudreau 2010).

Many celebrities leverage their reality-program experience to extend their reach in media and plant seeds for new enterprises. Rachel Zoe Rosenzweig used her experience in the fashion industry to market a series of looks and styles based on old Hollywood glamour. Her television show *The Rachel Zoe Project* on Bravo secured her a big market and ran for five seasons. However, her official Web site indicates that her television experience nurtured her move from merely fashion editing to establishing her own product lines, strategic tie-ins with Nordstrom, a newsletter that she sends to friends and followers about her take on the fashion industry, guest bloggers on her site who add to her image of the current fashion world, video reports featuring Zoe and others covering personalities and trends in the business, and a Web store from which you can order Zoe products and a membership gift, the Zoe Box of Style, a quarterly gift pack from her firm for $100 a quarter. Zoe has transformed a writing career into a strong fashion empire and used the Web to build a network of fans and contributors.

Another entrepreneur and author, Bethenny Frankel, has piloted her own talk show, been a contributor to the *Real Housewives* franchise, and was the topic behind *Bethenny Ever After*. Like Rachel Zoe, many women have gained insight, not just because of Frankel's television appearances, but because of the strong biography behind her work. A tough businesswoman who has endured many disappointing relationships, Frankel comes off as a scrappy survivor who turns lemon into lemonade. Frankel moved from being a contestant on *The Apprentice* to a celebrity on reality television in her own right. When she appeared headed toward matrimony, her appearances on *Real Housewives of NYC* spun off into her own series, *Bethenny Getting Married*. That didn't last, and her continual relationship disasters started to become fodder for her own talk show. Frankel wrote a book on relationship failures entitled *I Suck at Relationships So You Don't Have To*. Frankel sees herself helping to enfranchise women in a world where women are often viewed but sadly ignored in the boardrooms of America's largest firms. Frankel's empire includes a line of foods to keep women slim and healthy (Skinnygirl drinks and menu items), diet cocktails, continuous television appearances offering advice and stories of empowerment, business and start-up features, and ways to make women healthy (workouts, facials, and self-help tips).

While Ozzy Osbourne would not have been considered a natural for reality show celebrity, Osbourne's show *The Osbournes* was a big MTV hit, showing the general normalcy, to the surprise of fans, in his living environment. Osbourne has become bigger, given his almost 50-year career, through the use of Web technologies. His Web site offers a regular e-mail newsletter, music and DVD information, tour dates, fan links, a merchandise shop, photos from concerts, and links to Facebook and Twitter. Recently, Osborne, entering his late sixties, has embarked on a new enterprise: *Ozzy and Jack's World Detour*, in which Osborne and son, Jack, tour the world and perform a series of programs detailing their impressions of places both domestic (South Dakota and Virginia) and foreign (Cuba).

The Web's role in transforming our watching voyeuristic culture is powerful. A strong case can be made that Rob Dyrdek's *Ridiculousness* on MTV is one of the most influential shows on that channel. Dyrdek, in his own laid-back and unassuming way, has parleyed his skateboarding interest (started at 16) into a massive media empire. While Dyrdek, a working-class kid from Ohio, may not take the risks he shows on *Ridiculousness*, his video-hosting show keeps him on the forefront of outrage and connected to the youth culture he promotes. *Men's Journal* described him saying, "In truth, though, his enormous value as a media mogul, youth-culture impresario and all-around social media phenomenon—his 30 million followers include two million on Instagram, and his various TV shows reached 100 million unique viewers in the past year—have made him a businessman operating at the top of his game" (Sullivan 2014).

The relationship between other media and television has become so entangled that television is quickly becoming a mere destination on the Web. *The Guardian* reported that television, despite the wider and growing range of programming, has declined from viewers watching almost 5 hours of television a day to now only 4.5 hours. On the contrary, perusing information by smartphone took a jump in occupying consumers' time. Reality television can be partially blamed for the shift. What were once *consumers* could now be branded *prosumers*—people who watch, buy, and contribute to the media market by their own actions and commentary.

However, T. V. Reed points to the fact that this may not always be helpful to the consumers who think they are contributing to a democratic Web environment. It is only the five big station owners who are profiting from their digital efforts. Reality shows have been implicated with suggesting that they democratize television, when, indeed, the power and the selection of who gets a show and what message it sends are still concentrated in the hands of the few. Reed writes, "Much free pro- or con-sumer created content underwrites immense profits for major corporations not only one's like YouTube, but also for companies whose products are endorsed, sometimes through manipulation, via things like Facebook 'likes'" (2014, 44). Despite Google's $400 billion stranglehold on searching, consumers still wield considerable influence in making new connections with new reality stars who, at least, give viewers the impression they are choosing new television relationships.

Further Reading

Jenna Goudreau, "Big Families Are Back in Style," *Forbes*, July 29, 2010; T. V. Reed, *Digitized Lives*, 2014; James Sullivan, "Rob Dyrdek's TV Empire of Fun," *Men's Journal*, October 3, 2014; Sam Thielman, "Dragons, Nipples and Technology: Why the Real Mad Men Are on the Run," *The Guardian*, May 16, 2015.

AN AMERICAN FAMILY

An American Family is the archetypical reality show that problematized the entire history of reality television, that purported to get inside the story of people and tell the truth. The Louds were an upper-middle-class American family blessed with a strong income and comfortable surroundings in lovely Santa Barbara, California. They were anything but typical, enjoying a living environment that most Americans would envy. Yet they also had a father who was a cheating spouse, a mother who was anxious and on the verge of a nervous breakdown, and a gay son who advocated aggressively for his worldview—in essence, a frightened, confused, and mortified family who in the end probably did not know why they had subjected themselves to that sort of scrutiny. Theories for why the troubled family wished to endure the rigors of being the subjects of a PBS investigative documentary of American family life abound. One theory is that father Glenn Loud wanted coverage as he left the family, and documentation might help his divorce proceedings. Documents suggest that Pat Loud was seeking to hold her family together through the program. Many found the show fascinating and depressing, showing the ins and outs of relationships, and found commonalities with their own lives. Unlike the plethora of reality programming today, this show was decidedly un-goosed, and audiences benefited from watching real—although some would say choreographed and conveniently edited—programming that told the story of the dissolution of a family. The filmmakers never intended to get such juicy footage, and the bounty for them and the American people was a deeper insight into social problems and family issues that were rocking American in the 1970s. These issues continue to play out in the redefinition of family life and its topsy-turvy nature in the economic roller coaster we have arrived at in this early millennial period in which jobs are scarce, benefits scarcer, longevity non-existent, and the promise of a brighter tomorrow a dire struggle for most. What were once assured and dependable jobs no longer exist, and conditions for employment are woefully inadequate. By comparison, what was shown in *An American Family* looks like a golden age of prosperity.

The show set the stage for shows that went from the previous documentary tradition into the newly emerging reality tradition, where drama, melodrama, and contrivance vied with actual reporting and recording of real life. Derek Kompare, in his analysis comparing *The Osbournes* to *An American Family* writes, "As Jeffrey Rouff contends in his retrospective of the series, the narrative structure, the cinematic style, and promotional structure of *An American Family* indicate how the documentary ideals of the filmmakers—and to an extent, even of the Louds themselves,—was adjusted throughout the project to more closely adhere to the generic standards of television drama, and more specifically, soap opera, rather than documentary" (2009).

See also: Jersey Shore; Kate Plus 8

Further Reading
David S. Escoffery, *How Real Is Reality TV?* 2006; Derek Kompare, "Extraordinarily Ordinary: The Osbournes as an American Family," 2009.

AMERICA'S FUNNIEST HOME VIDEOS (AFV)

Before *Jackass* and other shows that valorized daredevils and quixotic stunts, there was the more middle-class pleasures of *America's Funniest Home Videos*. Oddly, this long-running, highly rated program from ABC had origins in Japan. The show *Fun TV* with Kato-Chan and Ken-Chan appeared on the Tokyo Broadcasting System in 1986. Producer Vin di Bona licensed the concept from the Japanese creators and produced a program for American audiences that would have a similar format in which people in the home audience could send in their own video clips. There was another precursor in Germany's *Pleiten, Pech und Pannen*. The program thrived on charming and clean-cut shots in which individuals would be undone by a slip, a pratfall, a mechanical failure, an unexpected door opening, or some other gag/prank/mishap that usually embarrassed the participant. The show was billed as a manner of individual democratizing power. Individuals and families could show they were as clever in real life as people who were promoted as professional entertainers. A child might tumble over while playing with the family dog, a father might take a slide while going down the family steps during a snow-shoveling session, or a diver might go flying into space when a water spout threw him off course during a regular dive.

Popular segments revolved around clever or disgusting baby behavior, wacky or especially thrilling prank or sports moments, meltdowns during wedding ceremonies, and the ever-popular groin punches. Of course, some of the segments appear clearly staged. *AFV* would show military planes jettisoning toilets, uncomfortable segments in which the host would share a humorous moment with a non-celebrity studio audience guest, and the classic volleyball-to-the-face slap. Some of the editing used to goose the most powerful moments depended on repeating the moment of impact over and over again. The ham-fisted use of repetition seems annoying by today's standards, but, during the program's run (from 1989 to the present), the technique worked to reinforce the show's popular disaster moments.

The show has segments hosted by a lightweight host/entertainer/emcee. For most of the 1990s, the host was the genial Bob Saget, who was followed by Daisy Fuentes, John Fugelsang, and Tom Bergeron. Since 2015, it has been hosted by Alfonso Ribeiro. The format of spills and accidents has been amended and changed over time to keep things fresh. Bergeron's era includes segments like "Vs," in which one segment faces off against another, and "A Moment of Eww," in which the videos focus on something gross. "The Dog and Cat Park" features animals. "What's behind the Blue Blob?" asks audiences to determine what is hiding behind the blob on the screen. Is it a person, an animal, or some other object? Initially, audiences had to submit videos by mail, but recently the program has accepted online submissions. In 2011 the show introduced an app that lets people make and upload videos directly from the their iPad/iPhone devices.

Wired magazine reported in 2004 that the show may never die. Apparently the producers have stockpiled thousands of videos from amateurs, and the show has thousands of hours of documentary-style footage to draw upon if needed. *Wired* also suggested that the show has been instrumental in creating/pioneering the new low-tech/high-tech style of filming that YouTube has popularized, saying, "It introduced a whole new accidental-auteur style, marked by wobbly camerawork and abrupt denouements" (Raftery 2011). Brian Rafferty sees the show as an innovative precursor to shoddy Web videos. For Rafferty, the show's speed, commonness, and laugh-at-ourselves, unselfconscious silliness harkens back to an era when sophisticated production was central and low-budget, gag-oriented videos were a guilty pleasure of the televisual mediascape. Rafferty suggests that AFV has devolved us back to an era where shoddy is cool. The raw, unvarnished, DIY spirit of *America's Funniest Home Videos* restores the notion of a documented American landscape that is largely free of the conniving and artifice that has tainted programs like *The Bachelor* and *The Real Housewives of Beverly Hills* that subsist through staged meltdowns, self-imposed traumas, and degrading journeys to deride American subcultures. Rafferty argues that the low cost and regularity of its laughs will keep it pungent until the Rapture. Bergeron quipped, "In my house we call this show the annuity" (Raftery 2011). *AFV* is an example of reality programming that isn't too slimy (except for the kids who fall in doggy doo-doo), remains endlessly entertaining, and has inspired a low-tech, quick-tech style of cinema that has become an American standard for speedy communication. Think of it as shorthand for laughter.

The show can quickly degenerate into families attempting to rival station programming by attempting dangerous stunts and absurd pratfalls and capturing the results on low-budget camcorders and phones. The program has been a ratings success for ABC and a transformative icon for an industry interested in trimming budgets. The show costs practically nothing, produces spectacular (if often sanitized) results, attracts family audiences, and features opportunities to truly democratize programming. The show has become ABC's longest-running entertainment program. Richard M. Huff defined it as a "clip show" and remarked that "it was built around video footage of funny moments" (2006). The program now competes with other clip shows that scour the Web for funny and goofy pranks and stunts. Producer Vin Di Bona luckily has thousands of older clips in his inventory, so the program has many stories yet to tell. With that much material in the can, the producers simply need to roll the footage, and the laughs will continue.

An added bonus and incentive for the citizen-journalist contributors has been cash prizes. The producers pick three videos out of each episode's clips. Clips are usually short (5 to 30 seconds), and the studio audience votes for the best video, which can win up to $10,000. At the end of a series run, there is a $100,000 prize for the best video of the season.

See also: Jackass

Further Reading

Richard T. Huff, *Reality Television*, 2006; Brian Rafferty, "Why *America's Funniest Home Videos* Won't Die," *Wired*, 2011.

AMERICA'S MOST WANTED

America's Most Wanted was an extremely popular docu-reality show featuring recreations of violent crimes and insights into the minds and misdeeds of master criminals, hosted and helmed by a host whose own family had been the victim of violent criminal action. The show had a tinge of authenticity, not only because of the host's experience but also because of the extreme level of cooperation witnessed with law enforcement officials during the filming. One of the first waves of reality programming that hit the United States and has remained a staple were programs that dealt with criminals and police work. The popular *Highway Patrol* series ran years and featured actor Broderick Crawford. Jack Webb brought a semi-documentary feel to his *Dragnet* for two decades. *Cops* was another series that used live footage of the police in action to give a real, documentary feel to a program about police activity. For one reason or another, Americans seem addicted to the grim reality of police business, whether by reality television or actual news reports. *America's Most Wanted* involved Americans in the search for criminals in the most visceral way possible.

The host of the popular show, John Walsh, arrived at his fame through the kidnapping and murder of his son Adam at the age of six. Walsh's wife, Revé, had gone to the store with Adam and left him alone for a few minutes while she went to another department to buy a lamp. Their son disappeared, and his head was found a few days later. After the horrific abduction and murder, Walsh became a strong advocate for victim rights and a staunch opponent of all criminals and any sort of criminal behavior. To many he became a hero, and his zealous pursuit of violent criminals made him a solid national advocate for a show that pursued the worst criminals in the country.

There was a sense that we were with an investigative team tracking the worst, most depraved, and violent criminals, and, through watching and witnessing we too, were helping the investigative process. The show successfully integrated the audience by giving them numbers to call if they witnessed suspicious activities. Like in films of the early 1930s that sought to turn regular kids at risk of delinquency themselves into Junior G-Men (slang for Government Men), the Junior G-Men Club tried to dissuade young people from lives of crime and move them toward lives of law-abiding citizenship and helping the police. This itself was a reaction to the lawless gangster era prompted by the highly unpopular Prohibition laws of the 1920s. The Prohibition era was called the Roaring Twenties for a reason, and Walsh's anti-criminal crusade seemed to parallel that time.

Daniel Trottier's article "Watching Yourself, Watching Others: Popular Representations of Panoptic Surveillance in Reality TV Programs" makes the case that such shows reinforce a mechanism that is at the heart of television: surveillance. As Alfred Hitchcock firmly conceived of films as "men watching women," Trottier discusses the ideas of French philosopher Michel Foucault and his idea of the panopticon, where, in society, surveillance becomes a norm. In the realm of CRTV (Trottier's term for "Crime-based Reality Television"), Trottier claims that "one of the many functions of CRTV is to implicate the audience member (the many) in the panoptic apparatus, in effect to situate them on the crimino-justice grid" (2006). So when shows integrate us by having us call in, vote, or report crime, the show is demanding a high degree of involvement and access to the criminal justice system. In a weird sense, we are players in the reality game of justice, and if we don't play, we are either guilty, helping the criminal, or acting as the indifferent Americans that we disdain in others.

The program has had a remarkable run on network television, running 23 years on the Fox Network from 1988 to 2012, then on Lifetime from 2012 to 2013, and in 2014, moving with a title change to CNN. The show holds the title of the longest-running program on the Fox Network.

Further the show may have a deeper impact on American society than many reality shows that are watched, absorbed, and discarded. The manner in which citizens were incorporated, literally recruited into the show and into the war on crime, encourages people to join up, and, by fighting crime, to become a better person. Trottier remarks, "It is worth noting that many police academy students have reported that show such as COPS and America's Most Wanted prompted them to enlist" (2006). In essence, the show sought to be an instrument for social justice and prompted a disturbing notion that vigilance and spying in your neighborhood for signs of suspicious activity was a good thing. The plus side is that criminals have been caught thanks to show, but the downside is that this can sponsor acts of vigilantism and violence against people in the street. The Trayvon Martin case, whether murder or misunderstanding, is the sort of incident that could be triggered by such interactive, hegemonic television messages.

The program was unique in that it did not lend itself to repeats, since the programming was mostly time sensitive, and if shows were repeated after the felon was caught, the show performed little function. Also, the show seemed to have a far better batting average than most reality dating shows. In its brief incarnation on Lifetime, the station ran 44 episodes, and their investigations led to 36 arrests.

But most importantly is the way the show configured space for the viewer and the broadcaster. Trottier discusses the issue of synoptic flow and communication, in which the few generate messages to the many. In some cases, the synoptic message was to show the actions of a few criminals to a great mass, but at a deeper level Trottier argues that this CRTV content "could be understood too as synoptically legitimizing panoptic control apparatuses through the particular content in which these apparatuses are presented" (2006). In other words, people who watched America's Most Wanted got used to the positive approval of surveillance and the constant polling of the populace to aid in police matters. That public involvement in surveillance and the state's ability to watch everything was seen as good and normal. In the end, despite the positive contribution of *America's Most Wanted*, maybe that is not necessarily a good message to normalize.

Further Reading

Daniel Trottier, "Watching Yourself, Watching Others: Popular Representations of Panoptic Surveillance in Reality TV Programs," In *How Real Is Reality TV?* (ed. D. Escoffery), Jefferson, NC: McFarland & Co. Inc., 2006.

BASKETBALL WIVES

Not all the women on *Basketball Wives* were necessarily wives. These were the stories of women who were *involved* with basketball players. If that sounds vile and cringeworthy, for the most part, it was. The series ran on VH1 from 2010 to 2013 and has been revived as *Basketball Wives: Atlanta* and *Basketball Wives: LA*. It dealt with the lives of wives, girlfriends, and exes of basketball superstars and what the women, as mates and as people, had to endure in their relationships with sports celebrities.

The program showed the pressure cooker of life in the public eye as the spouses or girlfriends of sports idols. None of the women seemed secure. Their place in the pecking order appeared to be at the will and discretion of their basketball sires, and the kings of the court seemed to rule who was privileged to cohabitate with them. Like sultans, they seemed to be able to exile a loved one at the drop of a hat. Family and spousal allegiances seemed to mean little here. The women were constantly brawling, and the fights seemed to be the self-inflicted wounds of poorly educated women who had valued their physical attractiveness and presumably their sexual prowess above other more substantial characteristics. In the meetings and events the women staged, or rather were staged for them, the discussions routinely devolved into screaming matches, name calling, and vile behavior. One could find little pro-social behavior to recommend. Clearly, money would be the only reason to subject oneself to this kind of abuse.

The show explored the intimate lives of couples in the basketball world. There were trust issues (surprise!), and a number of the wives feared their husbands falling into another woman's arms. One of the *Basketball Wives* stars, Gloria Govan, married to star player Matt Barnes of the Los Angeles Clippers, had had a tempestuous relationship with her partner. For years their relationship had been on again and off again, and it was only in 2013 that the couple married. Things hadn't been made easy by the fact that the player made $1.2 million a year, he had a roving eye for the ladies, and, in basketball years (he was 34), his career was in its senior years. The *Music Times* reported in 2014 that the couple was in trouble, but not as alleged because Barnes was unfaithful, but, as later reported: "Those issues have nothing to do with infidelity and are directly connected to Govan reportedly forging her husband's name on a loan" (Meighan 2014).

The show usually followed the weekly lives of these basketball concubines. Their hair appointments, business deals, and trips to the gym became the focus of the program. In one episode, Chantel and Draya became incensed because Draya accused Chantel of seeing some man behind her mother's back. The accusation had a pungent sting because Draya had been somewhat defensive since Chantel and Orlando (Draya's basketball paramour) had a fling. The show was a complete validation of heterosexual patriarchal relationships in which men (wealthy, attractive, talented, and obviously sexual) woo, control, and manipulate the emotions of an entire *squad* of women. As some sort of feminist horror story, the women built their lives, their female relationships, and their psyches around their fragile control of their men. It was like watching a group of futures commodity traders screaming, "Sell! Sell! Sell!" on a hectic trading day. All the women were anxious all the time due to their need and focus on one primary relationship.

Notably, one of the stars of the show, Malaysia Pargo, recently divorced her Charlotte Hornets star/husband, Jannero Pargo, and she had very positive things to say about her new life as a divorced woman. One could imagine that the payouts as the divorcee of a basketball star would be extremely lucrative, so perhaps the money had soothed the sting. Still Pargo opined, "I'm finding who I am without a man. I've been in a relationship since I was a little whippersnapper . . . I haven't dated in 12 years. That's totally new to me" (Connor 2014). It seems the former NBA wife is learning to live as a co-parent, raising three children alone, and embarking on a career as an entrepreneur. From the testy environment on the program, it can be argued that Pargo made the smart move, and that the rampant unhappiness of most of the wives on *Basketball Wives* bespoke a cloud over the program and perhaps over the pressures of sports relationships in general.

Objectively, the tone of the show was one of the most negative, prurient, racist, anti-feminist, lowbrow, trashy wallows one could experience in the genre. One assumes the entire affair was a scripted ruse. No one could be so continually ill-spirited. One could only dignify such a show by calling it an exercise in nihilism, but it is doubtful anyone on the show would understand what that was.

Further Reading

Star Connor, "Basketball Wives LA Star: Malaysia Pargo Says 'I'm Finding Who I Am without a Man, I Let God Guide Me . . . I Never Speak Fear in My Life,'" *Mstars News*, September 14, 2014.

CAKE BOSS

Cake Boss follows the ups and downs of life at Carlo's Bakery in Hoboken, New Jersey. It is a tale of a tempestuous Italian American family fronted by Buddy Valastro and his sisters, Lisa, Maddalena, Grace, and Mary. The program airs on TLC and debuted in 2009. It explores the work, challenges, and personal relationships of the crew working in a bakery. The show is a solid portrayal of the ins and outs of small business life in the United States and is popular for its no-nonsense look at how to negotiate the world of business and life. TLC renewed the show for an additional two seasons in 2015, attesting to its popularity and fan base. The program is supplemented by blogs and fan sites that follow the struggles of the family business.

The biggest issue in the program for initial viewers is keeping the massive cast of characters straight. Aside from Buddy, the central focus and owner, there are the four sisters, their husbands, and their kids. Between Buddy and his four sisters, there are 14 children and multiple family members and cousins. Many old family retainers work at the bakery. Due to their success and television exposure, they have opened a second location in another town in New Jersey.

The show has had a massively popular effect on the economy, drawing tourists to Hoboken, New Jersey, and many days there are lines around the block at Carlo's Bakery. The show has manufactured several successful tie-ins. The series celebrated the 100th anniversary of Carlo's Bakery (it has been a bakery for 100 years but owned by the Valastro family since 1963). Buddy has written several books, including *Cake Boss*, the story of the family and the bake shop, and *Cooking with the Cake Boss*, a book of recipes.

There have been several successful spin-offs, including *The Next Great Baker*, a competition show with the winner receiving an internship at Carlo's Bakery. While that show is already into its third season, a second show offering Buddy doing daily recipes from the shop, *Kitchen Boss*, shows in the daytime on TLC, and a makeover program, *Bakery Boss*, offers a kitchen-hell sort of atmosphere in which our star goes to troubled bakeries and tries to reform them. This is one busy baker. With a big family, lots of business, and a growing set of fans, *Cake Boss* has already generated 150 episodes and shows no signs of slowing down.

There is enough action and excitement in the day-to-day operation of the business to give crews lots to film, and, with such a large and broad family, there are lots of fights, squabbles, and disagreements to keep everything interesting. One minor controversy was that a company used the name *Cake Boss* in their software and sued Discovery Networks (who own TLC) for infringement. Another controversy was a prank in which celebrity transgender personality Carmen Carrera appeared on the show and went out with Cousin Anthony. Carrera did the bit to raise positive awareness of transgender people. Buddy announced to Cousin Anthony that he had gone on a date with a *guy*. Carrera was offended because, as a transgender person, he/she did not see herself/himself as a guy and saw the line as a cheap shot. Valastro apologized profusely for the misstep, and TLC even reedited the episode for the public.

Cake Boss is an example of reality television doing something that most reality TV is never accused of doing: *doing good*. The program has promoted positive values of American domestic entrepreneurship and hard work. It has taken Hoboken, New Jersey, a town that sired Frank Sinatra and Alfred Stieglitz, and made it a contemporary favorite for people seeking cakes and celebrities, when previously they would cross to Manhattan for those aspects of life. More importantly, the program situates location as an important focus of American identity. Rather than dwell on the freakishness and oddness of place, Carlo's Bakery exudes its common, medium-sized, congested, city charms with all the attendant headaches associated with it.

Valastro's family has been involved in baking throughout the century. Andrea Sachs, writing for the *Washington Post,* describes the celebrity baker: "Both his great-grandfather and his grandfather worked as bread bakers in Sicily . . ., and his father continued the tradition in New Jersey, his adopted home from the age of 13." The idea of a family business appealed to his father, who wanted a place for the whole family to work. Buddy fulfills the dream by "filling the bakery with his four sisters, his wife, his mother, one aunt, three brothers-in-law, two cousins and occasional cameos from his two sons and daughter" (2010). The bakery is bursting with family members.

When his father died, the young Buddy Valastro, not even out of high school, took over the family business, modernizing, creating new cakes and pastries, and transforming the business for modern tastes. He has been successful, and today the shop knocks out over 600 specialty and birthday cakes a week. Valastro says, "I am definitely hanging on to these traditions because I want to, not because I have to. I can't turn my back on the way we did things" (Sachs 2010).

On the show, Valastro tours the city with pride, pointing out its monuments, like Sinatra Park. He sometimes stays at an upscale Hoboken hotel instead of taking the 20-mile drive to be with his wife and kids. He admits he likes to get away from the family once in a while. With a crew and operation the size of Valastro's, who could blame him? Every once in a while, there is a comical and winsome moment of tenderness, and even occasional moments of sadness. One such moment occurred when 45-year employee Sal Picinich, a regular on the show, succumbed to cancer. The show even did a tribute to Sal the week he died. Occasionally reality television manages to birth an adorable show, and this is one of them.

See also: 19 Kids and Counting; Ramsay's Kitchen Nightmares

Further Reading
David S. Escoffery, *How Real Is Reality TV?*; Roxane Gay, "The Marriage Plot"; Andrea Sachs, "Reality TV's 'Cake Boss' Shows Off His Bakery and His Home Town, Hoboken, N.J.," *Washington Post*, March 14, 2010.

CANDID CAMERA

Candid Camera was one of the earliest and most successful reality shows of the golden age of television. The show actually originated with producer/creator Allen Funt on radio as *Candid Microphone* and gravitated to television in the fall of 1948. In various permutations, the humor and anxiety of the show produced ripples through audiences for generations, and it survived on television into the 1970s. It was revived again in the 1980s and 1990s, and a new incarnation surfaced on TV Land in 2014. *Candid Camera's* popularity has survived various network incarnations. It appeared on ABC, NBC, and CBS and briefly was featured on the PAX Network until that station was sold.

The show's concept was simplicity itself and involved ruses and a great mastery of the hidden-camera technique. Unsuspecting people would see outrageous and discourteous behavior enacted, and the unsuspecting witness or victim would respond usually in an embarrassing way. Often a person would intervene, or a pratfall or angry exchange would ensue. Then the hidden television camera crew would come forward and explain that the terrible thing had all been a joke or ruse. Usually, the chagrined citizen would sheepishly admit to his or her own bad behavior in response to the setup, and all would walk away in good-natured humor.

Unlike many producers who saw reality as a simpler way to generate capital through the TV medium, producers like Allen Funt saw great promise in the *Candid Camera* technique for improving society and making people more responsive to mistakes and misdeeds. For Funt, hidden cameras were not intrusive watchdogs but instruments for change and social adjustment. Anna McCarthy writes, "The appeal for Funt, was the way real life drama revealed the ever changing scenery and natural resources of the human mind" (McCarthy 2009). There was clear social science and social benefit to watching people. You could chronicle the anthropological aspects of culture. People's lives moods, methods, mores, and taboos rose to the surface, and Funt found that such programming was genuinely instructive, fascinating, and explanatory. McCarthy continues, "What he wanted to show the public was pure situations where the subjects are relatively unprovoked, or mood spots," that would tend to reflect a certain mood or tone in a person's life. These goals seem lofty, academic, and nearly scientific in comparison to the hijinks of *Jackass*, the chicanery of *The Bachelor*, and the scheming of *Survivor*. By Funt's comment of "relatively unprovoked," it means that he wished to introduce a stimulus to the subject to respond to something, but it was not the loaded, charged, dangerous, or conspiratorial form of temptation introduced in later reality television that thrives on baiting, defiling, and transgressive behavior. No, Funt's impetus was something simultaneously much purer and simpler than the type of programming. He believed that giving people a simple stimulus would make them exhibit natural behavior, not the extreme forms of behavior we see in the form of goosed hyper-reality that passes as reality programming. Funt's vision of reality, even reality that produces laughter, is far more consonant with French philosopher Jean Baudrillard's vision of reality. Baudrillard believes that our modern reality is often exchanged for an impure hyper-reality that feigns our reality and replaces it with an insincere substitute that becomes the new reality we recognize as real. Baudrillard writes, "It retains all the features, the whole discourse of traditional production, but it is nothing more than a scaled down refraction (thus the hyperrealists fasten in a striking resemblance a real from which has fled all meaning and charm, all the profundity and energy of representation)" (1992).

Interestingly, producer Allen Funt moved to a film setup in the early 1970s with the spread of filmed adult entertainment producing the film *What Do You Say to a Naked Lady?* that featured *Candid Camera* situations only in a more X-rated atmosphere. HBO and the Playboy Channel came into the act in the 1980s with a series of *Candid Camera* programs that featured nudity and adult situations.

Jason Mittell argues that shows like *Candid Camera* are probably underrated for their ability at making us reevaluate television genres. He writes, "Traditionally, critical media scholars have viewed television programming from a distance, commenting on that which has already been made" (2004, 200). Mittell suggests commentators can do much more by shaping the debate and arguments about such programming as the programming is being formed and created. For Mittell and others, now is the time for scholars to jump in and guide the view of what social impacts reality television has had and should have in the future. *Candid Camera* was an early show that illustrated the intervention of surveillance on our lives. Funt saw surveillance as a useful and positive tool for society, not the dark *1984*-style structure that we see today. Years after discovering the NSA spent over a decade reading innocent Americans' e-mail, we might see Allen Funt's view of surveillance differently, but Funt saw looking at us through the camera as a social experiment. Biressi and Nunn identify Funt's work quite differently, writing, "Programmes such as *Scare Tactics*, (Sci-Fi channel) which owe more to early American prankster television such as *Candid Camera* and guerilla radio than to game shows, target the unsuspecting" (2005, 15). For the authors, *Candid Camera* was a show about pranks and pranksters, and sometimes that might be the best way to view reality programming. Another darker vision is that reality shows that practice surveillance are vilely targeting the innocent.

See also: The Bachelorette; The Dating Game

Further Reading

Jean Baudrillard, "Simulacra and Simulations," in *Modernism/Postmodernism*, ed. Peter Brooker, Harrow, England: Longman, 1992; Anita Biressi and Heather Nunn, *Reality TV, Realism and Revelation*, 2005; Jason Mittell, *Genre and Television*, 2004.

DUCK DYNASTY

Duck Dynasty is a popular reality show that began in 2012 and has remained popular for the past few years, chronicling the lives and business adventures of a family of Louisiana duck-calling entrepreneurs. The family is a group of long-haired rednecks, no-nothings when we first meet them. However, as in so many reality programs, appearances can be deceiving. The family, brothers Si and Phil and their children Willie, Jase, and Jep are far more aware and industrious than they appear. Aside from their disheveled guise and long beards making them seem like leftovers from a ZZ Top concert, they have hidden strengths, potential, and insights.

First, the Robertson family owns a massively successful duck-hunting business with attendant related industries, everything from duck calls, duck blinds, and assorted equipment related to this recreational industry. They manage well, have strong family relationships, espouse deep Christian values, and, beneath their grizzled exterior, are clever, well-educated, and articulate businessmen.

The show chronicles their sometimes-eccentric escapades, and in common, reality television–style seeks to find comical or humorous sides to their business, their relationships, and worldviews. Malcolm Gladwell, in the book, *Outliers,* expressed an appreciation of groups that stood outside the mainstream of society and profited from their unique stance and vision of things. He mentioned splinter groups, which through their own industry, maverick status, and independence of thought manage to create a divergent means of life and livelihood. The *Duck Dynasty* clan is almost a textbook description of such outliers.

Criticism of the show has come in the guise of critiques of their clannish, almost cultish organization. Further, some have been offended and put off by their deeply conservative and Christianized views, suggesting that the *Duck* clan wishes to Christianize American society, a claim they would probably not shrink from. Further, the suggestion that this backwoods organization is doing something that much of American business and industry is not doing—making an honest profit and serving the public need—flies in the face of many who see the Robertson clan as either a rarity or simply an anomalous aspect of a society that finds pockets of wealth in unique businesses and leisure industries. In recent years, there have been sporadic attacks on the family, their comments, and their lifestyle. A part of the backlash against the *Duck* clan may be based on their success.

One element of the show that provides constant room for debate is the way in which masculinity is portrayed. Southern men are shown being brothers, hunting, wearing long beards, acting patriarchal, and shooting. Leandra Hernandez reports in "I Was Born This Way: The Performance and Production of Masculinity in A&E's *Duck Dynasty*" that being a Southern man is constructed in two ways: a Christian gentleman and masculine martial ideal. One stereotype is the Robert E. Lee figure of culture and refinement, and the other is the image of a crafty but poorly educated and Southern man of nature arts: hunting, fishing, and carpentry. Hernandez writes, "To the men of the Robertson clan, the term redneck is not a pejorative; rather it signified honor, love of one's family and dedication to their land and hunting" (2014).

The show has had other controversies. Duck Commander and family patriarch Phil Robertson gave a controversial interview to *GQ* magazine, saying that gay people were sinful and acceptance of difference was part of a slippery slope toward immorality. The remarks, made as simply statements of his own personal philosophy, made headline news, and the A&E Network suspended Phil from the show for a time. *The Huffington Post* wrote, "Robertson's anti-gay comments did not sit well with lesbian, gay, bisexual and transgender (LGBT) advocates. GLAAD called his comments some of 'the vilest and most extreme' uttered against the LGBT community, 'littered with outdated stereotypes and blatant misinformation'" (Sieczkowski 2016). Phil himself had been a drug user in the 1970s and turned his life around through religion. As many would say, it seemed strange that one who acknowledged his own sin felt so comfortable in pointing out the sin of others. Many fans questioned, Who was he to judge anyone?

The *Duck Dynasty* crew deals with religion in a variety of ways. In 2015, when Jep Robertson had a seizure and landed in the hospital, his brothers asked him if he had seen a light. He replied that he hadn't, and they suggested he might be having a problem with the Almighty. The serious hospital experience became a moment for mild humor. If Jep wasn't seeing a light at the end of his tunnel, he might be on the wrong road.

One can always count on the Robertson clan for good, juicy gossip, and during their television tenure they have provided lots of unsettling reports. Alan Robertson (another Duck family member) reported to Fox News that he had a lurid past as a wild teen, using speed and clogging the plumbing in his girl-friend's house because he used so many condoms. He escaped a husband out to beat him after having an affair with a nurse, and his current wife, Lisa, admitted to two affairs.

The show has benefited from many spin-off projects, including a newly proposed Duck Commander Experience, a touring exhibition featuring the science, lives, and careers of the Robertson family, produced by the same corporation that produced the Titanic Experience that successfully toured the United States two decades ago.

Interestingly, the wives of the Robertsons look nothing like their bearded back-woods spouses. Jessica Robertson, married to the youngest Robertson son, Jep, boasts that the family life and the close proximity of in-laws has strengthened their relationship, and the Duck wife has written a book about her spiritual life and faith and how it has strengthened their marriage.

Reality fame can be fleeting, however. The *Huffington Post* reported that a new Vegas musical, *The Duck Commander Musical*, flopped in 2015 and ended after one month due partially to "controversial comments from patriarch Phil Robertson, who compared homosexuality to bestiality" (2015).

See also: Shark Tank; Swamp People

Further Reading

Leandra Hernandez, "I Was Born This Way: Performance and Production of Masculinity in A&E's *Duck Dynasty*," 2014; Ed Mazza, "'Duck Dynasty' Musical to Close in Las Vegas," *Huffington Post*, May 4, 2015.

BETHENNY FRANKEL

Frankel has had a varied career as a contestant, talk show host, business entre-preneur, and professional celebrity through the reality show format. She appeared in the celebrity list of top-100 celebrities as number 42 and rose from a modest income to a top television star from 2005 to her own series of shows starting in 2010. Frankel came to fame as a contest on the reality program *The Apprentice: Martha Stewart* (2005). She has been a fixture of reality programming since and is one of the rare breed of reality celebrities who has made easy transitions from one type of program to another. She appeared for several seasons on *Real Housewives of New York* and was featured on reality specials such as *Bethenny Getting Married* and her own talk show on Fox, simply entitled *Bethenny*.

The talk show conveyed her success in the medium into a *nuevo*-Oprah program in which an invited guest audience responded to women who brought controversies, issues, and a variety of unusual professions/life choices to the program. Frankel was tough and asked intelligent questions, holding court as the main inquisitor, judge, and moral jury. In one episode, a group of young women determined to find sugar daddies argued that women should profit from relationships with older men. The women suggested their companionship was a business worthy of pursuit and guided by ethical standards. Frankel chided the women, accusing them of greed, gold-digging, and immaturity and suggested that such friendships had a hidden price tag in terms of diminishing self-esteem and the need to render sexual favors, turning the women into self-deluded sex workers. Frankel's talk show lasted for a year.

Frankel herself possesses a high degree of business acumen, jumping from show to show and marriage to marriage with ease. She married, had a baby, and divorced businessman Jason Hoppy within two years. She created a Skinnygirl cocktail company and sold it quickly for $100 million. She has produced DVD exercise videos, a series of Skinnygirl diet books, and other media as part of a large marketing empire. *Forbes* magazine described her as a "mix of burning ambition, self-effacing humor, and painful vulnerability" (2011). Frankel had a turbulent childhood, a daughter of divorce who was shuffled from residence to school frequently, Frankel lacked the stability that children crave. *Forbes* also commented on the fact that her life is an exhibitionistic display of her success. Megan Casserly writes, "With millions of fans cheering she's gotten married, given birth, and built her Skinnygirl brand of consumer products on camera" (2011).

Frankel is a marketing and productivity maven, receiving millions of hits to her Facebook and Twitter feeds, millions of viewers in her various reality programs (*Bethenny Ever After, Real Housewives of New York*, and her cancelled talk show, *Bethenny*), and scoring millions of readers to her bestselling texts, *Naturally Thin* and *A Place of Yes*.

Frankel appears the model of industrious self-promotion. She made $100 million by selling her margarita brand to Fortune Brands. By 2017 the *Sun* estimated Frankel's 2016 income as $6 million; other reports gauge her net worth as $25 million. Of the celebrity top 100, most performers and celebrities make their money by deals with studios and through performance contracts. This amounts to a sort of bondage. As long as they work with the studio or the industry, they make money. When they stop, the money stops coming in. Frankel is a new breed of performer who owns at least part of her own personal product brands. Like David Beckham and Diddy, Frankel is at least part owner in most of her operations and brands. This is a prime motivator to keep her active. Her career is not entirely dependent on whether a station or program hires her, since some of her revenue is derived from her own product lines. Frankel is unabashedly capitalistic in her drive to succeed. She pondered, "What's the point of being on TV if you don't have something to sell?" (Casserly). Certainly the TV market is and always has been a medium to market products (sharing a common heritage with radio, newspapers, and the Internet, television is principally a medium to move items to market and promote them, and that programming is a secondary consideration, a Judas goat to get the buyers to the market). In Frankel's case, the selling purpose is pungently clear and linked to the content of the program. As we watch Frankel sell her Skinnygirl line of products, we also watch her life progress. Frantic self-marketing involves and engages the audience in the competitive activity of rooting for this plucky underdog, this go-getter, this tooth-and-nail capitalistic animal.

Frankel isn't without her critics and detractors. Haters accuse her of whoring herself and her brands to earn a buck. This is a charge that Frankel doesn't flinch at. She welcomes the chance to continually market Bethenny and her brands. Further, because she has moved quickly from company to company (although retaining lasting relationships with Bravo and Fox Networks), she has attracted lawsuits. One business manager, Doug Wald, sued her for breach of promise for not allowing his company, Raw Talent. to share in profits from the sale of Skinnygirl products to Fortune Brands.

What emerges from all this is a woman who is no piece of cake. Sure, Bethenny is attractive, but she doesn't sit still for what she doesn't like. She moves on. She has fits of temper, and they don't seem tuned for the camera. She appears to be a real spitfire. When her last husband's family asked her to a get-together for the holidays, she blew up at them on camera. She has had to run for cover after a reality project falls through and she winds up back on Bravo's *Real Housewives* franchise. In this way, Frankel is captive to the public eye. If she doesn't keep high visibility, she cannot keep growing her empire. In essence, what we are watching, in her reality appearances, is a businesswoman doing business. The only difference is the product that Frankel promotes isn't computers or perfume but herself. Her complicated, gypsy childhood and her exposure to adult traumas and divorce made her ambitious and tough, and, while that is a turn-off for some viewers, true fans relate to her hard-bitten, driven determination.

See also: The Bachelorette; The Hills

Further Reading

Meghan Casserly, "Can Bethenny Crack a Billion?" *Forbes,* May 8, 2011; David S. Escoffery, *How Real Is Reality TV?*; Roxane Gay, "The Marriage Plot"; Sophie Roberts, "Living the High Wife: What Is Bethenny Frankel's Net Worth?," *The Sun,* August 13, 2017.

THE GIRLS NEXT DOOR

The program chronicled the careers and daily routine of a group of Hugh Hefner's girlfriends residing at the Playboy Mansion with Hugh Hefner. The girls, who were supposedly Hefner's girlfriends but appeared more as roommates at the Playboy Mansion were Kendra Wilkinson, Holly Madison, and Bridget Marquardt. The assumption was that Hefner was conducting relationships with many of these women, but it seemed unlikely that any man would have the energy for this many women. They all looked fairly high maintenance, and Hefner looked more avuncular than dirty old man.

In one episode, Holly was having a Marie Antoinette–themed birthday party at the Playboy Mansion. The girls acted as queen bees and portrayed life as simply concubines, but the reality was that they were models and professional escorts for Hefner. The program promoted the attractiveness of life at the mansion and espoused the Playboy philosophy of gentlemanly conduct surrounded by attractive females as appendages. The program confirmed male patriarchy, a culture of consumption and pleasure, and a vision of life ensconced in hedonism and self-pleasure.

Holly's day included a trip to the salon, and the other playmates hid a gift of a golf cart and a cake from another playmate, Laurie. The great drama here was who put a finger in the cake and what people will wear to Holly's birthday party. There was a surreal presentation of the guests in their pseudo-18th-century wardrobes. All the girls came in short-skirt 18th-century gowns, shared presents and gifts, and portrayed the adorable dolls that Hefner presumed men wanted to see. The surroundings were a fantasy, but in a sense, the show was a *show*, and highly meta-referential. Women were "playing" beautiful women.

The program was produced by executive producer Kevin Burns and Hugh Hefner and ran on the E! Network from 2005 to 2010. The women on the show were appropriately dippy, but one was always aware that this was their role as Hefner's representatives of his corporation's mantra and style. Hefner doddered around the mansion in his silk pajamas and held court over these young women. The emphasis seemed to be on having fun and living a life of luxury based on rituals of consumption, beauty regimes, and fine food in pleasant surroundings.

Frankly, the show was pretty noncontroversial. It was obvious these women were retained by Playboy to support the Playboy manifesto and to appear on the show and support charity events. There were charity golf and tennis tournaments, the Playboy Jazz Festival, the Fourth of July celebration, and the girls sponsored their own parties, including Holly's Marie Antoinette party and later a Bridgette-sponsored Clue-style murder mystery party. There was a bit of marginalization of the girls as only bimbos, but the reality was that the girls were social managers of the mansion, and they all add their own touch to the glamour of the mansion. Many people watching E! would see this as another validation of the lifestyles of the rich and the famous.

E! originally ordered a program about Hefner, but they found the perspective of the girls living in the mansion to be more exciting. The show was retooled as a female view of life inside the Playboy Mansion, and presumably much of its viewership were female.

See also: The Dating Game

Further Reading
David S. Escoffery, *How Real Is Reality Television?*

GIULIANA AND BILL

A mild-mannered reality show in which Giuliana DePandi, a reporter for the E! Network, has married businessman Bill Rancic, a real-estate mogul from Chicago. Bill was the first winner on the show *The Apprentice*. This was one of the early cases of a reality show siring another program. So both members of the couple had a celebrity side, and both believed they could beat the reality show curse where couples come unglued via the self-imposed pressures of living their life under pressure and constant scrutiny. Perhaps the tribute to the couple was that their program was cancelled. They had their individual challenges, bad moments, and trials, but frankly the two of them were too normal, too committed, and too rational to misbehave themselves into ratings glory.

Still, *Giuliana and Bill* did have some high moments. For one thing, Rancic is as wedded to Chicago as to DePandi, and getting him to leave was a no-go. Giuliana, on the other hand, had a rough fear of flying, and, since her E! News reporter job kept her in LA, flying back and forth to see her husband was a real challenge.

The good news is that, despite their brush with reality fame, the two are still a happy couple, if today, less in the public eye. Rancic told ABC News in 2015, "Looking back almost a decade . . . obviously it's gotten better every year, for us and especially for me."

See also: The Little Couple

Further Reading

David S. Escoffery, *How Real Is Reality TV?* Michael Rothman, "Bill Rancic: How My Life Changed Since I Asked Giuliana to Marry Me," ABC News, 2014.

HERE COMES HONEY BOO BOO (HCHBB)

Spouting wisdom like "go go juice" and "there ain't nothin' wrong with being a little gay," *HCHBB* has at once surprised and disturbed Americans seeking a reality program featuring trash-talking, lowbrow Southerners. *HCHBB* was derived from an earlier TLC program, *Toddlers and Tiaras*, which featured children involved in the lucrative beauty pageant industry.

HCHBB was aired from 2012 to 2014 and had a large and compelling audience. It was a ratings hit for TLC and corresponded to the interest in the field of child beauty pageants, both a popular pastime for some families and a cultural oddity to others. *Boo Boo* was one of TLC's most watched programs in its two-year tenure. The show was universally negatively reviewed and focused on the exploits of beauty pageant contender Alana Thompson (Honey Boo Boo) and her mother June Shannon (Mama). The producers noted the outrageous combination of Thompson and her provocative, and some might say, exploitive mother/ringmaster, Shannon. The free-spirited and unpretentious duo pricked the reality television cultural milieu of demonizing class distinctions, both rich and poor. The series showed the daily life of the family preparing for beauty pageants and the drama behind it. June Shannon relentlessly marketed Alana in a variety of child beauty competitions during the summers and appeared the quintessence of a bossy Southern matriarch. Her starkness added to the program's edge. At center is always Alana, aka Honey Boo Boo, spouting folkish wisdom tinged with irony and portraying the child brat/prima par excellence. Together with half sisters Jessica, Lauryn, and Anna and mother June's paramour Mike Thompson, the program examined the daily adventures of the (then) eight-year-old child beauty pageant contestant as the family prepared for competitions, performed family rituals, and dealt with domestic squabbles in the hot, rural, McIntyre, Georgia, summer sunshine. Viewers were treated to the family posing for a group portrait, Halloween decorating, eating "Sketti," a mixture of butter and ketchup poured over pasta as a meal, ATV recreation, and other delights.

The program partially derived from the winsome and ironic comedy of Jonathan Dayton and Valerie Faris's *Little Miss Sunshine* (2006), an independent, American road film about a family traveling from New Mexico to California to allow their daughter, Olive, to compete in a beauty contest. The film follows the dysfunctional tribe as they roll across Arizona and California in an aging Volkswagen microbus. Like *HCHBB*, the film features an assemblage of oddball characters.

Shannon and Alana were loud, aggressive, insensitive, ill-mannered, and ill-tempered. This made them keen subjects for voyeuristic mockery, and the sort of snide judgmental viewing that reality programming often exploits. However, both June and Honey Boo Boo occasionally surfaced as real people, not scripted, Southern, O'Connor/Faulknerian, Gothic archetypes. For example, when the family decided to take a family portrait on a hot 100-degree summer day in season one's episode 10, entitled, "It Is What It Is," the clan was justifiably worn out by the heat, but the desire to take a group family portrait was a relatively normal validation of family values. Further, the family occasionally shopped, and both June and Alana sang the praises of coupon clipping to economize on family expenses, allowing June to spend on costly costumes, choreography, travel, and entrance fees to facilitate Alana in her continuing quest to be a competition first-prize winner. At last count, despite numerous competitions, she had never won the top prize. Her striving in the face of rejection and continual self-doubt surfaced as a subtext of the show, and its message to American audiences—pummeled by a lackluster economy, marginal financial advances, and few real opportunities for personal and societal growth— was that trying ennobles.

Honey Boo Boo and shows like it address codes of behavior for families and especially roles of mothering and parenting. Brenda R. Weber explains, "The case study offered by Kate Gosselin (of *Jon & Kate Plus 8*) reveals a depressing familiar misogynistic backlash toward ambitious women particularly, since in Kate's case she actively defies norms of idealized motherhood even as she defines herself according to those same normative codes" (2011, 166). June and Alana also ran afoul of normative codes of behavior. Both were loud, boorish, frank about their love of money and material pleasure, pleasantly slovenly, woefully unsophisticated, and addicted to trash culture.

Simultaneously, *HCHBB* posited that hard work, goal-directed behavior, thrift, and a focus on fame/personal achievement were worthwhile strivings, and an American dream. Despite June and Alana's dubious accomplishments and qualifications, the goal of bettering oneself was routinely a core subtext of the program. Megan Carpentier, writing for the *Guardian*, praised the show, saying, "The Thompsons seem reasonably functional and supportive as a family unit, and that the women of the family don't despise their own bodies and despair over them, but actually feel good in them" (2012). *Atlantic Monthly*'s Allison Yarrow referred to *HCHBB* as, "Here is a loving, American family that adheres to its own standards. In the words of Mama June: 'You like us or you don't like . . . we just don't care'" (2013).

The show has been criticized for presenting a portrait of a neglectful American family as normal. Alana is the product of an unwed union between June and boyfriend Mike Thompson. Daughters Jessica (Chubbs) and Lauryn (Pumpkin) are allegedly the children of Michael Ford, a convicted sex offender. Daughter Anna is the daughter of a union between David Dunn and June Shannon. Thus, the show does not show a convivial portrait of sustained and sanctified parenting through matrimony. Shannon's association with known child molesters was undoubtedly creepy, but the accusations of June Shannon's licentious life failed to consider the mobile, tempestuous, and uncertain paths navigated by poor people worldwide. Fancy weddings and expensive divorces are the province of wealth, not the disadvantaged. The fact that the family had any unity or solidarity was as much a testament to June Shannon's fortitude and pluck as it was to any conventional sense of family values. More troubling were accusations that Mama June had reinitiated contact with convicted child molester Mark McDaniel, who allegedly molested Shannon's oldest daughter, Anna, when she was eight years old. Amid such swirling allegations, the show was abruptly cancelled in October of 2014.

HCHBB was often a course in self-abasement, which could provide audience pleasure. The term *schadenfreude,* derived from the German, describes this sense of joy gained from watching others suffer or embarrass themselves. It is common in Japanese reality game shows, such as Takeshi's Castle (1986–1990), in which contestants were put through extreme (almost insurmountable) physical challenges to conquer a fortress castle. The *HCHBB* clan appeared to be keenly aware of their freak value, sadly understanding that a temporal value for a capitalist society was better than no value in a disposable media environment.

See also: Takeshi's Castle; Toddlers and Tiaras

Further Reading

Megan Carpentier, "*Here Comes Honey Boo Boo*'s Surprising Home-Truth"; Brenda R. Weber, "From All-American Mom to Super Bitch from Hell: Kate Gosselin and the Classed and Gendered Politics of Reality Celebrity," 2011; Allison Yarrow, "*Here Comes Honey Boo Boo* Is a Fabulous Cultural Ambassador for America," 2013.

THE HILLS

The Hills was a documentary-style reality program chronicling the challenges facing young people from the community of Southern California. It was part of a series of shows that MTV debuted in the millennium that previewed life as wealthy, well-positioned, white teens in a privileged California environment. The show was probably more *a fiction of* reality than reality for most of us. The shows were parables of how to mature, and, in a way, kin to the afterschool specials of the 1970s in being near manuals for manners and mores of the emerging millennial generation. Another harbinger of this style of programming were fictional shows like *Beverly Hills, 90210*, a fictional drama that chronicled the many conflicts, encounters, concerns, and debacles confronting a series of teens in the exclusive environs of Beverly Hills, a luxurious enclave of Los Angeles known as a home to wealthy individuals and movie stars and complete with restaurants, shops, and neighborhoods that cater to this elite set.

The show began at Laguna Beach, California, at Laguna Beach High School. The program followed several high school and post–high school students from established Los Angeles families struggling to achieve fame in the music and fashion business while juggling life, romance, and family issues along the way. In the first season, we followed Whitney and Lauren as they committed to fashion school and internships at *Teen Vogue* magazine. Again, these were lucky job placements that most teens were not going to land. While the show was enthusiastically embraced by teens and MTV audiences, critics commented that the show was more of a dream of adult life for most high school grads.

We followed Lauren and her friends as they struggled with job interviews, boyfriend dilemmas, and daily life in Los Angeles. At the start, Lauren interviewed for a position with *Teen Vogue* as an intern. The girls, Lauren and Whitney, both applied to a fashion school to learn the fashion trade and become employable. Lauren had a 3.6 and seemed well prepared, but Whitney volunteered to the fashion school that she would not wish to work on a store floor as an entry-level worker. Both audiences and potential school admissions counselors questioned her commitment to the rigors of college and the rough-and-tumble fashion industry.

The program was a ratings hit and ran for six seasons from 2006 to 2010. The characters came and went, generally moving on to other positions and off the program as they found their place in education and employment and love. The storylines resembled traditional soap operas, and the producers clearly had *Beverly Hills, 90120* in mind when they created the show. Girls partied too hard, selected the wrong guy, and generally complicated their carefree lives. Ample amounts of time, evenings on the town, days at *Vogue*, and classes at the Fashion Institute were routine activities, and, when these pastimes were exhausted, the girls spent endless hours working on their significant tans, lounging around the pool in the most fashionable teen wardrobes.

The program was roundly criticized as being pretend reality. In essence it was a highly scripted, soap-operatic rendering of reality. *The New York Times* lambasted the show, saying that, for the most part, all it did was "looked, in all of its Antonioni-esque plotlessness and dreamy cinematography, at the ignominies of youthful friendship (that) has turned toward the more conventional cruelties that good-looking playboys perpetrate on young women who wear low-rise pants and put on boots in warm weather" (Bellafante 2008). Most saw it as a reality show that served young adult versions of adult life. James Cote observed that many young people had a negative vision of adult life. They saw it as a stage in which one "simply lose(s) one's youth and get(s) old" (2000, 49). Amanda Klein, in her article on the MTV brand of reality TV "Abject Femininity and Compulsory Masculinity on *Jersey Shore*," writes, "Instead, these scripted reality shows highlight their own constructedness by mimicking the editing and cinematography typical of glossy Hollywood films" (2014). The program reveled in the tribalism of youth culture—what writer Patricia Hersch described in her book *A Tribe Apart*. She argued that young people live in a culture so segregated from adults that "the effects go beyond rules and discipline the idea exchanges between generations that do not occur, the conversations not held, the guidance and role modeling not taking place, the wisdom and traditions no longer filtering down inevitably" (1999, 21). *The Hills* shows us such a culture where teen life dominates to the exclusion of any other view of life or culture. It was about teens, for teens, and developing teen images of existence.

Mostly the series portrayed people in a market-driven society who wished to be a part of the consumption food chain by being in the music, entertainment, and fashion industry. Neal Gabler, in his book *Life: The Movie,* argues that America democratized desire, the need for everyone from the top of society to the bottom to own things, and, "It was the desire that led to the fixation on owning material things" (1999, 199). The cast of *The Hills* were so strongly fixated on owning the environment, the nice abode, the great job, the perfect outfit, and the perfect mate, because, on the show, these items were rewards for winning at the game of life. There were material signposts in every moment of the show.

ABC ran a piece describing where the stars of *The Hills* settled. Not surprisingly, most of the girls on the show ended up in long-term relationships, which was the thing they all seemed to desire while appearing in the program.

Lesley Messer of ABC described Lauren Conrad's post-*Hills* career as evolving into the fashion field she was seeking during the show. She has a clothing line, runs a fashion blog, published a book, and became engaged to boyfriend William Tell. Series bad girl Kristin Cavallari married NFL quarterback Jay Cutler, designs shoes, and has two children.

See also: Laguna Beach: The Real Orange County; Real World

Further Reading

Ginia Bellafante, "Career Climbing with Claws Bared," *New York Times*, March 24, 2008; James Cote, *Arrested Adulthood*, New York: NYU Press, 2000; David S. Escoffery, *How Real Is Reality TV?*; Amanda Klein, "Abject Femininity and Compulsory Masculinity on Jersey Shore," 2014; Lesley Messer, "The Hills Stars Are All Settled Down: Where Are They Now?" ABC News, November 24, 2013.

JACKASS

Jackass was a groundbreaking and lawsuit-prone reality show presented by MTV from 2000 to 2002, featuring amateurs doing stunts that resulted in injury, embarrassment, and general stupidity. Several people, most notably Johnny Knoxville, obtained careers in television due to the program. Despite its limited run, its influence, both negative, resulting in injuries and lawsuits, and positive, the democratizing of TV and the Web, have been wide-ranging and profound. The program was produced by MTV and ran from 2000 to 2002. The unique setup was to give the impression of a cinema verité experience with a single camera and amateur-seeming lighting and framing of scenes. The original series ran three seasons and 25 episodes and spurred the movement toward DIY video that achieved fruition in sites like YouTube, where amateur videographers were encouraged to illustrate their arcane take on reality, feature stunt shots, and ultimately challenged themselves to death-defying comedy and variety antics.

The show generated a host of spin-offs, three films, and led to a generation of hapless teens thinking they could perform dangerous stunts because they saw it on television.

The program had its origins in skateboarding humor magazine *Big Brother,* which was edited by Jeff Tremaine. Writer and nascent video auteur Johnny Knoxville (aka Philip John Clapp) had the idea of doing stunts in which he would test self-defense devices on himself. Most people thought that it was daft, but Tremaine gave him the go-ahead and suggested he film himself being shot, Tasered, or maced to provide a more visceral experience for the viewers. At the same time, Bam Margera and his extreme stunts crew were making movies in Pennsylvania featuring goofy and dangerous activities, sports, and pranks. Knoxville and his friends thought the idea was the foundation for a new type of show. It would be a combination of crude home movies, extreme stunts, pranks, and mostly silly behavior that would appeal to a young daredevil crowd. Tremaine, Knoxville, and their friend, director Spike Jonze, pitched the idea to several networks. Both SNL and MTV bid on the show, with MTV winning the rights to the program. It is likely all the programmers saw this as a wacky new way to reach out and engage young viewers, who had soured on traditional television with its canned and clearly contrived programming. These videos restored a real, genuine element of risk in performance.

However, the business of doing crazy stunts for a living and being known as an insane clown willing to do anything just to be outrageous can take its toll. *New York Times* writer Dave Itzkoff spoke to Knoxville in 2013 to find out about his career and the physical and mental price for being the "king of TV outrageous behavior." He writes, "There are signs that the beatings his body and psyche have taken are starting to catch up with him, though he says he doesn't dwell on them. The person you see, whether cameras are trained on him or not, 'that's pretty much me,' he says" (2013). Knoxville's party persona and try-anything attitude is "all in a day's work" for the professional daredevil obscure stunt/prank guru.

Of course, because the show, whether knowingly or unknowingly, encouraged participation in extreme sports and worse extreme stunting, it resulted in massive controversy. This has caused stations to take precautions to prevent corporate entities from being blamed for the stunts, damage, and harm they might cause. Litigation and potential legal entanglements has prompted modern-day versions, such as *Ridiculousness,* which cleverly, through the use of viral videos that MTV merely selects and does not create, absolves the station of any charge in actually making dangerous stunt videos, maiming unsuspecting teens, or resultant (and inadvertent) suicides via stunting. MTV has had enormous success with such formats. It keeps people watching, exploits their ignorance, avoids any legal responsibility for encouraging dangerous activity, and continues to reap profits (while paying no one for personal risks) for the station. The station's only expense for the *Ridiculousness* program is host Rob Dyrdek, an experienced skateboarding celebrity. Dyrdek safely hosts the self-destructions, and MTV continues to serve gullible youth who believe they too can perform stunts.

In the early millennium, Senator Joe Lieberman attacked the show, calling it irresponsible and encouraging of dangerous stunts. MTV's standards and practices board found the show negligent and liable to incur legal entanglements. Though the show ran warning labels, though it was moved to after 10:00 p.m., and though the station tried to assert some control over the stunts and how they were performed, the program was eventually cancelled after its third season.

A man named Jack Ass, who had changed his name to protest the deaths of family members due to drunken driving, sued the show and blamed it for taking his name. Bad publicity and notoriety haunted the show at all turns. For example, a young man in Australia set another teen covered in gasoline on fire, causing dangerous burns, because he had seen the stunt on *Jackass.* Knoxville's dangerous stunts included being sprayed with mace and being shot. He was wearing protective gear at the time, but the stunts were dangerous and highly controversial.

After the show was dropped by the station, MTV offered $5 million to make a *Jackass* film. The popular feature made 12 times its cost, recovering $60 million dollars, and finished in the number-one spot at the box office during its debut weekend. Other sequels followed. Knoxville admitted that he was somewhat addicted to the stunt behavior, and it was reported he ran into street signs to net additional footage.

All of the *Jackass* movies and sequels have been incredibly successful, if appealing to a really lowbrow vibe. The essence is that these films contained gross and uncensored stunts and events. It has that "too hot for TV" label that attracts viewers. In 2011, the crew released a *3D Jackass 3.* This was also a success and secured additional revenue. In 2013, Jackass presented a spin-off, *Bad Grandpa,* their fourth film, and this time the film even scored an Oscar nod for best makeup. Even *The New York Times* took notice, reporting that Knoxville had assailed the character before. Itzkoff writes, "Zisman (the bad Grandpa) is a lascivious if well-meaning character whom Knoxville portrayed in 'Jackass' segments, and whom he reprises in the reality-based comedy movie 'Jackass Presents: Bad Grandpa'" (2013). Rumor has it, the crew would like to film a fifth *Jackass* film in Australia. In any event, despite the controversy, the series and films have a loyal fan base, even spawning a video game in 2007.

See also: Ridiculousness

Further Reading

David S. Escoffery, *How Real Is Reality TV?*; Dave Itzkoff, "Autumn of the Jackass," *New York Times*, October 11, 2013.

JERSEY SHORE

Jersey Shore was a mixture of fantasy and reality programming, taking eight transplants not from New Jersey and plunking them down in the Jersey Shore, New Jersey, to watch them interact in a sort of *Big Brother/Real World* fishbowl to see how they would adapt and react to the constant monitoring. The show ran on MTV from 2009 to 2012 and focused on the escapades of the eight residents first in Jersey, later in Miami, then back to Jersey, then to Italy, and finally ending the series in New Jersey.

The program sparked the usual controversies of MTV programming—contrived locations, encouraging meltdowns, provoking reactions, and bad, immature behavior. The participants seemed to suffer from a directionless ennui that may have been indicative of the age group or could have been a symptom of how the students were expected to respond, basically appearing in a state of inertia. More debilitating was the show's use of racial stereotypes, often referring to characters as "Guidos" or "Guidettes," a slur word referring to Americans of Italian descent.

The show scored with viewers, becoming the most watched program on MTV, ever. Despite its popularity, the program was known for its lexicon of phrases, and people would discuss the show and specifically how people talked on the show. Several universities featured classes or conferences about the importance of the show, its linguistic devices, and its important portrayals of ethnic enclaves. The concept of focusing on a small, ethnic group in a larger society has been picked up and broadcast as *Geordie Shore* in England, the *Gandía Shore* in Spain, and *Acapulco Shore* in Mexico. Needless to say, the program has been an international phenomenon.

The MTV network treated the show as a sort of experiment in a more honest, naked, and documentary-style format. After programs like *The Hills* and *Laguna Beach* had borrowed from a more soap-operatic mix of pretty, attractive characters, *Jersey* offered a chance to focus on a different direction. These kids would be tougher, realer, and grittier. This time reality players would not be getting an internship at *Teen Vogue,* but something altogether more complicated and everyday, like working at Uncle Vinnie's restaurant.

The average-looking crew was assembled at a summer rental in New Jersey along the shore. The house was equipped with over 30 remote-controlled cameras so the students could be surveyed 24 hours per day. *Rolling Stone* reported on Nicole Polizzi, one of the residents saying, "You're always being watched. . . . But that's why we go crazy. That's why we fight with each other. That's why we drink. We're living in a house for two months with that shit. We can't have cellphones, TV, radio or internet" (2011). So basically, MTV stuck these kids in a cooler, encouraged their interaction, and waited for them to explode after two months in lockup. The cast was a hit, and ratings rose every week they appeared. They asked for more money, and they got it. By the second season, MTV had moved the program to Miami to shoot in the winter, so they would not have to wait for another summer to start shooting the next season.

The denizens of the house all arrive from Italian American ancestry of some sort and it was clear that the producers were practicing some sort of racial/ethnic stereotyping in the assembly of this clan. Interestingly, while the United States preached diversity and freedom from stereotypes, MTV routinely practiced some of the most ruthless and vile stereotyping (*Jersey Shore, Girl Code, The Hills, Basketball Wives*) and regularly gained success with these ethnic- and gender-coded programs. MTV seems to follow the logic that payment to individuals who are cast for stereotypical reasons is all right for entertainment purposes.

The locale for this experiment in social surveillance was located in Seaside Heights in New Jersey. Like much MTV programming, a band of privileged teenagers were set up in a comfortable abode for a time and encouraged to act out, complain, and be obnoxious, fomenting interpersonal conflicts and struggles that lead to on-air personal traumas and crises. If these social experiments were conducted in a college and not-for-profit, the college would be closed and the professors jailed. It was a part of the plan that the house was set up as an experimental décor with images of Cadillacs and Scarface on the wall. The most leading item was a hot tub, brought in to tempt all the residents into getting naked in the tub.

A series of merchandise items were marketed in conjunction with the program, including seasons of videos, soundtracks, bobblehead dolls, Halloween costumes, calendars, and books of *Jersey Shore* phrases.

Although not all the cast members were directly derived from Italian American roots, that label stuck to the show, and Italian American groups protested the show and attempted to have it removed by MTV. The station stood behind the show, saying that the people on the show were proud of their ethnic heritage and that the show did not disparage the image of Italian American identity. Several Italian American sponsors, such as Dominos Pizza, removed their ads from the show.

Further, Governor Chris Christie felt the show blackened the reputation of the state by importing a bunch of New Yorkers into a dwelling and palming off their exploits as the real acts of young people from New Jersey. Christie refused to sign a bill giving MTV tax incentives to film in the state. They filmed anyway. A poll by a New Jersey university found that the show *may have* promoted positive views of the state, not negative ones, as Christie surmised (Parry, "Poll: 'Jersey Shore' Not Hurting New Jersey Image," *USA Today*, 2011).

The show has produced several actors who have had repeated success in the reality format. The program has been copied by foreign markets in at least six different configurations, attesting to audience interest in ethnic enclaves in their region. Gordon Alley-Young writes, "Constructing individual reality performers as personifications of regions, nations, and cultural frontiers" (2014, 136) is nothing new, and *Jersey Shore* was just one of a series of shows that used a few people to stand for an ethnic group. While the show may have been tokenistic, stereotypical, and perhaps even a bit racist, it became a stand-in for a certain New Jersey stereotype for viewers who crave seeing those stereotypes portrayed.

See also: Real World; Ridiculousness

Further Reading

David S. Escoffery, *How Real Is Reality TV?*

KATE PLUS 8 (AND *JON AND KATE PLUS 8*)

Jon and Kate Plus 8 has had a checkered career. Jon and Kate had twins and then sextuplets, making them a medical anomaly show. A special featured their complicated road to eight children, and a series evolved. In total there have been eight seasons and over 150 episodes shot. The Gosselin family specials and shows began airing in 2007, and the show was retooled and transformed when dad, Jon, flew the coop and left mom, Kate, to fend for herself and the eight children. Kate Gosselin has been described as a difficult mother, but on the program she seems normal and overwhelmed by the demands of raising eight bright, complicated, demanding, and smart children.

In 2000, the Gosselin family had twins. Their set of sextuplets was born in 2004. Two specials featured the Gosselins coping with the birth of twins, and expecting the sextuplets was presented in 2007. The Discovery Channel ran the shows and addressed the medical aspects of Gosselin's novel birth of so many kids simultaneously. The TLC channel took over from there, offering first a short eight-episode season of the family as they progressed from a household of two to a household of eight. As the family grew, the episodes grew as well, until season 4 created a whopping 41 shows.

The shows illustrated the typical, everyday issues of cleaning up a messy basement, Jon taking the kids to a minor-league baseball game, and the baking of cakes. There have been crossovers with baking shows and visitors from the *American Chopper* show. Interestingly, the show was often self-referential, and the family often reassessed where they were and what they plan to do next. For example, after the fourth season, they did a few retrospective shows and discussed whether they wanted to do anymore television. The kids talked maturely and honestly before the camera, and we had the sense that there were real concerns and stresses with a family that was on television 24 hours a day. Some shows featured big trips, like the girls going to a butterfly sanctuary in Florida, while others simply focused on Jon and the kids shooting off water rockets.

When Jon and Kate divorced in 2009, there were legal issues. Jon Gosselin issued a court order barring TLC from filming on the family property. However, the show was retooled, and Kate returned with the rebranded title *Kate Plus 8*. While Kate is still a reality celeb, her ex-husband has had a variety of positions after his reality show fame, including DJ, cook, and, according to ETonline, a stripper in Atlantic City.

Questions were raised over how fit a mom Kate Gosselin was and whether the children were being exploited. The crew filmed in the Gosselin household for three days a week. Lawyers suggested that Kate could be in violation if she overworked the children to achieve profit.

From what one can guess watching the most recent episodes, the children look like they are actively participating, but they don't seem compelled to perform. They seem honest and upfront about criticizing their mom when she is demanding, but mostly Kate Gosselin appears to be a mother surviving under extraordinary circumstances. How many people could raise eight children and not have problems? It seems that by the show, careful product placements in the show, and a series of four books that she has written, Kate Gosselin is doing everything she can to ensure her children's future and to provide the income they will need for an education. Reality television has made strange partners, and, in the Gosselin family's case, the mix of child rearing with television child-exhibiting (a quality shared by *Honey Boo Boo* and *19 Kids and Counting*) has allowed the family to survive.

See also: Keeping Up with the Kardashians; 19 Kids and Counting

Further Reading

Jenna Goudreau, "Big Families Are Back in Style," *Forbes*, July 29, 2009; Desiree Murphy, "Exclusive: Jon Gosselin Confirms He's Performing as a Stripper in New Jersey, Calls It 'a Blessing.'" ETonline, March 25, 2017; Rebecka Schumann, "Where Is Jon Gosselin Now?" *International Business Times*.

KEEPING UP WITH THE KARDASHIANS

Keeping Up with the Kardashians chronicles the struggles, lives, adversity, and activities of the wealthy and complicated Kardashian clan. The program has produced 10 seasons and over 120 episodes, focusing on the trials and problems of the family. Criticisms range from the show is scripted, to these people have no talent, to the entire thing is one grand soap opera. All charges are probably true, and all of them make the show more fascinating. Here is a reality show in which the difference between a surreal parody of a reality show and the actual lives of notorious celebrities merge. Truly, in the Kardashians, it is difficult to know where real life ends and fantasy begins.

The program arrived in 2007, a product of Ryan Seacrest of *American Idol* fame, and has been a major hit for the E! Entertainment Channel, producing numerous specials and spin-offs. While people complain they have seen and heard enough of the Kardashians, their fame and entrepreneurship continue to grow. *Keeping Up with the Kardashians* focuses on the lives of Kim, Kourtney, and Khloé, daughters of mom Kris Jenner. Becoming more controversial and more of a central figure is second husband Bruce Jenner and his children with Kris, Kylie and Kendall Jenner. Kylie and Kendall's stories are almost setting up a second-generation Kardashian assault.

The show labors with accusations that the program is a carefully staged soap with arranged plotlines. Considering the quantity of filming in the household, it would be surprising if they could generate the same level of constant romance, intrigue, anxiety, and anguish needed to fill a half hour of reality programming per week. Some people have blamed the Kardashians for falling into the trap of being famous for being famous. The popular show has developed several spin-offs, including *Kim and Kourtney Take Miami*, *Khloé and Lamar*, and *Dash Dolls*.

Despite the haters, the Kardashian clan seems to be a productive unit. Kristen or Kris, the clan mom was married to attorney Robert Kardashian, who helped defend O. J. Simpson in the murder of Nicole Brown Simpson. Kris had four children with Kardashian, divorced him, and married Bruce Jenner. Kris and Bruce had two more daughters (Kendall and Kylie). Kris ventured into fashion, becoming a shopper and stylist for some A-list clients, and her daughters opened a boutique in Calabasas called DASH. Kim had several high-profile entanglements with celebrities and performers. In 2007, a sex tape made years earlier when she was dating rapper Ray J surfaced, Kim sued—although the film seemed to do nothing but raise public awareness of her—and eventually Kim was paid $5 million for the leaked film.

In 2007, Ryan Seacrest, producer of *American Idol*, announced there would be a reality program concerning the Kardashian family. Seacrest suggested that the wealth, turmoil, and melodrama of the family would resonate with people viewing. He was right.

The family is rife with scandals and controversies. Kim married NBA player Kris Humphries. The union lasted less than three months. In 2014 it was leaked (in what appeared to be a publicity campaign that was carefully staged complete with pictures, interviews, video tapes, etc.) that Bruce Jenner was undergoing a transition to become a female. This was a shock, since Jenner was an Olympic gold medalist, married, fathered several children, and was established as a male national hero. Again, such provocative actions urged people to see the family as a corporation or publicity brand that exists merely to produce spin. The E! Channel reportedly paid $30 million for exclusive rights to Kardashian properties and spin-off shows through 2016.

Initial seasons focused on Kris's older children, Kourtney, Khloé, and Kim, but in more recent installments, Jenner's children are more prominent. The program continually generates new series offspring. *Kourtney and Khloé Take Miami* showed the Kardashian daughters opening a new DASH boutique in Miami, Florida, with all the attendant trials and traumas involved in starting a new business branch in another town. The show was later changed to *Kourtney and Kim*, as Khloé became over–reality committed. This show begat *Kourtney and Khloé Take the Hamptons* in 2014, when the sisters installed a new branch of their growing DASH empire into the luxurious Hamptons in New York. The girls had a shop in California, and the producers thought that the new locations would make an ideal places to expand the Kardashian franchise.

Say what you will, the family has energy and lots of enthusiasm for marketing their name, their brand, and a host of products.

See also: Khloé and Kim Take Miami

Further Reading

David S. Escoffery, *How Real Is Reality Television?*; Maria Pramaggiore and Diane Negra, "Keeping Up with the Aspirations: Commercial Family Values and the Kardashian Brand" (2014).

KHLOÉ AND LAMAR

Khloé and Lamar was a short-lived reality spin-off from *Keeping Up with the Kardashians* involving troubled (aren't they all!) Kardashian sister Khloé and her relationship to basketball star Lamar Odom. There were 20 episodes produced between 2011 and 2012, and this appeared as another franchise show in the Kardashian series of programs on their home network of the E! Channel.

The show illustrated the complications of Khloé's life with the basketball player and his struggles. Lamar was estranged from his father, and Khloé sought to bring them back to speaking and communicating. Lamar also had his own product line and subsidiary business interests outside of basketball, and episodes detailed Khloé's and Lamar's various business ventures and entanglements. Guest stars included the Kardashian clan (Kourtney, Kim, mom Kris, Lamar's dad, and Lamar's friends and business associates).

In the first season, the couple tried to conceive a child; Khloé tried to connect Lamar to his father; the couple considered opening a unisex salon; business associates became annoying; and family retainers were fired. Amid the anxiety, Khloé put on weight, worked on her self-image, and tried to maintain the quality of her relationship with Lamar. In essence, life here was a continual soap opera. Much of the intrigue centered around plots hatched by Malika Haqq and Khloé. Like a modern-day Lucy and Ethel, the two girls got themselves into pickles. Malika started dating a man with kids going through a divorce.

Things changed as Lamar began to feel he was being babied and controlled by Khloé. He had trouble with his team and knew he would be traded by the Lakers. He was offered a job playing basketball in Turkey and considered it. Eventually, Lamar ended up with the Dallas Mavericks, and Rob Kardashian came to visit, having a panic attack

The program is probably a better portrayal of sports stars' spouses and their issues than VH1's *Basketball Wives*, because the threat of being traded and the constant moving would drain anyone's energy. Sure, Khloé seemed a bit strident and hyperbolic at times, but her family was plenty of stress. Khloé came off fairly normal. Of course she wanted money and fame, but she struggled to create some semblance of a happy home life with the extreme pressures of a husband constantly on the road, friends like Malika with their own problems and agendas, and a controlling family unit that was alternately dysfunctional, embracing, and ambitious. As Khloé's appearances attested, she was a strong person grappling with a crazed lifestyle, entrepreneurial ambitions, stresses that exceeded the norm, and a public profile that made every move a showcase for newly discovered insecurities.

Maria Pramaggiore and Diane Negra in their "Keeping Up with Aspirations" article on the Kardashians writes, "In the heady atmosphere of powerful, fashionable, and glamorous femininity that this reality sitcom purveys, postfeminist celebrity eclipses the masculine world of high-performance sports." Khloé, for all of her insecurities, rants, and cries for help, seemed to be screaming all the way to the bank, and, while she suffered, legions of poorer, less privileged, dreaming women empathized and commiserated with her suffering over being betrayed, childless, angered, and embittered by the false dreams of fame and fortune. Nonetheless, whether it was for an actual talent or simply because she was part of a famous family, Khloé seemed to be pulling her own strings, and, despite the treacherous waters she navigated, she steered a steady course riding on drama and nerve.

See also: Keeping Up with the Kardashians; Khloé and Kim Take Miami

Further Reading

David S. Escoffery, *How Real Is Reality TV?*; Maria Pramaggiore and Diane Negra, "Keeping Up with the Aspirations: Commercial Family Values and the Kardashian Brand," 2014.

KOURTNEY AND KIM TAKE MIAMI (KKTM)

KKTM is another in the almost endless tabloid tales featuring the exploits of the ever-popular and ever-filmable Kardashian clan. This series is part–reality television and part–continual advertisement for Kardashian products. The Kardashian sisters, seeing themselves as fashion entrepreneurs, have opened a series of DASH boutiques, totaling four at present. There is a store in North Hollywood, the Hamptons, and Soho in New York City. The Miami store is a new enterprise and outside the normal areas the Kardashians have frequented, which marks it as an added challenge.

The show premiered in 2009 and ended in 2013, lasting three seasons and producing 30 episodes. Likely this was an intentional plan, launching the store, placing it in the public eye, and moving on to new territory once established. The Kardashians' hit-and-run strategy has not been universally attractive, and many have protested the clan's entry into high fashion. *The New York Times*'s Eric Wilson said people protested when Kim Kardashian adorned the cover of fashion guru journal *W* in the fall of 2010. People were further appalled by having a Kardashian enterprise next-door in popular Soho when the family opened a new DASH location in an attractive area. Wilson writes that a resident of the area pronounced the Kardashians' fan base "a generation of classless, tasteless and clueless sheep" (2010).

The Kardashians, long the heroes (and the punching bags) of the press, paid this tribute no mind. For the Kardashians, the gig was simply launching another store. While on duty running a store, Khloé stayed busy running a nighttime radio show, *Khloé After Dark*. Additional cast members included Kourtney's boyfriend Scott Disick and their daughter, Penelope. If anyone is looking for special ironies, Penelope is famous in classical Greek mythology as the faithful and long-suffering wife of Odysseus, away at the Trojan War for 20 years and eternally cursed by the gods for the Trojan Horse incident.

Despite what the Kardashian haters say, the program was a big ratings success for E! netting nearly 2 million viewers per episode during its first two seasons and upping that to 3 million in the third and final season. It is doubtful the show was actually cancelled and was thought to be a side project in marketing the Kardashian family's chain of boutiques. Other shows sponsoring store openings have taken the original series' place.

Wilson posits the obvious question about the family and their continual enterprises. "Why do people care?" (2010). Clearly the Kardashians' audaciousness and boldness has taken the public by storm. While they might not be the best role models of family values, they are strangely contemporary in that they are gypsies, they are mobile and circulate continuously, and they market their celebrity as a brand and commodity in and of itself. Taking a lesson from Warhol, the Kardashians have learned that, in essence, the product isn't a product but the essence of personality that makes a Warhol work famous. In the same way, the Kardashians create fame by associating themselves with anything that is celebrated or unusual. They understand how society types them, and they respond to the stereotyping of themselves and play that role for society. Their tag or attachment to the product (whether it's Kanye West, DASH, their television show, a fashion line, perfume, etc.) adds to its luster in some small way. John Berger, in his clever book on painting *Ways of Seeing,* writes, "We are accused of being obsessed by property. The truth is the other way around. It is the society and culture in question which is so obsessed." Sadly, Berger may be right. It is not the Kardashians and their sometimes trivial products that are the problem, but society's obsession with them and their products.

See also: Keeping Up with the Kardashians; Khloé and Lamar

Further Reading

John Berger, *Ways of Seeing,* 1990; David S. Escoffery, *How Real Is Reality TV?*; Maria Pramaggiore and Diane Negra, "Keeping Up with the Aspirations: Commercial Family Values and the Kardashian Brand"; Eric Wilson, "Kim Kardashian, Inc.," *New York Times,* November 17, 2010.

LAGUNA BEACH: THE REAL ORANGE COUNTY

MTV's *Laguna Beach: The Real Orange County* was an early MTV reality show supposedly following real teens in their quest for riches, success, and fame in the complicated and crowded environment of Laguna Beach, California. It helps that they are all young, white, attractive, connected, possess attractive abodes, have fashionable jobs, and are firmly positioned for success. The program aired on MTV from 2004 to 2006 and was related to *The Hills* and other shows featuring affluent, white, attractive teens dealing with burgeoning adult issues (life, jobs, living conditions, school, family, boyfriends, etc.). Here the focus was high schoolers at Laguna Beach High School and proposed a documentary look at the ins and outs of high school life. What was created was less an anthropological portrayal of American teens and more a soap opera of teen problems, not unlike *Buffy the Vampire Slayer* minus the vampires.

The principle star was Lauren Conrad, a senior at the high school, and she served as the guide, chaperone, and entre to the world of the high school and its denizens. As the seasons progressed, a senior class was replaced by the previous year's junior class, and viewers watched the classes (and issues) come and go as they approached their last year of high school.

The show was a typical MTV reality product, long on scripted and contrived scenes and situations and little that resembled the hardscrabble life of true high school students. These kids were all beautiful, perfect, intelligent, and well-supported by homes and families that already had them outdistancing over 90 percent of American high school youth. Most kids should be so lucky.

MTV had problems producing the show after the Janet Jackson wardrobe malfunction at the Super Bowl. That was likely a staged event itself, but it worried the school. If the station could not manage a dance scene for 15 minutes, how effectively could they monitor the school's students? The series began with a narrator/star for that season, starting with a narration overview that set the stage and tone for the episode. Most episodes concluded with a similar voice-over, putting the show and its lesson in perspective. Most of the first season revolved around Lauren Conrad's and Kristin Cavallari's interest in boy/toy Stephen Colletti. Several important steps were marked by the show. The women were in charge. Both initiated relationships, and both were manipulating events. The story of the boys and their interests were peripheral, if there at all. This was a show for girls about girls and their fate, and in a sense this marked the show as a third-stage feminist show. Men here shared what used to be more the female role in male-dominated films, basically, a moving prop.

Many organizations disdained the show. The Parents Television Council said the mix of tough language and sexual content made the show bad for the age group it was intended to reach. In essence, they found it too real. Local groups said the show championed Laguna Beach as a great place to live and own a business, while others thought it glamorized teen partying, drinking, and violent behavior. Many people saw Laguna Beach as a sleepy artist colony along the beach, and many blamed MTV for transforming it into a Hollywood-style teen hangout.

Many critiqued the show for using scripted dialogue and even performers on the show said they were manipulated by the producers to fabricate conflicts. A further accusation was that the show was merely a pseudo-reality version of a popular teen soap opera. Dana Heller writes in her article "Wrecked" that "a dominant trend in television programming in which scripted shows spawn reality-based shows—for example Fox's *Beverly Hills 90210* and MTV's *Laguna Beach*" (2014). That is, instead of paying for a property, MTV merely copied something popular and put a reality tag on it, thus avoiding costs and supposedly providing something genuine and original.

MTV wasn't sure it had captured the high school experience and retooled the show as *Newport Harbor: The Real Orange County*, which also failed to impress and was quickly cancelled.

Reviewing the individual shows, the big problem with *Laguna Beach* was that it played like a bad 1980s Brat Pack feature where being popular, getting the right boy to ask one to prom, having a cool car, and going to college were the big pursuits. Instead of showing an economically stressed, diverse, individualistic set of young people showing new interests and preoccupations, we were treated to a homogenized more-of-the-same. The girls stood around shopping, asking each other about who might ask them to prom. The scripting was like something a middle-aged woman would write whose last date memory was probably being asked to one of the *Back to the Future* movies.

See also: The Hills; Next

Further Reading

David S. Escoffery, *How Real Is Reality TV?*; Su Holmes and Deborah Jermyn, "The Pig, the Older Woman and the Cat Fight," 2014.

THE LITTLE COUPLE

Even on reality shows, reality sometimes intrudes. When *The Little Couple* premiered on TLC in 2009, newlyweds Bill Klein and Jen Arnold, 4' and 3'2" respectively, knew they would publically share some intimate concerns, notably the quest for a family. But as 30-somethings, the pair probably never dreamed they'd be filming their own life-and-death struggles.

The Little Couple followed on the heels of *Little People, Big World,* which has chronicled the lives of the Roloff family for eight seasons. Amy and Matt Roloff are little people, as is one of their four children. All participated in the family business, a pumpkin farm, that alternated as a seasonal destination and later a wedding venue. The audience watched the children grow up, the business expand, and the marriage dissolve. The can-do attitude exemplified by the parents and the relative normalcy of their lives (messy house, teenage sass, DUI) dispelled any ideas that little people were different.

The Little Couple goes further and shatters stereotypes. Not wrestlers or actors, these two little people are urban professionals. Dr. Jennifer Arnold is a neonatologist; her bedside manner is facilitated by a stool. Husband Bill Klein has been described as a "serial entrepreneur" (hence the reality show?). Klein was chief operating officer for Emerge Sales in New York and the owner of a start-up pet shop in Houston managed by his mother-in-law.

Both Arnold and Klein appear to be intelligent, energetic, generally positive people. Their complementary personalities make the show. Dr. Jen, when not being the consummate professional, would give the energizer bunny a run for his money. She does hula, yoga, and taken a self-defense class. Normal-height women will easily identify with her shopping addiction, although she sometimes must look for clothes in the children's department. In good times and bad times, her hair is done, in a variety of styles. Bill too is active physically, but more laid back in attitude than Jen. His easygoing nature balances Jen's enthusiasm. A typical guy, he's into sports and cars.

The series began with a TLC special that chronicled their wedding. Subsequent episodes revolved around typical new-couple concerns—moving, working, scheduling, and finding housing. Jen's new job was in Houston, so they moved from the northeast, but because Bill's business was in New York, he traveled frequently. His availability and Jen's work schedule did not always coincide. Eventually, they discovered they were not on the same page when it came to where they wanted to live. City or suburbs? Rent? Buy? Build? They do all three, but end up building a custom house that will make their lives easier.

The next quest was the desire for family. Given Jen's stature, there were concerns beyond the couple's fertility. They tried it all. Jen took fertility drugs, had an unsuccessful pregnancy, and employed a surrogate who miscarried. Adoption emerged as the best alternative, and the couple decided to adopt children physically like themselves, whose options may be limited by their culture. They found Will, who, aside from being Chinese, seemed exactly like the child they would have had— verbal, rambunctious, and generally cuddly. Soon, a little girl with skeletal dysplasia became available in India, and they made another trip to adopt Zooey. To their credit, after the adoptions, the couple took a hiatus from reality TV to concentrate on cementing their familial relationships.

Watching their parenting skills develop was instructive. While Will seem to easily bond with both parents, Bill, as a result of Jen's battle with cancer, had to complete the adoption process for Zooey alone. Initially Daddy was not Zooey's favorite person. Viewers later found out she didn't care for Santa either. Stoic Bill realized the bonding could take time and patiently filled the role of good father to little acclaim from Zooey. Eventually, of course, Zooey adapted. Jen seemed to be the activity parent, planning an elaborate tea and birthday parties. Holidays were celebrated to the nth degree. In general the kids assumed traditional gender roles. Jen and Zooey sunned on the beach while Bill and Will went fishing.

In India, when the couple was adopting Zooey, reality set in. Jen was diagnosed with a rare form of cancer, ironically caused by her unviable pregnancy. Surgery, chemotherapy, and wigs became part of the show. Jen recovered and was cancer-free when Bill's chronic back problems made surgery his only option besides a wheelchair. Spinal surgery has inherent risks, and the one Bill feared most was paralysis. The season ended as Jen sat stunned by the events of the past year.

In general, response to the show has been positive among little, medium, and tall people. Sarah Quick, a junior at Texas A&M and an achondroplasia dwarf says that shows like the *Little Couple* "normalize dwarfism for more people" (Wilkins, 2014). On the other hand, the high spirits and accomplishments of this little couple are anything but normal.

Liz Hufford

See also: Little People, Big World

Further Reading

Joan Ablon, *Little People in America: Social Dimensions of Dwarfism*, 1985; Betty Adelson, *The Lives of Dwarfs: Their Journey from Public Curiosity toward Social Liberation*, 2005; Yehuda Koren, *In Our Hearts We Were Giants: The Remarkable Story of the Lilliput Troupe, a Dwarf Family's Survival of the Holocaust*, 2005; Emily Wilkins, "Texas A& M Student Pushing for Respect for Dwarfism Awareness Month," *The Eagle*, 2014.

LITTLE PEOPLE, BIG WORLD (LPBW)

While The Learning Channel can be accused of pandering to popular curiosity about freaks, leading them to be called "the freak channel," TLC has also offered a deeper mission, calling attention to marginalized and underappreciated outliers in our society. While *19 Kids and Counting* could be grouped as a freak show because of some of the Duggars' obscure beliefs and unique ideas about parenting, the series does provide a complicated and compelling insight into the lives of people raising large families. Similarly, *Little People, Big World* has been termed by the IMDB "the most in-depth television documentation of the lives of little people." Despite the judgments people may pass on TLC, the series is a thought-provoking, nonexploitive, serious, and engaging look at people who happen to be small. Watching what the Roloff family endure daily makes viewers more aware of the struggles that other small-stature people endure, and perhaps in some way bring us to understand their project.

LPBW began as a series in 2006 and has continued through 2017. The program focuses on the Roloff family, who run a family farm outside of Portland, Oregon. The parents, Matt and Amy, and one of their sons, Zach, are diagnosed with a medical condition known as dwarfism.

TLC sought out the family in 2005, and Matt and Amy Roloff decided they would cooperate with the show since it was a chance to tell the story of people with dwarfism. They assumed that the public knew little about their condition, and it would bring awareness and understanding about their daily lives. It would also constitute a forum to illustrate how dwarves are similar and different than the rest of us, and in some small way it might help to transform how people see dwarfs.

The show is filled with ironic information that transforms how regular-sized Americans might see little people. For example, Matt and Amy have four children, but only one of them is also a dwarf. That is Zach. He has a fraternal twin brother named Jeremy who is normal sized (6'1"). Two other children, Molly and Jacob, are also normal-sized children.

The drama emerges from watching the family do everyday activities, such as shopping, school, vacationing, and working and the inherent challenges in these simple activities due to the parents' small stature. Matt and Amy are only 4'1", and their son Zach is 4'4". Life can be especially challenging when you are smaller than average. Matt and Amy run a 36-acre pumpkin farm in a suburb of Portland. Matt has designed a series of play stations in their yard. He wishes to give his children a fun and playful childhood, since much of his youth was spent in hospitals dealing with complications from his dwarfism condition.

Matt is a middle-aged computer technician who has been involved in various phases of sales, software, and computer applications. His form of dwarfism is fairly severe. He is somewhat disabled, must walk assisted by canes, uses a motorized chair on occasion, and had complicated surgeries in his childhood due to his dwarfism condition, known as diastrophic dysplasia.

His wife, Amy, though the same size, has a different and relatively more mild form of dwarfism and did not suffer any of the surgeries of setbacks that Matt endured in his youth. Her form of dwarfism is known as achondroplasia. She is athletic and has acted as a soccer coach and a preschool teacher to provide additional income, although she prefers to be a stay-at-home mom when possible.

Zach and Jeremy are both involved with soccer, but Jeremy competes as a normal-sized competitor and Zach has more difficulties competing because of his size. Like his mother, he is diagnosed with achondroplasia, but, unlike his mother, he has had lots of side effects and symptoms. His soccer playing was curtailed temporarily when he had to have an operation to correct his legs, which were bowing and interfering with his mobility and ability to run.

Drama abounds on the show through normal activities. Jacob and a family friend were playing with a family catapult used to launch pumpkins. The device went off, hitting Jacob in the head, and he had to have an operation to put his broken skull back in place. The Roloffs' farm has become an important tourist destination, and now many people flock to see where the tiny family lives. While the show has increased understanding of little people, some are still attracted because they want to see the farm where the "hobbits" live. Of course, the program has received charges of being voyeuristic for the way the family are viewed—shot from downward angles and narratives tend to focus on their differences rather than their similarity to other people. As with *19 Kids and Counting,* courting is an issue on the show, and, when son Jeremy married longtime sweetheart Audrey in 2014, the show produced the series' highest ratings ever, including the highest ratings among female viewers.

Some of the Roloffs of Portland may be small, but their popularity among Americans is huge. However size is no protector against the sudden fame and anxiety that arise due to reality television. Many have mentioned that the rigors of reality filming and work are difficult for people in marriages and relationships. Sadly, Matt and Amy underwent a trial separation in 2014, and *People* magazine reported Amy Roloff saying that after 26 years of marriage, "To tell you the truth, it's like a death. You get numb, you don't know what to do" (2014).

See also: The Little Couple

Further Reading

Sheila Cosgrove Baylis, "Amy Roloff of *Little People Big World* Says Separation Is Like Death," *People*, March 24, 2014.

MOB WIVES

Mob Wives from VH1 suggests an interesting idea: to tell the story of mob wives, girlfriends, and daughters trying to distance themselves from a life of crime and their felonious relatives. The problem is that doing so on television in a deeply public manner might not be the best way to avoid "sleeping with the fishes." The program was conceived by an ex-mob wife and picked up by VH1 and the Weinstein Company (makers of such gangster fair as *Reservoir Dogs* and *Pulp Fiction*) in 2011. The program has run five seasons, 66 episodes, and has a loyal fan following. The concept is derivative of *The Sopranos*, showing the inner workings of a crime family and the moral dilemmas occasioned by these anti-hero protagonists.

Of course, many criticisms can be lodged at the show, including that it shows negative portrayals of New England and New Jersey culture. Jennifer Graziano pitched the idea to VHI, and they liked the idea of a group of women trying to work their way out of the criminal underworld. Graziano is the daughter of a Bonanno family associate. Another cast member, Drita D'Avanzo, has a husband from the Bonanno family; another, Karen Gravano, has connections to the Gambino family; Carla Facciolo is connected to the Gambino family; Angela Raiola has ties to the Genovese family; and Natalie Guercio has connections to the Carto Funeral Home (convenient) and family. The show has guest visits by mob luminaries, such as Victoria Gotti, daughter of John Gotti.

The show is rough territory for some, including people who don't wish to see these women of Staten Island characterized as real New Yorkers. Further, the nearness of violent people and crime families makes the production staff nervous. Many critics have found the show far grittier than the usual *Real Housewives of Atlanta* variety fair. Some of the families of people harmed by family members of the wives are not so kind. They consider the show a validation and glorification of criminal lifestyles.

The women themselves are tough customers. When they talk, they throw around four-letter words and make big threats. Mostly, they are trying to make it away from the criminal world and the men who made them a part of that lifestyle. The opening credits show the women in heavy makeup and seductive dress against a tough, slinky opening number. They lift their wine glasses together and smash them, throwing glasses and wine everywhere. Their logo (*Mob Wives*) and their catch phrase (Trust No One) blaze across the screen.

In one episode, wife Drita D'Avanzo is pushing a line of cosmetics, Lady Boss, that uses her mob-connected status to market lipstick and beauty products. Her new plan is to improve her business by doing a calendar shoot to project the products to more potential clients. The other women squabble about presumed slights and insults and hurl threats at each other. *The New York Times* quoted Howard Abadinsky, author of *Organized Crime* as saying, "To have wives or daughters of organized crime figures appear at all is rather extraordinary, a breakdown in the idea of a secret society" (Billard 2012). These women, by their heroic action of stepping out, discussing the mob lifestyle, getting jobs, and leaving the criminal world, are trying to change things.

A major aspect of the show is that it is not a tell-all. These women are not ratting out their mob husbands or divulging mob secrets. For the most part, this is a show about the lifestyle of the women who have learned to live with gangsters, and they have to learn how to cope without their husbands, fathers, and male family members. In a way, this is more a tale of how these women get along, when they have been left behind for years at a time. Rather than betraying others, it is the women on the show who have been betrayed. If they are belligerent, it is because they have learned to cope with life through belligerence. Like a pack of dogs, when they are together, they bark loudly, not so much because they want to bite, but because they want to keep the other dogs at bay.

See also: America's Most Wanted

Further Reading

Mark Billard, "Silent Partners No Longer," *New York Times*, March 28, 2012; David S. Escoffery, *How Real Is Reality TV?*

MTV CRIBS

MTV Cribs looks like one of the Property Brothers from HGTV took a model McMansion two-story, open floor plan with new steel appliances and granite counters and then redecorated the same site for hundreds of rappers, sports stars, celebs, and rockers. The amazing thing about *MTV Cribs* was how homogenously wealthy, nouveau riche celebrities decorated their homes. They looked nearly the same. About the only difference between Lil Wayne's crib and Ludacris's crib was the color of their Escalades.

MTV Cribs (and later *CMT Cribs*) aired from 2000 to 2011 and featured over 150 celebrity homes and produced a whopping 100 episodes, many featuring multiple celeb pads. Some fun hosts, including Lil Wayne, made a ritual of revealing the contents of the starring guest's fridge. Many of the stars had a remarkable collection of good foods, health drinks, and haute cuisine in their pantries. Most of the houses were nicely decorated, tasteful, and only gave away that a rocker was the owner when the artist displayed gold records, sports trophies, and other memorabilia from their respective profession. Furnishings were elegant and new; the rooms were mostly bright and white. Many had children and most of the celebs doted like any parent, showing off their children's toys, their photos, and their family memorabilia.

Some of the fun episodes described famous homes that many would like to visit. Hugh Hefner's Playboy Mansion (see the *Girls Next Door*) was ornately and comfortably decorated, but it also was the site for the Playboy publishing and media empire and served multiple purposes in positioning the brand and their product. Despite the fact that it was portrayed as a pleasure palace, the truth is, it was a big complex. Of course, the MTV crew noticed panties strewn about the house in lighting and on furniture. Hefner strolled around holding court in an evening jacket. Fighter Manny Pacquiao had a variety of trophy collections and a nice assemblage of fight photos and poses. During the program's 17 seasons, there were many remarkable celebrity homes, including Babyface's antique-decorated mansion. The soulful crooner showed off a 21,000-foot complex with 10 baths and a tennis court. The entire spread had an engineered, decorator-designed layout directly from *Architectural Digest*. Babyface explained where President Clinton had sat, pointed out his Bosendorfer piano, a library, a room for his various Grammies, and a professional kitchen for his professional cook. Babyface offered class all the way and apologized for having junk food. The show derived directly from early television like *Person to Person,* in which Edward R. Murrow would enter the dwellings of the rich and powerful.

The original episodes of *Cribs* were reedited and distributed unsuccessfully for syndication sans music, narrators, and celebrity insights. The syndicated versions missed everything that made the originals so delightful. Wayne Newton's crib was an elegant mansion with Renoirs, other forms of fine art, classic racecars, and a horse farm. One doesn't associate Wayne Newton with cool, but his crib screamed affluence.

A number of controversies erupted over the program. For one thing, the emphasis on expensive housing caused MTV to start focusing on regular teen pads, but, as it turned out, when they went to viewers' homes, they were often treated to private mansions of rich kids. Another controversy was that many people passed off houses that were not their property as their property. Musician Robbie Williams showed off his beautiful home, only to later admit it was a property owned by Jane Seymour that he was just renting. 50 Cent showed three Ferraris featured in his episode of *Cribs* as his. They were not; they were cars loaned to 50 Cent for the episode.

In 2009, CMT took over the idea of a *Cribs* show only showcasing country music royalty, race drivers, and personalities popular in the Southern United States.

See also: The Bachelorette; The Dating Game

Further Reading

David S. Escoffery, *How Real Is Reality TV?*; Julie Gerstein and Adam Ellis, "41 Things Mariah Carey Was Definitely Hiding in Her Bedroom During Her Legendary 'MTV Cribs' Episode," *Buzzfeed*, June 24, 2014.

MY BIG FAT GYPSY WEDDING (AND *MY BIG FAT AMERICAN GYPSY WEDDING*)

My Big Fat Gypsy Wedding (MBFGW) was a series of specials and documentaries that dealt with the lifestyles and activities of Gypsy families in the European community. The earlier shows dealt with Irish Gypsies known as Irish Travellers. Later shows began to feature Romani Gypsies. Romani Gypsies are European Gypsies who have traveled around Europe and originated among the Roma people of Romania. They were Gypsy people, and they were dispersed after the Soviet Union collapsed in 1989 and began to circulate more widely around Europe. In film, the old Gypsy woman is a character in films like *Wolfman*, representing the Roma people. Brad Pitt played an Irish Traveller Gypsy in the popular caper film *Snatch* at the dawn of the millennium.

The channel 4 production of *MBFGW* was produced in 2010, ran 2 seasons, produced 18 episodes (thus far), and has spurred a variety of specials featuring supposed practices of the Gypsy community. Early criticisms of the show complained that the program dwelled in stereotypes, that the only sorts of Gypsies illustrated were Irish Travellers, and that programs presented caricatures of Gypsy people. Critics argued that the show portrayed them laughing endlessly, illustrated them as childlike and highly emotional, suggested that they were feckless and not hardworking, focused on their weddings and social engagements, did not focus on problems of the community, and didn't portray them as a serious ethnic enclave.

A standout for the show was the life and career of Liverpool dressmaker Thelma Madine. Madine was a self-made business woman who herself had had trouble with the law but had survived to create her own popular and creative dress shop. The Gypsies, mostly of Irish descent, came to her shop in Liverpool to get outfitted for their wedding dresses. Madine's creations were a highlight of the show, and the program focused on the outlandish creations and insane dresses that the girls wished for their wedding presentation. In one show, Madine had to make dresses for two Gypsy girls who wanted to resemble a pineapple and palm trees. Another dress required Madine to weave 200 pounds of human hair into a dress. The program was cleverly tied to current events in television culture. The marriage and fancy dresses of Irish Traveller Gypsy Mary was shown in a *MBFGW* special the night before Prince William's marriage to Kate Middleton.

Despite charges that the show misrepresented the Romani and Tish Traveller communities, the program won praise for bringing the stories of these clandestine and often marginalized communities to life. The series was nominated for several awards as a groundbreaking documentary showcasing underrepresented people.

My Big Fat American Gypsy Wedding was a spin-off from the Channel 4 series that aired on American network The Learning Channel. The series has run at least four seasons thus far and produced 32 episodes. Unlike the British series, the American version featured American Romani tribes living in the Middle Atlantic states in the United States. The program focuses on families in this community and again describes the ethnic issues, the persecution, the legal entanglements, and especially the courtship, dating, and wedding rituals of the Romani youth. Many family issues are discussed, and much of the programming illustrates contentious issues among family members. In one special, the Stanley sisters, a group who are often a focus of the series, are upset because a sister, Mellie, has taken a job working in a strip club, something her sisters fear will being shame and dishonor to the family.

See also: The Bachelorette; The Dating Game

Further Reading
"A Pineapple, a Pine Tree and a Cat!" *Daily Mail*, February 14, 2012.

MY SUPER SWEET 16 (MSS16)

My Super Sweet 16 is a celebrity-based or near-celebrity-based reality program from MTV that trumpets girls, fame, and selfhood through the vehicle of a sweet 16 party. In the past, being 16 was usually a time of a young woman's coming out as a dating woman. In previous centuries, a 16-year-old girl of a certain family status would announce that she was available through a party or a gala ball. The concept was courtship and marriage between two people who came from suitable homes. The notion in 19th-century culture was that a marriage between families would be a strategic alliance. Today, that idea has waned, but the notion of a big party for a girl turning 16 to celebrate her maturity and freedom is still fashionable. The notion used to be a subject for the wealthy and the privileged, but today the idea of a celebratory party for 16-year-old girls is gaining strength in all sections of society. MTV's *My Super Sweet Sixteen* was an attempt to lure the MTV demographic—12–24-year-olds—only this time for girls. The program was on MTV's rotation from 2006 to 2008, although new episodes have arrived at the MTV Web site in recent years.

MSS16 has had a resurgence in episodes popping up on MTV's Web site. Mostly featuring rap artists and their families, the series presents the demanding teen girl trumpeting her family and the lengths the family has gone to assure her of the ultimate sweet 16 experience. In one Web-based episode aired on February 2 in 2015, Reginae Carter discussed her father, Lil Wayne, and her *MSS16* party experience. Despite the fact the focus has moved from elite, old-school American families to new rap and pop stars, the demanding nature of the teen girls and their need for the ultimate party remains constant. Carter knew daddy, Lil Wayne, was loaded, and she pulled out all the stops for the most fashionable party she could create. The occasion was the sort of affair catered and brokered by Kleinfelds, the large wedding-dress supplier and party broker that arranges the big wedding celebrations for wealthy New Yorkers.

Reginae had the same sort of starstruck notions that many girls did when they saw the chance for a big party. It would be impressive. It would wow her friends. It would gain her new friends. It would be the social event of the season. Reginae came off as headstrong, like all teenage girls. She and her mother lived in Atlanta, and Reginae tried to talk about planning the party. Her mother suggested the planner who created her wedding in Los Angeles. Reginae wanted someone young and hip and immediately insulted her mother and declined her choice. She wanted to spend half a million on the party and invite hundreds of guests. Her mother vetoed the over-the-top expenses. Reginae told her mother she wanted a nose ring. Her mother knew she had a celebrity brat's child, but she argued that she was a straight-A student and, aside from the brattiness, she was a good-natured and intelligent little girl. Mom planned a party that included performances by Nicki Minaj and a new car.

What MTV provided was the other side of wish fulfillment for female viewers. For little boys, viewing involves watching living in your own place (*Real World*), skateboarding all day (*Rob Dyrdek's Fantasy Factory*), and listening to music and playing games all night. For girls, it is a lavish party with spectacular themes. Sophie Mitchell decided she wanted a *Moulin Rouge*–themed party, and the *New York Times* reported, "There (were) can-can dancers, a fleet of stretch limousines for friends and family and a $1,500 cake" (Ogunnaike 2008). The series articulated the needs of the very rich to be conspicuous with their spending, for the sweet 16 party to be a spectacular on the level of a Hollywood special effects epic. Ana Marie Cox, writing for *Time*, refers to the show as "celebrations of self" (2006), and she adds that such parties prolonged the infantile selfishness of childhood longer. Instead of girls hitting 16 and starting to grow up, such affairs keep them focused on the wonder of themselves.

The show was divisive. Lots of wealthy people wanted to celebrate their children and did so by having a lavish party where wild spending was encouraged. However, critics argue that such displays send a message that wealth thinks differently than the rest of the country and only wishes to celebrate itself. The hell with the poor. Or as one prominent cardiologist hosting a party for his 16-year-old daughter said, "It's the American way. You work hard and you play hard" (Ogunnaike, 2006). Perhaps, but what does MTV say to the millions of little girls out there who don't have anyone to give them a lavish party, don't have Kanye West singing at their gala, and lack a new car at the end of their special night?

See also: The Bachelorette; The Dating Game

Further Reading

Lola Ogunnaike, "MTV's 'Super Sweet 16' Gives a Sour Pleasure," *New York Times*, April 26, 2008.

19 KIDS AND COUNTING

One aspect of reality programming that is often underrated is the process of normalizing what might be construed as abnormal behavior. Such a show is *19 Kids and Counting*. The program looks at the complex workings of the family Duggar, who have 19 kids and are open to more. This seemingly, well-adjusted tribe, clan, town(?) appear to be a nice family *but* (and it's a big but) have a *lot* of kids. There are accusations that the show is not real or a stunt, but this may be a rare case of the truth being stranger than fiction. The Duggars were married in 1984 and practiced birth control to prevent unwanted pregnancies early in their marriage. However, after the birth of their first son, Josh, all hell broke loose in the business of birthing. The Duggars have had nearly yearly visits from the stork thereafter, and even their television series—*17 Kids and Counting, 18 Kids and Counting*—has had to work hard to keep up with the exponential growth of the family.

In recent years TLC has veered markedly from their "learning" label, unless you consider shows in which oddities of society are considered. Lately, their stock-in-trade had been either freakish behavior, odd physical abnormalities, medical conditions, and groups that could be considered outliers. The *19 Kids and Counting* show is a staple of TLC's oddities series (which features programs like *Little People, Big World; Sister Wives; Breaking Amish; My Six-Hundred Pound Life*, etc.) and has thus far produced nine seasons, filmed over 200 episodes and features a roster of activities that produce an attempt to show the unusually large family as a typical family that is larger in quantity. Common themes emerge, such as taking a group of family members to help at the family's church or taking the kids to the amusement park or a pretzel factory. The program seems content to barter tie-ins to supplement the family's income and to trade their notoriety as a productive family for product endorsements.

The Duggars have so many children because they are devout Independent Baptists and do little to forestall continual pregnancies. Their friendly but controversial view is that that this is what God wants. They make no defense of their breeding practices and believe that such decisions are left to a higher power. They practice modest dress, curtail their children from viewing harsh media, and seem to practice close parental control. Due to the massive numbers of their family, they practice child-on-child supervision, where an older child looks after a younger child. Their children practice chaperoned courtship, where there is no physical contact between daters, and the boys must ask the father's permission to date a daughter.

The program raises genuine questions about separation of church and state, as Jim Bob Duggar is a politician and served as a congressman in Arkansas. Due to deeply disturbing statements the couple made regarding gay people, the group Change.org launched a petition to have the show cancelled. *The Huffington Post's* Cavan Sieczkowski described the Duggars as "hav(ing) been using their fame to promote discrimination, hate, and fear mongering against gays and trans-gendered people" (2014). One can understand gay people feeling threatened by anti-gay statements, but it seems a little strange that any group should try to cancel another group's program because it disagrees with their philosophy. It is clear that the Duggars are conservative, and likely hold conservative views, but it is also likely that conservatives are a basic market for such a group, and the family's views are probably shared by their constituency. There is little clandestine in such viewpoints, and the family acknowledges that their own peculiar brand of fundamentalism may not be widely shared across the spectrum of American society. What Change.org and others might logically object to is that the Duggars promote their individual, decidedly unique view of the world as the norm. This is also probably not the case.

The London *Daily Mail's* David McCormack reported that "Michelle Duggar, matriarch of the conservative Christian stars of TLC's *19 Kids and Counting,* has an older sister who is a lesbian with a long-term partner who says she worries about the reality star's chosen lifestyle" (2015). Apparently, Michelle's older sister, Evelyn Ruark, is concerned that the Quiverfull Movement, which Michelle Duggar adheres to, preaches lots of births for mums and no birth control. Ruark and her partner have expressed fear the group is a cult that controls women and endangers them. There is further proof that the Duggars aren't perfect, don't claim to be, and don't care who knows it. They wear their prejudices on their sleeve. Earlier in 2015, their adult daughter Jill, a midwife, wished to aid family friend Susanna

Keller with her pregnancy, but she had refused to marry the father of the child. She wanted the baby by herself without the father. Most people would consider that a brave decision. The family refused to allow Jill Duggar to help, and Susanna hasn't been allowed even to visit on the show, even though she is an in-law, the younger sister of Josh Duggar's (the eldest Duggar son) wife, Anna. (Are you confused yet? I am!) The *Daily Mail's* David McCormick wrote, "All that changed in 2012 when she (Susanna Keller) became pregnant with daughter Noelle. Patriarch Jim Bob felt that 'Keller's slide into sin' warranted cutting off all contact and striking even the mention of Susanna's name from the family's show" (2015). Ouch. Jim Bob went on to explain that the girl would harm the Duggar family brand. Double ouch. So much for Christian charity and compassion.

The Duggars seem to be living their life in front of the public, warts and all, and they seem somewhat oblivious to public judgment as people of faith are often liable to do. There is a disturbing trend in American culture to desire to judge or blame people. The Duggars in their commonness and their unabashed celebration of their communal lifestyle (little different than *Honey Boo Boo*) somehow annoy some viewers and challenge perceptions of normalcy. In Helen Wood and Beverley Skeggs's *Reality Television and Class* text, the authors frame the way reality TV and people are viewed, saying, "First, there are many popular critical commentaries in which reality television as 'trash' inscribes a set of assumptions about participants and viewers based upon hierarchies of culture" (2011). That is why we as viewers tend to associate people on such shows with hierarchies of class. It is comforting to look down or look up to people who appear on television as either august role models or uncontrollable freaks. Undoubtedly, no matter what the Duggars do or say, they will be judged right or wrong by the left and the right. Still, the program holds a strong attraction for family groups and constitutes a continual source of curiosity for people who want to know what it's like to try to raise a family of 19 kids.

See also: Kate Plus 8; The Little Couple

Further Reading

David McCormick, "How the Duggars Banned Their Midwife Daughter Jill from Helping Relative Because She Was Not Married When She Got Pregnant," *Daily Mail*, January 27, 2015; Cavan Sieczkowski, "Thousands Sign Petition to Cancel TLC's *19 Kids and Counting* Over Stars' Anti-LGBT Sentiments," *Huffington Post*, November 19, 2014; Helen Wood and Beverly Skaggs, eds. *Reality Television and Class*, 2011.

THE OSBOURNES

The Osbournes was a complete surprise as a series and arrived as something not unlike the scripted family comedy dramas of the 1950s and 1960s, such as *The Donna Reed Show, Father Knows Best,* and *The Adventures of Ozzie & Harriet.* The central focus of the series and the star and house manager was materfamilias Sharon Osbourne. It was Sharon, strong, proud, theatrical, loving, and speaking firmly for family values, who glued the show together and kept the family a family unit.

In *The Osbournes*, we did not see the disarray that haunts most portrayals of pop music family units. True, the teenaged Osbourne children, Jack and Kelly, were hyperbolic, spoiled brats who had been wildly indulged since birth, but they were clearly a realistic portrayal of their lifestyle in Los Angeles. Ozzy and Sharon came off as two old fogies. Ozzy shuffled around mostly in an absent daze from one gig to another and one event to another, always the dutiful if slightly unconscious husband and father. Mostly we wondered how Ozzy could have stayed focused long enough to sire children, since for the most part, he wandered through the house aimlessly looking for things and munching in the kitchen.

In an episode revolving around Kelly's 18th birthday and Ozzy's concert in Las Vegas, we saw the brood boarding a personal jet, escorted by various retainers, body guards, personal assistants, and friends. We saw the Ozzman trundling through his typical performance with heavy metal backing band, and we saw Kelly and Jack complaining that they were too shackled by camerapeople and security guards. Jack and his crew decided they wanted to have more fun while in Vegas. Kelly spent the evening dancing, playing at the machines, and grousing to her mother and brother that she is 18 and she can do whatever she wants. She and a friend danced in circles, antagonized other parties in the bar, and almost encouraged a barroom brawl. Sharon did what she could to calm a hyperbolic 18-year-old prima donna (it was not Ozzy's show, it was Kelly's show, at least to Kelly), and even brother Jack had to intervene to keep her from acting out too loudly. By the evening's end, Jack and his friends looked very worn out and sat mindlessly watching *Teletubbies*, which Jack and his droogs found to be stoner-enchanting. The tribe flew back on the private jet, ready for another go-round in the Los Angeles sun.

The show arrived as one of the best-produced and most real appearing of MTV's docudrama reality programs. Osbourne's health seemed extremely compromised after years of drug use, and he spent considerable time under medical care with Sharon leading him from room, to car, and to his appointments, holding him like a crippled old man.

The original series ran from 2002 to 2005 and spawned over 50 episodes. The show was rebooted for VH1 in 2015, and it remains to be seen if the series will retain its earlier sparkle. Ozzy Osbourne has said that he was under the influence of drugs during most of the earlier show, and he would like to show his sober side during this new series.

Some interesting aspects of the show included that the Osbournes' other daughter, Aimee, disliked the show and refused to be filmed for it, or associated with it. When she did appear, her face was obscured, and she reportedly berated her parents for their absurd antics on the program. During the program, one of Kelly and Jack Osbourne's friends lost a mother to cancer. This other child, Robert, was reportedly adopted by the Osbournes, lived with them for a time, and appeared briefly on the program.

Ozzy's song "Crazy Train" was used as the show's theme, but it was reedited and sung in a big band and swing version that totally transformed its meaning in the context of the show, suggesting the family was just one big, crazy environment.

Osbourne cursed like a sailor on the show, and the MTV producers snipped out the offending dialogue, but it did permeate the show. Charges that the show was staged might have been true, but the show looked better than most of the plodding reality fair where unskilled actors were given wooden lines to read. One might assume if it was scripted and staged, that the Osbournes paid for better-quality scripts, because the dialogue at times sounded more dramatic. Further, the show had some quality editing, and the family, dealing with Ozzy's addictions and Sharon's bout with cancer, and the kids acting out served a real punch.

Despite accusations against the show, it scored the highest ratings up until that point in MTV history, and it won an Emmy for the best reality program in 2002, which perhaps was a dubious distinction. Several DVD collections and CDs of the show's music have been released.

See also: Keeping Up with the Kardashians

Further Reading

Leigh Edwards, *The Triumph of Reality TV*, 2013; David S. Escoffery, *How Real Is Reality Television?*

PUNK'D

Taking a cue from *Candid Camera*, *Punk'd* is a slang term meaning "you have been had," and has even a more vile meaning sexually. The pedigree of the show is from Hollywood performer Ashton Kutcher and his friend Jason Goldberg. Kutcher was the host of the program. The initial incarnation aired from 2003 to 2007, and the show returned in 2012, briefly.

The program had a rocky start. Kutcher staged a prank in Las Vegas involving a supposed dead body at a hotel. The victims of the prank were regular people, and they were mad to be so misused and sued the performer and production company for $10 million. Ouch. The program was retooled to focus on celebrity guests, to prank them instead. The logic was that since celebrities made their money from being in the public eye, it was unlikely they would sue or want to sue. Plus, the publicity from being the unwitting victim of a prank would continue to project them into the limelight, and they would be advanced by the free publicity. Everyone wins, and no one gets sued.

An early prank was a scheme to make Justin Timberlake think federal officials were in town to take his property for tax evasion. Yuck, yuck! A favorite segment was sending incompetent reporters or fake reporters to a public red carpet event to ask embarrassing questions of celebrities. This trick was revamped using child reporters and foreign reporters using translators to ask absurd or stupid questions. Many have commented that such practices seemed to derive their humor by introducing strands of racism into the show.

The show was revived in 2010 with celebrity hosts including Justin Bieber. *Vulture.com*'s Josef Adailan remarked, "The thinking was that the show, whose pranks had grown lamer as the years wore on (the final season included punks on Jewel and Freddy Rodriguez), needed time to rest" (2010). The idea of prank shows, though popular during the early days of television, is strangely popular to young audiences. It may be in a society in which so much is staged and contrived that prank videos show the rarest of reactions, a genuine moment of surprise.

See also: The Bachelorette; The Dating Game

Further Reading

Joseph Adailan, "MTV Bringing Back Punk'd with Host Justin Bieber," Vulture.com, October 5, 2010; David S. Escoffery, *How Real Is Reality Television?*

THE RACHEL ZOE PROJECT

Rachel Zoe is an effective entrepreneur and fashion stylist who has worked with a legion of celebrities. Due to her persistence and good management, she has had a lengthy 20-year career in the turbulent fashion industry and has prompted many new trends in the fashion world. Her work and celebrity status are certainly crafted on a media agenda and a strong work ethic, but Zoe appears to be an aberration in reality programming, in that she possesses actual talents in business and the fashion sector. Her program, *The Rachel Zoe Project*, was a serious enterprise that began in 2008 and was managed by her husband, Rodger Berman. Alongside her business endeavors, Zoe has had time to raise two sons.

Zoe arrived in New York in the 1990s and quickly shaped a career as a fashion consultant, working with an exclusive set of industry publications and fashionistas, including Miley Cyrus, Jennifer Lawrence, Jennifer Garner, and Pauly Shore. Her friendship with Nicole Richie led to the creation of a house style that is still emblematic of Zoe's projects. Zoe and Richie crafted what is known as the boho-chic look, which is a combination of cheap, big, oversized, and often tacky jewelry and dresses that accentuate the thin fit frame of the models and actors that conform to the style. Films like *American Hustle* that catalogue the fashion blues of the 1970s wallow in Zoe's wacky and successful style ideas. The combination of trashy wardrobe and extremely attractive models works, and Zoe has said, "Being a stylist is a lot like being a parent, you need to be patient. You need to step back and understand what's being communicated—whether you're dealing with a celebrity, a private client or a child" (2009). Clearly, Zoe is listening and produces interesting fashions and unique takes on our cultural turns.

Zoe worked as a fashion editor, learning along the way, despite the fact that she had little formal training in the fashion business. Her freelance work allowed her to interact with celebrity clients and allowed a wide range of collaborations.

Collaboration is what Zoe excels at, and she quickly learned that an idea or product line with just her name was vulnerable, but partnered with a powerful ally was a better shot at success. She has worked with accessory-maker Judith Leiber, fashioning bags, Samsung's cell phones, Gap's shoe and bag online presence, books, style guides, a style line from Lindex, luxe promotions with QVC, a line of salons, and, of course, her reality program.

Her Bravo program, *The Rachel Zoe Project,* aired from 2008 to 2013 and dealt with Zoe's constant struggles to move her product line and balance her home and business life. A fun part of the show was watching assistant Brad Goreski insinuate himself into Rachel's business, then exit and get his own show. Zoe set tasks for herself, like outfitting actress Debra Messing for the Golden Globes or attending New York's Fashion Week, looking at collections with Donna Karan, Michael Kors, Oscar de la Renta, and Karl Lagerfeld. Through the first season, turmoil was spread as assistants Taylor Jacobson and Brad Goreski sparred for position with the boss. Zoe had recurring bouts of vertigo from the stress and eventually fired Taylor. Amid all the turmoil, there was the backdrop of the fashion industry, show openings, and Zoe launching her own fashion line.

Zoe was a relentless worker and described her typical day as up at 6:00 a.m., reading *Women's Wear Daily* and checking out lookbooks (briefs of current fashion lines) to determine what would work best for her A-list clients. The morning continued with conference calls about her product line, editing fashion shoot footage, and dressing for a day on the run. She grabbed a quick lunch and a consult with a client about looks for the next month. Zoe and the client picked through 40–50 outfits to find the right 15 pieces for any press events during the next month. In the afternoon she hit vintage shops, filmed a bit of her show, and reviewed client looks pulled in her studio. She planned for the evening, dressed for an event, usually pulled something at random, usually vintage, and then ate with her husband. She was in bed by 11:00, with her phone at her side.

Besides the television program, Zoe issues a daily newsletter, *The Zoe Report.* Her clothing line is available worldwide and is growing. Perhaps the main criticism of the show and its shopping aesthetic was what Jennifer Pozner writes, "While shows like *The Rachel Zoe Project* and *WNTW* have been instructing us to model ourselves after 'how the rich shop,' Americans are drowning in credit card debt" (2010). Pozner sees a disconnect between the show's rhetoric and the reality of what people do.

See also: Queer Eye for the Straight Guy; What Not to Wear

Further Reading

Jennifer L. Pozner, *Reality Bites Back,* 2010; Adam Tschorn, "Rachel Zoe Talks Motherhood, Psychology and Styling John Wayne," *Los Angeles Times,* April 12, 2014; Rachel Zoe, "A Day in the Life of Rachel Zoe," *Los Angeles Confidential,* September 1, 2009.

REAL PEOPLE

Real People was a popular and early reality program that aired on NBC from 1979 to 1984 and subscribed to the *Ripley's Believe It or Not* theory that real-life experiences of people, their jobs, and their peculiarities were stranger than fiction. The program was a rare hit for NBC in the early 1980s, when the network's entertainment programming was briefly faltering, and it was one of their top-rated programs.

In that time period, writers' strikes had begun to plague the networks, and, since the writers were requesting more money and holding the networks and their programming hostage, the producers were looking for alternative ways to produce entertainment programming. Reality programming based on a documentary style of filming and featuring real people in unscripted formats offered a low-cost and stopgap solution until strikes and labor relations could be resolved. No one suspected that soon reality programming would evolve into a genre of its own, with its own variety of shows, stars, and formats.

In *Real People*, there were regular segments hosted like a *60 Minutes* news program, giving insights into people with odd careers, strange hobbies, or unusual lifestyles. When stations were seeking reality formats in this early period, *Real People* often appeared as the reality/news/documentary-style leader. Hosts included Fred Willard and Sarah Purcell. Segments would include odd headlines or funny pictures to indicate the type of story to potential audiences.

The cast and crew would travel the United States looking for cute, unusual, or bizarre people who could do unusual things. The show featured graphics like *Love, American Style* that offered images of supposedly real Americans in real jobs, flocks of people running in a group race, images of the flag, stars and stripes, and clips of upcoming segments for each episode. The emphasis was on curious or unusual people, and often there was an attempt at alliterative titles or titles that were scatological or pruriently suggestive. In one episode, there was a tale about women watching male strippers, a man who played music with his teeth, a group who snow skied on a single pair of skis, and a group of people who drank "piddle water." Host Sarah Purcell explored an old American railroad trip, and host John Barbour went hoboing with a professional hobo. Other hosts included Skip Stephenson and Byron Allen.

The show began like a less-formal *60 Minutes,* introducing the cast and the segments. Then there was a staged chat with an audience member as an icebreaker, making people think the cast were just *real people*, just like the loud and appreciative studio audience, who were constantly featured and surveyed.

There was a natural fun that the people and the hosts had in self-presentation. The program valorized self-presentation, and sharing with the studio and home audience was seen as communing with that group. Today, reality stars seem keenly aware of the pressure and the anxiety of the performance; however, the people on this show seemed gracefully unaware of the contrived pressure of the program. Clearly, this was an illusion of ease and grace created by the television studio, the training the performers and hosts possessed, and the writing and the direction of the show, but it gave an effortless and buoyant sense of reality that 30 years later appears as quite natural. Today's reality stars seem primed and tense by comparison. Neal Gabler writes about the way people present themselves in real life as a sort of life show in his text *Life: The Movie*, saying, "Though the personal lives (life pictures) were no less, and possibly even more, influenced by the movies than the public celebrity lives, they had actually been in performance long before the movies arrived, in fact since people first became aware of the power and pleasure of self-presentation and perhaps even before then" (1998). Gabler explores the phenomenon of self-presentation and how people presented the self prior to television and documentary forms of filming. To Gabler and others, television only accelerated the practice of self-presentation. Today, mediated technologies like YouTube allow people to share their lives in events like flash mobs, where a common activity can be enacted by a group of strangers through the use of a simultaneous network connection.

After the teaser, the hosts arrived and jaunted up to the stage. The hosts bantered with the audience, again seeking to achieve rapport. The jokes were usually banal and clearly scripted, but both audience and cast members endured the canned lines with good grace. One guy told Sarah Purcell, "I hear the oil companies are selling glue." Purcell responded, "Oh yeah?" The guy chirped, "Yeah, Sarah, so it's easier to stick it to us." The topical humor about gas prices received a big laugh.

Eventually, the hosts moved to the actual segments. However, the notion that the cast had to set the stage by revealing themselves as real people was significant to the production and reception of the show. The producers realized that it was instrumental to the program's reception that the hosts were seen as genuine to increase the reception of the segments as unscripted and real. In a sense, the program was clearly selling a vision of reality and what that meant to audiences in that era. The hosts exchanged a few lines to set up the segment, and then a big-screen television opened up to reveal a scene. In one segment, Purcell reported on two guys who skied in tandem and practiced navigating the slopes of Purgatory as a team on one pair of skis. They were trying to convince others that two people skiing on one set of skis was the future. There was even a segment of women on their backs, making a set of four people on two skis. Finally the daredevils tried a run off of Purgatory's famous Purgatory Point, and the two leapt the 125-foot jump and successfully landed without crashing. The combination of an odd avocation, team skiing, and daredevil stunts made the show a pleasurable mix of oddities and thrills.

Gabler gives us a sociological insight into why we like entertainment like this. He writes:

> An obscure Russian playwright of the early twentieth century, named Nicolas Evreinoff who was a pioneering theorist in the interplay between reality and imagination, believed theatricality was an "instinct" and called it a fundament of life, just as Johan Huizinga in Homo Ludens had called play one of the essentials of human existence—that is, an instinct to entertain as well as be entertained. (1998)

Gabler's view is that self-presentation or a type of acting is natural to us and that all people have a propensity for self-staging a view of themselves. Whatever prompted NBC to it, *Real People* illustrated an audience for the common and unusual in American life that prompted a new sort of television experience.

See also: America's Funniest Home Videos

Further Reading

David S. Escoffery, *How Real Is Reality TV?*; Neal Gabler, *Life: The Movie*, 2000; Jennifer L. Pozner, *Reality Bites Back*.

REAL WORLD AND *ROAD RULES*

Real World has an impressive lineage and really paved the way for MTV's entry into reality television. The show was and is universally panned as a convergence of a group of ill-tempered, privileged brats meeting in a rented mansion to wreak psychological havoc on a willing/unwilling series of like-minded abominations and to then whine and complain into the camera until another hard-pressed, luckless, pathetic rich kid wannabe throws a shoe at the whiner and invites the obligatory brawl, meltdown, group hug, or wayward pass that usually ends in embarrassment or disaster—preferably both. A perception of *Road Rules* is somewhat more charitable. *Road Rules* has been credited with revealing the thought processes and opinions of a generation, and the show has also been praised for its realistic and non-Hollywood, sanitized version of how young people, particularly the grunge generation and millennials, really are. The viewpoints and ways of dealing with life, media, and other people do reflect different views and methodologies than we see reflected in youth on television. In many ways, the *Real World* speaks with more honesty regarding the attitudes and perceptions of youth. Both descriptions of the program can be argued with equal effectiveness, but whether people like the *Real World* or denigrate it as a program of whining teens, the program is viewed by millions of MTV viewers.

Despite *Real World*'s mandate to hold a mirror up to the pressures of adult life (albeit adult life served in a palatial palace, surrounded by attractive, youthful, and corn-fed adversaries/friends with nothing but time to air one's dreams), the program does shine a microscope on the pressures and the challenges of teen life in hypercritical, hyper-self-analytical, microscopic California hip culture. Virtually none of the overnight-famous attractions of this program ever surface again. Unlike *American Idol*, where a game show contestant may actually rise to semi-star status for a moment or two, the contestants on *Real World* ingloriously serve their time in the sun, agonizing over serving their time in the sun. They are ravished, diminished, and debauched by their fame, but not each in the same measure. Many from the show become reality show castoffs, but many do return to play in *Road Rules* and former contestant reunions and matchups.

In one amusing season, (*Real World* has been an MTV staple for 32 seasons at last count, starting in 1992) Irishman Dominic describes his mission to survive the month of *Real World*. One isn't sure if the contestants on the show feel they are being tested and goaded by challenges, or if the real challenge is having the fortitude to put up with other people for a month. The fact that the teams have so little tolerance for each other suggests they are suffering from adolescent angst over being labeled, classified, and determined by their captors.

The show bears some resemblance to its psychological parent, PBS's 1973 remarkable sociological documentary *An American Family,* which purported to show the inner workings of an average American family (conveniently located in one of the wealthiest enclaves in the nation, Santa Barbara). What the show and later reality faire seemed to thrive on was the melodramatic meltdown of the participants as the surveillance and close scrutiny made all micro-aware of their every glitch and twitch. MTV perceived the program as an inexpensive, documentary-style, insightful vision of teen life observed up close under arbitrary settings. The plan was to do very little and allow the residents to interact, leading to explosions, disagreements, and natural conflict that might appear between roommates. Of course, MTV provided some goads and prompted some disagreements to stimulate rancor and discord. Accusations that the show is totally, or at least partially, scripted production has long been in the air.

The program holds many distinctions, including existing as one of the longest reality shows on air, the longest-lasting show on MTV, and a show credited with bringing many adolescent issues to light. Some not so charitable toward its vision of teen trauma would argue that it's a four-week wallow in teen self-wretchedness and bathos.

See also: Jackass; Ridiculousness; Survivor

Further Reading

Alicia Jessop, "Rob Dyrdek Expands Entrepreneurial Reach to Present Winning the Largest Winning Purse in Skateboarding History," *Forbes,* August 24, 2012; "Rob Dyrdek Gets Renewals, Pilot in MTV Deal, *Fantasy Factory, Ridiculousness* Renewed for 7th Seasons," *Adweek,* June 25, 2014.

RIDICULOUSNESS

Ridiculousness is another product from MTV moneymaker, entrepreneur, and sometime-skateboarder Rob Dyrdek. Dyrdek has built an empire around his skateboarding products, his reality television personality, and his entrepreneurial skill. He promotes the slacker, cool-dude façade to the MTV audience, wearing his personalized hat, T-shirt, and skateboard lines and promoting the extreme sports activities that propel him and keep him engaged. Dyrdek in *Ridiculousness* provides another show that promotes the MTV ethos of a couple of friends kicking back and having a good time, when, in fact, the show is a crafty promotion of typically free MTV videos (chosen from the Web) and shares the aesthetic of a couple of pals watching gross and dumb videos together on YouTube. Only in this venue, it is Dyrdek who is guiding the show.

Ridiculousness is now in its seventh season and shows no signs of slowing down. In essence the show is a steal of *America's Funniest Home Videos,* only MTV doesn't send a check to the Japanese company that thought of the idea, and, instead of simply appealing to the home audience, MTV adds the benefit of a studio team of pals (Chanel West Coast and Sterling Brim). The studio crowd does seem to enjoy watching the poor, unfortunate daredevils lose their cool when a stunt starts to spiral out of control. Despite the sense that what they are seeing is new and original, the stunts mirror the sorts of hairball goofiness that characterized *Jackass's* extreme sports team. Dyrdek is a great spokesman because he has been a risk-taker and a skateboarder most of his life. The audience and fans know that while he might laugh at another boarder blowing a stunt, Dyrdek's laughter is more ironic than condemning. He has been there himself and endured his own share of wipeout stunts.

An odd twist, unlike *Jackass*, which received strong criticism for encouraging dumb stunts from student viewers, *Ridiculousness* refuses to accept videos from viewers. The station won't even touch them. They say that this is because they don't want to encourage dangerous, irresponsible behavior. When has that ever stopped MTV? So to show they hold the ethical high ground, they take viral videos already submitted someplace else on the Web and show them. Fearing that the station will be sued over someone performing a stunt for the show, the station now has no liability for any of the stupid things people do. Instead, they steal the stupid things people do from other outlets, and they make revenue off this free programming while accepting none of the blame or responsibility for encouraging it. It's always good to know MTV is looking out for our best interests.

The programs themselves are a series of disastrous stunt clips, often endlessly repeated to the delight of the studio sidekicks and Dyrdek's wacky asides. Dyrdek and crew categorize the less-than-illustrious video performances by categories, like "redneck good time," "worst-case scenario," and, for juniors, "ridiculousness in training." The set appears to be the inside of a computer, with Rob mounted on a keyboard about to click the next video on or off. The audience can chime in, and Dyrdek seems to feed off the audience's responses to the on-air disasters as luckless videographers try to copy something they have seen on television or in movies and often fail savagely. Head dives into doo-doo and other gross-outs seem to be big audience favorites. The fact that the audience is participating and sharing makes the studio audience think these must be fun, because the studio audience seems to be enjoying the mayhem.

Dyrdek told *The Huffington Post's* Crystal Bell, "The show is made the same way you and your friends would all sit around and watch this stuff and what would pop into your head" (2011). Indeed the viewers seem to want to have the experience of sitting around and watching videos with friends.

See also: America's Funniest Home Videos; Rob and Big; Rob Dyrdek's Fantasy Factory

Further Reading
Crystal Bell, "Rob Dyrdek Interview," *Huffington Post*, August 22, 2011.

ROB AND BIG

This biography/extreme sports program features Rob Dyrdek, an MTV host and skateboarding celebrity, and his friend and bodyguard Big Black experiencing life as skateboarding extreme-sports celebrities. The show aired on the MTV network from 2006 to 2008 and explored extreme sports, stunts, animal tricks, and teen activities. The theme is Harry Nilsson's "Best Friend," a tune originally recorded for the television program *The Courtship of Eddie's Father.*

In one episode, Rob plummeted from a second-story loft onto a couch, a crazy stunt that seemed indicative of his daredevil personality. The duo seemed to be a madcap, fun-loving team who were addicted to finding strange pursuits. The show sounded scripted, but the two leads were charming and appeared to be having fun, so one easily bought their desire for goofy adventures. Dyrdek is a professional skateboarder, so he is no stranger to risk and daredevil events.

The shows focused around oddball trips that usually had to do with some extreme sports or pet event. They bought a tiny horse as a pet, they entered the horse, Mini, in a tiny horse show. They taught a dog to skateboard; they journeyed up the Californian coast to break a Guinness World Record; they solved mysteries (some unknown party left Dyrdek a gift?), and had a birthday party for their dog, Meaty.

Sometimes the smartasses got in trouble, like when they hassled a lady pulling out of her parking area under the duo's condo complex. Rob and Big talked the lady out of her angry tirade and gave her a T-shirt. On another occasion, the practical jokers were playing dodgeball in a sports complex and really bonking people ferociously. Their gal pal Chanel, a cute blonde Los Angeles coed, was having fun until a couple of stray kicks walloped her in the head and shoulder. She left the basketball court crying, and the boys were ultimately mortified at having struck a girl.

Dyrdek is quite a business phenomenon. He has an antiauthoritarian personality, and an anything-goes spirit, but he has picked up business acumen along the way. He has made many mistakes in his multimillion-dollar street-skating career, but he follows his gut instincts, and usually his legion of fans follows him as well. Early in his career he self-financed the skateboarding film *Street Dreams.* His error cost him millions, but he had the knowledge that he had failed on his own merits and through his own choices. Hannah Bailey writes in an interview, "For every failure, this serial entrepreneur has had countless successes as a businessman"(Bailey, 2015).

For all the goofiness of the show, there seemed to be a real camaraderie between Big Black and Rob. Rob bounced his sometimes-goofy ideas off Big Black, and on occasion, he rejected an idea as actually too strange or dangerous. In a season three episode, Dyrdek decided it would be cool to wrap a 20-foot python around his body. Black told him it was a bad idea. He did it anyway. For Dyrdek, it was about going the extra mile and giving an audience that thrill of doing something unreal and outrageous. It was really Dyrdek becoming a doppelganger for the audience. He stood in for all the wannabes viewing who wished they had the guts to balance a huge snake on their backs. When Dyrdek got home, he found a dead rat in the trough he had for his dog and miniature horse to use for water. A rat-throwing party ensued, and Dyrdek was tossing the rat around his big Los Angeles guy pad. With attractive architecture but a 10-year-old's sense of design, Dyrdek had skateboard and graffiti art decorating all the walls of this multileveled crash pad. One wasn't sure whether this was Dyrdek's real home or simply another MTV fantasy set provided to enhance the idea that teens watching MTV could invent their own environments and didn't have to be ruled by the standards of conventional homes that their families owned. It looked like an environment built for rebellion.

In an episode in which Rob believed his Los Angeles digs were haunted, he turned from his usual charming self to a paranoid character. He showed tapes of himself walking the perimeter of his mansion and, in *Paranormal Activity* fashion, he showed low-quality tapes of himself encountering what he believed were spectral presences. In his case, it could more easily be explained as the ghosts of bad taste. Big Black explained that the ghost was the smell of the bathroom. He called it a doo-doo-related ghost, or a DRG. Dyrdek hired a female ghost identifier wearing tribal dress. She explained to Dyrdek that we are all just energy. Big Black and Dyrdek decided that the rats and bad vibes in the house were there due to a carved wooden statue of a cat. They went to an exorcist for advice. They decided to have a tree cutter chop the offending wooden cat. Dyrdek returned home, found more rats, and was convinced he was being haunted. He took a sledgehammer to the bathroom, and Big Black tried to calm him down. He hired an exterminator and had a new bathroom installed.

The psycho Rob destroying his bathroom seemed absurd, nonrealistic, and scripted, as if teens who would destroy things and then whine were the target audience. Viewers noticed the carefully appointed slob crib that Dyrdek inhabited. Beds were a mess; an energy drink was always within easy reach; he was surrounded by a posse including Big Black continually; his collection of skateboarding gear, a collection of fashion sports hats, and attractive stereo gear was strewn everywhere. At times, we could be watching Dyrdek's real life or a carefully contrived set that played to the values, interests, and desires of a typical, young MTV viewer. Dyrdek's life appeared to resemble a skateboard fanatic's fervent dream of adult autonomy. Imagine a world where you could play endlessly, rise when you pleased, live on energy drinks, skateboard in your own park, live in a big open-floor-plan messy house you never have to clean, have exciting adventures with your friends, and never have a care for financing anything.

Dyrdek exuded a calm, understated, *Lebowski* sort of confidence. Aside from his skateboarding fame, he appeared as a likeable buddy kind of character, just the sort of person to attract the 12–24-year-old slackers whom MTV sees as its core audience. And unmistakably, MTV loves Dyrdek. His program *Ridiculousness* is the most watched Thursday night series on cable. Besides *Rob and Big*, Dyrdek has developed four programs for MTV, and *AdWeek* wrote that MTV president of programming Susanne Daniels called Dyrdek "an essential part of MTV," and said he "has an undeniable appeal to millennials" (Lefferts 2014). After three seasons Big Black moved on, and Dyrdek reupped with a new MTV series, *Rob Dyrdek's Fantasy Factory*. By this point, he has become an established MTV star and persona for his generation.

See also: Jackass; Ridiculousness; Rob Dyrdek's Fantasy Factory

Further Reading

Daniel Lefferts, "Rob Dyrdek Gets Renewals, Pilot in MTV Deal: *Fantasy Factory, Ridiculousness* Renewed for 7th Seasons," *Ad Week,* June 25, 2014.

ROB DYRDEK'S FANTASY FACTORY

Rob Dyrdek, skateboarder, MTV program guru, extreme-sports enthusiast, and million-dollar entrepreneur, uses his brand to spread an image of carefree, harmless fun and extreme-sports and crazy video madness. His concepts have entertained millions of MTV viewers. *Fantasy Factory* is one of his popular products on the network. The show began airing in 2009 and is currently in its seventh season.

The concept is that the show is a reality depiction of Dyrdek's real life as an entrepreneur and as a skateboarder. The *Fantasy Factory* is Dyrdek's 25,000-square-foot facility for work and pleasure. Inside, he has a full skateboard facility, studio, and office space for his many shows and enterprises. Dyrdek is not the freewheeling homeboy he appears. He is a businessman with a sharp acumen for putting his label on skateboards, shoes, hotels, films, and any enterprise that is profitable.

The *Fantasy Factory* may be a fantasy, but it is an impressive set. In this massive complex, Dyrdek has a corporate headquarters and office for family, business managers, assistants, graphics artists, and lawyers. On the other side, he has built himself an indoor skateboarding cement park with skateboarding ramps, attractive structures, and incredible inclines and traps. It is certainly a fantasy space for skateboarders.

What's fun about the show is watching the mercurial morphing of Dyrdek from skateboarding bad boy to focused, monetary mogul. In the opening episode, Dyrdek lectures his cousin about his dreams of opening a series of Asian fusion restaurants. The next minute he is dirt biking into a mountain of McDonalds Playland balls and shooting baskets while popping off his skateboard and landing in a soft crash area. The show is aptly named because everything in Dyrdek's world appears to be part of his successful fantasy/reality.

What the program explains is that Dyrdek is constantly dreaming of new enterprises and feeding off his regime of frenzied energy and fun activities. For Dyrdek, the skateboarding, racecars, dirt bikes, extreme sports, and dog skateboarding are what keeps his hyperpumped motor running. His highly active lifestyle feeds his creative ideas.

While Dyrdek's need for speed and excitement is fun to watch for a time, it is likely that a lifestyle this frenetic would wear out a lot of people. His business office is located far from him, and his proclivity for throwing things and tossing objects everywhere must be a lot to absorb. One pities his cousin, who must roll with his moods. One minute he is discussing ideas; the next he is in a tanning booth; and later he is shopping in downtown LA. When Dyrdek has friends over, they skateboard in his massive skate park and play basketball on skates.

Dyrdek shows his often-problematic relationship with his corporate people, the group he calls Corpo. At one point he hangs a basketball hoop in front of his lawyer's glass office window. The lawyer complains loudly that the arrangement is unsound and dangerous. Dyrdek seems to take great pleasure in torturing his corporate partners. While it looks like fun on film, either Dyrdek is a dick who is tolerated because of his incredible wealth or the idea of Dyrdek as a rebel is a manufactured construct.

It seems he is far less the rebel and far more the business tycoon from *Forbes's* serious article on Dyrdek. At an early age, as a skateboarder designing and selling skateboards while skateboarding himself, Dyrdek counted the profits and watched what was selling and what was needed. Alicia Jessop spoke with him, and he expounded on his natural inclination toward business, saying, "I started my first company when I was 18 and learned by trial through fire, having no formal education or entrepreneurial experience" (2012). He learned fast.

His best skill seems to be finding programming and product markets in which there is no natural solution and plugging those gaps. He noticed there were fast foods at convenience stores, but not the kind he liked. He debuted a form of burritos for Mexican and American audiences that had different ingredients for the different groups. His first show, *Rob and Black,* focused on his life as an extreme-sports enthusiast and a pranking crazy kid. *Fantasy Factory* merges his persona as a sports enthusiast and maverick with his interest in business and creating his own enterprises. *Forbes's* Jessop discussed this with him, and he explained:

> Anytime an opportunity presents itself, really what I'm trying to do is put an infrastructure around me to creatively operate at a very high level and be able to have the people who can execute the idea. My goal now is making it more scalable, so I can scale my creativity into all these different markets, brands and things in a more effective way. I operate best on big vision and creative detail. (2012)

In this sense, *Rob Dyrdek's Fantasy Factory* differs markedly from many other MTV fantasy shows. While Dyrdek can appear cartoonish, he clearly is focused on twin goals of having a good time and creating good business opportunities. Further, there is a natural simpatico between Dyrdek, a man who is never not selling, and MTV, a station that pioneered the 24-hour advertisement. Dyrdek's shows may appear to be entertainment, and sometimes silly entertainment, but underlying all his products is the presence of Dyrdek and his clever way of featuring himself (using skateboards, clothing, and hats he has designed) skateboarding (in his skateboarding compound barracks that he designed and that advances the agenda that skateboarding is a fun sport that everyone should be doing) and his pursuit of fun by shopping (which urges young followers and consumers to follow his lead). Like MTV itself, which markets lifestyles, dating, music, living environments, relationships, and products, Dyrdek is a continuing windmill of new products and things to buy.

MTV's shows featuring Dyrdek have somehow found a perfect figure upon which to hang rituals and methods and ideologies of consumption. Nick Couldry wrote in his "Teaching Us to Fake It" that ritualization "teaches us to organize our movements around space, helps us to experience constructed features of the environment as real, and thereby reproduces the symbolic authority at stake in the categorizations on which ritual draws" (2009). For all of his "dude" rhetoric, Dyrdek understands the deeper marketing potential of skating on TV and so does MTV. That's why the two are a perfect match.

See also: Jackass; Ridiculousness; Rob and Big

Further Reading

Nick Couldry, "Teaching Us to Fake It," *Reality TV* (Susan Murray and Laurie Ouellette, eds.), New York: New York UP, 2009; Alicia Jessop, "Rob Dyrdek Expands Entrepreneurial Reach to Present Largest Winning Purse in Skateboarding History," *Forbes*, August 24, 2012; Daniel Lefferts, "Rob Dyrdek Gets Renewals, Pilot in MTV Deal: *Fantasy Factory, Ridiculousness* Renewed for 7th Seasons," *Adweek,* June 25, 2014.

SAY YES TO THE DRESS (SYTTD)

Say Yes to the Dress is a show that needs little to make it dramatic. It is a story set in a bridal dress shop where the sometimes anxious, sometimes frantic staff is determined to outfit a series of brides who want their dresses and their marriages to be perfect. If there was ever a situation filled with hormonal-driven anxiety, this situation swims in it. The brides are uptight, fearful, sometimes obnoxious, and definitely edgy. The salespeople are seeking to close big sales in an environment where sales can mean keeping a job and failure to sell can mean unemployment. It is competitive and tense work. The show covers the bridal shop at Kleinfeld's in New York, arguably one of the best bridal boutiques in the nation. The staff of expert dressmakers, fashion consultants, and often, nonce family counselors, work overtime to make sure the young and often privileged brides receive the total bridal experience they are seeking. The staff works hard to make sure the wedding dress is the stunning item these women intend it to be.

In this environment, ritual and tribal bonding go hand in hand as mating, family convergence, and commerce coalesce into a new synergy of anxiety, neuroses, and agony. The program debuted in 2007 and remains a popular ratings winner up to this day, running on The Learning Channel, although some days with its mix of therapy, makeover, and self-help shows it could be translated into The (Women's Self-) Loathing Channel. After 10 seasons, the bridal showdown of wills, body-image fears, overwhelming amounts of friendly and unfriendly advice, and giant heaps of self-doubt take their toll.

We meet the bridal consultants/salespeople, and they are engaged in selling to the most customers and providing each customer with the best dress she can afford. Did we mention affording? If you think divorce is expensive, wait until you see the cost of getting married. The brides at Kleinfeld's can pay anywhere from $1,000 to $40,000—all for one dress for one event to be likely used for one day.

However, the show has a soft and very admirable side. There is a direct synergy and true documentary feel to the juxtaposition of salespeople, the bride, and the family/friends/onlookers. It is as if we are all devouring a spectacle in a Roman arena, and the lions smell fresh blood on the floor. These women are not all self-obsessed, prima donna bridezillas ready to devour anyone who threatens their special day. Most of the women on *SYTTD* are extremely normal (well-off normal) and really pleasant women. The drama erupts for a variety of reasons, but erupt it does, like Vesuvius, on a regular schedule of temper tantrums, self-doubt, expensive complications, and family skeletons.

These women are under the excruciating pressure of one of the biggest decisions of their lives, and they are being documented at a time of great emotional stress. The program should be lauded for portraying the women's backstory. These are not simply wealthy bimbos trying to look good, they are people with real lives and family concerns that project into the wedding/bridal experience. In one episode, a young bride is tortured by the loss of a sister in a car crash. As she searches for the right dress, she is troubled by remembrances of a sister who won't be there to share that special day with her as a bridesmaid. In another segment, a granddaughter raised lovingly with great sacrifices by her middle-class grandparents falls for a $7,000 designer dress. It is hard for the grandparents to tell her the dress may not be possible. Sometimes kind parents and grandparents offer helpful and, unfortunately, sometimes dreadful advice. Like the brides, we witness the good and bad behavior over their wedding traumas.

There is the element of sales and the direct tie-in to women watching TLC.

Viewers may be the prime age and the prime demographic to buy what the show is selling. In one episode, the consultants at Kleinfeld explain the value of "sample-sale madness," where brides can get the dress of their dreams for thousands less. What this presumes is that they are spending thousands in the first place. Jennifer Pozner writes in *Reality Bites Back* that "the sale staff of bridal behemoth Kleinfeld tell *Say Yes to the Dress* viewers that their weddings can only be perfect with this $12k Pnina Tornai ball gown or that $17k J'Aton Couture creation" (2010). It is hard to blame Kleinfeld's for commercializing the bridal industry anymore than one can criminalize Macy's for commercializing Christmas. But there is a problem with the massive costs of the wedding industry, in the same ways there are problems with the costs of life-saving surgery. In either case, a person should not have to lose their entire life's savings on a single, perhaps life-saving, event. When one surveys the Kleinfeld's site, it is indeed an elegant array of products and services, but immediately one is struck by the notion that the industry demands everything from the consumer for the promise of wedded bliss. The "partners" tab leads to wedding planners, photographers, jewelry, cakes, caterers, and, of course, the obligatory honeymoon contractors. The assumption is that you and your pocketbook will be whisked away on a ravishing event that is so sumptuous that you won't feel the pinch.

Still, unlike some reality programming that wallow in either extravagance or deprivation, *SYTTD* seems focused on its all-too-human subjects. Kerry Weber, writing for *America*, describes it by saying, "It can be interesting to see the range of emotions experienced while choosing a dress, even though they are, I am sure, amplified in the edit suite" (2013). Still with all the digressions, traumas, and anxieties of marriage, attractiveness, security, finances, and perhaps most importantly and most unknown: "What will the future hold for this couple?" the show has a very real core. This is a far cry from Fox's wince-some *Married by America,* in which the station threatened to marry couples by audience acclamation. Leigh Edwards writes, "The show had audiences pick mates for couples who could have gotten married on air" (2013). By comparison, *SYTTD* offers us the assurance that these troubled brides do have the power to say no to marriage fantasies and bloated-budget dresses if they so choose.

The popularity of the program has produced several spin-offs, including the *SYTTD Atlanta* sister show, where Southern belles shop for perfect wedding fashions, but usually with a more down-to-earth budget in mind.

See also: The Bachelorette

Further Reading

Leigh Edwards, *The Triumph of Reality TV*, 2013; Roxane Gay, "The Marriage Plot"; Jennifer L. Pozner, *Reality Bites Back,* 2010; Kerry Weber, "The Perfect Fit," *America,* June 17, 2013: 34.

SISTER WIVES

Kody Brown, the hero of *Sister Wives* if he can be called that, is the protagonist/father/patriarchal figure of a polygamous family living in Utah that, over the course of the show, has relocated to Las Vegas. Drawing upon dilemmas and storylines that are strangely reminiscent of HBO's fictional series *Big Love*, Brown has his own brand of Mormonism and practices it, seemingly, without incurring the wrath of the law or people wherever he and his tribe go. In fact, the show might be groundbreaking in its view that individuals practicing their religious rights and hurting no one in the process should be allowed to practice their religion with impunity. The Brown clan was forced to relocate to Las Vegas because they were being pursued by criminal allegations that their desire to live as a group family was a violation of Utah laws prohibiting polygamy. Oddly, the federal government has long fought against the practice of polygamy, as practiced by some religious sects. Brown was acquitted of any charges that he had broken state laws on polygamy. Brown's court victory was viewed by many as a surprise. The issue, according to federal judge Clark Waddoups, was that the state had no right to curtail the family's rights of free expression, practice of religion, and matters of personal association. The judge "ruled Utah's criminalization of cohabitation violated the due process and First Amendment religious freedom rights of the Brown family" (Nelson, 2013). In essence, what the Brown family did, such it was, was no affair of the federal government, nor should the Browns be subject to harassment on the basis of their living arrangements and who they wanted to marry.

The show may be a move toward more people changing accepted views of what constitutes marriage and a committed relationship. A report from the National

Center for Health Statistics reported in 2013 that more people were living together before marriage. Of women surveyed in the study, 48 percent lived with someone before marriage. The Browns have an arrangement where Kody is legally married to one wife while the other "wives" are merely wives by spiritual union, not state-sanctified marriages. This arrangement tends to avoid violations of existing marriage laws.

At present, it is assumed Brown has around 17 children from four different mothers. He seems a dubious catch of limited means and skill, aside from his remarkable ability to sire a squad of progeny. The show is another in TLC's range of programming normalizing obscure social behaviors, in which an unusual and perhaps dysfunctional family unit is shown as paralleling our straight universe. The series proceeds by turns to show how normal, average, and like us real people these polygamists can be. Kody has to struggle with his wives' struggles. The women need their own houses in Vegas, and Kody has to worry over whether they will be able to obtain separate mortgages. There is the added consideration as to how to afford the high expenses involved in caring for four separate households and of course the care and feeding of their own Brigham Young/patriarch, Kody the first.

Naturally, the show has stirred controversy for promoting polygamous lifestyles, deviating from accepted Mormon practices, legitimizing the unlawful, making heroes out of luckless, henpecked rebels, diminishing the position of women, and reducing American social culture to a crude tribal form of birthing and childrearing.

Family feuds and flare-ups are common and provide fireworks for the show. The series avoids (most) legal entanglements about polygamous relations and laws against them, because Kody is only officially married to one of his partners. Since the other three marriages are "spiritual unions" only, there is no legal paperwork tying Kody to anyone but one wife. Still, he practices his polygamous relationships out in the open, and he is proud to talk about the polygamous lifestyle as a supporter of it.

The life and lineage of it all gets rather complicated. Kody married Meri in 1990. He divorced her in 2014 and has since married Robyn. He has one child with Meri and one child with Robyn. Robyn has three children from a previous relationship. Kody has two other wives, Janelle and Christine, and he has six children with each of them. So altogether he has 17 children—14 of his own and 3 through marriage to Robyn.

Pamela Morris and Charissa Niedzwiecki in their article "Odd or Ordinary: Social Comparisons between Real and Reality TV Families" commented that shows like *Sister Wives* "are also chosen by producers for their deviance from social norms" (2014). The authors suggest that producers seek out the unusual so they can provide viewers with a way to stretch their perceptions of a normal American family. The researchers studied results of surveys from focus groups that were shown episodes of *Sister Wives*. Although initially the viewers were put off by the oddness of the families portrayed on the show, the viewers commented that "as the lifestyles were portrayed over a long period of time, viewer acceptance of the families' oddities may have helped change attitudes or created more acceptance of these types of families" (2014). The authors suggest that television could be a mechanism for conditioning audiences to accept difference and changes in society. In this sense, television may be able to perform a positive conditioning effect by using reality programming to transform perceptions of the normal.

See also: The Bachelorette; The Dating Game

Further Reading

David S. Escoffery, *How Real Is Reality TV?*; Pamela Morris and Charissa Niedzwiecki, "Odd or Ordinary: Social Comparison between Real and Reality TV Families," 2014; Steven Nelson, "'Sister Wives' Defeat Polygamy Law in Federal Court," *U.S. News & World Report,* December 16, 2013.

16 AND PREGNANT

16 and Pregnant created a variety of controversies. The program debuted in 2009 and is still active. It focused on different teenage girls, from four months' pregnant to several months after their babies' births, focusing on the mothers' struggles as teenage parents. The stories are largely horrific, with complicated and often unsupportive parents, deadbeat, immature teen boyfriends (if any boyfriend at all), and disturbing school and work developments that make the girls and their children's fates precarious at best. The girls allowed their stories to be broadcast in the hopes that such tales might discourage teen pregnancies. The outcome has been mixed. *In Touch Weekly* pronounced news that *16 and Pregnant* alum Kayla Jordan, aged 23, was expecting her second child. (Her first had just turned five.) This baby, to the still unmarried young adult, was from another boyfriend, and she posted the news and a baby sonogram on Instagram. If the rigors of early child rearing weren't enough, some of these young girls repeated the same behavior when they were older, and theoretically wiser. Why? In fact, *In Touch* boasted that as many as seven of the alums of *16 and Pregnant* (the show has only run four seasons and features four teens per season for a grand total of 16 participants) are pregnant again. Instead of warning girls from bad pregnancies under rough conditions, the contestants on the show seem addicted to procreation. Yet despite these odd stats, *The New York Times*'s Anne Lowery reports that the show pounds an incessant drumbeat of bad news about teenage pregnancy. She writes, "The depiction of both joy and hardship is unflinching, with angry parents, medical complications, lost sleep, financial difficulties and fights with absentee boyfriends" (2014), creating a large part of the show's dynamic.

Perhaps part of the problem isn't that "childbearing is addictive," but that celebrity is intoxicating. Farrah Abraham, a former *16 and Pregnant* alum, did a highly publicized sex tape, netting a million dollars for her and her offspring. Another alum, Jenelle Evans, battled drug addictions and scored a number of police arrests. Lots of the pseudo-celebs of *16 and Pregnant* learned that it paid to be bad, either in dollars or attention. Maybe such celebrity doesn't send the negative message that teen pregnancy is bad. It might be sending the idea that if you get pregnant as a teen you could get attention, a large sum of cash, and your own infamous hashtag on Twitter.

The New York Times's Anne Lowrey writes, "A new economic study of Nielsen television ratings and birth records suggests that the show she appeared in, '16 and Pregnant,' and its spinoffs may have prevented more than 20,000 births to teenage mothers in 2010" (2014). *Science Daily* parroted the good news, saying that research by Levene and Kearney led to a nearly 6 percent decline in birth rates and was partially accountable for the birth rate for teen girls falling to the lowest level in 20 years, from 62 pregnancies per 1,000 girls in 1991 to 29 out of 1,000 by 2012 (Wellesley College 2014). Another factor might be that teens are having less sex, overactive and programmed lives, more use of contraception, and fewer sex partners. But whatever reasons apply, it seems that some students may be rejecting the complicated life of teen moms for something less stressful.

All well and good, but others think the show may be inspiring young girls without the means to raise a child to have one despite the risks. A researcher at the University of Arizona, Jennifer Stevens Aubrey, explained that "Girls who watched '16 and Pregnant,' when compared with the control group, reported a lower perception of their own risk for pregnancy and a greater perception that the benefits of teen pregnancy outweigh the risks" (Harwood 2014). Considering the adversity presented in the show, it is hard to understand how teen girls could arrive at any conclusion perceiving teen pregnancy as somehow empowering.

A lot of the critics like *16 and Pregnant,* and the reason isn't that the show preaches, shows the real world, or scares kids straight The reason is simple. Like so much of MTV, the station gets kids and shows them as they often are: petulant, hormonal, obnoxious, sexual, crazed, maniacal—all the things that teens can be occasionally. Julia Bricklin in "Why We Need *16 and Pregnant*" writes, " MTV captures the essence of teenager to the extreme, complete with immature thought processes, selfishness, a hyperactive need to please one's friends and the opposite sex, and grinding opposition to whatever anyone over the age of thirty has to say" (Bricklin 2012). It is this waywardness, this annoying irascibility, this failure to think things through, this determination to have fun and gratification no matter what the cost that drives these teen daredevils to risk pregnancy and to screw up their young lives that gets people to view it. We are watching their self-destructive derby, which MTV has long exploited. MTV simultaneously expresses teen thinking and anxieties but also explores teen behaviors that can be troubling and risk-taking, such as *Jackass, Real World, Ridiculousness,* and *16 and Pregnant*. The station offers insights but also plays a role in exploiting dark and often unhealthy teen behaviors. One thing is for sure, MTV's *16 and Pregnant* offers a voyeuristic ringside seat to the demolition derby some teens call their lives.

See also: Real World; Teen Mom

Further Reading

David S. Escoffery, *How Real Is Reality TV?*; Lorrie Harwood, "UA Researcher Finds Negative Impact of MTV Show '16 and Pregnant,'" *UA News*, March 25, 2014; Anne Lowrey, "MTV's '16 and Pregnant,' Derided by Some, May Resonate as a Cautionary Tale," *New York Times*, January 13, 2014.

SWAMP PEOPLE

The History Channel, which prides itself on authentic and entertaining documentaries and docudramas of the nation's past enters into the reality television world with the bare-boned directness of *Swamp People*, trailing a family of Cajun, Louisiana denizens who survive in the Bayou and swamp areas of Louisiana through alligator hunting, selling skins, and fishing. This brusque set of freewheeling lifestylers works hard and has a strong sense of identity and honesty.

The program has a distinctive back-to-nature feel with lots of water and boating shots that cover the challenges of the swamp existence. The show debuted in 2010 and has enjoyed a strong following of outdoor enthusiasts, separatists, and devotees of the back-to-basics Americana lifestyle. The program is currently in its fifth season, and, while championing an iconoclastic and individualistic lifestyle, a theme of area reality shows, it lacks the goofy repartee, homespun philosophy, and overt conservative ethos of *Duck Dynasty* and other back-to-basics shows. The show debuted on Sundays at 10:00 p.m., a usually dull ratings area, but it was a ratings winner for the History Channel, and people have thrilled to the struggles and adventures of the Landry, Guist, and Kliebert clans.

Because many of the cast members speak with a Cajun/Louisiana patois and sound slightly French, the History Channel has placed subtitles below the dialogue spoken by the principles. Oddly, they are easy to understand, but many people have trouble because the principles speak very rapidly. Some have commented that the use of titles is insulting and makes the characters appear dumb, like they are unable to speak standard English. Others consider it part of the program's anthropological roots. The characters are given subtitles because their language and culture is unique.

The program is thrilling and features a down-home, countrified narrator who twangs his dialogue about the family and their pursuits. Again, the charge can be made that the tone of the narration is derogatory and casts the characters as dumb backwoods hicks, but in actuality the show has an anthropological feel more akin to Marlin Perkins's *Wild Kingdom* than the salaciousness of MTV's *Real World*. Part of the difference is that the characters of *Swamp People* are a family doing what they do to survive. Second, while some of the show may be manipulated, staged, or prompted, the actual adventure of hunting and subduing alligators is a high-risk entertainment. There are no stuntmen on duty, and there appears to be genuine danger around every turn. True, our hunters have guns, spears, rifles, hooks, and nets, but the gators are tricky, violent, and ferocious.

Despite the high energy level and the real look of the show, environmental groups have raised issues with encouraging people to hunt, poach, or eradicate animals that may pose little or no threat to men in their own natural environment. Ethicists have complained that such shows lionize hunting that in the context of the show seems practical but, in reality, may present dangerous and unrealistic images of people's relationship to the natural world.

See also: Duck Dynasty

Further Reading

June Thomas, "The Gator Good," *Slate*, April 12, 2012.

TEEN MOM

Teen Mom is one of MTV's reality programs that seeks to show the daily experiences of teenage mothers. It isn't a romantic picture. The program aired from 2009 to 2012 and followed moms from the previous MTV program *16 and Pregnant*. Here, the girls who had babies in their teens were tracked through their first few years of surviving as mothers. As with many MTV relationship programs, the relationships under scrutiny turned into train wrecks or were portrayed as such for audience enjoyment.

The program featured mostly grumpy, distraught people whose romantic and relationship lives were overturned by a pregnancy. If anything, such programs, while not preaching or saying "don't do this," explain in no uncertain terms the massive responsibility of childbearing. More importantly, they emphasize, in a world of *Jackass* and *Real World*, how completely unprepared and unable to cope with the demands of motherhood and adultness these teens are. They prove that bringing children into their lives horribly complicates and derails their lives and all their relationships.

The shows dwelled on the mostly vile and sensational aspects of the women's lives. These mothers were coping with unplanned or unexpected pregnancies and their dreams of living a life with a man who could take care of them were foiled on multiple levels. First, the men they had usually chosen were not men, but only larger boys, more adequate to handle skateboards than babies. In one episode, the father of Maci Bookout's child (Bentley Cadence Edwards), Ryan was chewing on some string licorice or chewing gum, driving around with his girlfriend, and failing to meet or pick up little Bentley. Second, the boyfriends seemed completely disengaged and uninterested in the child-rearing process. Their interest seemed to be rooted in videogames or other women. Finally, these dreamboats seemed to have invested little in self-growth outside of a nice set of bicep tattoos.

Bookout agreed to participate in both *16 and Pregnant* and *Teen Mom* with the understanding that being a teen mom is difficult and demanding work. For Bookout, dealing with lover/boyfriend and baby father Ryan was a gauntlet race, and repeatedly Maci was frustrated, angry, disappointed, and bitter about the experience. When she left the show, she was going back to college and preparing to write about her experience, but in 2014 she became pregnant for a second time. Audiences might wonder if she had learned anything from the negative experiences of her first pregnancy and testy relationship with a baby father. Apparently not.

The setup of the show was that it followed the daily struggles of four young women who were *16 and Pregnant*, another MTV reality show. The programs were popular as *Teen Mom 1*, *Teen Mom 2*, and *Teen Mom 3*. The fact that there were at last count three reiterations of the show suggested that the girls did not seem to be changing behavior because of these new complications in their lives. In the first season of *Teen Mom*, none of the girls who had children were married. The boyfriends, or fiancées, or extended families were supposed to be available to help with child-rearing duties, but this did not always work. One of the girls, Farrah Abraham, lost a boyfriend in a car crash while still pregnant. She had to undergo therapy to deal with it. Her mother hit her and was charged with assault. Her dead boyfriend's family sued her for grandparent visitation rights. She sold a porn tape for over $1 million to produce funds to pay for her child's well-being. One girl decided to give up her child for adoption, thinking that the best plan for the child's welfare. Her parents disagreed with her decision, and she wound up living with the boyfriend, getting a tattoo in honor of her baby, and having another child. Amber Portland was so frustrated she beat up her baby's father and left scars on him. She later served time in jail. In a word, the show was rough.

The shows were absolutely disturbing documentaries of debacles, posing as relationships. There may be one silver lining at the end of this ratings tunnel: teen pregnancies may decline due to exposure to this show. After witnessing the violence, anger, and outbursts on the show, why would anyone, let alone a teen, have a child? *The New York Daily News*'s Victoria Taylor writes, "The franchise was responsible for an estimated 5.7% drop in teen births between its debut in June 2009 and the end of 2010" (2014). This can only be good news to a society that seemingly is overwhelmed by the misguided onslaught of teen pregnancies that have reached epidemic proportion.

Still the situation of shows like *Teen Mom* is not clear. *Time* magazine's Eliana Dockterman writes, "But a different study conducted by researchers at Indiana University published Thursday found the opposite to be true: *16 and Pregnant* and its spinoff show, *Teen Mom*, lead viewers to think that teen mothers have an enviable quality of life" (2014).

See also: The Bachelorette; The Dating Game

Further Reading
David S. Escoffery, *How Real Is Reality TV?*

THIS IS YOUR LIFE
An early example of the reality impetus was this curio from the 1950s that provided a *Mr. Holland's Opus* look at the lives and careers of famous or ordinary Americans. The host of the show, Ralph Edwards, had worked on the popular radio program

Truth of Consequences, a strong game show format. At one point in the years follow-ing the United States' midcentury wars—World War II and Korea—Edwards was called upon to try to do something to improve the lives of veterans recuperating in veterans hospitals in the Los Angeles area after receiving life-altering wounds from the wars. Edwards did a tribute to a veteran who had lost limbs in the war, and the audience and network (NBC) were so moved by the program that Edwards was empowered and encouraged to create a continuing series.

Edwards developed a show concept in which the life of an individual could be shown through clips, remembrances, reenactments, and testimony during a seg-ment providing a capsule history of a person and their life achievements. Edwards carried a little red book on the show that contained the documented data of a person's life. The audience went on a journey of nostalgia, heartbreak, and remem-brance, reliving that person's life with the studio and home audience. The show profited from a mixture of sentiment, nostalgia, and historicism. The program moved strategically from everyday people to famous celebrities trying to express the common experience of all mankind. The original incarnation of the program was from 1952 until 1961, but there were revised attempts at the concept in the 1970s by Edwards in 1971–1972 and in the 1980s with Joseph Campanella, and Edwards returned for specials until his death in 2005.

The scheme of the show was a mixture of reality and setup. Usually, Edwards would begin with a bio of the subject, and then, in the first 15 minutes, the sub-ject would be ambushed, surprised, and told that this was "your life." Family and friends would be reunited with the subject in a studio setting. Sometimes, when they were doing the life of someone who was ill, they would announce to the recipient that he or she would be featured. At other times, the sometimes-reluctant honoree was showered with praise and accolades out of the blue. The resulting sentimental moments were pure television magic of real people in the entertain-ment business celebrating each other in a highly public meeting.

Most often, guests graciously responded to the tribute. Mack Sennett, the famous silent film director and producer, was put off by the ruse initially but warmed to it. Others were not so kind. Stan Laurel of the classic comedy team of Laurel and Hardy was horrified that he and Hardy were publicly embarrassed and humiliated by having to appear unrehearsed on television. Laurel's complaint wasn't that the tribute was lying, mean, or duplicitous; he was far more concerned as a profes-sional that people would see his unpreparedness as a symbol of his lack of profes-sionalism. Lowell Thomas was also dubious about being featured and felt the show and its sneak-attack chicanery was a sort of insult to honesty and privacy. Many offered that the show pulled unnatural reactions from people and that the show was padded out in uneasy sentiment.

Even Edwards was wary of his own ambush technique and apparently threat-ened to fire anyone who inappropriately ambushed him or his family. Edwards was never featured on his own show. Other criticisms were that the show bathed in a warm glow of untruthful bathos. Some tense and awkward moments were when a Japanese survivor of the Hiroshima bombing, a Japanese Christian named Rev.

Kiyoshi Tanimoto, was "reunited" with pilot Robert Lewis, one of the men who flew the *Enola Gay*, the plane that dropped the atom bomb. One cannot buy television more glaringly insensitive to history than that. By all accounts, the victor and victim had a cordial exchange.

Annette Hill in *Reality TV* comments on the fact that "at the heart of the debate about the reality of reality TV is a paradox: the more entertaining a factual programme is, the less real it appears to viewers" (2005). Edwards was able to develop a package that excelled at using real people, while appearing to be genuinely surprising and a revelation. One suspects many of the guests/victims despised a living eulogy, giving the suggestion their lives were over and already spent. Still others probably welcomed the publicity. Edwards was able to make the entertainment aspect tied to the discovery or the surprise of the guest. Controversy erupted over the program's use of maudlin and emotional frames. At one point, Edwards did a show featuring a concentration camp Holocaust survivor. The message seemed to be, "Way to go, you made it, you survived," which perhaps did not send a very comforting or compassionate vision of the horrific human suffering behind such an event. Nightclub singer Lillian Roth, an admitted debauched alcoholic, saved by Alcoholics Anonymous, appeared, prompting the biographical film *I'll Cry Tomorrow* framing her frightening and painful life story. Despite the massive criticism and the parade of has-been performers, pitiful bereft mothers, and hopeless cases, Edwards's show was an early attempt to merge human pathos with live events so that television audiences were able to accept the illusion they were seeing real life enacted, regardless of how staged, how hammy, and how emotional it all became.

See also: The Bachelorette; The Dating Game

Further Reading

David S. Escoffery, *How Real Is Reality Television?*; Annette Hill, *Reality TV*, 2005.

TOP GEAR

Car enthusiast shows. This sounds like a natural topic for American television. Yet, aside from a few shows, the love of the American automobile is something that audiences enjoy on the road but not on the television screen—at least that's the way it is in the United States. In England, where cars are rarer, vehicle ownership is more costly and problematic, and the variety of cars is exotic and enticing, the allure of the open road beckons in shows like the UK's *Top Gear*. *Top Gear* has aired since 2002 and, in its blend of daredevil stunt driving, exotic global locations, carefully orchestrated media controversies, exquisite high-end automotive machines, and smooth hosts who know a well-built vehicle, this program is stimulating eye candy for the perennial adolescent male in all of us. More interesting is *Top Gear's* status as the most watched factual television program in the world.

Don Kaplan, writing for the *New York Daily News,* calls the show "the coolest thing on television" and opines that "its irreverent hosts have celebrated and critiqued all the major carmakers" and "is seen around the world each week by 370 million people" (2013). However, the program is really about the cars, and the hosts do everything short of stripping the cars naked in what some refer to as automotive-fetish behavior, or worse, car porn. An amusing aspect of the show is the hosts' vile remarks about their sponsors and their products. One of the hosts, James May, insulted Mercedes Benz, calling their vehicle a "knuckledragger's car," and then they featured a commercial by Mercedes Benz. You can't say the show features in program promotions, because advertisers are as likely to receive cruel treatment from the hosts as they are to receive praise. Any sponsors take their lives and their products in their hands if they advertise on the tempestuous program.

The show knows how to court controversy, and when the cast journeys world-wide, they know how to stir the pot. In 2014, they were in hot water internationally. The program has been BBC2's traditional top performer, pulling in a whopping 6 million viewers a week. That would be healthy by U.S. standards, but in the UK, with a far smaller population, such numbers are outstanding. They were testing cars in Argentina, and host Jeremy Clarkson was driving a Porsche with the license plate H982-FLK. This was taken to be a thinly veiled reference to the 1982 Falklands War, in which Argentinian troops invaded the Falkland Islands, owned and governed by the British. In the 10-week conflict, the British soundly defeated and repelled the Argentinian forces, killing over 600 Argentinian fighters and prompting an international outcry. The Argentinians did not wish to be reminded of the insult or to be publically slighted by English television visitors. Clarkson's license plate enflamed the situation, and, when news of the inflammatory license spread, Argentinians rioted, attacked the hotel residence where Clarkson and company were staying, and threatened the crew. Clarkson and the principles hid in a series researcher's room. The crew fled the country in rented SUVs and ran for their lives.

Each week the hosts of *Top Gear* fly around the world, putting the top cars from the top manufacturers through grueling test drives and performance-bursting stunt drives to see if the cars live up to their makers' extravagant claims. In one episode, a show host, the popular Richard Hamilton, drives a Porsche 918 Spyder. He goes to a racetrack with a remarkably long, straight track in the desert. The footage is pristine, and the high-end auto looks exciting and brilliant.

The footage, which appears to be shot from a variety of cameras both inside and outside the car, looks striking and appears to emulate footage from a massive action-adventure film. Yet, while accelerating at speeds well over 100 kilometers per hour, Hamilton chats with the audience as calmly as a nun at choir practice. Intercut with the high-tech/high-def spectacular footage are animated shots of the car's features, engine, and internal devices.

The show has generated a variety of critical backlashes. The hosts are feisty and often make deprecating remarks about people and cars of foreign nationalities. Most of the tongue-in-cheek comments are blown off as the show's macho bravado, but sometimes nations and individuals are stung by the sharp-tongued test drivers. More disturbing are some anti-gay comments, like host Jeremy Clarkson referring to a Daihatsu vehicle as "gay." Equally disturbing was Clarkson's comments about a BMW Mini Cooper that was described as "British." Clarkson joked that a German-oriented Cooper would have Hitler salute turn signals, a navigation system that directed drivers to Poland, and fan belts that lasted 1,000 years. The hosts and their wicked kidding draw fire with their casual slurs. Rather than dropping their ratings, such controversies over the years have kept the show in the public eye.

The cast, including Jeremy Clarkson, James May, and Richard Hammond, spent an episode on the Mexican-designed Mastretta sports car, saying that waking up Mexican must be depressing. They made fun of Mexican food, calling it "refried sick," and commented that any Mexican car would reflect Mexican national characteristics of laziness and oafishness.

The show seems to use its constantly nasty and insensitive humor to prompt continual attacks and controversies. In a spoof ad of the Volkswagen Scirocco, the crew showed Polish people leaving Poland in advance of a German attack. At the end, the cut line showed a dark blue Volkswagen Scirocco and the line: "From Berlin to Warsaw on one tank." The spoof ad was released to YouTube. The Polish government and many other parties were outraged. Despite its controversy over cheeky humor, insensitivity, and cheap shots, *Top Gear* remains a top performer, drawing big audiences and offering thrills, aggressiveness, and its own brand of comedy to car enthusiasts globally.

Finally, in 2015, Clarkson's insensitive and oafish behavior had him canned from the show. The BBC had had enough from its boisterous and irrepressible star and dumped him from the show. However, in May it was announced that Clarkson was back on the road with *Top Gear* buddies for the Clarkson, Hammond, and May Live tour. One imagines it will be the loud-mouthed car enthusiasts spouting about their favorite rides and meeting with fans on a cross-country driving tour. When *The Mirror*'s Walker asked May about the tour, he said, "Occasionally they want to talk about cars, but actually not as much as you'd expect because they've probably worked out by now that we don't really know what we're talking about." Knowledgeable or not, the three British car knuckleheads plan to hit the road in 2015, and fans have lined up to hear their grumpy humor on cars, countries, and the driving life.

In 2015 the show was rebooted with a new cast of presenters, including Chris Harris, American Matt LeBlanc, and Rory Reid. Reviews were mixed, and the performers were said to have little onscreen chemistry; however, *Top Gear* remains a popular international driving entity.

See also: Duck Dynasty; Ridiculousness

Further Reading

Jeremy Clarkson, "Make No Mistake, Lives Were at Risk," *Sunday London Times*, October 5, 2014; John Plunkett, "BBC Top Gear: No Apology over Clarkson's Argentina Comments," *The Guardian*, October 31, 2014; Danny Walker, "Jeremy Clarkson Ready for Belfast Live Show," *London Daily Mirror*, May 14, 2015.

Chapter 4: Finding the One(s)—Dating, Matchmakers, and Hooking Up

A History of Romance

Shows that prominently feature romantic love, such as *The Bachelor* or MTV's *Dismissed* play into our societal fascination with the allure of romance. However, the notion of romantic love, being attracted to someone on the basis of physical and psychological characteristics, is a fairly new and novel construct and the history of modern romantic love is fraught with problems and often bad results.

Romantic love was idealized in myth and literature and held as an ideal. In mythology, we have the story of Leda and the Swan. Leda falls in love with the swan because it appears to be a gentle, kind, and loving creature. What she doesn't know is that that swan is a deception, and the real character in the guise of a swan is Zeus, using the ruse to effect a deception and another romantic conquest.

Romance is problematic in history as well as mythology. Despite people's attractions for one another, the outcome can be tragic. Julius Caesar and Marc Antony both fell in love with Cleopatra. She is at least partially responsible for distracting the leaders, if not totally responsible for their ends. Peter Abelard became enamored of his student, Héloïse, and her father was so enraged that he had the much-older tutor castrated. Abelard and Héloïse wrote letters to each other until the end of their lives, but they never met again. Both were mass media exemplars of the tragedies of romantic love in their respective cultures. Shah Jahan was so despondent when his wife Mumtaz Mahal died in childbirth that he erected a memorial to his third wife that took 23 years to build, the beautiful and elegant Taj Mahal, one of the most gorgeous monuments to a loved one in the world.

Romantic love has prompted wars and horrific mourning. Prince Pedro of Portugal so loved his consort Inês de Castro that his father had the lady banished and murdered. Pedro embarked on a civil war against his father. He won and demanded that everyone swear allegiance to his deceased love. The modern era has shown us still more forms of the devastation brought by romantic entanglements. The British royal family has suffered many love misfortunes, but Queen Victoria was the victim of one of the cruelest love matches. Her beloved husband Albert died 40 years before her, leaving her with a long, lonely reign. When Prince Albert was 42, he had severe stomach trouble and succumbed to typhoid fever. Perhaps one of the most tragic love affairs was between Andrew Jackson and Rachel Donelson. Jackson married Donelson, thinking her divorce from her previous husband was finalized. The ex-husband held on to the divorce papers and only filed later.

Donelson was accused of loose morals, which aggravated her heart condition. She died months before Jackson started his term as president. He was so shocked at her death that he held her for hours after her passing, thinking she might revive.

The concept of romance, as we know it, is relatively recent. The sex urge and the way people pursue sex have been hardwired into the human anatomy for at least 100,000 years. Toronto psychologist Edward Shorter said, "Just as our bodies tell us what we might like to eat, or when we should go to sleep, they lay down for us our pattern of lust" (Shorter 2005, 4). Scientists do think our way of looking at sex and our willingness to talk about it and demystify it has changed. This could play a role in why sex has had more notice in the media.

However, media has a way of making everything bigger, and the mass media has emphasized our interest in sexual and romantic encounters by strongly featuring that aspect of life in the media. Social theorists Adorno and Horkheimer feared the media's manipulation of our latent desires because the two German sociologists feared that these desires could be manipulated to encourage our consumption of products related to our desires. Andrea Schuld-Ergil writes that according to Adorno and Horkheimer, "Cultural commodities—those ideas manufactured into the forms of things for sale—are aimed by producers not to satisfy consumers' physical needs but to influence consumers' conscious and subconscious selves" (Schuld-Ergil 2006, 168). When we watch reality programming, are we actually seeing something approximating a true view of love and courtship, or are such programs merely a way to use those emotions and desires and transform them into cultural commodities that advertisers can sell to us? In other words, is *The Bachelor* showing love or simply stroking our vision of love to sell products to romantically enhanced men and women watching the show?

In today's world of reality programs, the notion of courtship is ritualized with a series of tests or conventions. In *Dating Naked*, contestants learn to cope with the potential partner's nakedness and to seek to disregard this unusual circumstance to find a compatible date. In *The Bachelor*, the awarding of a rose is a testament to continued interest in a participant. However, rituals of courtship were far harsher in the history of dating. In ancient times, writer Kimberly Powell reminds us that tribes would raid adjoining villages to find potential wives, and the hunter/tribesmen would have to hide with their contested/stolen brides until the rival tribes stopped hunting for the lost women. While hiding, the new lovers would drink a beverage called metheglin, a concoction made with honey. They laid low for a month while they avoided the raids of their rivals, hunting for them in the village. This period of drinking honey and settling in together to make a home became known as *the honeymoon*, a time where they evaded other suitors for a period of a month.

The opposite of stolen matches were arranged matches of "bartered" brides in which families negotiated for the best husband for a daughter. The hope was that daughters from privileged families would make good political and economic alliances for the benefit of both families. Both families would gain in stature, the girl would bring with her a dowry to underwrite the expenses of marriage, and the coupling would produce children for both family lines to continue and consolidate their various forms of wealth.

However, the arranged marriage was less a romantic institution than a practical method of maintaining wealth in influential families. An alternative to this economic reality was the ideal of chivalry, where the male would make complex and gallant declarations of love and sacrifice his own comfort and safety for the benefit of a woman that the lover desired. The courtship rituals of the chivalric tradition included writing poems, singing songs, performing dances, playing an instrument, and deporting oneself in a pleasing and courtly manner. It was thought that a woman's chastity and a man's honor were the most important qualities in a love match. The notion of romantic love conducted under the code of chivalry is lauded in literature and made popular in the 19th century most strongly in Sir Walter Scott's *Ivanhoe*, and the idea of romantic medieval love became fashionable through romances of that era. Ivanhoe is such a great hero that he defends people who have few friends in England. Among his great deeds, he champions the Jewish beauty Rebecca, who is falsely accused of witchcraft by Lucas de Beaumanoir, the grand master of the corrupted Knights Templar. He fights on her behalf, and, though he defeats his enemy Bois-Guilbert, he does not kill him. Ivanhoe is so noble that he battles for Rebecca despite the fact that he is destined to marry another, Rowena. Thanks to Ivanhoe's intervention, the innocent Rebecca and her father are able to escape to Granada where they can live in peace. While the chivalric tradition sounds completely foreign to our culture obsessed with external attractiveness, there is an element of the chivalric tradition in shows like *The Bachelor*, and even comical programming like *Queer Eye for the Straight Guy*, which offers a group of gay men who work to promote the attractiveness of other men who are unable or unwilling to make themselves attractive. The role of kindness and helping others is not lost on such programs.

This vision of courtly and romantic love is validated by the reign of Queen Victoria, where, due to the death of the prince consort, Albert, poor Victoria was forced to be a widowed queen for 40 years. Victoria, who reigned from 1837 to 1901, installed new codes of propriety to the courting rituals. Girls could not simply meet and talk to men of interest. They had to be formally introduced and chaperoned. At parties, girls would be presented to the world, and boys would present cards to a girl to request permission to escort a girl home. The girl would pick from her suitors and send a card to the boy selected to escort her home either by walking or, the preferred method, by carriage. During the journey home, the young man and woman might be allowed to talk but never to touch, and always and only in the presence of a family chaperone. Once smitten with one another, courtship would be conducted only at the girl's home and only with the family sitting in the room with the suitor and the girl, watching and listening to all transactions and conversations between them. More often than not, a boy would not ask a girl to marry him in person, but only in writing, often waiting weeks or months for a reply. These complex rituals are often mirrored in reality programming. In MTV's *Taildaters*, dates are conducted in full view of the couple's friends and family, and, as the couple is filmed, the party of guests watching from an adjoining area is encouraged to comment on the love match.

Today, many reality programs require such conventions for a relationship to proceed, and actions just as strange as chaperones are common on shows like MTV's *Next,* where a female contestant can boot an unpopular suitor by simply calling, "Next!" and the undesirable is removed in favor of a new and hopefully better suitor.

Sadly, there has been marginal commentary on these programs. Author Elizabeth Johnston writes, "Academia has overlooked reality shows because, like daytime television, they have been devalued as 'low culture,' watched primarily by women" (2006, 116). Perhaps the strangest change in the history of romance is the way the romance novel has been transformed by modern feminist authors. Once reviled for plunging women into old clichés of men raping women and women falling for older, ill-mannered, violent suitors, the scene of many modern romance novels is often female-centric. In Jennifer Luther's article on modern romance novels for the *Atlantic Monthly*, she describes the changes that have been brought by modern authors like Cecilia Grant, who wrote in her novel *A Lady Awakened*, "The heroine uses the hero in order to get pregnant. She is not initially interested in emotional intimacy or love. The heroine is the one taking charge of her sexuality and her future while it is the rake who we find crying about how he feels used and eventually begging his love for a long-term commitment." These images of males desperately in love likely do occur in society, but they are not championed in our literature or media. Even reality television still favors very traditional notions of male/female courtship, and only the slow awakening of feminist themes in shows like *The Bachelorette* or MTV's *Catfish*, with its duplicity about who one is really dating on the Web, tend to privilege female power in the dating environment.

In any case, the history of romance plays a major role in how dating and romance reality television programs are configured. It is only in the past decade that programs like *The Dating Game*, in which bachelors in the 1970s picked a date from behind a wall, sight unseen, have been changed. Today we have shows like *The Hook Up* and *Millionaire Matchmaker* that slowly and fitfully start to give women more to say about the business of romance. However, despite the changes in power structure, reality television still privileges the signed over the real, and this can create a rift between what we see in a televised form of the real and what we see in actual reality. Johnston writes, "Our real experience (the signified), becomes less visible, less important as it is gradually replaced by the representation of reality (the sign)" (Johnston 2006, 121). In other words, the more we watch romance in reality television, the less likely we are to see anything approaching real romance and instead will be confronted with producers' codes of romance, propounded to make us think this is how reality operates, even though such portrayals can be largely fictitious.

Further Reading

Jennifer Luther, "Beyond Bodice Rippers: How Romance Novels Came to Embrace Feminism," *Atlantic Monthly*, March 18, 2013. Web; Heather Powell, "Romance through the Ages," *About.com*, September 1, 2015. Web; Heather Whipps, "A Brief History of Sex," *Live Science*, July 27, 2006, Web.

THE BACHELOR

Gamification refers to the act of transforming every form of existence and cultural practice into the province of a game. This phenomenon may be related to the hypercompetitiveness of Americans, the popularity of gaming culture, or the manner in which competition makes us more attentive and responsive to our world. At the cutting edge of gamification are the forms of reality TV in which the most complicated and intimate relations in our life are progressively *gamified*. Gamification reaches a zenith in *The Bachelor*, in which a single man is pursued for an entire season in a formalized ritual of courtship by a group of as many as 30 women.

The Bachelor has a dark pedigree, a low (2.8 star) IMDB rating, a lackluster Google description: "A man chooses from a group of women," and many awkward moments that play upon the psychology of women who wish to see idealized relationships portrayed in the program. Emphasis is placed on moments of embarrassment, and many featured characters are exploited for comic and ironic moments. In 2015, when a Fox producer/contestant Jillian Anderson tripped on a carpet on the way to picking up a rose from Bachelor Chris Soules, her fall and humiliation were widely covered by the network's camerapeople. The program, a massive ratings hit, spawning over 10 seasons, providing countless tabloid speculation about potential winners, and infinite Web commentary about advancing players, exists as a psychological reservoir of romantic longings. Contestants often become short-term celebrities featured on magazine covers. A disparaging description of the program's content ran in *The New York Times* as writer Roxane Gay writes, "Since 2002, these two shows (*The Bachelor* and *The Bachelorette*) have offered a grotesquerie of the courtship ritual that is predicated on the fragile premise that '*the one*' is waiting among a carefully selected group of entrepreneurs, pharmaceutical reps, dental hygienists and personal trainers" (2014).

The show has a strong courtship message. However, the roles are reversed, and the man is pursued as the object. The women vie for a man's attention, and they plot and strategize ways to spend time with their intended lover. The pursuit of the male object is the sole goal. They seek one-on-one time while they express fantasies and longings for their potential love connection. A symbol of their continuance on the show is the awarding of a rose, which implies that the protagonist/object intends to keep the woman around for another episode. Otherwise, their ranks can be thinned by the competitions and cuts built into each segment. Like a date or a job interview, every social occasion is elevated to a complex spectacle. Despite the ornate theatricality of the proceedings, the effect of the ritualistic behavior mirrors real life. Just as people prepare for dates and assign great importance to being with a potential date, the producers of the show postulate that these romantic interludes need to be addressed with all the solemnity and seriousness of a real-world romantic encounter. At the same time, the spectacular elements of the encounter somehow render the event at once intimate and ultimately a gaudy defilement of date intimacy.

All the while, these television wife-hopefuls exist in a gendered dorm where they reflect on their various strategies, share intimacies with other competitors, and reveal their various moods, idiosyncrasies, and darkest secrets. In one episode, a dejected player feared to reveal she already had a one-year-old child from a previous relationship. The audience saw her as a threatened and lonely partner longing for the security of a truly spiritual communion. The show mixes the spectacular ritual of mawkish tribal courtship events and public romantic moments in an unsettling mix of sentiment and luxury trappings. There is an effort to normalize the often-bizarre and extreme settings and dress. David Escoffery writes, "Most of the contestants on reality television shows come from working class backgrounds," and the common origins of many of the participants and the exotic locales often signal a disconnect in the proceedings (2006, 119).

Throughout there are competitive bouts and bondings in increasingly surreal exercises of presentation and habituation where the man dines, dates, and progressively familiarizes himself with the cohort of potential wives/partners. The settings are surreal in their luxury and obscure lighting effects. If anything, the amount of ceremony and ostentation showered on these meetings probably dampens the most vigorous lover's ardor. At the center of the show's premise, there is the continuing problem of defining true romance in a world of extreme spectacle and surreal performance pressure.

The show, like much of reality television, is intrinsically tribal. The show portrays mating dances of attractive young people placed into awkward confrontations and competitions. However, the anthropological model of the show is sound. Just as the contestants feel uncomfortable exhibiting themselves in public as they date, the audience recalls their own dating woes in their youth and the sense of discomfort is a shared experienced between participants and viewers. Elizabeth Johnson remarks that reality shows are based on everyday occurrences. She writes, "Not only are the contestants 'ordinary folks'; many of the most popular reality shows focus on everyday experiences" (2006, 120). Part of the pleasure derives from viewing how others deal with everyday matters like dating. We are watching the contestants play the strong male and the attractive coed. We watch the planning and negotiation that produce the dating event, and we understand that this commonly private and intimate set of events is being conducted under the view of millions of watchers, which renders it odd and surreal at a very heightened level. The simple act of a date becomes a high-stakes, dramatic sporting event, and the audience becomes embroiled in trying to guess outcomes and chances for various competitors.

Women particularly see dating shows as symbolizing something familiar. They recognize the theatricalization of courtship rituals as a performance in which we are all involved at some time. Richard M. Huff writes, "Women, young women, tend to tune in to reality dating shows in larger numbers than any other demographic" (2006, 108). Despite the frame that the show is competitive and people treat the winning as a game, the underlying reality is that courtship is a high-stakes game for all people. Being involved with someone can make one secure or unhappy or wealthy or increase a sense of self-worth. Relationships are complex, and who we choose to spend time with is an important life decision. The show taps into that very real problem.

The program also recognizes that dating allure also translates into sales dollars, and advertisers selling clothing, makeup, and fitness products advertise heavily on the show, recognizing that the demographic of young female viewers are watching and may invest in beauty aids to help them in the competitive romance market. Elizabeth Johnson in her article "How Women Really Are" explains that *The Bachelor* shares a sensibility with a long tradition of romantic literature, saying that "both eighteenth century fiction and reality television also tend to celebrate the everyday, focusing on both domestic experience and the lives of 'ordinary' people" (Johnston 2006, 119).

Programming like *The Bachelor* is inspired by ideas from Jane Austen. Austen wrote, "It is a truth universally acknowledged, that a single man in possession of a good fortune, must be in want of a wife" (Austen, 1853, 1). *The Bachelor* describes that search for a capable and viable partner. For 18- and 19-century women, this issue was not only important, but often fatal. A failed match or no match would condemn an unmarried woman to existing on the periphery of society with no status, no employment, no purpose, and no protectors. If she survived at all, it would be merely at the mercy and charity of her male family members. The reality was that they would have likely preferred her to have succumbed at birth than to burden the family with caring for another maiden aunt. *The Times*'s Roxane Gay writes, "*The Bachelor* harkens back to Puritan times, when courtships were supervised by parents and other invested parties to secure wealth, land, social standing" (2014). Perhaps love is less a factor in *The Bachelor* than the serious matter of finding and securing strong relationships. When viewed this way, *The Bachelor* rises from a show about dating to a show about pivotal concerns in contemporary society. The underlying concerns are creating partnerships, making strong relationship connections, finding life partners, and avoiding alienation in a strongly alienated society. When viewed through this lens, *The Bachelor* rises from the trivial to an important program about self-image and finding solid partners to navigate society. This makes it more in tempo with the Harvard Business School and less about finding a date for the prom.

More often, contestants on *The Bachelor* are, like us, struggling to navigate a hostile and fragmented society to find normal, rational people to share their world. This is reminiscent of the Situationists, a political group in France in the 1960s who declared our society a society of spectacle. To the Situationists, we were living in a society in which image dominates. Similarly on *The Bachelor*, it is all the spectacular presentation of men and women in exotic locations that makes the romantic event seem special. Steven Connor writes, "Guy Debord, the spokesman of the (Situationist) group, . . . forecast that the image would replace the railway and the automobile as the driving force of the economy" (1998, 51). *The Bachelor* shows us that society has replaced other technologies with the image of romance, and that image of perfect love often dominates our psyche.

See also: The Bachelorette; The Dating Game

Further Reading

David S. Escoffery, How Real Is Reality TV? 2006; Roxane Gay, "The Marriage Plot," New York Times, May 11, 2014; Richard Huff. Reality Television, 2006.

THE BACHELORETTE

Giving a feminist view to the pursuit of reality television mating rituals, The Bachelorette was a spin-off from ABC's popular series The Bachelor (2002). The Bachelorette debuted in 2003, capitalizing on the same theme of achieving true love through screening a series of winsome and provocative candidates chosen by the show's producers. This notion was a springboard to stimulate lots many games, rituals, and rivalries to help a young woman obtain a good male paramour. There is a notable difference from The Bachelorette's parent show The Bachelor. In The Bachelor, the bachelor picks a girl to be with him, but there is no conditional acceptance or demand that he keep this choice. He doesn't have to marry. However, The Bachelorette usually culminates in one or two of the male contestants proposing to the eligible bachelorette, in keeping with the notion that an honest and noble female wishes to culminate a relationship in the bonds of matrimony, where carnality is sanctified in marriage vows. The show's success rate has been low, with only two of the eight seasons' couples progressing to marriage. In this way, the show realistically portrays the difficulty in finding a real love match. Certainly, the highly public fishbowl environment in which courting is conducted adds to the spectacular and often unsettling element of the program's courtship rituals. Cleary Hollywood, with its highly competitive entertainment industry, is not the ideal place for a tranquil coupling. This makes the difficulty of creating a lasting, stable, and happy romantic partnership in such surroundings difficult. C'est la vie.

Shows like The Bachelorette are one of the ways people use television to remember and reinforce their past. In Leah Rosenberg's "The Way We Were: Ritual Memory and Television," she talks with a focus group that tell her stories about their lives related to shows they watched during these pivotal times in their youth and early adulthood. Rosenberg writes, "I have argued that remembering through television enabled people to recall past time, place, identity, and social relationships" (2013, 23). The Bachelorette likely does similar work for contemporary young women. It provides them with a prototype or guide for contemporary courtship rituals. People forget that there are few manuals on such behavior in our society, and television or YouTube often fill the gap. So despite the ornate trappings of the program, The Bachelorette may serve as a training manual for young women confused by codes of courtship.

A typical season of *The Bachelorette* introduces the bachelorette and gives some biographical information to (1) help the audience build a bond with the player and (2) come to understand her worldview and (3) perceive what she seeks from a date/mate. The male competitors are introduced, and they range from charming men to rogues, bad boys, father figures, and fun-loving types. Over time, contests and challenges change, but the crux of the program is the staged romantic encounters between the bachelorette and her male harem. The producers and the women viewing are hoping for a spark, a moment of true delight between the woman and some man. Despite the fact that they are all vetted performers in the competition, it is difficult to find those real moments of connection, and the audience analyzes the men and their actions in minute detail. Blog posts, social media commentaries, and blow-by-blow show summaries catalog the seriousness of viewers' interaction. An offhand remark and a brush of flesh can ignite weeklong debates about the reasoning and gameplay of certain contestants.

Many aspects of the show are carefully stage managed. People make the assumption that real-life romantic encounters are spontaneous. As we might imagine upon reflection, few romantic moments occur without careful planning and anticipation. As in all reality programming, there are dubious claims of authenticity. While the contestants usually swear that their remarks are nonscripted, there are many who perceive a scripted guiding presence behind all presentations, meetings, and encounters on the show's stage. While some scenes may not be actually scripted, the contestants are so keenly primed and stroked to these frenetic performances that it is clear that every moment is managed, even if the contestants are not told what to actually utter.

Critic Umberto Eco makes the case that television and film are all about invented reality, no matter how real it appears. The people on *The Bachelorette* might appear real, but in some way they are all impressions of people; they are all robots. Eco writes, "As in certain horror films, detachment is impossible, you are not witnessing another's horror, you are inside the horror through complete synesthesia" (1986, 46). Eco thinks Disneyland does a great job of simulating real life, but he also believes that simulation can be a powerful lure into a fantasy world. The same is true of *The Bachelorette*. It may be totally fake, but, by the end of an episode, we are encased inside the drama. Like the Haunted Mansion, we have been locked in the show's fantasy.

As in much reality television programs, there are accusations that the reality portrayed is not real, but in *The Bachelorette* several previous contestants have come forward to expose show practices. Several have said that selective editing, scripted storylines, and producer nudges have created characters and storylines that deviated from the real people and their interactions. One critic, Jennifer L. Pozner, writing in *Reality Bites Back*, notes: "Female submissiveness is still imposed as a major theme, even when the roles are supposed to be reversed on shows like *The Bachelorette*, where many men pursue one woman" (2010). Pozner's point is well taken. If *The Bachelorette* is presumed to provide women with an avenue of power that is the selection of a suitor from the ranks of many competitors, the show has sadly not materialized a new sense of female empowerment. Old problems assert themselves. These new relationships, in which women are able to choose among a field of candidates, do not seem to promote healthier or more enduring relationships. Despite the notion that women on *The Bachelorette* are in the driver's seat, too often the women are shackled to seductive wardrobes, entrapping situations, and the often-degrading situation of pretending submissiveness to a man when they are clearly the final arbiter of when or if a relationship will be produced.

Perhaps there is a philosophical subtext as well. Famed French postmodern feminist philosopher Julia Kristeva called writing "clearly practical knowledge within the imaginary, a technique of fantasy" (Kristeva 1992). Perhaps these shows are just such a delicate juxtaposition of the practical and the fantastic. In that sense, perhaps that is why they appear so bizarre. Like a Warhol painting, they take the everyday (a Campbell's soup can), and they ask us to reimagine it as something bigger and more resonant. In such programming, the everyday, courtship rituals are exposed to massive audiences and critical reevaluation. The small is made large, and every aspect of what seemed common or even trivial is magnified in outsized proportion. As in Kristeva's explanation, television can merge the practical and the imaginary to make a fantasy.

Such programming tends to reflect conservative values such as marriage, heterosexual coupling, a prohibition on premarital intercourse, and a decidedly Victorian manner of puritan dating in full display of an audience. Such shows also dismantle progressive moves toward a diverse society. Michelle Brophy-Baermann writes in "True Love on TV" that "in a perfunctory nod to diversity, there are always contestants of color in the group of potential mates at the beginnings of these shows," but they "always manage to avoid parading interracial romance on prime time" (2005). The shows may appear to open the door to people's most private practices, but, in the end, such programs espouse a conservative social perspective.

One interesting aspect of the show was how *The Bachelor* and *The Bachelorette* provoked a synergistic utilization of the companion show. In season one of *The Bachelorette*, the first bachelorette was Trista Rehn, who had been a runner-up on *The Bachelor*'s first season. The 2015 season of *The Bachelor* featured Chris Soules, a successful Iowa farmer who was one of three finalists in the previous season's *Bachelorette*. When star Andi Dorfman decided to send the fan favorite, Soules, home, audiences were stunned, and the producers quickly picked Soules as the next bachelor. Soules, who appears every inch the warm-hearted romantic guy he portrays, jumped to play in the competition and has been especially poignant in his kind treatment of all the women contenders in his edition of *The Bachelor*. Lately, he has found continued reality show success by appearing on *Dancing with the Stars*.

Ultimately, *The Bachelorette* differs from *The Bachelor* in one key way that relates to the underlying message of all reality programming. Alison Hearn, writing in her article "Hoaxing the Real: On the Metanarratives of Reality Television," explains that a *metanarrative* is a statement made in the show about itself and the genre of television in general. She says, "Beyond the lessons about love or adventure, the transformation of the home or body, or the survival of deprivation or fear, reality programs are, for the most part, stories about television itself—its modes of production, its commercial and promotional logic, its specific privations and rigor, and its mechanisms for celebrity making and work" (2009). Some people watching *The Bachelorette* might be lulled into believing this is reality. But television at its core is about delivering audiences to advertisers and ultimately about selling products. Sometimes that product can be something as disturbing as the genuine nature of intimate human relationships.

The Bachelorette is engaged in the metanarrative of the commoditization of a product and at the same time a deception about the product. *The Bachelor* clearly treats people as objects and commodities, and whether a bachelor is going to choose one or another person is always part of the show's mechanism of consumerism. Basically, the bachelor is simply a cipher for any modern person who is consuming things in a store—groceries, cars, or people. In television, people are often reduced to consumable objects. But *The Bachelorette* differs significantly, because, in the psyche of women, there is clearly a double fear not only of picking the wrong object but the underlying psychodrama that pervades all relationships—that the potential mate, the man, may be lying, acting or simply "gaming" the female contestant. In this regard, *The Bachelorette* may comment on the mechanisms of television more than *The Bachelor,* because the participants may feel that there is a double game involving their emotions. This situation makes *The Bachelorette* fun to watch but more dangerous and untrustworthy.

See also: The Bachelor; Cheaters; The Dating Game

Further Reading

Michelle Brophy-Baermann, "True Love on TV: A Gendered Analysis of Reality-Romance Television," *Poroi* 4: 2 (2005); Alison Hearn, "Hoaxing the Real: The Metanarrative of Reality Television," 2009; Jennifer L. Pozner, *Reality Bites Back*, 2010.

BEAUTY AND THE GEEK

As the title suggests, this dating show explores relationships between studious and scientifically oriented males and attractive female partners. The program was a short-lived reality game show program created by actor/producer Ashton Kutcher (*Two and a Half Men*). The program was aired from 2005 to 2008 and appeared on both the WB and CW Networks and has been revisited on Fox Reality as a rerun. The program has spirited theme music by the Pet Shop Boys, shouting their 1980s hit "Opportunities (Let's Make Lots of Money)." The lyrics explain the viable combination of a team that has both attractiveness and intellectual ability. Neil Tennant wrote the lines, "I've got the brains, you've got the looks, let's make lots of money." The programming is geared to a demographic of young males. It promotes youthful, male intellectual models and lionizes male values. Leigh H. Edwards explains in *The Triumph of Reality TV*, "Reality TV reverses classic narrative. Instead of trying to make characters seem real, it turns real people into characters, using predictable and repetitive narrative frames" (2013). Here the stereotype of the physically meek and socially awkward male was magnified so that the most egregious aspects of stereotype (the thin physique, the poorly fitting wardrobe, the shrill vocal register) were key to the character/performer's performance. The show portrayed characters that existed as hyper-attenuated clichés. Stereotyping was used here to explore myths of how males and females interact. The cartoonish nature of the males revealed that society judges people by appearances. The accentuation of the male awkwardness and the extreme attractiveness of their female companions problematized the way society wishes to see romance.

The show used a light-hearted, comedic technique where the contestants were extreme versions of socially dysfunctional males. Episodes explored the irony of engendering romance between a socially dysfunctional young male and an attractive young female. Female contestants were brought to the show and hired with little academic knowledge. Comic interludes included asking questions of a female contestant, including, Who is the Secretary of State? And one female blurted out, "Let's just talk more about me." Stereotypical behavior was showcased, and there was a sense that the contestants may be actors portraying extreme stereotypes.

Jennifer Pozner argues in *Reality Bites Back* that the reality television trope of "women are stupid" is "among reality TV's basest notions." Further, she argues that these "dumb females" "exist for our comedic pleasure" (2010). The show opened with screen tests featuring the seven chosen males, who portray social awkwardness, and the seven inept female contestants, who introduce themselves. In one segment, a piano-playing, glasses-wearing, loud character who resembles a youthful Woody Allen described his attempt at getting drunk as "Kafkaesque." The program mixed comedic moments with actual competitions in which the intelligent young men mentored the hapless young women.

The show was structured through a series of encounters and competitions to bring the mismatched couples into a closer rapport. The males attempted to attract their potential female companions through witty banter, talent contests, and competitions. The show differed from reality fare, where spectacular behavior is often encouraged. There were efforts to provide a bit of empathy for the two groups during the hour-long interaction. In one tearful scene, a beauty from the show acknowledged that these young men were not the luckless, mindless, unhandsome fashion victims they appeared to be but were actually nice fellows who were not enslaved by notions of fashion and shallow physical attractiveness.

In one scene, Richard, a buttoned-down, collared, glasses-wearing thinker, became frustrated that his plans had not worked and his female partner had not followed his logic. He accused her of complacency, and she asked him what that word means. Bookending scenes of embarrassment and squashed plans and unsuccessful dating situations, there were some genuine moments of understanding, as when one of the girls defended Richard, saying, "He just doesn't understand that it's OK to make mistakes." The show refused to attack people who acted or appeared different, and the Beauties found value in their male partners and appeared to adopt motherly concern for their new friends' self-images and attempts at self-improvement. The show strove to provide interaction between these two groups and taught some common understanding. Jennifer Pozner writes that the show seeks to be socially constructive and does not simply wallow in unfriendly stereotypes. She writes, "The men instruct the women in math, science, grammar, geography, technology, and how to be stuck-up bitches. The women teach the men to find the right pair of good-ass jeans" (2010).

Despite the desire to include a socially redeeming message, the plot still utilized vestiges of stereotypical thinking. Women who are beautiful are often portrayed as less intelligent, and men who are smart are shown to have no fashion sense but must be conversant in all technology, auto repair, and other manly crafts. Perhaps the most disconcerting thing was how the reality world often divided characteristics into sharp, binary opposites. A pretty person could not be naturally intelligent. They must be trained to acquire a level of intellectual skill. Intellect came in for serious evaluation. While the male contestants appeared to be intellectually well-developed, their physical skills, sensitivity, and attractiveness were deeply critiqued.

The show featured elements of competition, and a highlight in the first episode was a dance competition in which the female contestants trained the men to dance. There were parallels to David O. Russell's hit film *Silver Linings Playbook,* in which a troubled young man played by Bradley Cooper must restore his sense of balance and self-worth by dancing with an equally troubled Jennifer Lawrence, herself the victim of a trauma when her husband, a policeman, is murdered in the line of duty. Here the civilizing force of dance was used to train the men to become more expressive and familiar with their bodies, something the female partners had mastered despite their academic shortcomings. When Richard, the archetypical epitome of geek culture, won, he complained that winning could make him more vulnerable to elimination in future rounds of the show. That is, the contestants feared that surmounting their geek status could harm their ability to advance in reality programming status.

The show produced a high degree of anxiety during a quiz competition when the tables were turned, and the men had to coach the women in academic matters. The trivia contest pitted the women against queries like, "What president appears on a one dollar bill?" and "Who is the prime minister of England?" Though not advanced questioning, the round proved problematic. The women flailed and groped aimlessly while cameras focused, not only on the agonized female contestants but also on their male coaches simultaneously. The programming illustrated that attractiveness was important in some aspects of society, but also made the case that intellectual skill was important as well.

However, the program wanted to have fun with both beauty and intellect. There was an alternative questioning round undercutting the males' coaching, and, in the reverse round, the male contestants were quizzed on their understanding of pop culture, presumably coached by their female beauty counterparts. Questions such as, "His song 'In da Club' is a hit in the clubs," and, "She danced in a school uniform in the video for her hit, 'Baby One More Time.'" The answers, respectively 50 Cent and Brittany Spears, were capably handled by the male contestants. The round showed the importance of the men's learning skills. Memorization was shown to be a transferable skill, and subjects like culture or pop culture could be quickly handled through the same study skills. The ability to learn popular culture merely reinforced that the men had some sense of study skills. However, such competitions showed that the female contestants were inadequately educated or worse that society had schooled these women in impractical and peripheral issues instead of details that mattered to society.

The reality genre often uses the mechanism of the stereotype that makes audiences aware of society frames and primes our reactions to people on the basis of appearances. Perennial perceptions of women as airheaded, thoughtless, idle, self-involved, consumed by simplistic diversions, and devoted to trivial forms of popular culture is challenged by such programming. Such programming questions such demeaning, reductive, and negative norms and encourages youth to avoid these forms of behavior and to move beyond them. Thus, the images portrayed in *Geek* make us rethink our perceptions of cerebral male students in a more positive light.

See also: The Bachelorette; The Dating Game

Further Reading

Leigh H. Edwards, *The Triumph of Reality TV: The Revolution in American Television*, 2013; Jennifer L. Pozner, *Reality Bites Back*, 2010.

THE BLAME GAME

MTV's *The Blame Game* was a clever mash-up of two reality genres, the court show and the game show and featured two individuals who had previously been in a relationship using the court tribunal to ascertain who was at fault for the failure of their tempestuous romance. *The Blame Game* aired from 1999 to 2000 and produced over 120 episodes in its two-season run. The show benefited from overheated emotions from the combatant former partners. The program benefited from showing examples of young people who were experiencing anxiety over relationship issues. This strategy mirrored MTV's target demographic of young people who were experiencing dating anxieties in their own lives. The large number of episodes (topping 130 in two years), a two-season run, and high ratings attested to the program's success.

To magnify the drama, the show often used courtroom tactics, including accusations of cheating and infidelity, included a judge character performed by Chris Reed, and provided counselors or defenders. In other words, the show created pseudo-lawyers to defend each participant in each case, and, of course, a live audience to hiss, boo, cheer, and prod the combatants to more outrageous accusations and behavior as the program progressed. Somewhere between the legalism of

Judge Judy and the shenanigans of combat-oriented shows like *Cheaters* and *Jerry Springer*, the performers did their best to have rousing debates before the cheering audiences. The rhetoric of the show was often criticized as transforming dating to a legally punishable affair, but the show also elevated the role of teenage romantic anxiety and provided closure to many who had suffered unhappy love affairs with frustrating partners.

Perhaps the most inciting aspect of the show was the inclusion of a DJ to provide musical accompaniment to the heightened emotions and speeches between contestants as they lodged accusations at each other. The DJ, Richard "Humpty" Vission, provided beats and pumped up the tension to increase the hyperbolic conflicts. More pungently, the show accentuated moments of drama by having "guest" or "surprise" witnesses suddenly appear to disrupt or overturn the testimony of one angry party. These unannounced witnesses could implode the testimony of one or another witnesses and could show an entire case to be built on fabrication and falsehood. Sadly, such extreme moments rarely followed logical courtroom procedures but mirrored a dramatic courtroom program where surprise guest stars could punctuate a tense court trial sequence and transform the outcome. Thus the show lampooned court proceedings, undercut respect for the legal system as a means of romantic redress, and heightened drama as the principle factor in romantic entanglements.

To add to the intensity of the program, the harshly colored lighting imitated that found at a boxing or wrestling match. The handheld camerawork stabbed the cameras in the faces of the hurt contestants. The players emerged from a long, recessed runway that snaked up to the docks like combatants in a physical match. Their counselors announced their grievances and explained why they believed the relationship ended. Far from hearing words like *incompatibility* or *different interests*, the usual culprits for relationship meltdown were more tawdry accusations like the boyfriend was "a stripper-obsessed caveman," or the girlfriend was a "jealous wacko" who had repeatedly trashed his car in one way or another.

The setting replaced aspects of a dignified court with values of sensationalism. *The Blame Game* derived more from the histrionics of an episode of *Perry Mason* than a courtroom. In that popular program, clever legal tricks and theatrical proceedings often prevailed over hard, factual evidence. Here, feelings surmounted reality. Often the theatrically staged contexts would pitch the program into open aggression, and defendants would attack one another. Thus, theatricality was championed over deeper issues, such as why the relationship failed in the first place. Producers used combat scenarios over human interest. This staging suggested that the participants were actors in the guise of lovers. Any real accountability for relationship failure was a secondary consideration compared with the show's potential for combat dynamics. The jury of peers, supposedly adjudicating the wrecked relationship, were arranged like a mob at a brawl. The judge appeared in the guise of a frat boy in a graduation robe as he belted out the accusations like an announcer at a World Wrestling match. Adding to the carnivalesque experience were robo-lights throwing color mixes and splashes of exotic high-energy lighting around the room. The sense of energy was further enhanced by roving, steady cam shots on cranes where the cameras flew over and around the participants like flying drones on remote control.

The idea of making a carnival space comes to us from Russian writer Mikhail Bakhtin. He writes in "Carnival and the Carnivalesque" that "carnival is the place for working out in a concretely sensuous, half-real and half-play-acted form, a new mode of interrelationship between individuals, counter-posed to the all powerful, socio-hierarchical relationships of non-carnival life. The behavior, gesture, and discourse of persons are freed from the authority of all hierarchical positions" (1998). *The Blame Game* utilized this carnival atmosphere to subvert norms by "playacting" the situation to make us consider how society situated relationships in a romantic encounter. Young people gained from seeing their relationships revisited in this less-threatening, theatricalized fashion. Kids could playact their failed relationships, and the world of real consequences could be mirrored in a grotesque way. MTV's *Blame Game* is a complicated reworking of relationship dynamics. The issues tackled are real grievances because a "crime" against hurt individuals. However, unlike a real court, the crimes of a broken heart aren't punishable on *The Blame Game,* except through the mechanism of mockery. Often, the wronged contestant on the show was allowed to hold her former lover up to public ridicule. Ultimately, the program did provide a form of punishment through embarrassment.

Thus, the program presented a theatricalization of real life where contestants do not behave conventionally. There they existed in a station, television, cultural space where the rules of the conventional world were replaced by the rules of a space where the individual was free to act out. Men were portrayed as boisterous, and girls could act freer because *carnival* wasn't the real world and didn't contain the real-world consequences of marriage, pregnancy, or divorce. Here, the characters could play at real life and learn from their errors.

Perhaps the most sophisticated aspect of the production was the graphics, which appeared as excited crowds cheered and howled in the background. The attractive graphics showed a multipaneled animation of flash images, featuring cartoons of tear-soaked girls, figures pointing fingers at each other, flags of broken hearts flying, and visions of heads served on platters. Over this flurry of images, a female narrator deftly announced, "The Blame Game." But aside from the cordial niceties of the introduction, the spirit of the show was engagement and ferocious combat. Here, romance was transformed into a contact sport to keep viewers interested.

The set of the show resembled a mock trial room with elements of an *Alice in Wonderland* magic kingdom where oversized, garish-colored witness chairs and a brightly adorned judge's throne held the center stage area.

The proceedings devolved into the sort of name-calling and theatrics that one might find in a minor domestic-disturbance call, which led viewers to think, if the characters were ever together at all, it was far better that they were now apart. The elements of verbal and suggested physical abuse were disturbing. Jennifer Pozner writes in *Reality Bites Back* that by presenting an array of physically, verbally and emotionally abusive men as the "princes" that "all girls dream of"—and by presenting women as only loveable if they are willing to give up their identities and their ability to make self-defined choices— reality television is reinforcing dangerous power dynamics that lie at the heart of violent relationships. (2010)

The show illustrated women willing to give up power for a place in a relationship with a man, and such programming often equated that with emotional success. As Pozner and others have pointed out, this might be a dangerous tradeoff for many young women.

When the contestants were urged to reveal the genesis of their relationships, they started with gender-oriented narratives. When a girl was asked how things started, she mentioned that they began dating on Valentine's Day. When the boy was asked how things began, he argued that they started "getting it on, after a road trip." The female rendition codified relationships around dates and mementos. The male compartmentalization focused on physical and sexual aspects of the relationship. If one looks closely, it is easy to see that the dysfunctional relationship began because the two people conceived their relationship in very different terms.

The program used the mechanism of a courtroom show transformed into a "he said/she said" series of recriminations with a musical score and leering jurors. Competitions included singing contests that pitted the parties against each other. The better performer scored points and won credibility, suggesting that performativity was more important on the show than the truth. If you sounded truthful and if you could sell your performance to the judges and home audience, it was likely your rendition of the relationship would be believed. These mechanisms of performativity also dominate *The Voice* and *American Idol*.

See also: Cheaters

Further Reading

Mikhail Bakhtin, "Carnival and the Carnivalesque," 1998; Leigh H. Edwards, *The Triumph of Reality TV*, 2013.

BLIND DATE

Blind Date was a reality dating show that aired in syndication from 1999 through 2006. Host Roger Lodge led the Universal series that paired two unrelated people and sent them off together on a blind date. The show was involved with seeing the reactions these strangers had when they were confronted with new and unknown partners for an evening together. The entire proceedings was taped for the show. Some shows were simply bad matches featuring people with little in common. The most thrilling episodes featured individuals who exhibited real chemistry and attraction or unbridled hatred for each other. Virtually all audience members could remember their own date successes and failures and warmed to the idea of two strangers trying to converse, eat, and become acquainted with each other.

Simultaneously, the show illustrated one of reality television's biggest issues, the constant and intrusive presence of a camera and crew. The presence of a team watching the couple's every move made it nearly impossible to obtain spontaneous and unrehearsed responses. Natural tension from the dating environment and of course the presence of cameras only made that situation worse. The host, Roger Lodge, appeared as an affable character who, with the audience, enjoyed the vicarious thrill in watching the dating process. The series ran an impressive 900+ episodes, and the show featured clever follow-up segments to see if individuals would continue dating or if the contestants would have bad dating experiences. Audiences warmed to the explosive mismatches and the rare couples who found a way to connect amid the show hype.

The program generally began with teaser clips featuring the potential dates and Lodge making witty retorts to the contestants' taped repartee. After a minute of footage, the audience was well briefed on the desires, habits, and needs of the contestants. With a baseline of knowledge about the two players, the audience waited to see if the date would either conform to the other partner's ideal or simply play the fool. Contestants usually tried to position themselves as fun-loving yet simultaneously serious about finding an attractive and wise partner. Some of the dates were hosted in prosaic surroundings, and some were set in exotic locales and settings like hot tubs and discos, where conditions could easily upset the participants. Richard Adler in *Television as a Cultural Force* remarks that "through displaced events and disguised characters, society uses television drama as a means of transforming its fears and unresolved into metaphorical forms which are less threatening than direct confrontation" (1976, 13). Reality television here does the same by allowing the viewers to enter the daters' experience, literally allowing them to follow along on the date with the couple without any of the fear and anxiety of a real date.

For some, the operative word behind *Blind Date* was *sex*, and some players thought they were *players,* usually with disastrous results. Most of the young women were more mature and were quietly shopping for potential relationships, and, of course, the cross-discourse conversations became amusing, since often men and women were speaking to cross-purposes. Many times the program had a look of a tabloid photo, where people were caught and photographed at their worst. Often drama was elicited by having a photographer cover daters at their worst and most vulnerable moments.

Misha Kavka writes that shows like *Blind Date* evolved from earlier shows like *The Dating Game*, but with an important difference. Kavka says, "Once absorbed into reality TV, the dating show was reconfigured as both contrivance and reality, both a competitive game and real life" (2012, 120).

Problems the show encountered and tried to overcome included the scenes where the date arrived. These scenes had to be planned and choreographed for the camera, but the partners had to appear that their bump into each other at a location was spontaneous, and they had not met before. How does one act the awkwardness of first meeting more than once? So despite claims that the show was not staged or planned, some elements, of necessity, probably had rehearsed components. Of course, the director had to direct that moment on film.

A feature of the show was highlighting a moment in stop frame and placing animation over the still figures. In one episode, a couple met in a very friendly way, and, when the couple shook hands, the look on their faces was mutual attraction. The screen stopped, and the characters were covered with test tubes that proclaimed, "Chemistry!" Many episodes relied on very unusual meetings. In another episode, a couple went to a gym, and the male had to give the female date a massage while she was naked. The nakedness was a ruse, and we only see the female naked from the back. However, this moment, like many others, appeared calculated to extract the maximum amount of awkwardness from the two strangers. The tension arose when the daters had to deal with the awkwardness through incessant chat and conversation. Again, these shows had to adhere to the rules of television drama. If there was no drama, drama had to be created, and *Blind Date* did this by making the guests participate in awkwardness-inducing situations.

The theatrical term for this technique is the *alienation effect*. It comes from German director and writer Bertolt Brecht, who believed that audiences could become too comfortable with reality and their sensitivity to a situation could be reduced. That is, familiarity deflated drama and tension, but unfamiliarity heightened tension and drama. In his plays, Brecht felt that introducing moments of strangeness or "alienation" in which some device might make the normal seem strange and new could heighten the drama of a scene. His goal was to rouse audiences from mentally sleeping through his plays. Brecht favored plays that aroused human intellectual focus on common and disconcerting problems of people. In an article entitled "The Street Scene," Brecht argued that this new theater must seem totally natural. Brecht writes, "It is most important that one of the main features of the ordinary theatre should be excluded from our street scene: the engendering of illusion" (1992, 122).

Shows like *Blind Date* seem like real life. If there is an illusion, there is an illusion that this is reality. At the same time, the producers, like Brecht, want the audience to be aware that what they are seeing is a highly artificial version of reality. What is real is underlying. The problem we all deal with is the fear of being uncomfortable, self-conscious, not fitting in, and failing to make some physical connection with another person.

While most of the dates were fun and the awkwardness was overcome by good-natured individuals, the show offered intrusive thought balloons. These Brechtian elements were injected into the show to remind audiences they were watching a staging of reality. In *Blind Date*, the Brechtian device of thought balloons not only told us what people were thinking but were a constant remainder of the madness and unnaturalness of the dating situation. The producers decided that humor would offset the awkwardness by showing the underlying thoughts of the characters during a scene. For example, during the awkward naked massage scene, the thought balloon read, "At least he doesn't have hairy hands." The thought balloons served to emphasize the awkward quotient.

The most satisfying episodes featured people who overcame the adversity of awkward cameras, events, and tension and somehow managed to have a pleasant time. This allowed the audience an opportunity to share a positive moment. On the other end of the spectrum, there were amusing moments when a male date became drunk or an female date became insulted and left. Mostly, the show produced amused viewers who were watching the difficulty of people seeking to connect.

See also: The Bachelor; Date My Mom

Further Reading

Richard Adler, *Television as a Cultural Force*, 1976; Misha Kavka, *Reality TV*, 2012; Anne Helen Petersen, "Entertainment Tonight: Tabloid News," 2013.

CATFISH: THE TV SHOW

Catfish is an MTV reality "dating" show that began in 2012, created over 30 episodes in its first season, and returned for a new season in 2014. *Catfish* builds upon a new awareness of an Internet society in which one's sense of identity becomes more fluid. Simona Sangiorgi explains in her "National Identities at Leisure" that "instability, distortion of meaning, and volatile identities seem to be rapidly spreading in the wake of globalization throughout the world in a multitude of forms" (Pultar 2014, 155). This new awareness complicates the proceedings of *Catfish* as a dating show.

Online dating has often been seen as risky, and *Catfish* takes that premise to a new level. One problem is we often do not know the real identity of the person on the other end of the conversation. What if the person you met was markedly different from the person you believed you were dating? *Catfish* is based on a weird reality film also entitled *Catfish*. It was a documentary about a young man named Nev in New York who began an online relationship with a girl he met named Abby. Supposedly, she was an eight-year-old child prodigy who could paint. Nev and his brother Ariel became Facebook friends with the whole family, including the mother, Angela, and the father, Vince, and an older, half sister Megan. Nev was really attracted to the older sister, Megan, and he decided to drive to Michigan to meet the family and learn more. When he arrived, he found Angela and Abby. He soon discovered there was no Megan, Abby could not paint, and Angela had concocted over 15 Facebook profiles and masqueraded as all of her aliases. As a compensation for a life as an overworked parent, she acted out various fantasy roles to satisfy a need to be different people. She wished to escape her overworked, burdensome life. In reality, she has been traumatized as a mother and foster mother to Vince's handicapped children. Her friendship with Nev, posing as other characters, and her painting (she was the painter, not daughter Abby) were ways to revitalize her otherwise depressing life and daily drudgery. Despite the seemingly shoddy premise of the film, the underlying truth was that role-playing online served a potentially reaffirming purpose for people suffering from unfulfilling life roles.

Many have commented on the Internet's ability to allow multiple identities to exist, and researchers have situated the Net as a place for experiments about the self. Rob Cover writes in "Becoming and Belonging," that

> when it comes to the relationship between the multiplicity of uses and identity, there is a common tendency in both scholarship and popular discourse to assume that the identities of users are fixed, static, and merely represented or expressed through online activities. An alternative view is to consider the ways in which social networking sites operate as a space for the continued, ongoing construction of subjectivity— neither a site for identity play nor for static representation of the self, but as an ongoing reflexive performance and articulation of selfhood that utilizes the full range of tools made available through common social networking sites such as MySpace and Facebook. (Rak and Poletti 2013, 55)

Cover clarifies some of the mechanisms at work in *Catfish*. Characters like Angela use the Web deception to broaden and deepen their lives so that they create dramas and a greater capacity to reach out to the world.

Vince explained the catfish allegory of the show. He tells Nev that when Cod were shipped from Asia to America in containers, the fish fell apart and became lifeless. The fishermen discovered when they put a catfish in the tank with the cod, the cod survived and retained their essence. Thus, the title of the film, *Catfish*, a clever deception to keep bored people involved in their otherwise dull and lifeless existences. However, more commonly, a *catfish* on the Web is someone who poses as someone different, usually more interesting and beautiful, to lure in some unsuspecting person to fall in love with him or her. Obviously, the idea of Web subterfuge is nothing new, but the heightened dimension of becoming emotionally involved with a deception is a strange and interesting phenomenon.

MTV's *Catfish* uses producer Nev Schulman as the investigator, and, with a camera crew, Schulman quizzes his guests on their true identities. Just like Schulman's film, where supposed cyber-daters are carrying on a relationship online, Schulman finds online daters who are interested in making the leap to an actual face-to-face relationship. Like Schulman's life experience, when he actually met Abby and discovered that Angela was the character behind the deception, Schulman created a program that is devoted to *the reveal*, the moment when the figures first meet. Of course, this wild, freewheeling world of Internet identities creates some drama. There are surprises, embarrassment, and strange experiences. The audience is voyeuristically involved in these online encounters and wonders, along with the subjects (and sometimes the victims), if the person on the other end is real. *The New York Times*'s Mike Hale described the process, saying, "The resulting encounters, with their tense moments in arriving cars and awkward hellos, are echoes of the film's 'reveal'" (2012). However, as Hale and others have mentioned, the sense of tension, fear, and anxiety is strangely reduced, since there is little at stake. The partners are either going to discover in real life that they get along and enjoy each other, or they don't. Further, without the element of mystery inherent in the Cyrano sort of literary relationship, the characters have no hidden agenda. Suddenly, what the characters see is what they get.

Schulman and associate Max Joseph, another filmmaker, pursue these investigative journalistic studies to find these "catfish" lurking on social media. As much as the reveal with dates is sometimes spooky and alarming, there is a second thrill generated. The show embraces the embarrassment of catching people in lies. One character is discovered to have only 10 friends on Facebook. The filmmakers recognize that as a warning sign of a con artist, because no real person would only have 10 friends online. They found he had lied about his positions and even had stolen pictures that were supposedly his by borrowing pictures from Switzerland. In one of the strangest reveals, a man pretended to be a woman and carried on an online covert relationship with a man for some time.

Like many MTV shows, the program capitalizes on the influence of technology and anxieties engendered by the uncomfortable demands of dating itself. The program utilizes techniques of subterfuge and fear, which produces a good mix of investigative journalism and romance dynamics. Cover comments that our sense of identity online and in the world may be changing due to the influence of technology. He writes,

> Indeed, as we have shifted from the text-based online world of Web 1.0 to a more interactive matrix of online behaviors in Web 2.0, characterized by social networking, audio-visual representation, and everyday tools for creative expression, we can see that online applications are taken up for anything but anonymity. Instead they are part of a complex response to an older, ongoing cultural demand that we process ourselves and our actions into coherence, intelligibility, and recognizability, and thus disavow the instability of identity. (Rak and Poletti 2013, 56)

In the end, *Catfish* isn't just another novel MTV spin on the dating show game format, it is an existential journey into truthfulness and an opportunity to uncover why someone might manufacture a totally new and novel identity.

See also: Date My Mom; The Dating Game

Further Reading

Mike Hale, "There's Always a Catch," *New York Times*, November 11, 2012; Annette Hill, *Reality TV*; Gönül Pultar, *Imagined Identities: Identity Formation in the Age of Globalism*, Syracuse, NY: Syracuse University Press, 2014; Julie Rak and Anna Poletti, *Identity Technologies: Constructing the Self Online*, Madison: University of Wisconsin Press, 2013.

CHEATERS

Cheaters is a reality show created by Bobby Goldstein in 2000 that has been continually aired and remained popular through 2017. A variety of hosts have presented the program, and the format has remained stable throughout the program's long run. It is a highly dramatic and emotional television show, and viewing audiences are captivated by the high-stakes drama depicted before them. Goldstein and his crew solicit contestants from regular people who believe their spouse or partner may be behaving unfaithfully. Producers send out a camera crew to perform surveillance on the individual, and, if they find evidence of misbehavior, they show that footage to the wronged party, who then has the right to a confrontation with the straying partner in front of a camera and in public. These are tense, dramatic scenes of confrontation that often erupt in violence and fisticuffs.

Cheaters contains elements of reality television that render the genre unpredictable and simultaneously complicated. First, there is an invitation to share something personal about a real person's life. The program identifies a couple and chats with one partner, who thinks their spouse or significant other is cheating. The show starts with an official caveat. It reads, "From *Cheaters* surveillance cameras. You are about to view actual true stories, filmed live, documenting the pain of a spouse or lover caused by infidelity." Such descriptions clarify for the audience immediately that this program will not be fun and games, but stands to be a bruising personal experience. While the subject matter might be distasteful to many, the ultimate payoff is to see the confrontation between the cheater and the betrayed spouse. In this sense, the program mirrors traditional and historical television logic. There is a protagonist and a villain who must be punished, and the program often provides a fight scene at the end that provides ample punishment for the offending party.

Cheaters has run continuously from 2000 and has filmed over 290 original episodes. It is commonly programmed for late-night syndication. Goldstein, a Dallas attorney cum television producer features the theme "Broken Hearted" by Bill Mason, which adds to the program's ironic tone. The show has survived three hosts, 15 seasons, and well over 500 breakups. There have almost been as many near homicides when one partner catches the other dallying with an outsider. The show has filmed and marketed special unexpurgated versions that featured more wild cursing, sexuality, and violence, and there are special 10-minute segments of brutal confrontations available for DVD sale and download from various online markets.

The program is intrinsically tied to the hidden camera genre, where people act out their worst behavior, and these moments of video angst are recorded unbeknownst to the perpetrator. *Cheaters* is especially brutal and crude, and it isn't uncommon for the program to require security and police in the background. The program thrives on realistic cinema vérité camera techniques in which a handheld camera is brandished and bashed by both combatants. This allows the viewers to have the sense they are in the center of the storm as the participants madly thrash at each other. Often police must separate incensed lovers and brawlers, particularly when one partner catches another in the middle of a tryst with a third party.

The German term *schadenfreude*, or horrific embarrassment, is important to the program's success. The battle portrayed is horrific and comical, eclipsing many things on fictional television. For example, a woman bursts into a fury when she finds her husband half undressed in a car with another woman. Other gruesome encounters ensued when a wife finds a husband gambling with a sister in a casino. Some of the scenes are comparable to tragic operas in the wide range of reactions recorded. In one scene, a wife is out on a date when her husband runs into the scene and throws a glass of wine in her face.

Many have written that these events are staged and that producers have provoked confrontations to derive better television. The true amount of manipulation of events is unknown, but it does seem that people act out at extreme levels. The cheating is uncovered by the Cheaters Detective Agency. They either follow or find the lying partner at a hangout or club and turn on the camera at the moment of greatest drama. The producers bring in the angered party, and, while watching the act of infidelity or cheating, the producer questions the outraged spouse to inflame and enrage the cheated party. Producers whisper messages like, "How does that make you feel?" or "Do you believe your wife is cheating now?" or "Do you still love her now?" The result is usually a fiery and violent eruption.

The show treads into fights, violence, and sexual situations, so it is labeled TV-MA and appears late at night. DVD packages proclaim that these sale packages include *more* violence and nudity. The producers play with notions of reality. If television can only show certain aspects of a tense situation, they offer the DVD version to provide a more in-depth experience, providing more scenes of outrage and anguish. In a way, *Cheaters* makes the argument that true reality programming should be more involving, and the best way to achieve that level of absorption is by showing the most sensationalistic aspects of something that will increase the viewers, the anger, and the interest level.

Richard Huff argues that such reality programming is always questionable in our society. We have to decide if what is shown in *Cheaters* is real or perhaps only a carefully contrived version of events. Huff writes, "Reality TV reflects an anxiety about truth claims that have become increasingly suspect in our digital era of easily manipulable images" (2006, 179). The show is structured to lead our assumptions about events. The wronged partner describes in an interview the early period of their relationship and what has led them to think there is infidelity. The other partner is called a "suspect," and the alleged lover of the suspect is referred to as "the companion." The investigative team trails the suspect and looks for suspicious activity. When the investigators find enough evidence, the producers arrange a moment of confrontation when the wronged party will confront the suspect and companion, either in an act of infidelity or on the verge of it. The censored TV version blurs the semi-nude couple caught in some love act. DVD releases show partial nudity as the parties scramble to look presentable to the camera. Some scenes depict men in S and M masks, whips, vampire capes, and animal costumes, and women in comparable cosplay (nurses, teachers, tramps, furries, etc.). These costumes add to the embarrassment and spectacularity of the encounters. The show concludes with all parties having commentary. Usually, the complainant describes their heartbreak and surprise, while the suspect attempts to justify his or her actions. Most often the companion, the third party in the affair, simply wants to be out of camera range.

To blunt criticism that the show is just shock value and appeals to basic vileness and revels in depravity, the producers post the message, "*Cheaters* presents to you inspirational chronicles of humankind. The heroic men and women of these stories overcame the challenges of relationships" (Teachout 2002). The content rarely shows people overcoming anything but a poor relationship choice. The content suggests the provocative. The characters are in a heightened state of agitation, and feelings of persecution, betrayal, or righteous indignation prevail. People are unceremoniously stalked and ambushed, and often someone on the program is physically attacked and/or partially disrobed. Despite the vile actions portrayed and the fact that the show deals in acts of lying and untruth, the tone is carnivalesque. Viewers of *Cheaters* are treated to another's misfortune, and they can vicariously experience betrayal with no consequences from the tragic play before them. The betrayed and the suspect seem to survive these encounters, lending weight to the charge that much of the carnage on the show is indeed staged and choreographed. The surreal aspects of the bad behavior render it more comical than realistic.

The show has prompted people to be concerned about the growth of a surveillance society in which our every move and action is recorded by someone, somewhere. Feminist social critic Naomi Wolf wrote an article for the *Guardian* entitled "*Cheaters* and the Sinister Normalization of Our Surveillance Society." Many take these fears of growing surveillance as a real threat to our lifestyle, and reality television in general gets blamed for the tendency. Despite such concerns and criticisms that segments are staged, the program is a consistent ratings winner. The program airs in many markets during late nights on Saturdays. The audience appears to be late-night viewers. The program has sired a massive online community (known as Cheaterville), and nearly 500,000 people have liked the *Cheaters* Facebook page. Feminist writer Naomi Wolf is especially horrified over how easy the show makes surveillance. She comments that the Cheaters Detective Agency (CDA) is available for hire and "does not just play a starring role in a series; it actually also advertises on the homepage of the TV show, and the site makes it so easy to invite an investigative team to stalk or surveil a lover or spouse that the one-page application can be filled out in minutes" (2012). Not only is Wolf concerned that the show makes stalking people you either trust, don't trust, or obsess over *normal*, it encourages law breaking, since such action is nominally illegal everywhere. The Web site is packed with ads for spy equipment, sponsored as *Cheaters* products. Audiences at the Web site can buy products that secretly record cell phone calls or track GPS for the wayward spouse, and individuals can grab data from SIM cards, can record information from all the data on a cell phone to a USB drive, can record directly from a USB drive, or can spy using an audio-recording pen. Wolf writes, "Nowhere on the site that I could find, in the promotion of the TV show or the sale of the recording and spying equipment, does it warn that many laws prevent surveillance, theft of computer or phone data, or monitoring someone else's phone without a warrant" (2012).

Shows like *Cheaters* have prompted real people who have been betrayed by lovers to out their duplicitous spouses on Facebook. Caroline McGuire reports that "many decide to take action after browsing their partner's private messages on the site and discovering they have been using it to send love letters" (McGuire 2015). So *Cheaters* may actually perform some public good for people who have been the victims of liars. Further, the show illustrates a dramatic confrontation based on the idea that spouses may not always be trustworthy.

See also: Singled Out; Taildaters

Further Reading

Anita Biressi and Heather Nunn, *Reality TV, Realism and Revelation,* 2005; Joseph C. Harry, "Cheaters: 'Real' Reality Television as Melodramatic Parody," *Journal of Communication Inquiry* 32, no. 3 (2008): 230–248; *Academic OneFile,* Web, January 22, 2015; Naomi Wolf, "Cheaters and the Sinister Normalization of Our Surveillance Society," *The Guardian,* November 26, 2012.

DATE MY MOM

Date My Mom was a reality dating show that was produced by MTV and ran from 2004 until 2006. The program produced three seasons and over 100 episodes. The insignia for the show was a graphic of a tattoo with the words "Date My Mom" through a tattooed heart. In the tradition of dating shows, *Date My Mom* adds a unique spin to the genre where children of single parents try to find dates by their moms dating for them. In most episodes, the children are either lesbian or gay. Thus, the mother must date a partner of the same sex as their dateless child, trying to find a potential partner for the lovelorn young person. They must participate in games or activities that the potential partner would like to do, such as shopping, getting tattoos, going to a water park, or cheerleading. The program was produced by Kallissa Productions and ran from 2004 to 2006.

A difficulty the show encountered was that the child never met the intended date, and all negotiations to obtain a date for the child were conducted by the parent. The difficulty was that this diffused the interest for the teen seeking the date and for the dater wishing to secure a new date experience. In other words, the principles in the date were one party removed from the action. The potential date wasn't courting the mother, but the mother's good will of the date. Thus, the date was only trying to make a positive impression on a parent. This made all transactions secondhand and far removed from a real date. You never knew how accurate the parental impression was until you saw the date for yourself. This sort of long-distance dating might be a shock to the teen being dated.

Following the date, the parent would report on the qualities of the intended date. The finale of a series of dates would be the dater presenting a formal analysis of the child (still unmet) via their parents, thus arriving at a rationale to choose one of the contestants as the winner. It seemed the contestants were so removed from their potential dates that the analysis could only be cursory.

In an episode featuring Megan and Jane, the daughter, Megan, sent her mom off to date Lara, who was an attractive, young blonde lesbian woman. Her mother, Jane sold her daughter's good qualities. This Lara took Jane on her boat and the two had a nice, sophisticated lunch. It was very convivial, but the aspects of the show that sounded scripted undermined the concept. Megan told her mom that she wanted Jane to tell Lara that she has a "big rack," and the crudeness of the suggestion conflicted with the nice rapport between daughter and date. When Jane volunteered this to Lara, you could hear the audience wincing. This upset the equilibrium of the dating experience and introduced an element of shallowness and crudeness that, though real, seemed especially dark and off-putting. It lacked a ring of truth and seemed somewhat forced. Jane seemed uncomfortable with such lines, and it showed. When Lara heard the crude comment, she was notably cool. Jane returned to her daughter and reported the news of the date. She extolled the virtues of Lara, the lesbian woman, and explained that she told Lara that her daughter (Megan) looked like a Cabbage Patch Doll. Lara went on dates with two other potential candidates, again just dating doting moms. Finally, the three women met Lara at a beachfront. Each mother expressed the wonders of her daughter to the camera. The mothers all looked like respectable, middle-class moms. MTV worked to broaden its demographic to female audiences and the LGBT community through the program, and overall the show expressed some sensitivity to that audience.

This program had a complicated premise, using surrogates to do the dating for the children. It was not only difficult for the contestants, but complicated for the audience to grasp. Lara gave her synopsis of the three mom dates, but some of the dialogue sounded goofy and written by writers. When Lara told one mom she didn't want to date her lesbian daughter, there was a furious outburst that conflicted with the attractive setting.

The show sought to normalize the role of gay and lesbian people as just people, but instead of making them mainstream American, the program seemed to call attention to difference more by trying to make the dating process seem natural. It didn't become more natural in this contest. It only became more strange and surreal. MTV used a mix of generations and a kooky pairing of lesbians and gays dating moms to invoke a sense of honesty, intimacy, and feeling of association these love lost teens were seeking.

Date My Mom UK was a spin-off of the original MTV show, targeted to MTV UK and Ireland. The program was a production of Princess Productions in the UK and ran from 2006 to 2007. The premise was in some ways more conventional than the American version. A young teen male would date three moms, who each had a daughter that this lad would want to meet. However, the British and Irish mothers would be reluctant to tell the young man anything about their daughters until they had a chance to check him out. The young man would spend his time with these older women hoping to learn more about the respective daughters of each. After his dates with the mothers, he would have a meeting with all three to determine which of the daughters he would like to meet and date. Only at this point would he get to see the girls in reality.

See also: The Bachelorette; The Hook Up

Further Reading
Troy DeVolld, *Reality TV: An Insider's Guide to TV's Hottest Market,* 2013.

THE DATING GAME

The Dating Game, which originated over 50 years ago, was the progenitor of many of the reality and dating programs that have appeared in the last few decades. The format brought in one fortunate male or female contestant. This person was separated from three eligible dates of the opposite sex by a wall. Writer Pat Perry described the basic mechanism of the game. He writes, "The interviewer would ask each of the three candidates straightforward questions that presumably would assist them with making the right choice for the 'perfect date'" (Perry 2016).

It was a product of the zany and profitable mind of Chuck Barris, who was a master of game shows and a producer of many formats and loony concepts. Misha Kavka, in her *Reality TV,* described the show's format as a staple of the 1960s game show style. She says, "In its earliest configuration, developed by US television producer Chuck Barris in 1965 as *The Dating Game,* the dating program was a studio-based show presenting a bachelor and a blind selection of a romantic partner based on answers to a series of usually whimsical questions" (2012). The program was featured on ABC, and later in syndication from 1965 through 2000. The show had Jim Lange, a charming and witty host with a twinkle in his eye, as the moderator who used innuendo effectively to ask risqué and provocative questions of the contestants. Here, the emphasis was always on humor, and the romantic angle was subordinated to entertaining the audience.

The dates all knew they were on a game show, and they knew the objective was to please their intended date. They tried to be charming and comply with funny and hopefully truthful answers to the questions posed them. After Jim Lange's death in 2014, Margalit Fox wrote a tribute for the *New York Times.* "The men, known as bachelors numbers one, two, and three, were sitting behind a screen visible in the audience but not the contestant" (Fox 2014). The idea was that the girl had to pick her date on the basis of their concepts and answers, not on the basis of their individual attractiveness. The same rules applied for males choosing a female date.

While some might see *The Dating Game* as a reflection of the swinging 1960s, in reality it reflected a gentle time where, at least ostensibly, both genders received respect in the competition. Boundaries for relationships and images of what was allowable or acceptable are far more elastic today. *The Dating Game* even expressed a feminist agenda. *The New York Times* writes, "In an era in which a woman was expected to wait for a man to ask her out, *The Dating Game* billed itself as a blow for progress" (Fox 2014). In essence, the program presented the idea that a woman could ask a man for a date. In the 1960s, this was considered female empowerment.

Of course, *The Dating Game* had its perverse side as well, including strange revelations about producer and sometime show chaperone Chuck Barris. Supposedly, the successful television executive moonlighted as an undercover agent. Barris proclaimed in his 1984 memoir, *Confessions of a Dangerous Mind,* that he had been contracted as a CIA assassin while chaperoning couples on *The Dating Game.* The *Times* quoted Barris as saying, "That's possible too, because you're not with a couple constantly, you would have some free time, so I don't know how much time it takes to kill somebody" (Fox 2014). No one has been able to authenticate the dark revelations, but Hollywood took it seriously enough to mount a film of the book, directed by George Clooney.

The Dating Game was provocative fun. Occasionally guest celebrities, including Arnold Schwarzenegger and Michael Jackson, would appear as potential dates. The show was always popular in its use and trivialization of the dating experience. Many modern dating shows derive from *The Dating Game*'s often satirical look at dating culture. The show portrayed rituals of dating as often comical and absurd. It was always fascinating to go inside the mind of the player and try to determine who he or she would choose for a date. Some of the date choices were bizarre and seemed unlikely to make a good pairing, but the logistics of love and the show's upbeat sense of humor avoided the tawdry. There might be some occasional saucy humor, but the show never devolved into smut.

The signature of the show was the set, which was filled with psychedelic daisies, and a theme song derived from the brassy sounds of Herb Alpert. The swirling lights, the applause, and the cheerful faces provided the background for a comedic dating experience. The show had a colorfully produced style. The questioning was prepared in advance, and the comical answers provided by many contestants appeared coached or scripted. Susan Douglas writing about *The Bachelor* said, "It was not unlike a 4-H competition of prize heifers, except the women did weigh less, got to go to fancy resorts, and had not been dragged there against their will with a rope" (2013, 226). One could say the same of *The Dating Game*, in that it was similarly conceived as an exercise in finding partners. However, *The Dating Game* always placed sexuality in warm light. Responses may venture into naughty territory, but most remarks were laughable and silly. Little in the show ever veered toward offensiveness.

Yet for all of its ease, *The Dating Game* did signal a strange reconfiguring of television aesthetics. Richard Adler writes, "Television is not simply a 'medium,' but a 'mediator'—between fact and fantasy, between our desire to escape and our need to deal with real problems, between our old values and new ideas, between our individual lives and the life of the nation and the world" (1976, 13). *The Dating Game* participated in that mediation between our lives and the outside world. It exists as postmodern television, theatricalizing the event of viewing and simultaneously being viewed. People watch people in an intimate situation (starting the dating process) while we, the viewing audience, watch from a far. Not only do we get to participate in the pre-date selection process, we also watch the studio audience spy on the prospective couple and ask sexy questions. If television had not normalized the display of people, the voyeuristic aspects of the medium could be disturbing. Stephen Connor, in his *Postmodern Culture,* discusses the dangers of theatricality. He says, "Theatricality stands for all those falsifying divisions which complicate, diffuse and displace the concentrated self-identity of a work of art, and so encompasses a number of different effects, including self-consciousness of the spectator, the awareness of context and the dependence upon extension in time" (1996, 133). Connor sees that theatricality problematizes a work of art. Where the work of art is thrust out into a theatrical space, it has to take into account people watching, the time it occurs within, the context of the era, and various opinions about what it is. So reality TV began to debate the concept of watching the self perform the self.

Did *The Dating Game* prepare audiences for today's reality game shows? Are modern dating shows like *Next* and *Disaster Date* here because *The Dating Game* produced a model of dating reality that is still considered the heritage of dating behavior passed down to a new generation? Further, have reality shows provided an illustration of possible behaviors or produced a template for how people think dating should work?

See also: The Bachelor; Taildaters

Further Reading

Steven Connor, *Postmodern Culture*, 1996; Troy DeVolld, *Reality TV: An Insider's Guide to TV's Hottest Market*, 2013; Susan Douglas, "Reality Bites," in *Popular Culture in American History* (Ed. Jim Cullen), Wiley-Blackwell, 2013; Misha Kavka, *Reality TV.*

DISMISSED

Dismissed was one of a number of MTV themed dating game shows. MTV experimented with the genre to explore how dating was conducted and how modern dating practices were changing. This was a serious question to youthful MTV viewers, who themselves had to navigate the strange waters of the dating world, and such shows provided insight into dating behaviors and provided a humorous manual of things to do on a date and activities to avoid. *Dismissed* applied the dating concept to a larger entity, a trio of people. *Dismissed* ran as an MTV program in 2001, with an international edition debuting soon after entitled *Globally Dismissed.* The international edition was similar in content but featured performers and contestants from many foreign countries. The show was eventually reconditioned and retitled *Next.*

The show featured an unusual condition of a contestant going on a date with two people at the same time. The idea was a testing ground for young people who prided themselves on their multitasking abilities. The program tested youthful competitors to see who could watch and interact with two dates at the same time and meanwhile form an opinion of the two potential matches. A participant would have to decide which person was most desirable. All of the dates had a timeout card that would allow them to have 20 minutes alone with the player if they so chose. At the end of the date, the contestant kept the date he or she liked more and dismissed the other. In Benjamin Solomon's article "A Complete History of MTV's Dating Game Shows," he discusses the mechanism of *Dismissed.* Solomon writes that this was the "network's first attempt to merge the old and the new, taking the dating show out of the studio and into the 'real world'" (2013).

In this sense, the network succeeded in revitalizing the game show by placing it in a lively context outside the confines of MTV's cramped and generic-looking sets. This production placed the players in real locations, and this added a level of reality, vulnerability, and artificiality to the show all at once. The setup was a preconceived situation. Solomon surmises that at best "the highly structured (and most likely partially scripted) show followed one contestant on a date with two singles. After the date the contestant would dismiss one single, and go on a date with the other" (2013). The process sounded simple, but the awkward juggling of two people on the date led to intentional and sometimes unintentional slights to one or another player. Also, audiences were unclear on the amount of coaching one or another player received. If the date was conducted completely by the principles, it worked rather smoothly; however, if moments were processed by the producers to create a fictitious encounter, with manufactured drama and conflict, the show could have the appearance of a highly artificial environment. Many shows never struck a balance between feeling natural and contrived, and many of the contestants were baffled over the difficulties of conducting a two-way date.

Often this reality process encouraged players to become highly competitive in the dating frame. Tanja Aho writes that "reality TV has become an extremely popular television genre partly because it mediates a supposedly 'authentic' representation of reality . . . and partly because it offers voyeuristic insights into people's private lives" (2013, 205). *Dismissed* accomplishes that by taking people into the center of a complicated dating experience. Instead of enjoying the company of their companions, the daters become competitors, and they alternately tried to undercut one another. This antagonism appeared manufactured, and perhaps showed a part of reality that made aggression look surreal. Since the players didn't know each other and had no reason to undercut their competitors except through the ambition to win, any sense of aggression would seem unwarranted. While this process created some tension, it also undercut the proceedings, making the dating seem stressed, and sometimes disturbing.

The program shared specific characteristics with many MTV game shows. For example, when the characters met, the girls wore provocative clothing. The male, who must pick between them, was highly attractive and seemed interested in a good-looking date. He was not looking for somebody especially interesting in conversation. The intellectual aspect of rapport was avoided in favor of visual traits. This reduction of people to attractive players in a maze turned the entire enterprise into a social experiment in which subjects acted out aggressions in a controlled environment.

The girls in this process immediately accessed their competitor, launched retorts and asides to the producer disdaining their competition, and determined their own chances for success. Immediately, words like *aggression, attractiveness,* and *competition* entered the show. The show became a competitive sport, and sniping commentary ran throughout the encounters.

In one episode two girls dated a man at a roller skating rink, and their first impulse was to fight it out, roller-derby style. There were shots of both of the girls falling on the floor, and friendly combat ensued. One doubts that most individuals would spar over a person they had never met before, but the show explored primitive animal impulses that underscore the conventions of dating. Certainly the behavior sought to illustrate the dangers of teen passions to younger viewers. In episodes viewed, the girls derived pleasure from awarding their rival a timeout card so the player could spend extra time with a male date. Many techniques of bullying and intimidation were explored. Girls launched e-mail and text taunts at each other, and the show explored the mean-girls syndrome that pervades many high school social cliques.

MTV utilized these encounters for maximum impact, showing the absurdity of such behavior. Often women on such shows depict negative stereotypes of women. This depiction of women as negative, hostile, and territorial played into depictions of women as window dressings for male fantasies. Female viewers were warned that such behaviors were self-defeating and often self-destructive. One senses that MTV was using such programming to explore teen female lifestyles and to push women to more appropriate behaviors that benefit them and their peers.

The show explored the manner in which modern audiences were growing more comfortable with self-presentation and postmodern issues of surveillance. For this generation, creating a character on screen was commonplace, and the performers were continually watching themselves being watched by reporting everything as it happened. The program illustrated the delicate balance between living one's life and reporting that constructed life via the use of continual social media feeds. Rob Cover, writing in "Becoming and Belonging," states that "the ways in which social networking sites have been taken up and become popular as an efficient, effective yet also problematic site for the performance of coherent, intelligible, and recognizable identities and subjectivities" (Rak and Poletti 2013, 57).

Dismissed also explored the difficulty in maintaining both an online life and an actual existence. For example, in January of 2016, rock performer David Bowie died of cancer, but since his death his Web presence has been vibrant and his staff have preserved his memory by exhibiting a wide range of posthumous releases and commentary on the dead star. In contrast, the live players of *Dismissed* narrated an online life while living an actual existence. The players constantly narrated every activity they did. Audiences received an almost-direct newsfeed of their activities. The viewer was treated to a constant and continuous Facebook post. The e-mail competitors gave a blow-by-blow description of their strategy and their anxieties during each part of the process. Thus players must negotiate a ground game and an Internet game. The entire process became a chess game of waiting for moves by their competitor. An interest in people barely known dominated their consciousness. Further, such interactions were framed as paranoid and antagonistic. While the players may not harbor such feelings, the program desired to engender interactivity between filmed players and a home audience. Women were drawn into combat mode about a potential date. Yet the males in these competitions seemed routinely oblivious to such mechanizations.

In one segment of the series, one of the dating girls decided to take her date and her competitor to her house for a hot tub experience. The presumption was that the competitors wished to turn the competition into a swimsuit pageant. Sidone Swift and Julia Watson commented that

> Opportunities for composing, assembling, and networking lives have expanded exponentially since the advent of Web 2.0. The sites and software of digital media provide occasions for young people to narrate moments in coming of age; for families to track and narrate their genealogical histories; for people seeking friends and lovers or those with similar hobbies to make connections; for political activists to organize around movements and causes. (Rak and Poletti 2013, 70)

The competitors acquired an aggressive stance toward their dating duties. Added to this was the generational tendency to report and narrate their life adventures. The allure for viewers and contestants was seeing, being engaged, and being involved in the date. Such dating reality programming took the viewer along for the experience. Many of the most provocative moments were strategic. After the hot tub get-together, one of the girls called a timeout so that she could spend more time with the potential date in the hot tub. In a discussion segment following the date, one of the girls retorted, "It was a tough race, I think he's got his work cut out for him." At the show's closure, following the methodology of *The Bachelor*, the male contestant told both girls that he had a good time, but that now he had to choose. He chose the more flirtatious girl. He dismissed the more reserved girl. The suggestion was that the attractive and aggressive girl would win due to her aggression and grooming. *Dismissed* promoted a sense of intimacy not only with the competitors but with home audiences who shared the dating competition. Smith and Watson argue,

> The selves produced through various sites can convey to visitors and users a sense of intimacy—the intimacy of the quotidian details of daily life, the intimacy of shared confession and self-revelation, the intimacy of a unique voice or persona or virtual sensibility, contributory to the intimate public sphere theorized by Lauren Berlant (1997) and Anna Poletti (2011).

Dismissed does something similar by creating an authentic dating environment, a virtual world of gaming, and demonstrating interest in another (Rak and Poletti 2013, 75).

However, the fear for viewers was that they would stay perpetually outside the arena of dating open to attractive and privileged youth featured on the program. Viewers never received a deeper insight into any of the characters. Their purpose was to provide us with a facsimile of our own experience. We often gained disturbing insights, such as that a compliant, submissive, sexually available woman was what men desired. It is unclear whether such programming advances viewers' sense of the mechanisms of dating. Smith and Watson suggest that "if authenticity can be 'manufactured,' if it is an effect of features of self-performance, then credibility, veracity, and sincerity acquire a slipperiness that can prompt suspicious readings" (Rak and Poletti 2013, 75). As the authors indicate, if these roles of reality can be acquired and shed rapidly, they become less real and less reliable. The performance of the date may be a distant version of the real thing.

The show possibly participated in a videogame performance of the dating game; dating became a game to be won with the right moves. Steven Connor, writing about postmodern society, explains that a "simulation takes the form, not of unreality, as so many of Baudrillard's followers wish to believe, but of manufactured objects and experiences which attempt to be more real than reality itself—or, in Baudrillard's term, 'hyperreal' (Connor 1996, 57). Here we could see hyper-real people providing a simulation of the dating experience. As MTV created *Dismissed* and other reality programs, they experimented with images of reality that functioned as genuine to viewers. *Dismissed* was an early experiment on how to configure images of youth in a dating situation. As MTV became more aware of the mediated sphere that many youth inhabited (cell phones, video games, social media, brief video culture), they carefully tailored progressive dating shows to capture elements of the online experience in a broadcast format. *Dismissed* was a step toward courting the online student audience.

See also: The Bachelor; The Dating Game

Further Reading

Steven Connor, *Postmodernist Culture*, 1996; Richard M. Huff, *Reality Television*, 2006; Julie Rak and Anna Poletti, *Identity Technologies: Constructing the Self Online,* Madison: University of Wisconsin Press, 2013; Benjamin Solomon, "A Complete History of MTV's Dating Game Shows," The datereport.com, November 12, 2013.

THE HOOK UP

MTV's *The Hook Up* is the newest derivation of the old dating game format. The first thing was that in slang teen language a "hook up" can be a no date, date where individuals hook up for sexual liaison with no idea of a permanent relationship. Despite the provocative and disturbing connotation, here MTV departed from that meaning and produced a show about people looking for actual dates.

A bachelor and bachelorette were placed in the studio with a live audience and confronted with four candidates for a date. Initially, the potential dates were asked questions and the player could throw out one candidate without ever seeing or meeting them. The conditions were fairly harsh for the potential dates. After the first elimination, candidates were brought out for a face-to-face chat. The candidates provided pictures, videos, and intimate knowledge of themselves through a quote. Jennifer Slack argues that such extended portraits have always been part of the human phenomenon and we are all composites. She writes,

> Indeed, arguing from the logic of articulation and assemblage, which insists that we consist of a range of connections to language, technology, bodies, practices, and affects, we have always been cyborgs. Our bodies can change and incorporate technologies (this alters action and perception). We can grasp that idea pretty easily. Even more radical, however, is the idea that technologies extend how we think; that they are extensions of our mind. (2015, 211)

On *The Hook Up,* various technologies helped to write a person's autobiography and to market the players to the potential date. Sometimes these segments told the contestants that one of the candidates might not be right for him or her. After this second elimination, the contestant had two candidates to choose.

As the show progressed, the player learned more about the candidates from their social media. Again the show focused on the constructed extended persona that the person had created online. If the candidates had posted a questionable video or written something that sounded odd, the player may pass on them. In a sense the entire show was a warning about what to share on social media. Basically, through its surveillance and the willingness of the potential dates to share information, the player could find out much about the potential dates. Many times it was more information than the contestant wanted to know, and this may transform the potential date into a potential risk. The Web site *The Wrap* commented that "MTV proves that nothing posted online is truly secret with its new dating show" (Nededog 2013). The scrutiny a guest received could cost a potential date that one chance to make a good impression. *The Wrap* goes on to argue that MTV's new show set boundaries on the positive minutes of social media and suggested to viewers that sharing too much information might prohibit one's ability to be socially acceptable. In other words, the show assumed a fairly conservative ground that sharing too much could be disadvantageous and not a sensible choice for individuals.

In the teaser trailer for *The Hook Up*, MTV revealed that social media would be used *against* the potential dates. After all of the embarrassing data about two finalists, the player finally picked one for the final date. However, the show didn't stop there. Potential dates now had a chance to turn the tables, and the player's chosen date could now look at the social media of the player to determine whether he or she actually wanted to go on a date with that person. Again, the show suggested that social media exposes all people to scrutiny they might not want. This may be a case of MTV urging more responsible behavior from youth when they are on the Net. This contrasts with shows like *Ridiculousness* and *Jackass*, where outrageousness is coupled with popularity and humor.

The Hook Up appeared to pick people who were practically looking for dates. David Hickley, writing for the *New York Daily News*, comments, "We see nothing that suggests they (the players) have any higher ambition than to do some skateboarding, pop open a 40, and have their friends call them 'Dude!'" (2013). The contestants were largely a congenial lot of players. Richard M Huff, in his book *Reality Television*, describes how shows protect their intellectual property and keep the surprises fresh. He writes, "By eliminating key details, it makes it a bit difficult for contestants to play to the concept of the show during auditions" (2006). The result was a program in which the contestants seemed like real people seeking a real date. In an era in which we are suffused with reality programming, this sort of naïve natural performance is lacking. It becomes increasingly hard to tell the difference between real people and people appearing to be acting in a game show. Here, there was at least the sense these were people seeking dates, not professional game show actors.

Each segment was entertaining. Again, embarrassment and finding out secret facts about people provided a voyeuristic and probative function for the show. What secrets might they be hiding? One of the funny segments in the first season involved a contestant seeing a video by one of the potential dates in which he meows like a cat for several seconds. The contestant thought that the video was just weird. Viewers agreed. In another segment, the contestant read an online report by a candidate that said a condom dropped out of her suitcase in front of a family member. The contestant suggested to the candidate that she might keep that information to herself. While the show was lighthearted and in many ways reminiscent of *The Dating Game* from the 1960s, there was an aspect of the show that placed the viewer in a position of judgment. It was easy for viewers to feel morally superior by watching somebody else's poorly formed Web content. The question most viewers must consider was, in their own immaturity: "Have I posted something I will later regret?" In this sense this was a meta-referential TV show. The people watching, presumably 18–30-year-olds, displayed the same behaviors as the contestants and potential dates. It may be an attempt by MTV (like *Teen Mom* appears to be) to offer socially responsible advice to a generation that the station has courted for over 35 years. It is thought-provoking to presume MTV, not as the rebellious child, but as the caring parent.

See also: The Bachelor; The Dating Game; Dismissed; Next

Further Reading

David Hinckley, "The Hook Up: Television Review," *New York Daily News,* October 14, 2013; Richard M. Huff, *Reality Television,* 2006; Jerry Nededog, "MTV's New Dating Show Proves You Shouldn't Social Everything," Dailies, *The Wrap*; Jennifer Daryl Slack and J. Macgregor Wise, *Culture and Technology: A Primer,* New York: Peter Lang Inc., International Academic Publishers, 2015.

JOE MILLIONAIRE

Joe Millionaire was a show produced by Fox that began broadcasting in 2003 and ceased broadcasting in the fall of 2003 after a second season, *The Next Joe Millionaire*. It dealt with coupling women with a millionaire. The premise of the show was a deception or ruse. Real-life construction worker and (sometimes underwear model, it was later revealed) Evan Marriott pretended to be a millionaire when indeed he was not a wealthy character but a mere day laborer. However, Marriott was very handsome, well-spoken, and seemingly could affect the guise of a millionaire handily. A problem with the show was that once it obtained wide popularity and notoriety, it was nearly impossible to repeat the trick. Any woman who had been around during the first show would have caught on to the idea and recognized the premise.

The concept of the first season was clever. It removed women from the domestic media for a month. Twenty women were whisked off to a romantic month in

France at the chateau of a supposed millionaire bachelor. The show featured *Bachelor*-like challenges and events in which the bachelor would squire the women on dates, and each would try to find ways to spend more time with him. The show derived sympathy for all players in the game. In real life, a man who deceived women into thinking he was a millionaire could possibly be liable for criminal charges, but, in this theater, the audience had sympathy for his predicament. He had to play the millionaire yet watch for signs that the women only liked him for his money. Neither role was without problems. At the same time, the women were pitiable, since they were being lied to on a regular basis about a man with whom they seemed to have a genuine bond. At the same time, the idea of deception in a romance is common. Males and females often lie about their financial standing in a relationship. Of course, women's groups objected to the framing of the show around notions that women are inherently gold diggers and only interested in a man for his money. The transparentness of this premise disturbed many social groups, who found the show an objectionable bit of sociopolitical theater seeking to indict the feminist movement as flawed and hollow. However, *People* magazine did a follow up in 2015 and investigated the recent activities of contestant Zora Andrich, commenting that, "for her part, the winner—who now goes by Zora Sabrina and works as a yoga instructor and model—'never felt bothered by the premise of the show'" (Steiner 2015), she told *People* last year.

At another level, the program may have resonated with audiences because the assault on women and the assault on our sense of propriety made the show interesting. It transgressed our common sense of decent behavior. In fact, the program benefited from a transgressive format that benefits many reality programs in which people display disturbing or antisocial tendencies in a manner that was embarrassing but also revealing. This was a factor of early reality programming such as *Candid Camera,* in which contestants were baited and then embarrassed by their outbursts of bad behavior. *Joe Millionaire* adhered to the format of using television to prompt social experiments in human behavior.

The finale of the show drew enormous ratings. The star had to choose one woman and admit to her that he was not a millionaire and the whole program had been an elaborate hoax. At this point, the woman had a complex decision to make. Should she stay at all connected to a man who had systematically lied to her with complete knowledge of his deception for a month? How trustworthy would such a person be, and what sort of date or mate would that person be? Further, she was deceived about his finances, not an unimportant part of the equation. So the chosen woman had ethical dilemmas to consider. Further, the man had to consider beyond the deception. Did he, in fact, wish to be with any group of women whose only purpose was to date and marry a millionaire? Further, how would the women react when they learned their dreamboat millionaire was an average construction worker, albeit a handsome construction worker?

The show dealt with a sociological investigation of American values related to wealth and capital. *The Wall Street Journal* reported the show as more of a marketing concept for Fox than a true bid at entertainment programming, saying, "'Joe

Millionaire' may have found his mate Monday night, but it was Fox who found true love" (Nelson 2003). They were jokingly referring to Fox's love of revenue, and *The Wall Street Journal* was happy to ponder such ironies. The idea of a massively elaborate ruse employing attractive locations, a romantic setup, psychological deception of a high order, and careful post-production and editing to frame the content seemed calculated to stroke audience notions of wealth and luxury. Fox used the show to comment on contemporary values related to wealth and station in our society. Producing courtship shows under such conditions implied that marriages were linkages of fortunes and income. The program allowed both the viewers and the subject, Joe Millionaire, to ponder the value of money in our courtship rituals.

An issue that the show was unable to resolve was the ability to replicate the results. Once the deceptions implicit in the show's constructions were revealed, it was nearly impossible to repeat the ruse for other audiences. Word had spread, and the ability to pull such a sting a second time became more challenging. Thus within two seasons, the program was retired. The *WSJ* pointed this out in their critique, stating, "The show marks the triumph—and fundamental vulnerability—of reality shows. While viewers clearly loved it, they know the ending, so Fox can't bring it back" (Nelson 2003). A flaw in this form of programming is that it often does depend on an implicit deception.

Watching a segment in the second season (a ratings failure after the secret of the first season was revealed) in which the millionaire was courting a group of European courtesans illustrated the difficulties with the show. The women were filled with tension due to the motive of money, and all reactions were calculated on the basis of the monetary issue.

At the time of the broadcast of the first *Joe Millionaire* series, the program created quite a stir. Again, notions of a long-term deception, the women's fear of a relationship deception, and of course the dramatic reveal that Marriott was not a millionaire produced great drama and excitement for audiences. In fact, *Joe Millionaire* helped to secure the future of reality television by garnering large ratings and impressive reviews from audiences and critics alike. The concept was novel at the time. The idea of long-term deception was new, and the drama in the situation recruited many female viewers who saw in "the millionaire" parallels to their own experiences with men and deception. Misha Kavka in her book *Reality TV* writes about the show, saying, "The trick of the program, having a manual laborer masquerade as a millionaire, created the conditions for an implicitly conservative moral message about money and romance, it also produced a double mode of address—A limited story for the viewers—which lent the program an ironic tone" (2012).

A logical problem is defined by such programming. People watch reality programming, ostensively to partake in real-life entertainment. However, in programs like *Joe Millionaire,* conceptions of reality were contrived and duplicitous. This may move viewers farther from reality, not closer. Again, reality programming had been built on deception as far back as *Candid Camera*, in which a camera caught someone in embarrassing behavior by setting up a fake situation. However, through shows like *Joe Millionaire*, the producers of the show may have been sending the unintended message that *all* of society is deception and that reality shows simply reveal the deception in our own lives. Such scenarios could depict negative self-portrayals of the United States as a nexus of duplicity.

These ideas fly in the face of reality programming *theory* that suggests that audiences in reality television wish to have more examples of real, unscripted, unconventional, nonfiction programming. What audiences may desire is the mess of life bustling all around them in their daily existences.

Interestingly, an article for *Jezebel* written by Jenna Sauers, entitled "The Guy from *Joe Millionaire* Apologizes for Being a Total Douche on *Joe Millionaire*," provides a letter from Evan Marriott in which he apologized for his behavior after the show and said the character he was back in 2003 was not a tribute to what his parents wanted him to be. He disparaged the mechanisms of reality shows and added he wasn't proud of his behavior at the time.

When Fox tried for a second season of the series, it became difficult to find a group of women who were not aware of the show and its disturbing setup. The second season moved the show to Europe and utilized a real cowboy who had earned around $11,000 the prior year. The level of deception was still there. After an exhausted, low-rated, enervated season, David Smith, the cowboy from Texas, selected a contestant who eliminated herself from the proceedings as his special woman. Apparently, she had moral qualms about snaring a millionaire. Like the first season, the coupling didn't last long after the broadcast, and Fox shelled out for Smith to buy a ranch and gave contestant Linda Kazdova, a Czech citizen, a $250,000 prize. The wonder of the *Joe Millionaire* phenomenon faded quickly.

See also: The Bachelor; The Dating Game

Further Reading

Richard M. Huff, *Reality Television;* Misha Kavka, *Reality TV*, 2012; Jerry Nededog, "MTV's New Dating Show Proves You Shouldn't Social Everything," Dailies, *The Wrap*; Emily Nelson, "Joe Millionaire Turned out Cash Poor, but Ratings Rich," *Wall Street Journal*, February 19, 2003; Amanda Michelle Steiner, "What Does *Joe Millionaire* Look Like Now?" PeopleTV Watch, *People*, March 20, 2015.

LOVE CONNECTION (LC)

Love Connection was a syndicated game/reality show that ran for nearly 20 years in incarnations from 1983 to 1999, spawning over 2,000 episodes. Host Chuck Woolery would interview potential dates. Most of the contestants were young people, unmarried, who were in their twenties and thirties. The program was a popular game show in the 1980s and 1990s. Perhaps part of its appeal was the hope of matching two lovelorn people through a process in which an applicant could have some understanding of the potential date before the date.

The contestant seeking a date would appear on the show and watch segments of interviews with the three candidates. In this program, the date had already happened. Prior to the show, a contestant had to complete interviews with all three candidates and had chosen which one he or she would date. Following the date, that contestant would appear to be interviewed on the show to be debriefed. She or he would explain what she or he had looked for in a date. While watching clips of the three candidates in the contest, the player would explain what had happened on the actual date. Then the candidates would be brought out on stage to meet with the player. For the player and the candidate that had been selected, this would be their first meeting since the date. Sometimes the dates were strong successes, and the player and candidate would be happy to see each other again. Sometimes the date and the contestant had been unsuccessful, and some awkwardness ensued.

A key factor in the show's success was the way in which audience suggestion and interest was funneled into the show's choices. Prior to the Internet, this program predicted later forms of reality television in which audiences clearly became a factor in the dating experience. Often the audiences lampooned the dater's choices of dates. The show suggested that viewers at home and in the studio would have a better idea of the quality of the various dates than the actual individual involved in the dating process.

The program offered an early form of interactive television in that the audience could participate in dating decision making. This made *Love Connection* an early precursor to MTV dating shows, where performance and participation were a standard feature. Both *LC* and the later MTV programs suggested that modern audiences saw courtship rituals as a matter of public display and something well-suited to the mechanism of a surveillance society where most public actions were monitored surreptitiously.

The audience was given a role in helping the contestants choose their dates. The audience would watch parts of the interviews with the player, and they would choose who they believed the contestant should date. When the contestant chose the same candidate as the audience and the date had gone well, the show would offer the couple a second date. This situation would be considered a "love connection," and the show would claim that it had put two people together in a positive way. If the contestant had chosen someone else and the date had gone poorly, the show would usually pick up the tab for a second date with a candidate chosen by the audience. If the contestant and the audience selected the wrong individual and the choice went badly, the show would generally pick up a second date for the contestant and one of the two previously disqualified candidates. The show dealt with issues of misdirection and poor decision making but also allowed for course corrections and revised choices made on more solid, later-uncovered evidence. The ability of audiences and players to correct decisions allowed for the show to provide a little diagnostic diversity in the dating environment.

Both home and studio audiences enjoyed the selection process, and meeting the contestants, judging the candidates, and picking the best performer for a date were real goals. There was a sense of civic pride in finding a good match. Psychologically, the audience tried to reach inside the mind of the participants and seek the best and most appropriate choices for the players. Occasionally the show would focus on an older couple and would try to match up mature adults who were either widows or who had never married. The show placed nearly 20,000 couples together during its production years. In all that time, there were reportedly 29 marriages, 8 engagements, and 15 children created from the coupling. Despite the show's successes, the complicated mechanics of coupling illustrated how difficult it was to actually make a real love connection.

A problem of the series was that some questions were unrevealing and didn't serve the contestant's quest for knowledge or insight into a contender. Again, the program's inability to discover the best matches mirrored the continuing problem that single people have in finding a successful and long-term partner. The program resembled the first date jitters, when daters are groping for conversation topics but have no common language. Sometimes the studio audiences made selections that were odd, erratic, or simply vindictive. Some of the matches seemed doomed to failure because interests and tastes appeared woefully mismatched. In the later edition of *Love Connection* (1989–1994), audiences could contribute via the Web. Unlike the more interactive and comical MTV dating programs that tended to evoke passionate responses from contestants and guests, Chuck Woolery and the guest/contestant appeared placid and controlled in the aftermath of the date. The shows reflected little animosity or anger over the dating experience. This may have been a factor of a slightly older demographic dating. MTV's programming targeted late-teen and early-twenties contestants. *Love Connection* skewed toward mid-twenties and thirties candidates, taking dating to a different audience and level.

In the post-date wrap-up, sometimes dates could be caustic about the dating experience. This produced a heightened sense of drama for the show's resolution. Jennifer Pozner wrote in *Reality Bites Back* that shows that destroy the myths of "happy ever after" dreams don't do women any favors. Pozner writes that such shows leave "female viewers with the impression that exploitation, contempt, and emotional abuse are just par for the course of women's romantic experience" (2010).

See also: *The Dating Game; The Newlywed Game*

Further Reading

Jennifer L. Pozner, *Reality Bites Back*, 2010; Ethan Thompson and Jason Mittell, *How to Watch Television*, 2013.

MARRIED BY AMERICA

Married by America was an odd show with an odd concept: Let the state pick your spouse. The game show paired up five couples by popular vote. The program was host by Los Angeles DJ Sean Valentine. The program, produced by Rocket Science Laboratories, was aired by Fox Television and ran in 2003. A group of five unmarried strangers agreed voluntarily to allow the viewers watching the show to pair them with a partner of the viewing audience's choice. Through the intervention of family members and phone calls from the audience, the singles were paired with others to become couples. The result was five new couples who were instantly engaged on national television.

These couples were then rushed to a resort to endure weeks of couples therapy by licensed therapists. Participants agreed to this intrusion into their lives. Clearly the inducement was money, but the madness of the idea seemed completely un-American. The idea was to learn with the television audiences about the individuals' tastes, views, and lifestyles. The audience would then decide whether the couples should remain together or separate. Weekly, the therapists would make a determination as to which couples would be eliminated and therefore separated and which should proceed down the aisle. At the end, two couples were remaining, and the therapists determined that they might be suitable for marriage.

There was a strong dream-like quality about the surreal situation given to the couple. Peter Wood, writing about the association of television and dream worlds, explained that "both TV and dreams involve a high degree of wish fulfillment" (1976, 21). It seemed as though the participants in the show were acting out the wishes of the home audiences and the public, and not acting through their own volition. What seemed to be missing was decision making on the part of the couples. They were totally manipulated by public opinion. Then the couples were victimized by medical professionals, who told them whether they were fit to be married. The show suggested human decision making was flawed on every level. It was curious that participants allowed themselves to be subjected to this level of meddling in their private lives. At issue was allowing a game show to dictate decisions about a person's lifelong commitment. The premise stretched the concept of reality television to include issues of rights of self-determination. In the end, none of the couples decided to marry, even though their coupling was sanctioned by the public and confirmed by professional therapists.

The program might have claimed some ethical and scientific high ground by arguing that the program was an experiment in how outsiders could dictate and control people's behaviors. In truth, such a program might have had value. Professor Paula Foss wrote that shows like *The Mary Tyler Moore Show* participated in the frontier myth of rugged individualism and illustrated visions of the American psyche that portrayed "self-sufficiency, independence, personal virtue and courage," but *Married By America* appears to argue for conformity, agreement, and complicity with experts that tell daters what to think (Foss 1976, 40). However, the program made the argument that coupling people via audience involvement and negotiating couples through couples therapy was a legitimate means of social engineering. The public rejected the show quickly.

The show spawned other controversies, including the notion that marriage should be transformed into a game show. Fox was censored by the FCC for violating standards of public decency for showing partially clad strippers and a woman licking whipped cream off a man's body. However, this controversy was itself overturned. A blogger discovered that the FCC had received very few complaints and that those complaints were generated by a handful of people who resubmitted the same complaint multiple times to make the event seem more remarkable than it was. Eventually, the FCC fine was reduced to under $100,000.

Slate magazine's Virginia Heffernan wrote that the show left her depressed. She explained that after the couples were placed together by an audience vote things began to fall apart. She writes, "Soon they were scrutinizing each other for faults, panicking at their implied sexual obligations, and—most surprising of all—losing sight of the prize money" (2003). The money to be awarded to each couple did not entice them to stay in the relationship, and the couples seemed to bristle at the fact that they were being forced together against their will. The drama turned the show from a boldly fresh idea to what *Slate* called a "tragedy." The program ended after a single season. Though watching dating programs can be fun, Fox learned that marriage shows might not prompt many laughs.

See also: The Dating Game; The Newlywed Game

Further Reading

Virginia Heffernan, "The Ring Cycle," 2003; Ethan Thompson and Jason Mittell, *How to Watch Television*, 2013.

MEGAN WANTS A MILLIONAIRE

Megan Wants a Millionaire was a reality show programmed on VH1 from August 2 to August 16, 2009. Megan Hauserman was a castoff from *The Rock of Love* reality/game show. She made an offhand comment that she would like to be a trophy wife, and she would like to marry a millionaire. The producers thought she would make an attractive star for another fantasy/dating program, so they pulled together the premise for a new VH1 program and entitled it *Megan Wants a Millionaire*. The station sent out a casting call for men who had a net worth of at least $1 million.

The structure of the show began with Megan meeting 17 millionaire suitors. First, there was a greeting and gifts from the millionaires. Then there was a mixer so that everyone could get to know each other. Megan then had a conference with her colleagues, Randy and Cecile. These two girls helped guide her in her decisions about the men as the camera glided around the room. Megan was followed during the mixer as she interacted with various millionaires. Some of the dialogue sounded scripted. In one brief segment, a movie director suggested he could get her placed in films. Other men suggested they could provide her with a massage, a comfortable life, and all kinds of business propositions. However, Megan had to make a cut the first evening. She determined who would be sent home from the competition. The elimination ceremony involved handing out special credit cards to all the players. Some would quickly discover their accounts were empty. During a weeklong process, on Thursday, she eliminated another three men from the room. For this crew, her decision was based on common interests. In a Valentine's

Day round, all the men had to buy Megan Valentine's Day gifts. The men groveled because they feared being suspended from the show. A criteria seemed to be cash wealth. If a gentleman had enough wealth, Megan would retain them, but players without sufficient cash resources would be cut.

The third round of the show and the final episode was a billion-dollar doggy competition. All of the contestants were arranged in groups to create a marketing campaign to make Megan's dog Zoe a household name and a marketable item. The teams of men were given two hours to prepare a presentation. Again, more men were eliminated. Although there was a "battle royale" segment planned and presumably shot, the show was suspended after the third episode due to unforeseen adverse circumstances.

The show ended in adversity and tragedy when one of the players from the show was found dead. Only three episodes of the series aired prior to the death. VH1 promptly canceled the show and shelved any previously unscreened episodes. Apparently one of the contestants on the show, Ryan Jenkins, had been accused of murdering his wife, Jasmine, who had previously worked as a swimsuit model. The show commenced broadcasting on August 2, 2009. Jenkins was found dead, apparently of a suicide, on August 23. With this cloud hanging over the first season of the show, the producers did not think they could continue the series. Tracie Egan Morrissey wrote an article about the scandal entitled "VH1 Scrambles to Distance Itself from Reality Star, Murder Suspect." According to the article, "Shortly after he was eliminated, Jenkins went to Las Vegas by car, and married Jasmine two days later" (2009). The facts suggest that Jenkins was unstable and that Jasmine Fiore was an innocent and trusting victim of a man she didn't know well. Under pressure, something went wrong, and he snapped.

As for the reality star, Megan Hauserman, she was no example of female independence and seemed to be constantly playing with her little dog, posing in preposterous outfits, and looking uncomfortable in the confines of a mansion with her concierge. She guided these men in a competition to compete for herself. Megan appeared deeply self-absorbed. In every sequence, Megan seemed self-engaged and more into her wayward quest than the men themselves. Megan became a cautionary tale of female characters who see dependence on a man as the means to fulfillment.

The show had a strong production style typical of MTV's and VH1's house set construction. Flashy and cheap sets, lots of glitzy lights, and roving cameras dominated the proceedings, but there was little attention to acting or realistic reactions. Misha Kavka in *Reality TV* writes that "the editing pace combines the choppiness of MTV music videos with the rhythm of emotional climaxes familiar from soap operas" (2012).

See also: Survivor

Further Reading

Misha Kavka, *Reality TV*, 2012; Jennifer L. Pozner, *Reality Bites Back*.

MILLIONAIRE MATCHMAKER

Millionaire Matchmaker was Bravo's exploration of marrying that involved investigations of wealth and affluence. A charming trash wallow, the program aired from March of 2008 through 2015. The program was a sole proprietorship owned by Patti Stanger, known for her organization the Millionaire's Club, a matchmaking service that purports to unite two like-minded, wealthy individuals. The advantages of such an arrangement provided both parties with capital, and there was none of the seeking of fame and fortune inherent in other wealth and marriage programming. Here, there was a match among privileged, entitled, highly capable, and cocky people. The concept manifested over 90 episodes, and the series has been popular for nearly a decade.

Still, despite the arrangement between equals, lots of critics find such programs promote the surveillance of women. Rachel Dubrofsky, in her book *The Surveillance of Women on Reality Television,* writes, "My approach underlines the need to question the logic that makes things appear real, authentic, rational, and necessary" (2011). Dubrofsky points out that in so many reality dating shows, the programs construct a world in which things seem genuine and real, but they are not. One major aspect is how women are viewed or followed by the camera. The proof of Dubrofsky's point is that men are not handled cinematically the same way.

Further, Paige Albiniak, writing for *The New York Post,* argues that what one would think about this show and the people in it is often far from the truth. She writes, "It seems like they would have little problem luring one (a date that is . . .), the truth is that figuring out how to make a big buck doesn't necessarily translate into having any relationship skills" (2008). We have arrived at another game orientation in which the contestants paid to feel the same tensions that all lonely dating people do. First, Ms. Stanger's Millionaire's Club (located appropriately in Beverly Hills) had a starting membership fee of $15,000. Rates could rise to $150,000 per annum for billionaires. In essence, good love came at a price, and, even then, there were risks.

Stanger, a brash, ex–New Jerseyite, joked about being mean to her wealthy charges and worked hard to beat them into shape, so they wouldn't destroy their next relationship. In the *New York Post* story by Albiniak, she jokingly states, "I'm the ghost of Christmas past, present, and future for them." In essence, she haunted them into behaving properly in a dating situation.

The show firmly managed the un-romantic men. These successful guys needed real help rethinking their relationship issues. They lived with infantile fantasies of women too young for them, and they desired unrealistic things in a partner that neither respected reality, their age, or their ability to nurture a meaningful relationship. The tasks they seemed to fail at included conversation, commitment, and intellectual respect for another person. What emerged were men old enough to be grandfathers of the daters on MTV's *Next,* but men who also acted more like the young, inexperienced daters on an MTV program.

When one looked at the contestants, money apparently was no barrier to stupidity. One debutant beauty said she wanted a love that was perfect like her parents. What we discovered was that many women suffered from the same reality deficit that men suffered. Those smiling pretty women appeared far too self-obsessed to find anyone to fulfill their image of a relationship. The show implicitly critiqued society's vision of a relationship and suggested that no one had an accurate perspective on how to create good relationships. Stanger talked tough to some tough personalities. These were bratty women and men who could have someone. However, their courtship behaviors needed some work. A big problem for the members of the club was they wanted someone on their own terms. Stanger bluntly told them they could get money in a relationship, but the guy might not be all that great. She asked them to make some realistic dating choices. She had terms for women who keep picking the wrong guy. She told them they were collectors, but collecting the wrong object. The show explored the reality that very smart people could make deeply ill-informed romantic choices. Stanger sought to cut through all of that, but sometimes her clients didn't help, but instead impeded her work.

The interview segment was a key part of the show, and when the audience saw what the matchmaker was up against, it was less a matter of finding a good match, then it was of finding therapy for a group of headstrong, spoiled, wealthy misanthropes.

See also: The Dating Game; Singled Out

Further Reading

Paige Albiniak, "Mister Lonely," *New York Post*, January 20, 2008; Jennifer L. Pozner, *Reality Bites Back*, 2010.

THE NEWLYWED GAME

The Newlywed Game is an American game show that was devised by Robert Nicholson and Roger Muir. It debuted in 1966 and has been around in various incarnations for over 50 years. The show was originally hosted by Bob Eubanks, and the popular host has returned to helm the show on many occasions over the years. The mechanism of the show was presented as a quiz program, pitting couples in amusement park carriages against each other in a competition; the couples answered questions that indicated the depth of their understanding and knowledge of their partner. Laughter ensued when one partner did not know some obvious intimate detail of his or her spouse's life. The show received attention for its probing questions about the secret intimate lives of couples.

The comedy erupted when the program asked embarrassing questions about the contestants' sex lives or details about their private lives that often baffled one or the other partner. In fact, many times, the couples did not seem to know much about each other, and audiences could only wonder how they could be married.

The show was suffused in tinsel and glitter, embracing the newness, hope, and wonder that young marrieds enjoyed in their early relationship together. However, in reality many of these young people still didn't know their partners, and sometimes their answers were not only surprising and shocking to the audience, but also to each other. Many of the questions revolved around the concept of "making whoopee," or another term for sex. Audiences enjoyed the humor induced by a couple's learning what they did not know about their loved one and partner. *TV Guide* called the program the number-10 top game show of all time in a 2013 poll (Fretts, *TV Guide* 2013). The program first aired in black and white and quickly turned to a color format at the end of 1966. The program was a daytime comedy game show aired by the ABC Network. It debuted opposite CBS's *Password* game show and eventually defeated it, forcing *Password's* cancellation the next year. The program ran as a popular game show until 1974, making it one of the longest-running game shows of all time. It went into syndication production and was revived in the late 1970s. The show reappeared on ABC in the 1980s. It went back into syndicated production in the late 1980s, the 1990s, and has been revived again in the post-millennial era.

The game play was highly structured. In the first segment, women were sent from the stage, and the husbands were asked three questions about their wives. The women were brought back to the stage, and the questions were asked to the women. The husbands had their answers written on a blue card. If the wife's answer matched the husband's answer, the couple received five points.

The program espoused the comforts of marriage, of knowing your spouse and having an intimate friend. Elizabeth Johnstone in "How Women Really Are" proclaims, "Not all the contestants are 'ordinary folks'; many of the most popular reality shows focus on everyday experiences" (2006). Here the questions often centered on the mundane aspects of marriage. Morning rituals, who takes out the trash, and what is on the menu were questions that dominated the interrogation. The second round exiled the males, and the females responded to four questions regarding their husbands' habits and behaviors. The husbands returned and answered three questions. Each question was worth 10 points, but the last question was considered a bonus question and was worth 25 points. The maximum score was usually up to 70 points. Prizes were awarded to couples on the basis of items they had requested before the show. Often prizes included a home entertainment center, a second honeymoon, or furniture.

In the 1990s, the format was changed to include video segments. Spouses were shown their "other" on video, and they would have to predict how the other would complete a segment discussing their spouse. A 2009 edition of the show returned to the original format but included returning couples called "goldyweds." In the 2009–2010 season, same-sex couples began appearing as newlyweds, and *Star Trek* actor George Takei and his spouse appeared. They actually won their round and donated their winnings to a charity. Non-celebrity same-sex couples were featured again in the next season.

There were a number of urban legends surrounding the show and various onstage encounters. Apparently some participants misunderstood questions and gave comical answers to questions. Host Bob Eubanks denied such events transpired, but several contestant responses have been bleeped and their responses censored.

The history of the show is somewhat difficult to chronicle, since many of the early episodes were recorded on tape, and apparently those tapes were wiped or lost and thought to be of little historical significance. The Game Show Network has aired surviving episodes where they could obtain them.

The Game Show Network has been keenly involved in the program's revival and showed new episodes starting in 2009. Carrie Wilson of the singing group Wilson Phillips hosted the show for several seasons, and *The View*'s Sherri Shepherd took over as a host in 2010. The new version of the show has produced over 400 episodes.

See also: The Dating Game; Parental Control

Further Reading

Elizabeth Johnston, "How Women Really Are: Disturbing Parallels between Reality Television and 18th Century Fiction," 2006; Ethan Thompson and Jason Mittell, *How to Watch Television*.

NEXT

Next provided some changes in methodology from MTV's previous dating game show *Dismissed*. The procedure was marked by attractive young participants, a degree of audience involvement, and reality contexts. It ran from 2005 to 2008 and featured two segments per airing, showing a dating experience between youthful male and female contestants. The *Next* van hovered in the background and contained potential dates. The date for the episode would begin the program by describing himself or herself and respective hobbies. A key factor would be the dater describing his or her greatest dislikes in a date. If the potential date committed any of these offenses, they could be banished immediately. Then the dating ritual would begin, with the hitch that the date could end anytime the dater called out, "Next!" Without warning, the dater could cancel the contestant's opportunities by summarily ending the encounter. The sequence was usually a series of introductions, and the dater would assemble several candidates to be tested through the dating experience.

The show tended to participate in the process of the young people finding a dating identity. Many did not have extensive dating experience, and the program helped them find an expression for their personality in dating. While we assume that people bring readymade psyches to the dating game, there is much evidence that identity is a constantly changing part of a person's psyche and that personas are more fluid then we once imagined. Alessandra Micalizzi, in her article "Cyber-Self," comments, "In recent developments across a range of disciplines, the idea of a monolithic identity, stable and predestined, has been replaced by a perspective that sees identity as a 'process,' a complex and constant ongoing work that regards the individual, his relations, and the contexts hme moves in" (Rak and Poletti 2013, 217). If indeed identity is a shifting construct, it received a thorough investigation in *Next*. Once the date commenced, the dater invited their prospective date to an event in their interest range. In one episode, Vanessa escorted her young friends to yard sales and asked them what they would buy to impress her with their decorating skills. Thus, one of the competitions impressed the girl by showing social and aesthetic skills in decorating. Such a challenge asked men to participate in design cultures, social cultures, and expertise in which they might not have had formal training.

The show had some carefully scripted and choreographed moments with girls, like Brittany saying, "I'm for a guy who knows life is way too important to take seriously." Benjamin Solomon writes in his "Complete History of MTV's Dating Game Shows" that "the show prided itself on caricatures and silly, sex-forward dialogue that helped it last for six big seasons" (2013). In one anxious moment, a frustrated date who had to drive a bike around a pylon threw a ball at his date and was immediately "Nexted." The other contestants quipped, "You got beat by a girl in a tricycle race?"

Many of the contests were arranged to tax the patience of the contestants. Opponents in the competition vied for position via boasts and bravado. The potential daters were introduced to the audience with dialogue boxes beneath their names, stating their statistics (likes fast food, falls in love too easy, thinks he looks like Bono, etc.). The parading of the contestants like warriors invoked the image of a competition or a gladiatorial match. Audiences received an ESPN-style wrap-up of the dating action by the contestants as their date ended. Television graphics blacked out faces of all competitors eliminated in rounds. Line-ups outside the *Next* bus made competitors appear as captives more than potential concubines. The show skewed toward speed dating and suggested that the players chosen by the dater were difficult to please. The expression of ostracizing a date within minutes spoke to the anxiety of the dating experience.

One of the funniest aspects of the show was the process of "instant nexting," when a contestant would "next" someone upon seeing the candidate. It was a funny and provocative moment, but it explored the idea of matching identities. Jennifer Slack in her *Culture and Technology: A Primer* argues,

> It's not just that we (ourselves and our bodies) are caught up in assemblages, but that our very sense of self is already an assemblage, it is already an arrangement of things, expressions, affects, and so on, a part-hardwired/part-contingent collaboration of body, technology, and environment. In terms of the idea of self, this would include the idea that our sense of self extends beyond our mind and even beyond our bodies, to encompass tools and other features of our environment. (2015, 208)

This sense of assembled personalities was strongly represented on *Next*. The candidates had to conform to the dater's vision of a good date. If that match of assembled personalities didn't exist, there was no way that that the dating environment could be sustained.

The program illustrated that bad behavior and acting out could draw attention to some candidates, and their outrageous antics could result in a date. Misha Kavka wrote in "Reality TV and the Gendered Politics of Faunting," that "there is . . . broad agreement that Reality TV shows are becoming more and more sensationalist, encouraging participants to 'revel in bad behavior'" (Kavka, "Faunting," 2014). *Next* allowed bad actors to profit from their exhibitionist behavior.

See also: The Dating Game; Dismissed; Score

Further Reading

Misha Kavka, "Reality TV and the Politics of Gendered Flaunting"; Julie Rak and Anna Poletti, *Identity Technologies: Constructing the Self Online,* Madison: University of Wisconsin Press, 2013; Jennifer Daryl Slack and J. Macgregor Wise, *Culture and Technology: A Primer,* New York: Peter Lang Inc., International Academic Publishers, 2015; Benjamin Solomon, "A Complete History of MTV's Dating Game Shows," 2013.

PARENTAL CONTROL

Parental Control was another in a stream of dating shows created for MTV by directors Brenden Carter and Bruce Klassen. The show was an intervention show in which parents decided to take action against their teenagers' dating desires. With the help of MTV, the parents recruited several alternative dates for their son or daughter. The idea of the show was that the parents so despised their child's current date they would do anything to dislodge that person from their child's life. Not only did the parents support the alternative date, they demanded that the current boyfriend or girlfriend watch as their child went on a date with someone else. It seemed unlikely and unnatural that any teen would obey their parents in their desire to unseat their current love interest. Further, it seemed like a move determined to greater alienate children and their parents. The program initially ran from 2006 to 2010, and the target audience was rebelling teens with a need to reject their parents' visions, particularly ideas about their dating life.

In one sense, the program was a commentary on parents' desires to control their children's social lives. In another sense, the program posed as an ethical intervention by parents to ensure that their children had the best mates and friends surrounding them so they did not get into trouble. Clearly, aspects of the program appeared to be heavily scripted and offered heavy-handed solutions. The interventions suggested that if parents' ideas were dreadful, home audiences of young people would feel justified in rejecting such "home management." The specter of the show was that parents appeared determined to reengineer their children's lives.

There were light moments. The scenes featuring the outcast boyfriends and girlfriends having to watch the alternative dating partners provided requisite sounds and commentary to show their annoyance. However, their reactions were so generally mild that they seemed unbelievable. If the original dates were so benign, then why did the parents oppose them? Further, it is unlikely that children committed to a relationship with one dating partner would gleefully go off on alternative dates to please their parents at the risk of offending their current love interest. The premise of the show lacked credibility.

There was the sense that the parents were trying to control their children's lives. It seemed likely that teens watched the show aghast at how insensitive the parents could be. This reflected the mind-set of a teenager, who perceived their parents as being extremely intrusive. Far from championing the new age of surveillance, the rhetoric of *Parental Control* strongly denied the work of parental interventions. The program portrayed parents making impractical interventions in their children's lives. Neither most young people nor most parents would believe such a form of behavior modification could succeed.

Accusations were lodged that the shows were largely scripted and fake. *Complex* magazine wrote an article on the 15 worst dating shows on television. *Parental Control* appeared as number two, with the article reporting, "While *Parental Control* was undoubtedly scripted as hell, it's purely the concept that earns the MTV time killer a spot on this list" (2012). Truly, the concept was a unique one. It was one of the few shows on MTV that ever mentioned parents. Jonathan Gray, in his article "Cinderella Burps," explained that much gender programming, including dating-themed shows, relied on scripted dialogue. He writes, "These scenes are marked by heavily-scripted outrageous behavior. In one episode the mother asked candidates if they were a love doctor, what would they prescribe for their daughter?" (2009). Gray pointed out the absurdity of such a performance.

While the actual dates promoted by the parents were rather tame, there were some disturbing scenes at home. In a series of probing interviews, parents grilled the prospective new dates, looking for information that would reveal these young people. It was insulting and unpleasant work. It was doubtful any parent would ask these questions of a prospective young person they wanted to have in the presence of their children. Further, it seemed disrespectful of the young people they were interviewing. In essence, it made the parents and young prospective dates look awkward.

The dating segment of the program was usually a simple activity with little remarkable footage. Usually the child, being forced to date by the parents, behaved decently on the date. Also the new dates, thrust into this awkward situation and knowing that his or her current date already has a boyfriend or girlfriend, tried to comply by being a good companion. It was almost like both of them were complying with the criteria of good sportsmanship. Nothing about the date looked genuine, and they appeared as people going through the motions.

However, back at the house, the despised boyfriend or girlfriend watched the progress of the date with the parents. Since there was already antipathy between the girlfriend or boyfriend with the parents, the parents would routinely praise the behavior of their new choice in the dating video feed. Indeed, rudeness escalated, as the parents would often ridicule the disparaged boyfriend/girlfriend while watching the date with him or her. They would insult their child's choice in that person's company. They would act rudely toward their child's friend. They would lionize the new date as a better choice than the existing paramour. This behavior appeared contrived. Again, the purpose of such scenes seemingly was to inflame teen anger at parents and to conclude that parents were clueless. Such provocative footage played into visions of adolescent rebellion against parental sanctions. Older viewers would be cognizant of such manipulations. They might see the parents in a more positive light. It is doubtful most teens believed their own parents such ogres. The show seemed intent on vilifying parents and playing into youthful rebellious images of parental rejection. Further, most people wouldn't imagine a chosen boyfriend or girlfriend sitting through such an excruciating experience.

Much of the dialogue seemed staged. One contestant said, "My parents do not like my girlfriend, so I'm here today to get set up on two blind dates. My mom's pick is almost here, and I hope she's hot." It is suggested that the teens are colluding with their parents' plotting. It seems completely unlikely that a teen love interest would discharge a lover due to a parent's request.

However, the program did exploit issues of parental control over teen behavior. Also, the show provided an experiment in social conditioning. The show posited that children's behavior could be reshaped by parents tuning their children's relationship choices. Another lure was the view that the audience could participate in experiencing this social work. Mark Andrejevic writes, "The value of this experience, calculated within the context of the therapeutic ethos, represents an important part of the promise of reality and provides one more ostensible benefit of entry into the digital enclosure" (*Reality TV* 2004, 143). While *Parental Control* might not solve problems between parents and teens, it exposed the experience of that conflict about association on screen. People might also find the proceedings humorous. It is possible that some reality TV is seen as Jean Baudrillard described it as "hyper-real"—that is, such shows are such overblown transformed restatements of reality that their coarse outline replaces the real in reality. Baudrillard argued that reality had been overtaken by simulations. At a certain point, people began to enjoy the simulations more than the real. Perhaps what we see today is not a defection from fictional TV, but that fictional TV and its professionalism approaches reality too carefully. The hyper-reality of reality programming doesn't delude itself that it is reality. It looks nothing like reality. It is its own hyper-reality world. It is a world that doesn't exist. The question remains whether viewers understand this hyper-reality world is manufactured or whether they wish to participate in the hyper-real as an alternative to actual reality.

See also: The Dating Game; Dismissed; Next

Further Reading

Tanya Ghahremani, "The 15 Most Ridiculous Dating Shows," *Complex Magazine*, 2012; Jennifer L. Pozner, *Reality Bites Back*.

ROCK OF LOVE

VH1's combination dating and game show *Rock of Love* appeared from 2007 to 2009 and featured performer Bret Michaels, lead singer of the pop metal band Poison, popular in the 1980s. The 25 ladies on the show competed with each other to win a date with Michaels. Michaels was a middle-aged rock star, in the business 20 years with substantial property and security. He had two daughters (from previous relationships), and he was the type of performer that VH1 skews toward to reach an older viewing demographic (men and women 25–40 years of age). Audiences might have been interested because they were fans of his career, but some may have been intrigued to see the competitive rounds between the women. The contestants had in common two characteristics: a love of rock music and, more importantly, a love of Bret Michaels. Michaels was a more-than-adequate host and ringmaster, presenting himself with the sort of rock star swagger acquired from years in a highly competitive business environment. Michaels made no hash of the heavily scripted show, and he read his lines like a pro. The setup was that Michaels had supposedly rented a Hollywood bungalow with his manservant and security guard, and they had prepared it for a visitation of 25 women who would try to win Michaels's heart. He claimed that he was looking for a girl who could make him laugh and could simultaneously be attractive. It sounded like a fairly upfront sort of arrangement.

The program ran for three seasons, spawned 40 episodes, produced CDs and spin-offs, and Michaels actually dated a few of the contestants after the show ended. As with several reality programs, there were lawsuits. Michaels and his production team were sued for damaging the rented mansion, and a crew member of the show was injured in a multifatality car accident while the show was filming, but all and all, the show had a very professional sheen and was parodied in films and on *Saturday Night Live*.

The program featured competitions between women escorting Michaels in activities they might encounter while dating a popular rock personality. Michaels went to other reality projects and seemed content with his popularity in the reality genre.

The program had some surprises. Jes Rickleff, who was selected as the winner of the competition by Michaels, refused his affections, telling him he should have picked the runner-up. A report in the *New York Post* argued, "She said she did not think she could handle the rock-star lifestyle he led" (2007) and decided to return to her old boyfriend. If nothing else, it sounds like the show at least clarified for some women what they really wanted, and, for some, it was not a life with a rock god.

However, the production team must have loved the girls assembled for the first series because many of these ladies appeared in later iterations of the show as contestants.

Programming featured many dates fussing with their appearance, flexing their bosoms, and trying to appear attractive. The essence of the discomfort was that none of the women were rocket scientists, and the gig was working with and being with a middle-aged rock personality. In one sequence, the girls were photographed by Michaels and his crew, and the contestants had to kiss him. Clearly, there were some awkward moments, but throughout it appeared that Michaels was seeking humorous women, willing to forget themselves and have fun in the activities.

Like many dating shows, the awkwardness experienced by the online crew was mirrored by the audience. The program probably played on fan nostalgia for Poison and also drew upon viewers' own awkwardness in dating. There were also correlations between the viewers' dating remembrances and the sadness of watching Michaels, who at midlife was still struggling with finding a good relationship fit. This reminded audiences of all ages that relationship foibles plague all demographics and leave no one untouched. VH1 viewers had enough life experience to know that midlife could be tough enough without exes, children, and financial liabilities in tow. With that in mind, it must have been difficult to revisit Michaels, although he didn't seem to mind the attention.

See also: The Dating Game; Singled Out

Further Reading

New York Post staff, "Bret Will Rock Again," October 10, 2007; Jennifer L. Pozner, *Reality Bites Back.*

ROOM RAIDERS

Room Raiders was a reality dating contest show that continued MTV's clever variety of dating shows that packaged dating around new twists that related to young-adult lifestyles. Most reality shows have grown out of a society where watching and being watched, the voyeurism of everyday life, has gradually been accepted as a part of modern technological society. At MTV, an emphasis was on creating reality entertainment for young adults that participated in a surveillance-oriented society. It was a quite natural evolution to voyeuristic themes for MTV viewers, who often were conditioned to being watched at schools, jobs, and in leisure activities. For a generation who had been supervised in their early lives, it wasn't difficult to watch shows where surveillance was an aspect or even a requirement of existence.

Room Raiders transformed dating into a show that privileged snooping and stalking behavior. The program featured four contestants. A male or female who was a room raider or snooper who would spy on three potential dates. The dater/raider was allowed to search and study the contents of each girl or guy's room. The contents of the room that would indicate an intended date were cleared. When the potential dater visited the rooms of the three contestants, he/she studied the rooms for compatibility features. The students being checked by the potential dater watched the inspection on video from a nearby van. They commented on the investigation as their potential date looked into their private room. Many were uncomfortable with someone rummaging through their intimate possessions. After the inspection, the students who were snooped had a chance to snoop in the room of the room raider who had rifled through their rooms. Again, such mechanisms reflected the rise of social media, where a potential dater could scan information about a partner. Facebook and other entities allow friends or acquaintances quick access to the details of a person's life that an individual may have shared online. Finally, the potential dater makes his or her choice on the basis of what was discovered in the rooms. The raider meets with the hopefuls and explains the reasons for choosing one person over another. A clever aspect was that the parents of the snooper were onboard and helping the youth to detect flaws in the potential date. Again, like other aspects of the show, this integration of the parents into the teen's life is more and more a feature of young adulthood. In previous generations, youthful adventurers would tolerate no interference from their parents in their complicated teenage matrix of friends and potential mates. Today, teens often share intimate details of their friends' lives with parents, and parents today often delight in having intimate knowledge of their teen child's love life, social scene, and social practices. This practice has transformed the "breaking away" phenomenon of teen life to something more akin to chaperoned ventures into the outside world.

Room Raiders opened a dialogue about how much snooping was permissible or allowable in teen life. *Raiders* had a large following, beginning as a popular game program in 2004 and producing over 30 episodes between its debut and its retirement in 2006.

In a way, the program valorized voyeuristic behavior as a means of expressing interest in a prospective date. Players normalized the activities of the show, and it didn't seem strange or perverse at all. In *Room Raiders*, the parents were also engaged in investigating teens by invading and raiding the room of potential dates to determine whether the date might be suitable for their child. So the program allowed a stranger who might be a date and that person's parents into the investigation. In essence, the show was a participatory burglary. This meant that a total stranger actually burglarized the house of another teen and their family. They went into a teen's bedroom unaccompanied by anyone but the camera team. They did their own investigation into a person's life, uncovering anything they found in the room and using it as evidence.

Such mechanisms for legitimizing snooping and surveillance behavior are not new. In the 1950s, Alfred Hitchcock's films (*Strangers on a Train, Dial M for Murder, Vertigo*) often had long sequences of stalking behavior, largely legitimized as investigative or police work. Today, parental interventions are seen as protecting a child from potential predators or unsavory types. In MTV's *Room Raiders*, what legitimized the intrusion was the wiling participation of the three candidates for the date.

Naturally the show explored issues of privacy concerns. The team of investigators used various means to discover things about the items they found in the room. They could look through drawers. They could investigate underwear. They could read diaries. Often they employed an ultraviolet lamp to look through the bed to uncover telltale signs of romantic coupling. The entire process complicated the dating process and problematized the way we see teenagers and their private lives. Privacy advocates could argue that such intrusiveness suggests a commentary on surveillance issues. The program's lack of legal proceedings reinforced the concept that MTV was not really making reality TV but was tagging the intrusion to increase the students' sense of violation and increase viewer interest. Since such violations might prompt legal recourse, the explanation may be that these people were either paid actors or willing participants in such a ruse who believed that such exposure was to their benefit. They may have known that their privacy wasn't really that disrupted. Further, many objects that make the investigation tantalizing may have been planted to suggest disturbing behaviors and to maintain audience interest. At its base, *Room Raiders* was a highly theatricalized version of reality, enticing viewers to participate in the snooping experience. The lack of legal action suggested that releases had been signed prior to filming to protect participants and the station from prosecution.

MTV has adopted reality programming as a highly cost-effective manner of providing insightful programming that uncovers the issues of teen existence in our society. The use of everyday spectacle is produced on a frugal budget and allows producers wide latitude in staging and arranging encounters for shows. The station continually leverages programs to sell items (product placements, DVDs, games, energy drinks, clothing, trends), making entire shows into a panorama of modern teen life. Thus *Room Raiders* casts students, parents, and potential dates in a program that literally investigated the range of teen life in the suburban United States.

Marc Andrejevic in his article "Visceral Literacy, Reality TV, Savvy Viewers, and Auto-Spies" discusses *Room Raiders*. He writes, "Raiders . . . provides a pop-culture portrayal of do-it-yourself detection in practice: viewers get to watch the spies as they 'investigate' the bedrooms of potential dates before meeting them" (2009). There are risks in such a situation. The candidates were investigated prior to meeting their potential dates. Not only was there spying, but they were spied upon prior to knowing who these dates might be. This provided a creepy stalking knowledge of the potential dates. The show closely circumvented laws about stalking and burglary and undermined principles of privacy. Allowing such investigations treads close to issues of obsession, stalking, and deviant behavior, where an unhealthy obsession about a stranger becomes a dominant reason for viewing. Because students have to learn about such behaviors, cope with obsessed teens, and learn to avoid such behaviors in their own conduct, the program acted as a cultural barometer, showing society's tolerance for snoops in our schools and in our own private life.

In practice, the mechanism of the show was fairly simple, when the raider for the prospective date, male or female, was (somehow) given access to the rooms of three people who were possible dates. The raider went undercover into their bedrooms and did an investigation of the potential date while the player, who wanted to know about the potential date, sat in the van listening to the raider's commentary as the raider surveyed the contents of the room. Again, such mechanisms mirror the common methodology of the crime-and-detection show, one of the oldest forms of television entertainment and one widely recognizable to most audiences. The only redeeming factor was that the subjects under surveillance were also able to see what the raider was doing in their rooms. So both the potential date and the player were hearing the outcome of the investigation. Both could get some insight into what the investigation was like and the qualities of the person under investigation. Often the worst issue discovered was that many teenagers were slobs. They didn't put away their clothes. They didn't do regular laundry, and they piled things up in their rooms. Thus often, students watching were reassured that many people in their age group were similar in their behavior. So the violated date was not totally unaware of the investigation of his or her life. Another redeeming principle of the show was that those who are raided get to perform a similar surveillance on the bedroom of the player. The investigation cut both ways. The subject paid with his or her privacy, but the investigators pay him or her back in kind. At the end, the raiders confronted all three contestants. The player explained in detail who he or she wants to date and the reasoning for the choice.

Occasionally there were some funny moments, such as when, early in his career, actor Zac Efron appeared on *Room Raiders* and went through the rooms of three girls. The fact that people can go back and look at those early scenes of Zac Efron acting as a "nonactor" was an amusing insight into the show. A more unsettling aspect of the show was an abduction scene. In many places, this would get the crew shot. It was clear that these scenes were staged and planned in advance. In the footage, a suspicious-looking man wearing a black bodysuit, a hat, and dark glasses would run into an apartment complex of some young woman, grab the woman, and bodily throw her into a van. Fun stuff for play acting, but highly dangerous actions that even in a staged incursion would be considered highly antisocial and threatening. Why this horrific mockery of an abduction and the potential for bodily harm? The producers wanted to assure the sanctity of the bedroom without changes. The idea was that the bedrooms could not be changed by the women because they've been kidnapped before they can alter anything in the bedroom. Further, all pictures of the women that might be in the bedroom are covered so that the raider doesn't see them. Then, of course, the roles were reversed when a man was the subject of the room raid.

In the Zac Efron episode, MTV had a very experienced actor who actually described himself as an actor in the episode. Of course, this was before he achieved worldwide fame in Disney's popular *High School Musical*. Efron went to the girls' rooms and conducted an investigation. The investigation didn't seem to be a witch hunt, and most items found were typical teen girl materials. He did find condoms and handcuffs in one girl's room, but they appeared to be staged props and not any disparagement of the potential date. His greatest complaint was about the girls' hygiene. One girl had a dirty hairbrush, while another had her clothes squeezed together. He critiqued the girls who were self-absorbed. Even though the girls were able to watch the investigation and survived the scrutiny, there was a sense of intrusion and violation implicit in the act. The girls didn't take it that way. They seemed to be so pleased that any man would look favorably upon them, and they were happy to have their personal items critiqued. The suggestion was that the girls were coached or had prepared for their inspection. How well would they have responded to a police raid with weapons drawn? The girls were extremely good-natured on the show. The content of the program considered the issue of how our whole society would welcome such intrusion into their lives. MTV, through its dating programming, makes us keenly aware that surveillance seems to be a standard part of reality life.

See also: The Dating Game; Parental Control

Further Reading

Mark Andrejevic, "Visceral Literacy, Reality TV, Savvy Viewers, and Auto Spies," 2009; Jennifer L. Pozner, *Reality Bites Back.*

SCORE

Score was an MTV dating reality show that debuted in the fall of 2005. The show was hosted by youthful and spiky-haired Ryan Cabrera, who was 22 when the show aired. Cabrera was a celebrity because he was a singer/songwriter with a popular album on Atlantic Records, *Take It All Away.* He was also the ex-boyfriend of then-popular teen icon Ashlee Simpson. Cabrera was selected for the dating show because it was dealing with the topic of writing and performing songs, and Cabrera had experience as a writer and performer. Unlike other MTV dating shows that used humor or a social interplay to explore dating relationships, *Score* explored the musical context of romance.

Originally MTV stood for Music Television, and for its first 10 years, the cable station featured music-oriented programming. However, in the past 25 years, reliance on reality programming that included a series of documentary/hybrid reality formats, including *Real World*, *Teen Mom*, and *Jackass*, moved the station from a music base to unscripted fictional and nonfictional television. This programming has consistently been popular among males 12 to 24: MTV's target demographic. Popular programming has included *Spring Break* and the aptly named *Score*. *Score* was a clever combination of two or the station's primary concerns. One aspect of the program was displaying young men having fun, and another aspect was the program's exploration of how to be popular with women. A third aspect was men's relationship to popular music. Here music was used as a vehicle to impress a young woman and gain status.

Score debuted in 2005 and lasted a single season until 2006. The concept featured two musicians who were commissioned to write a song. They had a single 24-hour day to compose a song and sing it. The idea was to compress the creative process to a day of writing, singing, and producing a finished song with a performance that evening. The recording of the song was then played for a young woman, and that woman decided which person she was going to date based on the quality of the song. Obviously, most of the songs were love songs in their orientation, tempo, and atmosphere. The show allowed guest host Ryan Cabrera to sing and perform with two potential male dates. Both of these men hoped to impress a date with their song. Of course, up to the meeting, the girl had no idea which of the two men had written either song. Her choice of someone to date was based purely on her selection of the best song. Whoever wrote the song she chose became the date. The show was fun, offered some clever melodies, and appeared charming and tender.

This might have worked to the show's detriment. What the *Score* did was demonstrate that MTV's democratizing mythos allowed students to dream they could be like the stars they saw on TV and the demi-stars of MTV's reality shows. Mark Andrejevic writes, "In keeping with this line of shows, MTV's website features a game called 'fantasy music tycoon' that, in imitation of popular baseball and football fantasy leagues, allows viewers to 'buy and sell' bands to see whether they can create a successful talent roster" (*Reality TV* 2004, 5). Just as the online game allowed viewers to enter the music business, the *Score* provided an entrance to television, performing, impressing girls, and a potential career as a "real" rock performer. In this sense, MTV's *Score* was an almost perfect blend of dating and pop music game shows.

Some of the moments between host Ryan Cabrera, the guests, and their potential dates were funny. During the supposedly impromptu jam sessions between the contestants and Cabrera, there would sometimes be funny exchanges. One fellow asked, "Dude, what do you want this song to be?" Often, ingenious contestants would respond with something equally pithy like, "Oh man, I wanted it to be, you know, upbeat!" Usually 15 minutes of bashing would turn out another strong song. Instead of crafting a unique love song to a potential date, what would generally happen was that another commercial, up-tempo pop rock song would be born. In essence, the show had to manufacture new material weekly, a tough order for any program. Television's constant flow and the concept that one program would quickly be replaced by another thwarted efforts to make musical material that was lasting in a dating program format.

As with most reality programming, there were some critical moments, and the most memorable moments were when the guest had to give an emotional response to a song on the show. Potential dates had to respond to the song in real-time. That took some effort. Further, Cabrera asked each potential date what they were going to be looking for in the two songs they heard.

The song competition was the final tie-breaker between the two remaining challengers, and it was the emotional impact of this single song that would determine whether a date would win the girl or guy or would go home alone. Most of the time, the male or female listener said they want a rock song. Further, there were extended rules to the competition. The listener/potential date told the songwriters that they must include certain ideas or keywords in the song. In most cases, the essential quality was the girl or guy's name. So a faceless, anonymous pop song basically had to include the name of the potential date. Then the potential date had to listen to the song and try to get a winning response with a new song that no one had heard before. Further, the program demanded that there be a response from a live studio audience, the player, and a professional pit band. The results were sometimes difficult and stagey. In general, MTV's questioning in such reality programming always lacked. Limitations included the fact that most songs were rock songs, which left little variety for the show. No matter how sincere the guest was, there was a world of difference between being a rocker and producing something that actually rocks. The reality of a rock lifestyle versus television conceptions of such a persona were tough to create. One had the ring of truth, and the other felt like a comic impression of rock music.

The most forceful moment on the show was when the two performers sang their songs. Watching the studio audience, the house band rocking, and two bedroom-performing Mick Jagger clones was fun. This modeled MTV's vision of every teen being a DJ, a rocker, or a skateboard entrepreneur. Many young men might fantasize about performing live to a roomful of women. The result was that the show was short-lived, and the dream of rock stardom was shelved in favor of less lofty goals. Later shows simply had guys and girls trying to get a date. Most of the heavy theatrics were replaced with even more surreal rules and codes for the next generation of MTV date programs.

See also: The Dating Game; The Newlywed Game

Further Reading

Mark Andrejevic, *Reality TV: The Work of Being Watched*, 2004; Jennifer L. Pozner, *Reality Bites Back*; Ethan Thompson and Jason Mittell, *How to Watch Television*.

A SHOT AT LOVE WITH TILA TEQUILA

A Shot at Love with Tia Tequila was an interesting spin on the dating show. Tila Tequila was a bisexual reality star. She hosted a show in which 16 heterosexual men and 16 lesbian women shared a house with her. In a weird, irreverent parody of *The Bachelor*, both the women and the men pursued Tila Tequila. The idea was that both genders were courting the star. Only at the end of the first episode was it revealed that Tila was bisexual, and that both the males and females were seeking her attention. The 10-episode series garnered a lot of attention and criticism for its portrayal of heterosexual, bisexual, and lesbian relationships. *MTV* parodied both homosexual and heterosexual relationships, mocking all real relationships in dating shows like *Dismissed* and *Next*. The LGBT community was not as amused at what it saw as offensive stereotypes of gay characters. The program ran in the fall of 2007 and ended in the summer of 2008. It received a 3.0 rating from the IMDB. Despite the controversy, the program returned again in a 2008 spin-off. This time it was called *A Shot of Love II with Tila Tequila*. The show evolved into a third version, entitled *That's Amore* in 2009.

Throughout the early millennium, MTV date and romance shows progressively interrogated modern relationships. In an effort to provide new perspectives on old romance themes, the producers stretched credulity to new formats. After about five minutes on Tila's show, the crowd of bachelors and lesbian bachelorettes were confused by the mix of genders dating one person. Was the subject gay or straight? The reveal at the end of the first hour stating that Tila was bisexual and wanted to be courted by people of both genders seemed distressing to all potential suitors. On paper, it might have been interesting, but Tila didn't represent a strong bisexual presence, and the audience suspected this was simply a game-changing ruse to throw off the contestants and the audience, the intellectual equivalent of the "surprise ending" at the close of horror films. Jennifer Pozner, in *Reality Bites Back*, writes about gay dating shows and argues that the networks have had difficulty reaching out to the LGBT community without exploiting the group as being strange or exotic. Pozner writes, "Among broadcast and widely viewed cable networks, only four high profile queer-themed reality TV dating shows have aired in the genre's first full decade, two starring gay men and two starring bi-sexual women" (2010, 49).

Despite people's reservations about the show and later criticism, the show was quite successful in its timeslot and was a highly rated cable show during its time on the air. Its finale was one of the highest-rated shows for MTV that season.

The show encouraged gender confusion and ambiguity in its opening moments. The group of males and females could not figure out why they had both been invited to court a single woman. Both males and females had an opportunity to spend time with Tequila, compete for her attentions, and build a relationship with the reality star. It is presumed that having Tequila be the object of both the men's and women's affection would be a younger, postmodern spin on the strongly conventional and heterosexual positioning of *The Bachelor*, a show that posits that every man and woman needs to find true love in the arms of that special someone.

The show basked in sensationalistic displays of sexuality. Michael Slezak, writing for *Entertainment Weekly*, commented that "16 lesbian contestants arrived on the scene and put on a lingerie fashion show ripped from the mind of a 12-year-old boy (it's a naughty nurse! and a naughty schoolgirl! and a naughty, um, construction worker!?); and Tila declared (very seriously), 'I never, ever told anyone this before . . . I'm a bisexual'" (2008). Slezak, like the audience, doubted the claim and believed that the producers knew this in advance and planned the revelation as a surprise to the audience. The show toyed with sexuality by having Tila tongue-kissing a girl one minute and then a boy the next minute. The show didn't seem to have any reverence for either gay or lesbian sensibilities but appeared designed to appeal to young boys who believed it would be exciting to watch a girlfriend make out with another girl. This show was thus less about liberating sexuality for individuals and more about teen boy fantasies. Further, because the acts of sexuality were so random and unwarranted by anything the audience witnessed in group or individual interactions, it didn't make a lot of sense. It looked as if Tila Tequila was simply directed to go through staged encounters with a variety of male and female suitors to fulfill a sex-encounter quotient for each episode.

Controversy surrounded the show, and religious groups found the show objectionable. Many found the living conditions on the show strange. There was Tequila and her brood all living in a mansion. While an aspect of the show was maintaining a closeness to Tila and pursuing her, the arrangement seemed claustrophobic and almost prison-like. LGBT groups found the way the show treated issues of bisexuality offensive. It applied a cookie-cutter mentality to all bisexual women, assuming they all liked the same thing and that all bisexual women would immediately be attracted to Tequila. These groups saw the presentation as pandering to the old negative stereotypes that lesbians and gays were simply perverts and not interested in serious and mature human relationships.

Also, accusations abounded that the show and Tequila's sexual preferences were fake, that she had a boyfriend, and that the show was a sham. After the program finished, Tequila revealed that the producers did engineer some show decisions. Tequila admitted that she would have rather picked the female contestant in the finale, but the producers forced the choice of a male contestant. Later, she also admitted that she was a lesbian, and that the male aspects of the show were not her idea.

Benjamin Solomon in "A Complete History of MTV's Dating Game Shows" remarks about the show and its issues. Solomon writes that MTV "had bisexual Internet personality Tila Tequila choose from a house full of guys and girls. Despite the toying with gay and straight issues the producers had Tequila choose a straight male partner. The show was a success often winning its cable time slot, and inspired a slew of spin-offs" (2013). What emerged was that MTV had no politics on gay or straight issues but simply wanted to raise issues about the idea of dating for LGBT groups that had not been raised before.

In fact, the show did widen the concept of dating and relationships in a nation-wide forum. Even if Tequila and her desire for bisexual dates was a false premise, witnessing the normalization of bisexual attractions on television and performing such images for young impressionable men suggested a show could begin to change attitudes about same-sex conduct. In comedy shows like *Will and Grace*, the action was far removed from young men's own experiences. In a dating show, the concept of alternative sexuality was far closer, and also more threatening to many heterosexual males. Though Tequila's adventures eroticized and exhibited bisexuality in an exploitive way, it provided such examples in close quarters to ostensibly straight males. It has been suggested that MTV might have hoped that such exposure might make the males less opposed or fearful of such behavior and could begin the process of a dialogue. Pozner cautioned that "while these hormonal performances may help destigmatize hookups between mostly-straight sorority girls who enjoy teasing their boyfriends with a little 'hot girl-on-girl action,' they hardly validate authentic lesbian and bisexual desire" (2010, 49). Despite Pozner's caution, the show did act as an important bridge to help society deal with such individual choices and differences.

Sometimes MTV has shown insight by producing a show that was difficult to produce and had a limited run but featured an interesting premise and unusual provocative characters like Tila Tequila. In the promos for the second season, we witnessed images of 15 attractive males and 15 attractive females in cages spraying each other with seltzer, dressing in provocative outfits, and groping each other and Tequila as part of the competition. The show's success was in normalizing same-sex attraction in the context of a heterosexual society, but it may have failed in that the star, Tila Tequila, portrayed little substance that would attract any mate, either male or female, to her.

See also: The Dating Game; The Newlywed Game

Further Reading

Jennifer L. Pozner, *Reality Bites Back,* 2010; Michael Slezak, "Someone Please Explain a (Penicillin) *Shot at Love with Tila Tequila*," *Entertainment Weekly*, April 7, 2008; Benjamin Solomon, "A Complete History of MTV's Dating Shows," 2013; Ethan Thompson and Jason Mittell, *How to Watch Television.*

SINGLED OUT

Singled Out was an early game show on the MTV network that appeared between 1995 and 1998. It was a flagship show in the dating genre, featuring several of MTV's best DJ personalities, including Chris Hardwick, Carmen Electra, and Jenny McCarthy. The show portrayed the mockumentary format that MTV game shows cultivated in which mocking the game show style became as important as playing and winning the game. MTV differentiated itself from other programmers of gaming shows by commenting on the programming meta-referentially within the show itself. MTV's canny approach to game shows included commentary on game show style. MTV took a youthful, parodic vision of the game show phenomena, thus revitalizing game programming and making it new. Such programming relied on stereotypes of rebellious youth, and rock and roll's theatricality. MTV utilized outrage in its reality programming but cautiously framed programs using its standards and practices personnel to censor videos that parents might find objectionable. MTV reasoned that content had to reflect youth themes but also had to be understood by families who understood the logic of game shows.

MTV's dating programming emphasized audience involvement. Programming of the 1990s experimented with new aspects of audience participation. The psychology of featuring cheering crowds was that such demonstrations would prime home audiences to also champion the players. As on other dating shows, the sets were posh, tacky, and filled with clichés. This created a stage for a commentary and for acts of derision, violation, and mockery. The contestant, the person who was going to be picking a date was blindfolded and led onto a stage. Usually, they were driven around in a golf cart by a fat, bearded cupid wearing a diaper. The potential dates were described by the host, and the 15 contestants of the opposite sex were situated in the room during the description. A series of reality TV programming elimination rounds proceeded that revealed the personality of the contestant and provided humorous comments to deflate the fear involved in the dating ritual.

Benjamin Solomon wrote a description of the show, saying it "featured a single guy or a single girl weeding out a crowd of horny hotties by choosing a series of attributes (hair color, body type, 'package size') and asking erotically tinged questions" (2013). The contest board listed a group of five categories. These could include physical qualities, age limits, or preferences in lovemaking. The contestant then picked characteristics. After picking characteristics, the player was allowed to open one category. For example, if the characteristic was blondes, brunettes, and redheads, the picker could choose to remove one group. The specific group under that limitation departed from the theater. After several limitations via categories, there were only a handful of contestants left to consider. When Jennifer Love Hewitt (early in her career) appeared on the show, she eliminated both older men and younger men.

The next round advanced players closer to a date. The player asked suggestive questions such as, "If you had me in a room alone, what would you give me?" Or the picker could ask comedic questions like, "How well do you play ping-pong?" forcing the contestants to have to play ping-pong. Lots of spectacle balanced with fun activities kept the show light and interactive. The contestants who either performed well or answered the questions well remained while the rest were eliminated until they were only three left. Finalists in the game were put on a series of steps leading to the player. Each contestant was asked to choose a question. If the choice of the contestant matched the player, the contestant would be advanced closer to the player. The first contestant to reach the player won a date with the player.

Occasionally, the show would benefit from celebrity guests. As mentioned earlier, a 1996 episode featured Jennifer Love Hewitt. Even as a teen, she was a charmer. When presented with categories, she chose quickly. After exiling older guys, the boys each presented her with a heart. The theme of the special show was Valentine's Day, so special decorations from Valentine's Day were strewn throughout the set. Each older guy paraded by her and left her a heart. All the while, Love Hewitt howled with laughter. Next, Hewitt chose the category of height. She dumped all short guys. Finally, her last characteristic was facial hair, and she deleted any males with beards and mustaches. A fun segment of the show was the entrance of the star parade. A fat angel rode the player in a golf cart. The spectacular angel wore a halo, shorts, T-shirt, and a gaudy-but-falling-apart set of sparkly wings. He was an obnoxious, rude, fat, ugly character, but he suggested that love was blind and that the entire show was just in fun.

For the final round, Hewitt was situated in a giant red throne that was at once tacky and surreal. The contestants answered questions similar to Hewitt's responses to be advanced into the winner's circle. In the end, the winner provided Hewitt with flowers. A rose petal shower met her and the date as they were paraded off the stage.

MTV worked to reinvent the game show as something fit for youthful audiences. Sometimes embarrassment and strange tastes helped to make the situation fun. There was the fun of embarrassing people and putting two people together in the same room, but nobody took this too seriously, and there was no sense of a long-term commitment in the highly public dating forums. An actress like Jennifer Love Hewitt was perfect for such a show because she could have fun while performing the role of a charming teen girl. As in all MTV programming, there was some suggestive dialogue, but the emphasis was on goofy couplings, a clever, competitive spirit, mockery of the old quiz game show, and an observation of the tropes of reality programming.

MTV saw the program as a way to explore issues of teen dating, and many watching found the show instructive about the context of a relationship. Many preteens might have had little idea of what to do in a dating situation. As always, the show was skewed toward male viewers, particularly younger teen viewers. Courtney Enlow wrote a tribute to the show's strengths in 2015 saying, "In 1995, a little MTV dating show premiered and changed our very lives (or at least amused us greatly for 30 minutes a week)."

See also: The Dating Game; The Newlywed Game; Next

Further Reading

Jennifer L. Pozner, *Reality Bites Back*; Benjamin Solomon, "A Complete History of MTV's Dating Game Shows," 2013; Ethan Thompson and Jason Mittell, *How to Watch Television*.

TAILDATERS

Taildaters was an MTV reality show that explored issues of dating from a voyeuristic perspective. The program was a progression from earlier MTV dating game programs and was the first series to involve a car in the dating process. The program followed the progress of a couple on their first date. *Taildaters* aired from 2002 to 2003 on the MTV network and offered a variety of new spins on the dating show. Friends and family could ride along and watch the proceedings. The cast of close friends and family members observing the date from a van following behind the couple were encouraged to make commentary about the date as the couple progressed. The friends weren't actually invited on the date, nor did they even have seats at the restaurant or some other aspect of the date. Instead, they were doing covert surveillance in an MTV mobile studio van. The show allowed both players/dates to have two family members watching and commenting during the event. Thus, the date became a set of six people, each date and their chosen "seconds." Besides watching each player and providing coaching to their respective friend/family member through the dating experience, the program revealed how the family responded to the date and the potential relationship. Thus, rather than seeing how the actual couple was responding to each other, we received commentary from people who know the daters well and could discuss their interests, views, and anxieties during the date. *Taildaters* allowed family and friends to contribute commentary to the date while it was in progress.

Ben Solomon, commenting in "A Complete History of MTV's Dating Game Shows," reports that the inclusion of a vehicle in dating shows was "soon to be omnipresent in all MTV dating shows" (2013). Solomon and others discovered that shows like *Taildaters* had a broad, anthropological mission in MTV's dating programming. Hirsch and Wardlow, in their text *Modern Loves,* explore the unusual ways that love and dating are viewed in our society and suggest that programming like MTV can be instructive to confused young people. The authors explain, "The role of romantic love as the social and emotional context of sexual behavior is largely absent from the public health and clinical discourse on adolescent sexual behavior, pregnancy, and childbearing" (Hirsch and Wardlow 2006, 118). Owing to the lack of healthy and reliable information on dating and sexual behavior in society in general, programming like MTV's dating shows provide a less-complicated and less-intrusive way to deal with issues of dating, courtship, and sexuality. Satirizing, sending up, or dethroning the importance and solemnity of dating rituals can reduce teen fear and anxiety about such rites of passage. By inviting family and friends along for the date, the ritual of dating became normalized as a family activity that was open to scrutiny and slowly debunked.

Taildaters interrogated the mythos of perfect dates and showed aspects of human behavior that were instructive to young viewers. There were some creepy sides to the show. In an episode involving Matt and Michelle, the friends of Matt were not all friends, and included a girl who knew Matt. This girl appeared to have an emotional attachment to him. It was possible that they might have had an earlier romantic relationship. In fact, she seemed to be a date-in-waiting, and her commentary appeared stern and disturbed, as if she could not bear the thought of him having a good time with another woman. This seemed to make the show more about obsession and voyeurism and less about positive shadowing of a relative or friend to ensure they were having a positive relationship with a good-hearted person. However, in Matt and Michelle's case, the instance of a girl "friend" exhibiting anxiety and possible stalking behaviors became evident. Thus, the show actually portrayed negative outcomes of the dating environment. Further, in the case of the female dater, Michelle, her backup friends were equally disturbing. One fellow named Forrest appeared to be her roommate, while another friend she had only known for a single year. The show created a clear vision of the role jealousy and anxiety played in the dating system. Researchers Sobraske, Baster, and Gaulin, studying threats to relationships in a psychology analysis, reported that their research led to an understanding of three key features: "These three components—severity, specificity of rival, and deception by partner—are consistent with the view that jealousy functions to avoid harm to romantic relationships, a view shared by appraisal theory and evolutionary psychology" (2013, 265). Perhaps, inadvertently, *Taildaters* revealed this jealous behavior in people who were introduced as friends but appeared to have romantic involvement with those experiencing the date.

Part of the program's appeal was the engagement aspect of experiencing the date with the participants. We saw how the two people were relating and felt empowered to inject our own views about the date. However, the surveillance camera may have also allowed too much intrusion, privileging the friends/viewers so much that their commentary seemed to compete with the date participants. One question raised by the series was a consideration of the role of surveillance in American life. Do we need that many cameras in all aspects of American life? Some would say we already have too much surveillance in our lives, and inviting surveillance into something as private as a date reflects the desire for people to share intimacy. Whether the surveillance is on MTV or Facebook, it might still produce negative results, and over time people may wish to reject the loss of privacy occasioned by sharing private moments with a larger public.

In episodes of *Taildaters*, the couples seemed quite conditioned to expect cameras following their every move, and little discomfort was detected. This suggested the rise of a new generation comfortable with a surveillance society. Such shows pursue the idea of lifecasting, in which individuals decide to broadcast their daily lives around the clock, often documenting mundane and uninteresting aspects of their life, such as taping their whole sleep cycle. Wade Roush, writing for the *MIT Technology Review,* describes the growth of lifecasting, "Thanks to cheap hardware and several new free or low-cost video-streaming services on the Web, the technological and financial barriers to amateur video webcasting—whether one hour per day or 24—are quickly disappearing" (2007). Roush described pioneer Webcaster Justin Kan as a voluntary 24-hour star of his own lifecasting service, Justin.tv.

Taildaters predicted a time when surveillance was simply a part of existence, and as the program explained, sometimes living in public was not easy. When daters met for the first time, we sometimes heard weird and detrimental commentary by family members and friends. The audience was treated to undercutting commentary that betrayed the couple's characteristic dating moves. Michelle was described as a hippie by her friends, and they jokingly referred to her lack of shaving her legs. Matt's friend commented on his cute, unassuming, and cheery "hi," suggesting his dialogue with women was consciously heavily scripted.

While on their limousine date, Matt and Michelle attempted to talk, but the screen became crowded with commentary from the four taildaters, who began describing the flirtatious behavior of both partners. In the technology of the early millennium, pagers were often used prior to powerful smartphones, and, during the show, the assistant daters sent "text messages" to the official daters using a pager. Things became more aggressive when the friends continued to text throughout the date, offering instruction and advice, where sometimes it was not needed or could harm the date. Finally, the evening struck a romantic note, and Matt grabbed Michelle for a dance. The program had a dramatic climax when Matt's female friend, a taildater, became visibly shaken, upset, and left the confines of the mobile recording rig to confront Matt. She apparently had unresolved issues regarding the new date and Matt's apparent romantic success.

Taildaters provided real anthropological insight into the forum of dating and included dramatic and confrontational encounters. *Taildaters* was part of a movement of postmodern scholarship that absorbed the study of women's issues into American culture and examined it with the seriousness of other aspects of common American life. Elizabeth Johnston, writing in her article "How Women Really Are: Disturbing Parallels between Reality Television and 18th Century Fiction," describes the matter thusly. She writes, "Only in the 1980s on the heels of the 1970s feminist movement, did scholarship begin to emerge suggesting that works about courtship and family did indeed, perform important political work which both impacted and reflected the cultural imagination" (2006). Like Johnston, the viewer can see the work of *Taildaters* as being a more serious analysis of dating and courtship rituals that previously had been disregarded. In this sense, *Taildaters* provided a way to watch and reflect on how we conduct our courtship behavior.

Like French critic John Baudrillard, we can see the rituals on *Taildaters* as a simulation of the dating process that perhaps, for this generation at least, may replace the real thing. What so many MTV shows teach us is that this concept of dating and sexuality is still an extremely problematic ritual of bonding for this cultural cohort.

See also: Cheaters; The Dating Game

Further Reading

Leigh H. Edwards, *The Revolution in Reality TV*; Jennifer Hirsch and Holly Wardlow, *Modern Loves*; Wade Roush, "Broadcast Your Life Online, 24-7," *MIT Technology Review,* 2007; Ben Solomon, "A Complete History of MTV's Dating Game Shows," *The Date Report*, 2013; Ethan Thompson and Jason Mittell, *How to Watch Television*.

TOUGH LOVE (AND *TOUGH LOVE COUPLES*)

Tough Love is a reality couples therapy show on VH1 that debuted in 2009 and continues to run in various configurations on the channel. It was hosted by celebrity Stephen Ward and Ward's mother, JoAnn Ward, and it offered relationship advice on each segment. Ward was a harsh critic, and he told women all the things they did wrong in trying to achieve a relationship and to derive romance. He sought to give them tips and advice that will set them on the road to a truly fulfilling relationship. This was not easy work, and the show tended to dwell in the cruelty that has made women suffer from issues of low self-esteem. Both Ward and his mother are involved in the business of being master matchmakers. The show took women to a lovers' boot camp. There, women were instructed in the ways in which they could be better daters and seek partners who were good complements to their qualities.

The shows were a pretty tough drill. On the first episode, "What Men Really Think," Ward took the women in hand when they arrived at the boot camp. He gave them an analysis of their appearance. He provided a course, explaining first appearances were everything. He explained that men judged appearances first and looked at the internal woman later. He gave them a grueling exercise to work, in terms of their own appearance, and gave them a firsthand analysis of how they appeared to others. It was not a pleasant experience. Many women were upset by the commentary, and one woman was hospitalized for not being able to deal with the analysis of how she appeared. The women reviewed their appearance and even watched tapes of themselves walking and moving. Ward was no cupcake, and talked to the women seriously about how they appeared and their attitudes toward men. His mother offered relationship advice as well. Many of the women didn't want to see themselves as they were. In this show in successive seasons, the program moved from individual to couples relationships and began to resemble the advice of Dr. Phil, in that it attempted to provide therapy in a few minutes to (1) aid appearance and (2) aid in finding true love. The emphasis of the program moved from finding a date to the task of finding someone to love. Later it provided analysis of the problems the couples endured in the hopes the couple could be more happy.

Jennifer Pozner summed up the problems for many of the couples in reality and relationship shows. The problem was that many of the contestants were very unrealistic about what they expected from a relationship on a day-to-day basis. The reason shows like *Tough Love* bit so hard was because they tried to provide people with a little bit of reality therapy. Pozner writes, "With few exceptions relationship and lifestyle shows frame women as unaware that there is anything more to life than tossing back martinis, lounging in hot tubs, and as Bachelorette Christine suggested, 'greeting husbands at the door with dinner and a foot rub at the ready'" (2010). Clearly, many people suffer from dysfunctional descriptions of reality. People watching the shows have little frame of reference for relationships, because they haven't been in one or because they sense the programs are idealizing the concept of relationships.

At the same time, one of the positive aspects of reality television is this diversification of our culture. Exposing a variety of people from different backgrounds who have problems in their relationships does make people aware that people of all races, classes, ages, and varied social groups suffer from similar vexing problems. Critic Susan Murray reported that "one of the most compelling aspects of reality TV is the extent to which its use of real people or non-actors contributes to the diversification of television culture" (2004). That is, seeing real people enduring real problems, even if they are scripted and even if they are poorly done, at least makes people aware that real people deal with these problems every day. In some sense, this may be a form of therapy for all viewers. Their problems are everyone's problems, and, by watching people like ourselves, these universal problems become less insurmountable.

See also: The Dating Game; The Newlywed Game

Further Reading

Susan Murray and Laurie Ouellette, *Reality TV, Remaking Television Culture*, 2004; Jennifer Pozner, *Reality Bites Back*, 2010; Ethan Thompson and Jason Mittell, *How to Watch Television*.

WANNA COME IN?

Wanna Come in? is a reality program broadcast on MTV from 2004 to 2006. It provided a new spin on the old *Cyrano de Bergerac* story of a handsome guy paired with an ugly guy dating a beautiful woman. Cyrano provided the poetry and the charm, and his companion, the less-articulate friend, Christian, provided the beautiful facade that Cyrano lacked. In the MTV version, the roles were somewhat reversed. A nerdy fellow was paired with a smooth ladies man. It was the charming companion who must coach the nerd via hidden microphone through the steps of the date, arriving at the moment of truth, when the attractive date must ask the nerd, "Do you want to come in?" The pairing of the "dud and the stud" used the technology of a hidden ear microphone to make sure the dud could communicate with his stud master during the date.

Different challenges forced the team to come up with creative ways to impress their female companion. At one point, there was a self-improvement challenge in which the unattractive male must admit to some bad habit and gain the date's advice on how to correct the same. Another challenge was even more complex. The team must find a way to sweep the woman off her feet. They literally had to get her *off* her feet. Such a task was almost impossible without the dater creating some ridiculous ploy to make the woman jump. The show presented nearly insurmountable challenges for coaches attempting to convert the nerd into an attractive date. If the male guide could pilot his nerd to an invite to a girl's house, the winner and his handsome counterpart would share a cash prize. Benjamin Solomon in his "Complete Guide to MTV Dating Shows" commented that "the clearly scripted formula, possibly inspired by then Bravo hit *Queer Eye for the Straight Guy*, might not be as fondly remembered as some other shows . . . , but it hit on themes that would be major reality successes later on dating shows like *The Pick-up Artist* and *Beauty and the Geek*" (2013). Solomon caught onto one of the show's strange allures. If the program could transform the undateable guy into a male that a female would want, perhaps home viewers might feel they too could become desirable. Such shows intrinsically unwrapped the definition of *reality* in reality television. Barry King writes, "If reality participants are manifestly perceived as performing for the camera, does this not serve to underscore that documentary, as in Grierson's famously ambiguous definition—the creative use of actuality—has always created the performances it records and observes?" (2006, 42). In other words, are the men in *Wanna Come In?* really nerds, or are they simply performing as such for the camera?

While some experts found ways to accomplish the complex tasks and unusual challenges of the date (like making a woman jump), many found that gaining points and cash during the date lost them the trust and attention of the female subject. That is, fulfilling the strange requests of the date made the oddballs seem even odder. The tasks demanded that these men sometimes had to make quick, strange choices or erratic actions that might frighten their date.

The real payoff was when the couple returned to the woman's house, and she either invited the man in to continue the date or she chose to conclude things at the door. Sometimes the outcomes were very surprising, as when a rather awkward date provided a man with an invite into the house. We can only imagine that outside the scruffy exterior, these women had the kindness to see the good-natured, klutzy prince beneath the rough veneer.

The show exploited MTV's interest in questioning self and roles of the self expressed in our society. Rose Niklas writes in *Governing the Soul* that "It is through the promotion of lifestyle by the mass media, by advertising and by experts, through the obligation to shape a life through choices in a world of self-reflexive objects and images, that the modern self is governed" (Niklas 1999, 256–258). That is, MTV discussed roles and self-presentation that young people displayed as they were forming their adult personas, and the characters of "dater," "nerd," and "voyeur" or "watcher" were depicted as prominent roles that young people play. The programming's spy-cam segments created suspense and excitement. The participants were stuck with tough challenges, and it was only an act of inspired cleverness and winsome charm that could make the female open her home to the questionable male presence. Thus, there was an element of trust and authenticity in the personas created and displayed. Unlike MTV programming in the style of *Ridiculousness* or *Jackass* that portray absurd or superhumanly dangerous behavior, here the characters were at a human level. Without parading buffoonery, the station can often produce the experience of being in the viewer's shoes, allowing the viewer some relationship to a reality contestant very much like themselves—filled with anxieties, doubts about their adult competency, and confused over complex dating and social issues. We, like anyone, can feel the self-consciousness and neurotic side of being subjects on the show. *Wanna Come In?* allowed the audience to experience the agony of winning someone's trust and affection. Here, MTV chose people who were nearly real, and for that we feel a close identification with them.

See also: Cheaters; The Dating Game

Further Reading

Leigh H. Edwards, *The Revolution in Reality TV*; Barry King, "Training Camps of the Modular: Reality TV as a Form of Life," 2006; Rose Niklas, *Governing the Soul,* 1999; Ethan Thompson and Jason Mittell, *How to Watch Television.*

Chapter 5: International Reality Television—America's Reach

Going Global: Reality Programming on a World Stage

In his book *World Television*, Joseph Straubhaar explained that television is for many people their central media experience of the world. In fact, the notion of reality television is literally indicative of what many world cultures see on their screens; for them, television by its very nature is a representation of reality, of the real. Straubhaar writes, "Television still forms a dominant layer of media experience for most people" (2007, 2). Albert Moran in *New Flows in Global TV* relates that there are at least seven regions of global markets across the globe, but that the regions have groups that have social, cultural, language, historic, and economic ties that make them more likely to trade television content (2009, 98). British television is widely viewed and heralded in the United States. Egyptian television is viewed favorably in Syria, simply because these cultures have languages and practices in common. At the same time, certain cultures dominate because they arrive at more original ideas for programs. Moran writes, "British broadcasting is the world's largest devisor and distributor of contemporary TV format franchises" (2009, 91). Why the British have claimed this position is unknown, but they seem clever at finding marketable concepts that world audiences enjoy.

The history of reality television globally has been markedly different from its arrival in the United States. For one thing, many of the ideas for our reality programs were generated abroad and imported to the American market. At the same time, reality television is extremely transferable to other cultures, and often American shows survive and prosper in foreign markets. Heather Timmons, writing for *The New York Times,* explains that many recent reality programs debuting in India originated in our culture. She writes,

> These new reality shows reflect a uniquely Indian form of chaos. But they are often a product of deals with foreign networks: "Bigg Boss," for example, is a result of a partnership between the local station Network 18 and the media conglomerate Viacom. Star, a unit of the News Corporation, has "Master Chef India" and "Perfect Bride," where mothers choose brides for their sons, and Sony's channels in India show "Kaun Banega Crorepati" or "Who Wants to Be a Millionaire," "Indian Idol" and "Maa Exchange," where, yes, mothers change places. (Timmons 2001)

Another factor is the enormous wealth of the U.S. television market. The industry, derived largely from radio and film companies, has billions in assets and caters to a population wealthy enough to subscribe to a wide and expansive field of programs. More importantly, this population is wealthy enough to buy and subscribe to the products and advertising that have traditionally underwritten the costs of expensive American fiction programming. Foreign cultures often lack the assets that support American television. In the United States, a strong consumer economy underwriting the costs of production has underwritten technically complex and ambitious television. Other states have not been so fortunate. For example, the concept of the BBC has often been held up to American producers as an exemplar of how television programming should be constructed using public monies. For many years, the BBC held a virtual monopoly on broadcasting, which held off competition. Further, the BBC and its expensive and expansive international news operations are extremely costly, and British citizens have had to pay large taxes to underwrite the television in their nation. Though the BBC has launched fine programming and ventured into reality programming, it has not always had the capital to challenge the most expensive of American programs (*Survivor* is a good example) that are able to underwrite programming with private funds from advertisers and production assistance from various corporations in exchange for on-screen advertising embedded in the show.

Finally, the United States has been rooted in the criminal and the fantastic aspects of programming far more than the rest of the world, so it is no surprise that American programs focused on different subject matter than their world television counterparts. What we have seen overseas is a more modest, small-sized industry either allied with governments or strong capitalist entities that have funded fiction programming. However, due to the constraints of cost, amateur, less-sumptuous, and reality-based programming has always been popular in non-U.S. markets.

Another factor in the growth and dissemination of reality programming was the fact that much of the basic research and creation of television itself was an international effort. Since all nations contributed to the medium, it was only natural that many different nations contributed their own spin on television programming. In fact, considering the popularity of reality programming abroad, it might be safer to suggest that the United States entered into this realm rather later than the rest of the world. The United States' technological prowess and already strongly developed film and radio industry led to a robust commercial environment for television broadcasting. Joseph Straubhaar, in *World Television,* describes the way television was organized throughout the world. He writes, "Nations poured much of the effort to unify their peoples and to become modern into developing national television, which is eclipsed now in some countries by a much more fragmented, postmodern form of television" (2007, 55).

For example, a Scotsman, Alexander Bain, figured out how to send images using telegraph lines in 1843 and created the first facsimile machine, a precursor to sending moving pictures. Frenchmen Georges Rignoux and A. Fournier sent the first mechanical television pictures in 1909, and that was only possible because American Lee de Forest made the vacuum amplification tube possible in 1907. In

Russia, Vladimir K. Zworykin made an early cathode ray tube that made television more practical. So you see, television was an international enterprise from the start.

However, to understand the growth and maturation of reality television, it is important to see the roots of world television. Andrew Anthony wrote a retrospective of the medium for *The Guardian*. He writes, "Not only did television re-envision our sense of the world, it remains, even in the age of the internet, Facebook and YouTube, the most powerful generator of our collective memories, the most seductive and shocking mirror of society, and the most virulent incubator of social trends. It's also stubbornly unavoidable" (2013). Television broadcasts began in 1929 in Great Britain and ran up until World War II (going into hiatus during the war for security reasons), but even then the roots of the medium in England were tied to reality programming. On September 30, 1929, the first British broadcast according to Anthony featured, "A Yorkshire comedian named Sydney Howard performed a comic monologue" (2013). Sydney sang, "He's tall, and dark, and handsome" in what was perhaps the earliest progenitor of *The X Factor*. Even then, the impulse was to find some real person performing in some reality medium; this indicates that even in its earliest days, television was engaged in live, amateur competitions.

Professor Zia Ahmed, in his *History of Television* course, provided a good overview of the issues that have long-faced foreign television. In his discussion of Asian programming, he notes, "In Asia, television has traditionally been state-controlled, although the number of private stations is increasing, as is competition from satellite and cable television" (2011). The fact that states dominated the television realm tended to reduce private investment and the variety of programming. Ahmed's report on the Asian scene shows the strong influence of reality and documentary programming. He cites that particularly in India under the state-controlled regime, run by the Doordarshan Corporation, or DD for short, programming was dull and skewed toward informative and nation-building fare. However, the Gulf War, with its real world-changing events, was an impetus for programming to change for the Indian audience. Ahmed writes,

> When urban Indians learnt that it was possible to watch the Gulf War on television, they rushed out and bought dishes for their homes. Others turned entrepreneurs and started offering the signal to their neighbors by flinging cable over treetops and verandahs. From the large metros satellite TV delivered via cable moved into smaller towns, spurring the purchase of TV sets and even the upgradation from black & white to color TVs. (2011)

Boom, in a single event, Ahmed showed how the reality of the Gulf War and the need to know spurred a whole market and audience for programming in India. This emerging reality marketplace became a new area that private industry and government fought to fill.

The *global* in global reality occurs because shows that are to be shown worldwide have to be tailored to global markets. Amir Hetsroni, writing about reality TV, explained,

First, reality programs are global media products that need at least some cultural adaptation to succeed outside their habitués. In the vast majority of cases, franchised or non-franchised formats are locally produced rather than shows are imported and broadcast in their original version—as often happens with other TV genres such as drama. (2010)

Hetsroni points out that reality as we think of it means very different things to international markets.

The roots of reality television were sewn in European cultures from the beginning, sometimes with a totally benign purpose, like the BBC's programs to inform and enlighten post-war audiences, and, sometimes, as in Russia and Germany, to spread messages of propaganda. In Germany the roots of television were tied to the intentions of the state to produce propaganda for the German people. Knut Hickethier, in his essay "Early TV, Imagining and Realizing Television," points out that early German TV "would serve the propaganda of the Reich and was pompously advertised as a 'German invention'. In Hadamovsky's words: 'Fight for Germany to become the first nation in the world in which all our "national comrades" can watch television'" (2008).

Zona Latina, a Web site specializing in reports of media usage in Central and South America, ran a report entitled "Television Program Preferences in Cable Households," illustrating cable television usage trends in Argentina, and showed percentages of programming that received large viewing audiences. Throughout the statistics, nonfiction programming that fell into the range or what today we would consider reality programming (cooking, home improvement, shopping, science and technology programs, documentaries) all scored higher than the national viewership of non-reality-formatted programming. The researchers framed the question as, "What television program types do people in cable households watch more than those in non-cable households?" The resounding answer was that many Argentinian families already enjoyed reality program 15 years ago. Dror Abend-David wrote an article about the influence of reality TV in Israel and concluded that reality TV may be changing non-reality television. He says, "What I wish to demonstrate in this article is that the gap between reality and reality television is narrowing, as the news—not less a form of entertainment than other programming—is adopting some of the techniques and styles of reality programs" (Abend-David 2010, 116). Ironically, the reality of the news and how it was being presented, according to Abend-David, was being transformed by the practices and techniques of reality programming, suggesting that reality programming isn't about "actual" reality but involves a form of "staged" reality.

The overall picture is that reality programming has always been a part of world television culture, and that many of these programs—such as the popular ninja competition programs, the romantic bus ride series, the haunted house paranormal shows, the slow television spectacles, and the funny and embarrassing naked shows—were all world television phenomena before they became stateside hits.

Further Reading

Zia Ahmed, "A History of Television in Asia," Course Materials for a History of Television Course, Blogger, October 9, 2011; Andrew Anthony, "A History of Television: A Technology That Seduced the World, and Me," *The Guardian*, September 7, 2013, Web; Amir Hetsroni, *Reality Television: Merging the Global and the Local,* 2010; Knut Hickethier, "Early TV, Imagining and Realizing Television," in *A European Television History* (Jonathan Bignell and Andreas Flickers, eds.), 2008; Albert Moran, *New Flows in Global TV*, 2009; Joseph Straubhaar, *World Television: From Global to Local*, 2007; Zona Latina, "Television Program Preferences in Cable Households," Zona Latina, Latin American Media and Marketing, March 5, 2000.

AINORI (JAPAN)

Ainori was a comic and sometimes tragic reality program focused on love and finding the right one. The meaning of the word *ainori* in translation literally means "ride together," but really is about a "love ride." However, instead of focusing on the game show aspect of *The Bachelor* or turning love into a competition, the Japanese, in a very philosophical manner, turn love into a trip or journey. A group of seven people would get on a small pink tour bus and embark on a globetrotting tour across the world. As they went from place to place, they became more engaged with their co-riders. Bonds were formed and friendships developed. At some point, when a rider felt an emotional bond had formed with another rider, the lover in private admitted these feelings to the home-viewing audience and submitted the feelings to a diary. The lover must then confess his or her love to the object of his or her affections. The object, hearing the declaration of love must sleep on it a night and decide if the feelings were reciprocated. If the two matched up, they were given tickets home to continue their relationship. If the player rejected the love proposal, the lover must pack his or her bags and head home as a love reject. The situation was cast as a poignant encounter and not played for laughs.

Before the trip started, friends and family members would comment on the player's love life and joke about how successful their friend would be on the trip. One colleague joked that his friend on the bus was likely to commit suicide like a samurai if he was not "love successful." The family and friends seemed to take great pleasure in bemoaning the love life of their colleagues committed to the road trip.

The program was a product of Fuji Television and began broadcasting in 1999 and ended in 2009. The program was so immensely popular that it was reborn the next year in 2010 as *Ainori 2*. As in many Japanese programs, public displays of emotion, crying and laughing were encouraged, and illustrated a level of drama that was absent from most polite society. There is an element of emotional revelation in Japanese programming that is absent from American programming. While American dating programs like Fox's *Temptation Island*—a program that Richard Huff describes as "a series that was a mix of *Survivor* and a dating show" (2006, 111)—purport to portray real intimate encounters in an island setting, it is hard to avoid the high-level production values that suggest such American shows are largely staged. *Ainori*, instead, had the ring of truth.

The show was featured late in the evenings on Mondays, a prime time to drag in viewing audiences. The program was so popular that it spawned many franchise series in Southeast Asia and the rest of the globe.

An interesting dynamic of the show was the group composition. Each tour bus in each country that the guests visited contained only seven passengers. Regardless of the pairing off and the romantic interests of the passengers, someone would always be left out of the romantic engagement. From 1999 to 2008 the bus visited 90 countries, and the tourists saw monuments and famous locations and took out-of-the-way side trips to unusual places. Part of the charm of the show was the travel, where the guests saw a new part of the world and learned about new places. It is a value of Japanese culture that an insular island culture must seek out the world and explore it. A similar ethic pervades English adventurism, but the Japanese explore that urge today through rituals of tourism. As they approached the border of a new country, they must change tour buses (always pink buses), and they acquired a new guide and friend to escort them on the next leg of the trip.

Of course, audience were attracted by the fact that all the participants on the journey were young, pretty, single people looking to return to Japan as part of a couple. The rules required the guests to pine in silence for their love object. They were forbidden from telling others on the bus that they had fallen in love. Instead, they confessed in a diary and to the TV audience what they felt. After they confessed their love, the object had 24 hours to reflect on the proposal and either agree to be the lover, leave the bus and return to Japan, or stay on board and continue the journey. If the lover proposed and was rejected, he or she must return to Japan in disgrace to be replaced by a new passenger. The love declarations were given directly to the home-viewing audience when no one else on the bus was around. It was as if the home audience was the person's confessional and only friend/confessor/priest.

New tourists were added after someone was tossed, as hitchhikers found on the road. After a brief self-introduction, they were taken on board. The bus really got around, circumventing the world several times. The first complete world tour ended in 2003 and the second in 2007. The show has been a massive success. After twice around the world, the tour bus has gone off the strict around-the-world tour and has visited countries not on the globe-circling journey. Over 400 episodes were filmed by 2008 and over 40 couples had found love on the show. There have been eight marriages and four babies birthed by lovers united on the pink bus. There have been some remarkable turnarounds, like people who jilted a lover and then decided to leave the bus to be with the person they had rejected. Even staffers who were strictly forbidden from engaging with the players on the bus have had relationships with the players. It was a regular *Peyton Place* on the love bus, and, in one country, a female player fell in love with the tour guide and declared her love for him. In another segment, a female player fell in love with a sound technician on the show whom she had never spoken to and who also had a girlfriend. The girl, the sound technician, and others were sent home after the mishap.

The show has had international fans and created international incidents. A group of players shook their buttocks at a group in Costa Rica, and, because kids were in the crowd, the offending guests were arrested. Later, they were rescued by the pleading of the crew. When the show decided to forego Nicaragua because of the political troubles in the nation, the government of Nicaragua was offended and begged the show to return. The passengers did stop off in the nation and were treated as goodwill ambassadors from Japan. The Nicaraguan government didn't want to lose the partnership of the powerful Japanese economy.

Interestingly, the Japanese do not like to see themselves as idle tourists and dislike the notion that the show exploits poorer countries to bring comfort to young Japanese dating singles, so the show had adopted a program of collecting money and establishing schools in poorer countries. Thus, *Ainori* had acquired the unlikely status of a non-governmental organization. The *Ainori* fund has made the tour, the show, and the bus very popular when touring countries around the world and has helped the show shed the image of spoiled, rich kids globetrotting for love.

See also: Anthony Bourdain; *Dismissed*; *Next*

Further Reading
David S. Escoffery, *How Real Is Reality TV?*

AMAAN RAMAZAN (PAKISTAN)

Amaan Ramazan was a Pakistani game show that has raised controversy through the practice of awarding orphaned children to childless couples as a prize. The program was mostly a *Price Is Right* quiz show, and the content was mostly religious and Muslim in origin. For the most part it was a respectful and pious show. The program translated into "Peace in Ramadan." Ramadan is a high holy month for people of the Muslim faith, and they are required to fast during the ninth month as part of the Five Pillars of Islam. The program was produced as an afternoon-long marathon program that aimed to be the most popular program in Pakistani culture. It aired in July and August of 2013 during Ramadan. The program aired live and was hosted by popular Pakistani celebrity Aamir Liaquat Hussain. It was the most popular program of the year produced by Geo TV.

A controversy erupted because the show decided to bring joy to couples by giving away babies to childless couples on the air. Hussain, the host, handed abandoned babies to childless couples. The parents had requested babies, and the babies had been obtained by the Chhipa Welfare Association. The Chhipa Welfare Association is an NGO (non-governmental agency) that provides social services in Pakistan. Apparently, that agency ran background checks on the prospective parents prior to the adoption. However, the idea of a baby giveaway on television presented problems. One issue was turning a living child into a product like a car or a laptop. Many people objected to *objectifying* the child. Another concern was to the lack of confidentiality. Exposing the family and the baby on television could lead to later harassment and a stigmatizing of the family and/or the child.

Generally, *Amaan Ramazan* was a conventional quiz show in which guests received awards for correctly answering questions about the Koran. Mostly, the show was filled with respectful rhetoric, but even domestic critics were concerned that babies were added to the prize mix. Prachi Gupta, writing for *Salon*, explained that the baby giveaway was actually awarded to vetted parents who were selected before the show and subjected to a rigorous study for fitness. The surprise both for audiences and new parents was that the show producers chose to do the giveaway on the air in front of millions. This sensational shock value prompted the outcry. If the baby exchange had been done off camera, it is doubtful that a controversy would have erupted. Raman Chhipa, from the NGO responsible for saving these abandoned children, explained, "Our team finds babies abandoned on the street, in garbage bins—some of them dead, others mauled by animals. So why not ensure the baby is kept alive and gets a good home?" (Mohsin 2013). The host offered that such babies might end up "used for suicide bombing attacks" (Mohsin 2013). Given the dangers of life for abandoned infants, the move was viewed as controversial, but perhaps intended as charitable, not as a means to create controversy.

Despite the controversy, the popularity for game shows has shown international reach. Chalaby remarked that "The environment is far more favourable than it has ever been for transnational broadcasting operations" (2009, 59).

See also: Game Shows

Further Reading

Jean K. Chalaby, "Broadcasting in a Post-National Environment: The Rise of Transnational TV Groups," 2009; Prachi Gupta, "Pakistani Game Show Giving Away Babies as Prizes," *Salon*, July 30, 2013.

DATING IN THE DARK (NETHERLANDS/UK/ UNITED STATES/OTHERS)

Dating in the Dark was an idea that arrived from the Netherlands, known there as *Daten in het Donker*. The simple premise was what if two singles were introduced to each other and had to enter the blind dating (no pun intended) experience without seeing the person they were dating? This was the situation that stimulated viewership behind the Netherlands' popular *Dating in the Dark* program, where contestants agree to not see their dates.

The staging is rather elaborate. The lonely individuals are separated in a larger house. There are three male contestants in the male wing, and three female contestants in the other wing. When the couples are paired up for a meeting, they must journey to a central room where it is dark. In this dark room, they stumble about, find chairs, chat, and try to have intimate, revealing time together. Activities like movies, smoking, or anything that could emit light are barred from the agenda.

At the outset the contestants sit in the room at a large table together. They accustom themselves to the sound of each other's voices and grow to know the personalities of the other potential dates through remarks that reveal their attitudes and worldview. After this initial group experience, they can decide to go on another date with one of the people in the room by choosing to return to the room with that party and have another sit in the dark to talk. Of course, the producer/ hosts try to fill in a picture of the potential dates by showcasing what the men and women brought with them to the house in terms of luggage and personal items. They presume that the more they learn about each other, the more likely it will be that they will form a bond. The only prohibition is physically seeing the other gender in the flesh. Sometimes artists are brought in to sketch a conception of what the potential dates look like in the minds of their potential suitors.

If the first date alone with a player goes well or badly, there are further options to fill. In any case, the player can ask for a private date with another member of the opposite sex. Finally, the six players are placed in the dark room one last time to reveal their true visual identity. At the revealing, the players are not allowed to speak or react to the actual physical size or attractiveness of another resident.

The program toys with the notion that allure should not be simply skin-deep, and potential mates should achieve a mutual understanding before physicality enters the picture.

The Guardian loved/hated the British edition of the show, saying that "it also throws in one brand new ingredient: total, soul-crushing, emotional rejection" (Heritage 2009). Unlike some dating shows, this program allows the contestants to choose to totally reject the suitor at the program's end. The novel notion is that one can build up a nonphysical emotional image and relationship with a player over a series of meetings, and either the guy or the girl can reject the player out of hand by responding to their appearance. However, Stuart Heritage, writing for *The Guardian,* sees the show as massively rigged and fraudulent, since it pairs an average-looking character with someone clearly in a supermodel class. The outcome will surely be that the supermodel will instantly reject someone not on his or her level. Heritage writes, "It's a methodical psychological dismantling, a stern lesson that you should know which rung you belong on and jolly well stay there" (2009). In essence, Heritage sees the show as a cruel example of bait-and-switch tactics in the sense that a golden girl or boy is held out to an individual as a lure, and immediately the foundation of a true and meaningful relationship is ruptured by the physicality of one player or the other. Other experiences of the show looking at various episodes do not always subscribe to Heritage's observation. In past episodes, one often sees a plethora of average-looking people discovering each other at the program's end. Certainly some are disappointed that they have not found a Venus or an Adonis at the end of the rainbow, but even the attractive must follow their instincts, and often dates occur following the final reveal because the two did find a spark that surmounted their contrasted physicality. What *Dating in the Dark* does show is that not everyone is carnally engaged by pure physical attractiveness and that many on the show find pure mental mates, which is a possible if often elusive outcome.

See also: The Dating Game; Next

Further Reading

Stuart Heritage, "Seeing Is Rejecting When You've Been Dating in the Dark," *The Guardian*, September 10, 2009.

DRAGONS' DEN (JAPAN) AND SHARK TANK (ELSEWHERE)

Dragons' Den is a popular Japanese reality program that originated in 2001 and explores the very real world of entrepreneurship. The contestants on *Dragons' Den* are seeking financing from well-positioned investors to make their product successful. Each believes their unique product, idea, or service can grow and prosper with sufficient seed capital. Therefore they are willing to pitch their product to a team of investors in the hopes that their pitch and the uniqueness of their product will entice an investor to provide much-needed capital to make their start-up business a raging success.

The program originated with Nippon TV, and it has franchised the program to over 30 countries, including several spin-offs in the same nation. The show has had a wide range of names, including the Japanese show originally called *Money Tigers*, basically a pun on the name of a famous Japanese general who operated in the Pacific region during World War II. The term *Dragons' Den* was ascribed to the show in Britain, and that name has been popular and variations of that name have been used in many countries.

In the United States the program is called *Shark Tank,* because of the notion of dealing in high finance and business. The executive producer behind the program is Mark Burnett (*Survivor*). The contestants likely think they are submerged in the business world of dangerous waters with many predator companies stalking the small ones. *Shark Tank* originated in the United States on ABC in 2009, has been a consistent ratings winner, and has successfully navigated eight seasons. The program has been nominated for Emmys as the best reality program, and it has won twice.

The format of the show is fairly simple and straightforward, and there is little of the false dramatics associated with some reality programming. The crucial element is the pitch of entrepreneurs to gain cash. Businesses can make deals with the sharks/investors on the spot, and some products and services go home without a bid. Here, the drama is the pitch and the pursuit of capital. A series of contestants who are providers of a product or a service believe they have a good idea and a good chance in their chosen industry. What they do not have is capital or backers. Each contestant, either an individual or a team, make a pitch to a panel of five investors who are known as the sharks or dragons. The contestant explains his or her product or service and dramatizes what it does and how it works. The seeker has already stipulated a sum of money that he or she wishes to procure and in return the originator will give the dragon/shark a percentage of the company's worth for the investment funding. The goal is to entice these wealthy investors to contribute to the funding of the product/service. If the originator does not achieve the goal, the product is passed and receives no funding. At other times, several investors are interested, and a small bidding war can erupt between investors who see potential for the product.

The theme of the show is that venture capitalists, those willing to invest in a largely untried and unresearched product, are the well-spring of economic and capitalistic self-development and that through perpetuating small businesses we help society to thrive.

The structure of the program uses several entrepreneurs to pitch their products to the team of sharks. Each of the *Shark Tank* panelists, like *The Voice* panelists, has the potential to bid for a percentage of the corporation in its infant form or to pass. In *The Voice*, the judges/coaches have to determine if the singers have talent. Here, the contest is to determine if the idea has merit. Often times, violent bidding wars for a smart idea will erupt. Some ideas find no backers. Mark Cuban, millionaire owner of the Dallas Mavericks, opted to pass on a product called Scrub Daddy, basically a super sponge that worked in a solid and resilient manner. Cuban was turned down for his offer of $100,000 in backing to own 50 percent of the company. Today the company generates $50 million a year, is sold in Wal-Mart, and nets inventor Aaron Krause a cool $20 million per year in revenue. Despite the show's ability to recognize and benefit new products and services, many good business ideas do not achieve attention from the investors on *Shark Tank* and do well despite the snub.

Perhaps some of the fascination with the program derives not from the products or deals pitched on the show, but from the personal stories of the youthful businesspeople who have created a product and often a vision. One lady in season eight wanted to sell stock in her company Sealed by Santa, which provided personalized replies to children's letters to Santa. The team asked her many penetrating questions about her business model and looked for worrisome signs in her structure and databases. She had been carving out the business for 10 years and had made the jump to a professional business 5 years prior. Several sharks showed great interest in her business idea. A key component in her winning pitch was her personal biography, which included two small children and a recent divorce. Her appeal, colored by the emotional aspects of her role as a principle breadwinner for her family, made her a successful candidate.

The program has had a therapeutic impact on some businesses. Mark Cohen in *The New York Times* reported in 2013 that the owners of VerbalizeIt, an online instant human-based translator system benefited from *Shark Tank* exposure. The owners accepted a bid of $250,000 from show shark Kevin O'Leary, but later they turned the offer down in favor of other investors who had offered a deal with better conditions. The owners utilized the exposure on the show to solicit other offers. So even an unfulfilled bid can arrive at capital and exposure for a smart business proposition on *Shark Tank*.

As the show progresses, we learn about the biographies and experiences of the sharks, and they too emerge as solid businesspeople with maverick approaches to their various fields. Mark Cuban discussed his propensity for being fired by multiple firms before starting his own company. His maverick personality was a great fit for the entrepreneurial model that the show espouses and fits the spirit of a nation that seems impatient with Washington-based answers and longs for the capitalist zeal of an earlier United States.

The show has had vocal supporters and imitators. Writer Sri Ravipati reported that Boston high-tech content-management firm Salsify was hosting a STEM day for middle school children to make them interested in new entrepreneurship.

See also: The Voice

Further Reading

Susan Adams, "Ten of the Best Businesses to Come out of *Shark Tank*," *Forbes*, March 18, 2016; Mark Cohen, "A Small Company's Reality Is Altered by ABC's 'Shark Tank,'" *New York Times*, June 12, 2013; Sri Ravipati, "Boston Tech Company to Host 'Shark Tank' STEM Competition," *The Journal*, December 7, 2016.

EPIC KNITTING (NORWAY) AND OTHER SLOW TELEVISION FARE

Epic Knitting was an eight-hour marathon program watching a sweater being made, from the shearing of sheep to the actual completion and modeling of the finished product. This national Norwegian broadcasting program was a massive hit, obtaining nearly a quarter of the Norwegian population watching the program through the night. In a sense, such programs are used to create a national consensus and to bond people in a natural synergy of their interests and the interests of the nation. It isn't created so much to produce a sense of nationalism as to create a sense of community and to create a closeness and sense of belonging. The show began on the farm, where the wool used for the sweater was actually sheared in real time from a sheep. The wool was transported to a factory and conditioned into a product with natural dyes and colors added so that it was ready for real-life knitting. Then the wool was given to master knitter Elga Fongswoggle, and the wool practitioners began the painstaking job of initiating the creation of a finely tailored sweater. All the while, the master knitter described the process blow-by-blow to the television audience as the work proceeded.

The program was part of a movement that has been quite successful in Norway and other places. The movement is known as *slow television,* or *reflective viewing,* in which a subject that is not known for being fast moving or endlessly compelling is chosen as the catalyst for reality programs. The format of slow television has been around for a time. It was popularized by artist Andy Warhol in the 1960s when he began making long feature films of still or relatively still objects. In 1963, he composed the film *Sleep,* which chronicled six hours of a man sleeping. His controversial *Blow Job* simply showed a man's face in a variety of expressions over an hour, and the audience was left to conjecture whether there was a sexual encounter taking place or not. Warhol gave us very few clues, and only the title suggests salacious or sexual content. Nothing the subject did suggested anything sexual was happening. The entire film portrayed only the subject's face and neck area, and, from what we can see, the subject could be entirely alone. Warhol's lengthy *Empire* was an eight-hour-long standing shot of the Empire State Building with planes and birds passing in the background and little else to suggest that the film was anything but a still shot of the building for eight hours.

Slow television evolved out of these early experiments to convey lengthy, and what some might term boring, experiences as a communal bonding experience. In

Norwegian television, the experience of doing something as a nation has become a national pastime. Famously, there was another show that prompted a strong national following. In this experiment, the people of Norway went on an ocean cruise for eight hours, and strangely, about half the population of the country tuned in to watch. There was a camera positioned at the prow of a boat, and the audience observed the cruise from departure to arrival at another port in real time. The notion was that everyone would have the experience of going on a cruise together in real time.

The concept of slow TV is that the world rushes by quickly and that so much television broadcasting tends to increase our pace, rush us, and demand we engage in a speedier life cycle. Slow TV is a recipe for moving the opposite direction, a reaction to hyperbolic lives, and for reducing the speed and anxiety of daily existence. By forcing the population to relax and enjoy communal hours together, the programmers hope to engender better life coping skills and to encourage better living in the moment.

Interestingly, the slow TV movement has been around for over 50 years and has spread from Warhol's initial slow videos to station broadcasts, to video experiments in the 1980s, to network broadcasts in the last five years. The initial experiment in Norwegian television was an extended broadcast of a complete train journey across Norway that followed the Bergen line for a seven-hour trip. This was followed by the journey of a boat trip, the *MS Nordnorge,* which traveled from Bergen to Kirkenes for a 134-hour (5 and a half days') experience. Both broadcasts were given extensive press coverage and received viewership in excess of the best television programming the station had provided. It proved that audiences had an appetite for slow television, not just high-speed action viewing.

One of the first incarnations of the slow television movement was station WPIX's *Yule Log* broadcast. The station filmed the burning of a Yule log, looped it endlessly, and played recorded Christmas music behind the broadcast. The piece could run hours at a time for late-night viewers.

See also: Most Haunted

Further Reading
Gerard Gilbert, "Slow Television: The Latest Nordic Trend," *The Independent (UK)*, February 11, 2014.

FOOL AROUND WITH . . . (BRITAIN)

Fool around with . . . was an engaging British show about truth and reality and involved a person who was single (maybe . . .) trying to convince a guest that they were, indeed, single. The setup was that there were four males or females in the competition seeking to convince the contestant that they were indeed a single person. The women and men masquerading as single would try virtually anything to get the contestant to select them as the single culprit. If a non-single person was able to make the contestant believe that they, in fact, were single, the non-single person and their loved one (boyfriend and or girlfriend) got to split $10,000. If the officially single woman or man could convince the player that they were the single person, they split the $10,000 with the contestant. So everyone had an incentive to be convincing, whether lying or telling the truth. The show took a cue from the 1993 film *Indecent Proposal*, since the accent was on lying for money. In the film, Demi Moore thinks she can make herself sleep with an attractive older man for a million dollars, since her family needs the cash. The journey is harder than she thinks it will be. In the television program, the candidates assumed that they could flirt and lie about their attachment to a significant other in order to make some fast cash. The program tread tricky moral ground, in that it involved lying about intimate relationships. This transgressive quality may have been a factor in the program's green-lighting and popularity.

Usually the show pit a celebrity or semi-celebrity (a club owner or DJ) against a roomful of average women or men. They were placed in an isolated room/apartment/living space for a week, and, within that time, they had to convince the contestant that they were the single one. The contestant could flirt with all four. The contestant could ask the competitors to bed, and the contestant could obtain kisses, sexual favors, and lap dances from the assembled women or men. Meanwhile, the women/men could be in contact with their boyfriends/girlfriends. The audience knew from the get-go who was lying and who was telling the truth. Part of the fun came from watching the boyfriends coaxing their girlfriends to try and be sexy. Some boyfriends bristled watching their mates ape sexually explicit behavior, but some were staunchly cool about the experiment in trust and lying.

The name changed with every contestant. If there was a girl named Fran, the show became "Fool around with Fran." The show has become popular in Sweden as well. The game is a very intense psychological experiment, and there is a continual sense that the players are engaged in some form of social research to investigate lying and truth telling and how to differentiate between the two. Laurie Ouellette and James Hay in *Better Living through Reality TV* comment, "Personal advice and instruction are part of the mix, but they are infused with, and tempered by, elements of voyeurism, suspense, humor, and emotional intensity" (2008, 4). It was somewhat wrenching to see the guest, Ian, ask one of the women to the bedroom on "Fooling around with Ian," and to know that he has a girlfriend and is still willing to carry the ruse that far. The show furthered its power to disturb by allowing the audience the opportunity to voyeuristically watch the couple under low-lighting conditions interact in the bedroom. A further upsetting aspect was the manner in which the women's boyfriends were displayed before us. They watched from a distance in a secluded screening room. This provided us, the audience, with a doubly voyeuristic experience. First, our player Ian had taken a girl into the bedroom to test her. Second, we observed the boyfriend observing and reacting to his girlfriend's possible infidelity. The sense of anguish and torture could be quite intense and compelling for viewers and contestants alike.

See also: Ainori; Dismissed; Next

Further Reading
Laurie Ouellette and James Hay, *Better Living through Reality TV,* 2008.

MOST HAUNTED (UK)

Most Haunted is a British-produced paranormal investigation series that aired in Britain from 2002 to 2010. The show was revived as an online entity on 2013 and picked up by the Reality Channel for broadcast in 2014. The series is currently in production in 2016. The program has benefitted from female hosts, a less-glitzy format than other paranormal series, and moody ethereal scores that provide a sense of ennui and atmosphere. Unlike its American counterpart *Ghost Hunters*, the hosts of *Most Haunted* do not take the stand that they are combatants and investigators struggling to undercut the view that ghosts do exist. The hosts of *Most Haunted* seem to be devout believers in the supernatural, and they consider part of their work to be involved in conjuring and inspiring the appearance of said beasties.

There have been multiple special episodes of the crew visiting suspected haunted places, and in its (thus far) 17 seasons and almost 200 episodes, the show has sponsored many sites of the dead and spectral. A striking episode was "In the Land of Hell" in and around Turin, Italy. Turin was long reputed as the "hell-mouth," or the most haunted city on earth, and home to the famous Shroud of Turin, a burial cloth supposedly used to cover the face of the deceased Jesus prior to his resurrection. The shroud is considered one of the holy places of Christendom. But, according to the show's logic, where there are holy artifacts, there are forces desiring to destroy the power of Christianity. The *Most Haunted* crew did a five-night stand in the city of Turin, broadcasting underground specials in the city's eerie catacombs. The crew was startled by electrical equipment not cooperating, loud sounds erupting out of nowhere, and spectral appearances by unexplained phenomenon that sent the crew running. There were several injuries, and the crew was visibly shaken.

Paranormal shows are always subject to accusations of staging and setups, but *Most Haunted* takes the heightened realism of their investigations quite seriously, and less time is spent on equipment than groping around in the dark seeking to speak with the undead. The production style of the series has evolved over time. The first few seasons featured elaborate, steady cam shots and lots of spooky-colored blue and green lighting with dry ice and many scary environments. Moving from Sky Living Channel to the Reality Channel in the UK and the Travel Channel in the United States, the show became grungier and more cinema vérité over the seasons. The show usually claims to present 24-hour visits to a location to investigate psychic phenomenon, and the producers Yvette Fielding and Karl Beattie both swear that nothing on the show is staged. The program has featured mediums, offered performances of spiritual possessions, shown fleeting images of something creepy, and provided a real sense of eeriness and unease in the proceedings.

A high point of the production was the original scoring by composer Alan Clark, who used a wide range of atmospheric effects and mood music that set an original tone for the program. In the first episode, the team investigated an appearance by something at Athelhampton Hall in Dorchester, England. The family that owned the facility was engaged in the episode. Fielding led the team through the house, and a local medium named Derek Acorah experienced a bout of spiritual possession, and the team heard strange noises that sounded like a woman's voice. They heard the rocking of a cradle from another room. During the 24-hour visit, the team performed a night investigation with growing uneasiness about the locale. Their hosts, and the house's owners, explained the home's history. The crew confessed to feeling uncomfortable in certain rooms, and their cameraman refused to go in specific areas and believed he saw a dead man walking in the hallways. The lights were turned off, and the crew began broadcasting in infrared format; the low lighting gave off a creepy green glow. The late-night hours contributed an added dimension of creepy dynamics.

All paranormal programming depends on creating sensations of unease, but *Most Haunted* does it quite effectively. As the crew toured the house, they learned about former owners back to the 17th century. Acorah sensed various animosities and spirits that lived in conflict. Acorah used a spirit guide named Sam, and, throughout the episode, Acorah turned away from the camera and thanked Sam for the information.

There are plenty of debunkers who doubt anything on the series can be believed. Filipa Jodelka wrote an article for *The Guardian* calling the program "still the market leader in ectoplasmic claptrap" (2014). Many feel that this and other paranormal shows are all staging, special effects, and a scam to make us think the paranormal really does exist. Jodelka writes, "*Most Haunted* has been the subject of a *Daily Mirror* sting, AKA 'ghosts aren't real-gate', as well as the less shocking claim that Yvette and the rest of her Spooky Gang create the knocks and creaks all the scary shit relies on" (2014). Yet even a cynical read by Jodelka cannot deny the show's appeal. While the ghosts may be hokey; the spiritual possessions, doubtful; the undead sounds, mechanically produced; and the ambience of normal houses enhanced by mood lighting; the show provides what most paranormal entertainment creates—a sense of unease and a transportation of the audience into another realm of imagination. Even hardened cynic Jodelka remarks that she can't resist the show's mix of creeps and obvious tricks. She writes, "At the best of times, *Most Haunted* is 98% standing around in the dark, the remaining per cents given over to theatrics from some necromancing scam artist and their dramatic interpretation of Peg, the Cantankerous Murdered Matchseller. I loved it" (2014). While the truth is unknown, the show does seek to find scary aspects in common places and asks the crew and participants to look deeper and more historically into the genesis of these houses and the events that happened there. Faulkner said, "The past is," and, in a deeper way, the *Most Haunted* programs ask us to look at what happened in a location centuries ago and view how that created the ambience of the place today.

In fact, doubters may have made the show *more* fashionable. Matt Roper, writing for *The Mirror* in London, penned an exposé in 2005 saying the show was largely faked. Audiences didn't seem to care. They also discounted Roper's story and motives appearing two days before Halloween. Was it a story cashing in on the horror season? The story claimed that a parapsychologist on the show, Dr. Ciarán O'Keeffe, came forward to blow the whistle on the show, saying the ghosts were all theatrics and special effects. He accused Acorah of learning about places and events before the show and using his coaching to enact spiritual possessions.

While claiming that Fielding and her husband Beattie had been caught adding and creating sounds off stage for scenes in the filming, Roper also reported on the show having a four-day special event broadcast tracing the reign of Jack the Ripper in London and visiting all the places that the Ripper had been known to frequent. Was Roper ripping the show for presenting false information, or was he using the accusation of a scam to somehow reverse-promote the program's upcoming Ripper series? Either way, audiences were guaranteed to watch more carefully after the accusing story that dared to criticize the popular series. Roper claimed that the show did not show credible skeptical voices, that the program lied and misled the audience. He writes, "One of our clips, later edited out, shows Karl push an unwitting sound man in the dark and pretend it was a poltergeist attack" (2005). Whether there are real ghosts or just garish production tricks, *Most Haunted* is an engaging thrill ride into the paranormal. Whether one believes or not, it can give chills and nightmares.

See also: Ghost Hunters

Further Reading

Filipa Jodelka, "*Most Haunted* Still Market Leader in Ectoplasmic Claptrap," *The Guardian*, August 18, 2014; Matt Roper, "Spooky Truth: TV's *Most Haunted* Con Exposed," *The Mirror*, October 28, 2005.

THE NIGHT BUS (UK)

Channel 4's 2015 documentary series *The Night Bus* explored the strange and unusual world of passengers and passersby on a night bus in London. This documentary-style series mounted cameras in a bus to capture the behavior as people interacted and found out about each other on the night bus. Channel 4 explains, "An ordinary night bus has been kitted out with cameras for this series, witnessing the funny, surprising, and sometimes moving interaction between passengers after dark" (2014). The programmers were happy to promote the night travel experience by focusing on the bizarre and esoteric. A picture showcasing the third episode featured two brawny trans dressers in full female outfits and hair extensions with Egyptian-themed makeup.

The Night Bus was an eight-part documentary reality series chronicling happenings on board the night bus routes through London. The series premiered in

May of 2015 and ran amid much hype and fanfare during the spring of 2015 as a weekly program. *The Guardian* commented that the N29, the bus under scrutiny, was the last place someone would look for love—a grimy engine of dirt and tired travelers winding up at the uneventful station of Wood Green. Throughout the journey, audiences were treated to the commonplace and the typical. For example, we saw boys, probably having had one too many ales, throw cheeky lines at girls, who look bored and appeared ready for a TV dinner and an evening in front of the telly. *The Guardian* snagged high points, such as bus driver Tony, who's driven for 30 years, yelling out, "Next stop: Holloway prison for naughty ladies" (Jodelka 2015).

The night bus is a standard part of travel for London's working poor, who need a way to and from work in the wee hours. The bus is used for West End revelers who can't find an underground station and can navigate better above ground. The first bus to be profiled was the infamous N29 route, which travels from the north London suburb of Enfield to Camden, the fashionable shopping district with lots of outdoor booths, boot sales, and corner merchants, to Trafalgar Square, where many tourists congregate for evening outings and fun.

The show was composed of a series of clips that were carefully assembled by an editor with an accompanying voice-over that built a narrative. Channel 4 did a canny job of turning random, sporadic action and goofing on a night bus journey into a partying atmosphere that extols romance, excitement, and licentious behavior. One fears the reality of the experience is a lot tamer than what we saw here, but the producers went for narratives that told an egalitarian story of people who ride the bus for fun and pleasure. The perspective was that people rode the bus on a Friday or Saturday night in the hopes of getting lucky and meeting someone. We followed a few party boys, one turning 19 who wants to celebrate. He asked a girl to join them, and, though flattered, she passed on their drunken offer. Two girls discussed who they would date. "Ryan Gosling, definitely," said one young lady. The narration tells us that London is a singles capital in the UK and that lots of people may not get lucky but they look for love on the night bus.

See also: Dating in the Dark; Ready for Marriage

Further Reading
"Channel Four Boards the 'Night Bus' for Brand New Rig Documentary Series." *Channel 4*, December 18, 2014; Filipa Jodelka. "The Night Bus: Nocturnal Naughtiness on the N29." *The Guardian*, May 11, 2015.

READY FOR MARRIAGE (ZAMBIA)

Ready for Marriage was a complicated program for a complicated reality audience. Zambia is a poor country with a problem of girls marrying at very young ages to avoid poverty. *Ready for Marriage* was a program that complicated that complicated life even further. Many women in Zambia who were subjected to poverty turned to sex work or the sex trades to be able to provide for themselves. Muvi TV, a Zambian channel, wanted to help these women. It created a reality show competition that featured 18 women contestants from the sex trades. The goal of the station, according to spokesperson Corrine Paolini, was to "make a difference in these women's lives. These are people after all" (BBC 2011).

While the program was filled with hot-button issues, there were many questions that could spur an audience to watch. Could women in the sex trade adapt to marriage? Would they want to be wives? Would Zambia's culture accept them? A local preacher Jeff Musonda seemed to voice qualified support for the program during the time it was in planning. He argued that if the show appealed to prurient motives it would achieve little, but, if the show helped women to reform, it could benefit society.

Many of the women found for the show were wandering the streets of Zambian cities. Many claimed to enter lives of prostitution to feed starving infants and because the fathers of these children did not marry them. They were left with no family support, no resources, and no job, alone with children and destitute.

The producers chose to concentrate on the challenges facing the women. The program wasn't an easy road to marriage and happiness. Consolation prizes for women who did not succeed were only around $1,000 per player. This was still more money than these women had before, and in Zambia may be an investment toward a business out of the sex trade, but it was a poor start in any culture. The producers also provided the women with jobs as a more important consolation prize. Jobs could lead the women out of poverty and the slavery of being a sex worker. Mutuna Chanda, from the BBC, argues, "So they're more or less being given a second chance at life" (BBC 2011). Sadly, when a woman in Lusaka, the capital of Zambia, was questioned about the show, her response was "once a prostitute, always a prostitute" (BBC 2011). The view of some people is that it is difficult for women in that line of work to change their employment. Beyond the real struggles of the women, there are deep societal prejudices against prostitutes.

The program was popular, but it did not cover the racy issues of prostitution, only showing the women competing in dull chores like cleaning a house or making a meal. These may seem like slow and meaningless challenges to us, but to the people of Zambia they were real-life struggles. The women who mastered these commonplace and routine household skills stood the best chance of finding a husband and becoming married.

The show used a sad theme song to tell the women's stories. The singer sings, "The world is cruel, so hard to survive. What do you do when there's no one to turn to and understand what you've been through?" The program explained the struggle of the women, introduced them as prostitutes, and the women explained how they came to their current state. In this sense, the confession of hardship was reminiscent of the 1950s American reality program *Queen for A Day*, where a woman who had suffered intense hardship told her story to evoke audience sympathy and win a washing machine or some other material device.

The trailer for the first season encouraged prostitutes to be contestants. The ads went further and advised these luckless women. According to Mutuna Chanda, the ads read, "Are you interested in changing your life around, are you interested in settling down to lead a decent and respectable and responsible life? Here is a super brilliant and bright opportunity" (2011). The winner of the competition won $9,000, which was a tidy sum in the poor African nation, and the station paid all the expenses of the winning girl's marriage. That is, if after their training, their prize winnings, and their exposure, they could find a good husband ready to marry them. It was sad to see that in this nation, women had few chances to take care of themselves and their families except through the institution of marriage. Still, the program made it clear that even after finding a spouse, there was no guarantee of life success.

See also: The Bachelorette

Further Reading

Mutuna Chanda, "Zambian Prostitutes on Reality TV," *The World*, PRI, July 14, 2011.

SEX BOX (BRITAIN)

Sex Box was a short-lived and controversial show from England. Despite the sensational title, the program was a far more informative and serious social experiment and talk reality show from Britain than it was sensational, although it could easily lay claim to the latter. Contestants on *Sex Box* agree to enter the stage in front of a live studio audience and a panel of social sex therapists and have sex on stage. The show is desensationalized a bit by revealing that the contestants were to enter a dark room "box" on the stage and perform their act of sexual congress in the privacy of this darkened room. Thus, the contestants did not have sex in front of anyone but instead performed in the safety, security, and secrecy of the box while the audience is largely oblivious to what is transpiring in the box. After the apparent sex act (viewers did not have any idea of what did transpire in the box except for the couple's report to the therapists), the couple would emerge and discuss their sexual experience. Rather than make the entire experience extremely freakish and unnatural, the therapists asked pointed questions to try to find out why they were willing to appear and what the purpose of having sex in public achieved for them.

One immediately discovered that many people openly admitted they could not have sex with their regular partner under such conditions. They sheepishly admitted it made them feel weird and voyeuristically exposed. They talked about what turned them on and what they got from their relationship. After a few minutes, the audience seemed to forget that they had supposedly just had sex. More often, it was the commentators who kept bringing up that the sex had given the players a fresh glow and a charming flush of energy. It seemed the show's hosts and commentators were willing to make the subject matter more salacious and scandalous than the guests. The therapists claimed that they called the couple's attention to their appearance to be able to "describe and reflect on the experience of sex" and what it meant to that particular couple.

The show was considered a bold experiment in reality television—a return to the documentary roots of such programming and a serious Kinsey-esque approach to studying human sexuality in a frank manner. The program only ran for one week in October of 2013. It hasn't returned. It ran a total of seven episodes. One of the interesting things about the show was the remarkable number of people it showcased. The first couple was the conventional WASP, young, attractive couple. However, they were quickly followed by a middle-aged gay couple. Another couple followed, and both suffered from physical disabilities. One quickly began to see that this show did not rely on shock tactics but took the question of sex very seriously. This may have accounted for its short run. Some might have expected something far more vile. Instead, the program approached sex from a therapeutic context. Leigh H. Edwards writes, "Reality TV reflects an anxiety about truth claims that have become increasingly suspect in our digital era of easily manipulatable images" (2013, 179). While the claim to have had semi-public intercourse might have seemed questionable, the emotions of the couple appeared genuine, and perhaps too real for audiences hoping for innuendo and hype.

The show has been proposed as an American program and supposedly has been in development. Critics largely panned the show, and ratings were not high. Still, the show presented sex seriously, and the programmers at Channel 4 in London proposed to treat sex in an adult manner, and, for the most part, the show achieved that goal.

The press dismissed it with gusto. *The Guardian* thought it provoked sleep and said the best part was the therapists' views. Sam Wollaston wrote, "There's something about the three Gs from Dan Savage—nothing to do with phones, it means Good, Giving, and Game, which is what we have to be, in bed" (2013).

Underlying the spicy nature of the program, the theory behind the show—that couples will be more forthcoming about their sex life after a bout of sex—seemed to make sense. The framers believed that people (1) refreshed from a sexual experience, and (2) with the idea of sex still in their minds as they discussed it would be clearer and more conversant on the topic immediately following the experience.

The plan for the American version, debuting in the future, was that the couples would follow the same regime and that the panel of experts would include a relationship therapist, a sex therapist, a minister, and a comedian. It is assumed this combination would bring out more varied aspects of the experience, and the comedian could lighten the mood.

See also: Survivor

Further Reading

Sam Wollaston, "Sex Box: TV Review," *The Guardian*, October 7, 2013.

SUSUNU! DENPA SHŌNEN (JAPAN)

Susunu! Denpa Shōnen is a reality show that featured comedians struggling for fame that aired on Japanese television from 1998 to 2002. The title means "Forward! Signal Youth," or it also could be translated as a Japanese pun: "Not Forward! Signal Youth." The show was popular because it placed the performers/players in raw and tough situations and extreme challenges. It raised controversy because there were accusations that some of the segments were staged and fixed. An even grosser accusation was that the producers would precipitously change the rules when performers were doing too well to retard their progress in the show.

The show was cancelled, and that type of programming was discouraged when the Japanese government cracked down on so-called torture-themed programming, where contestants were made to endure harsh conditions for money. The show was revived on the Web in 2009, causing more comedians, anxious for fame, to endure extreme challenges. Again, many of these shows depended upon schadenfreude, or deriving pleasure from someone else's misfortune or anguish. Biressi and Nunn comment that "contestants on shows . . . often speak of their voluntary self-imprisonment in a media created community as a challenge but also a way of confronting or finding themselves" (2005, 99). The comedians on *Susunu! Denpa Shōnen* presumed that the suffering they endured on the show would draw media attention and eventually enhance their career.

The show utilized gruesome punishments more befitting prisoners than offering a road to cultural fame on television. One challenge, known as Denpa Shōnen teki Kenshō Seikatsu, required a comedian to live for a year in his apartment naked, existing entirely on commercial prize foods. That is, the contestants had to write to contests to hopefully win food to make it possible for their continued existence. Nasubi, an aspiring comedian, auditioned for this chance and applied to do the task. The assignment required a year of imprisonment in a secret location. He was filmed 24 hours a day naked in this environment and had only a radio, a rack of magazines, and a stack of postcards for his amusement. The title of the challenge, Denpa Shōnen teki Kenshō Seikatsu, means "a life out of prizes." Nasubi had to write to commercial sweepstakes and magazine games to win prizes for everything he needed. Presumably, he found the sweepstakes' information in the magazines. He had to win contests to obtain food, toilet paper, and other essential items. It was ten months until he won toilet paper. He wrote a diary that was published during the year in captivity, and he became a popular celebrity and eventually somewhat wealthy from the proceeds from the book. The Denpa Shōnen teki Mujinto Dasshutsu challenge trapped two comedians on an island with no food and no idea where they were or how far from Japan they were. They had to fashion a raft on the island and make it back to Tokyo. This took them four months. Then they were given a paddleboat and had to navigate from Indonesia to India. Another extreme challenge was requiring a radio DJ from Hong Kong to hitchhike from South Africa to Norway. A sports-related challenge was Denpa Shōnen teki Pennant Race, in which sports fans had televisions that only showed their team's games. They were only portrayed by a small part of their face on the television screen. If their team won, they would be further revealed on the screen. A small portion of their face would be featured each time the team won a victory. They would receive food, and, the more victories their team won, the better their food would become. However, if their team lost, they would receive no food, and the lights in their room would be turned out. They would be hungry and in the dark until the next day's game. It was easy to see how the show could be construed as cruel and unusual punishment for the gaming audience and the contestants. The Web site *Dangerous Minds* commented, "Even for a culture well-known for its sadistic game shows, Japan's *Susunu! Denpa Shōnen* still stands out" (Metzger 2014).

See also: Survivor

Further Reading

Anita Biressi and Heather Nunn, *Reality TV, Realism and Revelation,* 2005; Richard Metzger, "Psychological Torture Makes for Good TV: Japan's Demented Real Life *Truman Show,*" *Dangerous Minds,* April 22, 2014.

TAKESHI'S CASTLE (JAPAN)

Takeshi's Castle was a popular Japanese game show that ran originally from 1986 to 1990 and has been copied, revived, and revised for various games in various countries as a flexible and popular franchise of competition shows.

The fictional backstory of the program was that some inept lords were defending a castle against an invasion by ninjas, rebels, or ronin (masterless samurai). The defenders were charged with keeping the invaders out, and their defenses were created to repel the invaders. Of course, this thin narrative held the premise of the game, in which a series of enthusiastic players valiantly sought to bridge the castle's defenses and thus win prizes and glory. The defenses around the castle created a giant obstacle course that formed the basis of the challenges for the game itself. The players, acting as an invading army, responded to the call to attack the castle, and the team threw themselves into the battle. As with all Japanese game shows, there was a high degree of embarrassment, debasement, and chagrin. Jennifer Pozner reflects on the fact that much of reality television is predicated on embarrassment. She writes, "Sometimes it makes us laugh, sometimes it shocks us, but we're unable to turn away from the cathartic display of other people's humiliation" (2010, 16). The players are subjected to painful falls, uncomfortable plunges into cold pools, and disorienting poundings by vicious machines intended to deter them from taking the castle.

The program was a competitive elimination program in which the attacking challengers had to surmount the challenges to win the prize. The metaphor of a castle siege, through a highly competitive obstacle course, was grinding. The original program ran over 100 episodes from 1986 to 1990 on the Tokyo Broadcasting System. The program starred Japanese actor Takeshi Kitano as lord and owner of the castle, and he set up the difficult challenges for the volunteer army to get at him. Sometimes over 100 contestants would start the endurance race and face the various challenges to reach the lord. The ending turned goofy, comic, and childish, as the final team of regulars assaulted the castle complex with water pistols. Those who could breach Takeshi's defenses could win. Later, the show progressed to paper rings and laser pistols. If the rings could be punctured or lasers could hit the paper targets or capture Takeshi's little go-cart with a laser blast, the castle would be taken and the show would end. Rarely did the army beat Takeshi, and only nine people won in the show's history. Winners would win around 1 million yen, or closer to $10,000 in American money.

One of the big features of the show and its later American version was the construction of an extreme obstacle course. The original Tokyo Broadcasting System's engineered environment, Midoriyama (Green Mountain), included massive obstacles, manmade moats, rubber pounding devices, and plastic obstacles. All were constructed to unbalance and topple players, but to do so playfully and hopefully harmlessly.

Some of the challenges on the program became popular and were repeated weekly. A highlight of the program was the constant plunging of contestants into mud, water, or goopy slime. Like the contestants on Nickelodeon, it was almost required for unlucky players to become mired in muck somewhere along their quest. Again, the emphasis was on comical chagrining of contestants. Pleasure came from watching the battlers get soaked in their struggles. This enjoyment derived from our sense of the term *play,* activity that is absorbing but far different from the everyday activities of most people. Misha Kavka writes in *Reality TV* that "Huizinga's core premise is that, 'we find play present everywhere (and it) is a well-defined quality of action which is different from 'ordinary life'" (2012, 100).

The show had a range of regular characters. At the top was Count Takeshi. He was in charge of the castle, made commentary about the contestants, and eventually was the one being stormed at the game's end. The actor playing Takeshi became embroiled in some one-on-one confrontations with reporters from scandal magazines and was banned from the show for a time. Other players took over, wearing a big, fake Takeshi mask and a fake green robe. These players were called the "Takeshi Dolls," because they appeared as big rag dolls filling in for the count. Saburo Ishikura was Takeshi's counselor who filled him in on the contestants and provided comedy skits. Another important set of players were the Emerald Guards, who protected the castle and sought to stop the contestants from taking the castle in the final round of the game. General Lee guided the players in their assault and through the various rounds of the competition.

The show became a worldwide phenomenon with editions created in the United States, Canada, Britain, the Middle East, Australia, Brazil, the Philippines, France, Greece, and Malaysia. The Indian version became so popular it played for two hours each Sunday. Many of the international versions used the original Japanese footage and dubbed them, either out of order or in the original sequence with comedy dialogue or lampoons of the original show. The Finnish version was subtitled *the Crazy Japanese*. The Philippine version added new actors for Takeshi and his aides and had dream sequences in which Takeshi woke to a nightmare of the contestants winning the battle. The British version mostly lampooned the original show with new voice-overs. The program proved so popular over the years that the British version was revived as *Takeshi Rebooted* in 2013.

The U.S. version aired as *MXC* (*Most Extreme Challenge*) and played over 80 episodes from 2003 to 2007. The show was a spoof of the Japanese show, with voice-over commentary and dubbing used to provide humor. Americanized versions were created by Fox and CBS, but both failed after single episodes.

See also: American Idol; Survivor; The X Factor

Further Reading

"About Takeshi's Castle," keshiheads.co.uk; David S. Escoffery, *How Real Is Reality TV?*; Misha Kavka, *Reality TV*, 2012.

Conclusion: Reality's Future

Many pressures drive the business of television, and many of those pressures are intensifying and are likely to drive existing stations to economize. First, the stations are driven by profit. Not just profit for the five large corporations that own most television broadcasting (News Corp/Fox, NBC/Universal, Viacom/Showtime/Paramount/CBS, Disney/Marvel/ABC, Time/Warner/DC/Turner/CW), but there is the factor of the stockholders who want to see profit and shows that bring in advertising dollars. This will drive a need for more reality programming, and it will likely mean that even popular but expensive reality shows like *Survivor, The Voice,* and *The Bachelor* and others that (1) pay for expensive hosts and talent, (2) film at exotic locations, and (3) use expensive sets and studios will have to cut back. Thus, it is likely that the type of reality shows will change to what we might term "chamber reality shows," using more complicated and obscure concepts but filmed with a lower budget in mind. Consider that much of reality programming in foreign markets originated because foreign producers could not produce shows with the level of production sheen that most American studios could muster. Filming in the United States is performed with a thriving economy and a massive entertainment industry, infrastructure, and subscriber base to underwrite costs. Such opulent conditions rarely exist in foreign markets.

Instead of winsome concepts like *The Bachelor,* which put the dreams of matrimony at the forefront, we are likely to see more comical MTV dating shows that depend on surprise, outdoor filming, common spaces, and amateur/young talent. The day of high-budget reality filming is likely coming to an end, simply because costs are high and profit uncertain. There will be more amateur or lesser-known hosts, more common guests/players, and more around-town filming, not requiring complex sets or specific locales, simple filming setups, and one-set productions.

Another condition that will drive viewers to reality programming will be the disintegration of networks and regularly scheduled viewing times into more niche-programming bundles. Audiences wanting more freedom to determine their own entertainment in their own manner are likely to reject the conditions imposed by networks that they must watch certain shows at certain times. The rise of video wholesalers such as Hulu, Netflix, iTunes, Amazon Prime, and others will change who watches what and when. Reality programming, with its fast turnaround and speedy seasons (many reality programs have two seasons a year) will fit perfectly.

Reality shows can be produce more quickly and cheaply than scripted TV. Currently, these non-stations have bought and paid for fiction programming, but, though this prestige programming may attract initial customers, these new start-up providers working directly from subscription viewers will have to find ways to satiate a public hungry for quick and enjoyable entertainment. It won't always be prestige shows, and reality programming will find a quick market on these non-stations. Many are already showing repeats of popular reality series, and the demand for more reality programming more quickly could drive these mini-majors to invest in creating their own reality programs or outbidding the networks for existing reality programming.

Intellectually, the world population isn't always interested in fiction broadcasting, particularly the glitzy sort of epics that American studios produce. Many nations and regions have larger problems than *The Bachelor* or *Real World*.

Many nations (including those in the Middle East, Africa, South America, parts of Asia, and Europe) have a need for more basic programming that includes educational shows, cultural and religious series, and socially focused programming that addresses local and regional problems of violence, human trafficking, drug cartels, corrupt governments, wars and terrorist organizations, potable water/food supplies, prostitution, spiritual and political leadership, and other woes the people living in the West don't have to confront on a daily basis. This emerging generation and population will have needs that compare favorably with what reality programming can provide for their societies and people. Reality programming will address needs like Zambia's *Ready for Marriage* program, which prepares young Zambian prostitutes for marriage, or Norway's *Epic Knitting,* which teaches common people about the market chain of the making of simple apparel products. Further, the process of globalization, often accused of driving down prices worldwide, should stimulate growth in the reality television market. Not all of it will be low budget or drive the price of production down. In fact, some reality programming could increase production, create new jobs, and enhance the chances for new programming, creating a greater demand and perhaps higher prices for reality programming professionals.

Finally, the confluence of the Internet and television will evolve in postmodern times, repositioning how people see and conceive reality. Michael Benedikt in *Cyberspace: First Steps* writes that the new reality will be very different from what we see as reality today. He explains, "A distributed cyberspace fashioned from real-world object with virtual attributes and behaviors will be the preferable alternative for some activities" (1994, 414). What Benedikt and other see in the new virtual world is a mixture of videogame logics and appliances applied to the real world. We may not have music-playing devices like cassette players or CD players, simply files of songs accessed through Spotify or another service to provide a route to hearing music everywhere. Similarly, the world of reality programming may be a streamed service without much relation to what we term as "television" today. There may be screens or kiosks in every city where people can access their favorite programs publically. Phones will allow people to call up their favorite programs on the run. People will have a whole new way to find out how their teams are doing on *The Amazing Race*, who's been booted from *Survivor*, who is Kim Kardashian married to this week, and who was picked on *The Bachelorette*.

Some complain that even reality shows are remote and still don't reach the common people. To combat this, another likely outcome will be that games and reality competition will become even more democratized and localized, so that *Survivor* might become a state-by-state game. *The Voice* or *American Idol* might be a county competition (there is that aspect now since competitions and screenings are held across the nation). So people will have local and national figures to cheer, just as music has moved toward more democratic characteristics. Many Americans today listen to local area bands and songwriters in their region. Communities in Nashville, Atlanta, New York, and Seattle have their own sets of popular bands. It's nice if they make a national noise, but it is no longer an essential aspect of band or performer success. Reality shows will progressively democratize away from large corporations toward smaller, local entities. The forces of economics will help. If the shows cost less, if there is less profit and less overhead, such shows can survive on a more meager budget with only local support. The money will spread from entertainment capitals and filter into local municipalities, at least that is the hope.

As the world transforms into the simulation world that Baudrillard envisioned, postmodern dreams and nightmares will emerge. Until people learn to manage the physical world better, people will have to take enjoyment from theme parks and online fantasy worlds, games, and reality programs that substitute for our ability to travel and explore. Mark Andrejevic in his book *Infoglut* determined that the world will change in unexpected ways soon. Many changes are inspired by the market society. He writes, "If the internet has helped to create the conditions for the revamped populism of the postmodern right, it has contributed a substitute for the void created by generalized debunkery in the form of the non-expert expertise of the marketplace" (2013, 64). Andrejevic argues that the amount of information confronting us is deafening and that we require apparatus to help us make sense of the quantity of information. For Andrejevic, he fears we trust too much in the marketplace, the place where reality shows exist. We can argue that reality television presents us with such apparatus. It allows us to choose and focus on a specific reality. Too busy to date? Watch *The Bachelor*. Confused by home prices and repair? Watch HGTV. Don't understand fundamentalist Southerners? Watch *19 Kids and Counting* or *Duck Dynasty*.

More and more, reality television tends to serve as Baudrillard's notion of simulation. As many scientists have expressed concern that we are approaching the singularity—the moment when AI becomes a rival or superior to human intellect—society might almost be concerned that the cartoonish and amateurish presentation of the commonplace expressed in early reality shows like *Real People* or *The Dating Game* is quickly achieving the level of an effective simulation. If we trust the complicated and myriad motivations behind reality television to substitute for a confusing real world, we might be deceiving ourselves and constructing a very flawed doppelganger universe. T. V. Reed discusses our acceptance and reliance on cyberspace ICTs (Internet communication technologies). Reed cautions, "Specifically in time (history), and place (geography) and social context (culture) all matter greatly in talking about ICTs" (2014, 22). We can apply Reed's thinking to our understanding of reality television. To some degree, we can use reality television as Andrejevic suggests to screen out the amount of information that overwhelms us, and we can appreciate this genre of television, providing we view it through the lens of culture, geography, and history. MTV's *Teen Mom* would mean little and provide poor understanding of U.S. sex and maturity issues to unwed mothers in Asia, while *Wipeout* might be highly relevant to Japanese game show enthusiasts. Reality television can be relevant and effective, and, alternately, it can be misleading or puzzling.

While reality programming is likely to be a larger part of the entertainment marketplace and the mix of global Web programming, the fear that such programming will be mistaken for competent information and an actual form of reality suggests society should take a cautious approach to such programming and recognize its marketplace, simulating, hegemonic, cultural origins. If we understand it in these contexts, it becomes less monolithic, less unassailable, more entertaining, and less likely to be confused with our often momentary and fictive grasp of the real.

> *The sky above the port was the color of television, turned to a dead channel.*
> —William Gibson, *Neuromancer*

Further Reading

Mark Andrejevic, *Infoglut*, 2013; Michael Benedikt, ed., *Cyberspace, First Steps*, 1994; William Gibson, "Neuromancer," in *Storming the Reality Studio* (Larry McCaffery, ed.), 1991; T. V. Reed, *Digitized Lives*, 2014.

Bibliography

Abend-David, Dror. "Reality vs. Reality-TV: TV News Coverage in Israeli Media at the Time of Reality TV." In *Reality TV: Merging the Global and the Local*. New York: Nova Science Publishers, 2010.

Adalian, Josef. "MTV Bringing Back *Punk'd*, with Host Justin Bieber." Vulture.com, October 5, 2010.

Adelson, Betty. *The Lives of Dwarfs: Their Journey from Public Curiosity toward Social Liberation*. New Brunswick, NJ: Rutgers UP, 2005.

Adler, Richard. *Television as a Cultural Force*. Santa Barbara, CA: Praeger, 1976.

Adorno, Theodor. *The Culture Industry*. London: Routledge, 2005.

Aho, Tanya. "Juno for Real: Negotiating Teenage Sexuality, Pregnancy, and Love in MTV's 16 and Pregnant and Teen Mom." In *Television and the Self*. Edited by Kathleen Ryan and Deborah Macey. Lanham, MD: Lexington Books, 2013.

Albiniak, Paige. "Mister Lonely." *New York Post,* January 20, 2008.

Albon, Joan. *Little People in America: The Social Dimension of Dwarfism*. Santa Barbara, CA: Praeger, 1985.

Alley-Young, Gordon. "Bigger, Fatter, Gypsier: Gender Spectacles and Cultural Frontlines in *My Big Fat American Gypsy Wedding*." In *Reality Television: Oddities of Culture*. Edited by Allison F. Slade, Amber J. Narro, and Burton P. Buchanan. Lanham, MD: Lexington Books, 2014.

Andrejevic, Mark. *Infoglut*. New York: Routledge, 2013.

Andrejevic, Mark. *Reality TV: The Work of Being Watched*. London: Rowman and Littlefield Publishers, Inc., 2004.

Andrejevic, Mark. "Visceral Literacy, Reality TV, Savvy Viewers, and Auto-Spies." In *Reality TV: Remaking Television Culture*. Edited by Susan Murray and Laurie Ouellette. New York: New York University Press, 2009.

Arellano, Jennifer. "Queer Eye for the Straight Guy Reunion: The Fab Five's Legacy." *Entertainment Weekly*, October 20, 2013.

Austen, Jane. *Pride and Prejudice*. London: RD Bentley, 1853.

Bailey, Hannah, and Renhard, James. "The Day I Interviewed Rob Dyrdek." *Behance*, March 27, 2015.

Bakhtn, Mikhail. "Carnival and Carnivalesque." In *Culture Theory and Popular Culture*. Edited by John Storey. Athens: University of Georgia Press, 1998.

Baudrillard, Jean. "The Automation of the Robot." In *Storming the Reality Studio*. Edited by Larry McCaffery, 178–181. Durham, NC: Duke University Press, 1991.

Baudrillard, Jean. "Simulacra and Simulations." In *Modernism/Postmodernism*. Edited by Peter Brooker. Harrow, England: Longman, 1992.

BBC. "Zambian Prostitutes in Marriage Appeal on Reality TV." *BBC News*. BBC.com, July 14, 2011.

Berger, John. *Ways of Seeing*. New York: Penguin Books, 1990.

Bernstein, William J. *Masters of the Word, How Media Shaped History from the Alphabet to the Internet.* New York: Grove Press, 2013.

Biressi, Anita, and Heather Nunn. *Reality TV, Realism and Revelation.* London: Wallflower Press, 2005.

Bourdain, Anthony. *Medium Raw: A Bloody Valentine to the World of Food and the People Who Cook.* New York: Ecco Books, 2011.

Bourdain, Anthony. "Under the Volcano." Tumblr Blog post, May 3, 2014.

Brecht, Bertolt. *Brecht on Theatre.* Edited by John Willett. New York: Hill and Wang. 1992.

Bricklin, Julia. "Why We Need MTV's '16 and Pregnant.'" *Forbes,* May 30, 2012.

Brodie, Richard. *Virus of the Mind.* Carlsbad, CA: Hay House, 1997.

Brooker, Peter. *Modernism/Postmodernism.* Harrow, England: Longman, 1992.

Brophy-Baermann, Michelle. "True Love on TV: A Gendered Analysis of Reality-Romance Television." *Poroi* 2, no. 4 (2005): 17–51.

Callahan, Maureen. "The Brutal Secrets Behind 'The Biggest Loser.'" *New York Post,* January 18, 2015.

Carpentier, Megan. "Here Comes Honey Boo Boo's Surprising Home-Truth." *The Guardian,* August 13, 2012.

Carr, Nicholas. *The Shallows.* New York: Norton and Co., 2011.

Chalaby, Jean K. "Broadcasting in a Post-National Environment: The Rise of Transnational TV Groups." *Critical Studies in Television* 4, no. 1 (2009): 39–64.

Clarkson, Jeremy. "Make No Mistake, Lives Were at Risk." *Sunday Times* (London), October 4, 2014.

Connor, Steven. *Postmodernist Culture.* Cambridge, MA: Blackwell, 1996.

Corner, John. "Performing the Real." *Television & New Media* 3, no. 3: 255–269.

Couldry, Nick. "Teaching Us to Fake It." In *Reality TV.* Edited by Susan Murray and Laurie Ouellette, 82–99. New York: NYU Press, 2009.

Cox, Ana Marie. "Sweet 16 and Spoiled Rotten." *Time Magazine,* April 16, 2006.

Cullen, Jim, ed. *Popular Culture in American History.* West Sussex, England: Wiley-Blackwell, 2013.

Currell, Susan. *American Culture in the 1920s.* Edinburgh, Scotland: Edinburgh UP, 2009.

Defino, Daniel J. *The HBO Effect.* New York: Bloomsbury Academic, 2014.

DeVolld, Troy. *Reality TV: An Insider's Guide to TV's Hottest Market.* Studio City, CA: Michael Wiese Productions, 2013.

Dijck, José van. *The Culture of Connectivity.* Oxford: Oxford University Press, 2013.

Dockterman, Elana. "Does *16 and Pregnant* Prevent or Promote Teen Pregnancy?" *Time Magazine,* January 13, 2014.

Dubrofsky, Rachel. *The Surveillance of Women on Reality Television.* Lanham, MD, Lexington Books, 2011.

Duca, Lauren. "What It's Really Like to Get Extreme Plastic Surgery from a Former 'Swan' Contestant. *Huffington Post,* October 27, 2014.

Eco, Umberto. *Adventures in Hyperreality.* Translated by William Weaver. New York: Harvest Books (Harcourt Brace), 1986.

Edwards, Leigh H. *The Triumph of Reality TV: The Revolution in American Television.* Santa Barbara, CA: Praeger, 2013.

Enlow, Courtney. "Let's Look Back at *Singled Out,* The Best Dating Show Ever." VH1.com, April 30, 2015.

Escoffery, David S. *How Real Is Reality TV?* Jefferson, NC: McFarland & Co. Inc., 2006.

Essany, Michael. *Reality Check: The Business and Art of Producing Reality TV*. Amsterdam: Elsevier/Focal Press, 2008.

Foss, Paula S. "Television as Cultural Document: Promises and Problems." In *Television as a Cultural Force*. Edited by Richard Adler, 37–57. Santa Barbara, CA: Praeger, 1976.

Fox, Margalit. "Jim Lange, 81, Genial Host of the *Dating Game*, Is Dead." *New York Times,* February 18, 2014.

Fretts, Bruce. "The 60 Greatest Game Shows of All Time." *TV Guide*, June 12, 2013.

Gabler, Neil. *Life: The Movie: How Entertainment Conquered Reality*. New York: Vintage Press, 2000.

Gay, Roxane. "The Marriage Plot." *New York Times*, May 10, 2014.

Ghahremani, Tanya. "The 15 Most Ridiculous Dating Shows." *Complex*, July 12, 2012.

Goodspeed, Michael. "The Cultural Plague of Reality TV." Rense.com, April 15, 2004.

Gray, Jonathan. "Cinderella Burps." In *Reality TV: Remaking Television Culture*. Edited by Susan Murray and Laurie Ouellette, 260–277. New York: New York University Press, 2009.

Hale, Mike. "There's Always a Catch." *The New York Times*, November 12, 2012.

Hall, Stuart. "Encoding/Decoding." In *Media Studies: A Reader.* Edited by Paul Marris and Sue Thornton, 51–61. New York: New York University Press, 2000.

Hart-Davis, Adam. *History from the Dawn of Civilization to the Present Day*. New York: DK Publishing, 2012.

Havrilesky, Heather. "Three Cheers for Reality TV." *Salon*, September 13, 2004.

Hearn, Alison. "Hoaxing the Real: The Metanarrative of Reality Television." In *Reality TV: Remaking Television Culture*. Edited by Susan Murray and Laurie Ouellette, 165–178. New York: New York University Press, 2009.

Hedegaard, Erik. "Snooki: America's Number One Party Girl." *Rolling Stone*, March 17, 2011.

Heffernan, Virginia. "The Ring Cycle, Heartbreak on Fox's Married by America." *Slate,* April 15, 2003.

Heller, Dana. "Wrecked." In *Reality Gendervision: Reality and Gender in Transatlantic Reality Television*. Edited by Brenda Weber. Durham, NC: Duke University Press, 2014.

Hendershot, Heather. "Belabored Reality: Making It Work on *The Simple Life* and *Project Runway*." In *Reality TV: Remaking Television Culture*. Edited by Susan Murray and Laurie Ouellette, 243–259. New York: New York University Press, 2009.

Henricy, Shana. "The Cutting Room: Gendered American Dreams on Plastic Surgery TV." In *How Real Is Reality TV?* Edited by David Escoffery, 149–166. Jefferson, NC: McFarland, 2006.

Hernandez, Leandra "I Was Born This Way: Performance and Production of Masculinity in A&E's *Duck Dynasty*." In *Reality Television: Oddities of Culture*. Edited by Allison Slade, Amber J. Narro, and Burton P. Buchanan, Burton P., 21–37. Lanham, MD: Lexington Books, 2014.

Hersch, Patricia. *A Tribe Apart*. New York: Random House, 1999.

Hill, Annette. *Reality TV, Audience and Popular Factual Television*. London: Routledge, 2005.

Hilmes, Michele. *The Television History Book*. London: The British Film Institute, 2004.

Hirsch, Jennifer, and Holly Wardlow. *Modern Loves*. Ann Arbor: University of Michigan Press, 2006.

Hollinger, Veronica. "Cybernetic Deconstructions: Cyberpunk and Postmodernism." In *Storming the Reality Studio*. Edited by Larry McCaffery, 203–207. Durham, NC: Duke University Press, 1991.

Holmes, Su, and Deborah Jermyn. "The 'Pig,' the 'Older Woman,' and the 'Catfight': Gender, Celebrity, and Controversy in a Decade of British Reality TV." In *Reality Gendervision: Reality and Gender in Transatlantic Reality Television*. Edited by Brenda Weber, 37–53. Durham, NC: Duke University Press, 2014.

Holmes, Su, and Deborah Jermyn. *Understanding Reality Television*. London: Routledge, 2004.

Huff, Richard M. *Reality Television*. Westport, CT: Praeger, 2006.

Hutcheon, Linda. *The Politics of Postmodernism*. 2nd ed. New York: Routledge, 2002.

IMDB. "Little People, Big World." Plot Summary. http://www.imdb.com/title/tt0782374/?ref_=nv_sr_1.

Jenkins, Henry. "Buying into *American Idol*: How We Are Being Sold on Reality Television." In *Convergence Culture: Where Old and New Media Collide*. By Henry Jenkins, 59–92. New York, New York University Press, 2006.

Jessop, Alicia. "Rob Dyrdek Expands His Entrepreneurial Reach to the Largest Winning Purse in Skateboarding History." *Forbes*, August 24, 2012.

"Joel Osteen Tells Larry King ' Scripture Says Homosexuality Is a Sin … But I Don't Want to Preach About It." *Huffington Post,* January 23, 2014.

Johnston, Elizabeth. "How Women Really Are." In *How Real Is Reality TV?* Edited by David S. Escoffery, 115–132. Jefferson, NC: McFarland & Co. Inc., 2006.

Kaplan, Don. "Why the BBC's Top Gear May Be the Coolest Thing on Television." *New York Daily News*, August 28, 2013.

Kavka, Misha. *Reality TV*. Edinburgh, Scotland: Edinburgh University Press, 2012.

Kavka, Misha. "Reality TV and the Gendered Politics of Faunting." In *Reality Gendervision: Reality and Gender in Transatlantic Reality Television*. Edited by Brenda Weber, 54–75. Durham, NC: Duke University Press, 2014.

Kellner, Douglas. "Critical Perspectives on Television from the Frankfurt School to Postmodernism." In *A Companion to Television*. Edited by Janet Wasko, 29–50. Chichester, West Sussex: Blackwell Publishing, 2010.

Kiesler, Sara. *Culture of the Internet*. Mahwah, NJ: Lawrence Erlbaum, 1997.

King, Barry. "Training Camps of the Modular: Reality TV as a Form of Life." In *How Real Is Reality TV?* Edited by David Escoffery. Jefferson, NC: McFarland, 2006.

Klein, Amanda. "Abject Femininity and Compulsory Masculinity on *Jersey Shore*." In *Reality Gendervision*. Edited by Brenda Weber, 149–169. Durham, NC: Duke University Press, 2014.

Kompare, Derek. "Extraordinarily Ordinary: The Osbournes as 'an American Family.'" In *Reality TV: Remaking Television Culture*. 2nd ed. Edited by Susan Murray and Laurie Ouellette, 100–122. New York: New York University Press, 2009.

Koren, Yehuda, and Eilat Negev. *In Our Hearts We Were Giants: The Remarkable Story of the Lilliput Troupe, a Dwarf Family's Survival of the Holocaust*. Boston: Da Capo Press, 2005.

Kristiva, Julia. "Postmodernism." In *Modernism/Postmodernism*. Edited by Peter Brooker, 196–203. Harlow, Essex, England: Longman, 1992.

Lawson, Mark. "Ten Years of *The X-Factor*, the Show-off Show with a Talent for Survival." *The Guardian*, August 29, 2014.

Lefferts, Daniel. "Rob Dyrdek Gets Renewals, Pilot in MTV Deal: *Fantasy Factory, Ridiculousness* Renewed for 7th Seasons." *Adweek*, June 25, 2014.

Lenthall, Bruce. *Radio's America*. Eugene: University of Oregon Press, 2007.

Luther, Jennifer. "Beyond Bodice Rippers: How Romance Novels Came to Embrace Feminism." *Atlantic Monthly*, March 18, 2013.

Malykhina, Elena. "Fact or Fiction?: Video Games Are the Future of Education." *Scientific American*, September 12, 2014.

McCarthy, Anna. "Stanley Milgram, Allen Funt and Me: Postwar Social Science and the 'First Wave' of Reality TV." In *Reality TV: Remaking Television Culture*. Edited by Susan Murray and Laurie Ouellette. New York: New York University Press, 2009.

McClain, Amanda Scheiner. *Keeping Up the Kardashian Brand: Celebrity, Materialism, and Sexuality*. Lanham, MD: Lexington Books, 2013.

McGuire, Caroline. "'It's Not Complicated, You Got Caught with Numerous Men:' Cheaters Who Are Exposed by Their Partners in Hilarious Facebook Status Updates Revealed." *The Daily Mail* (UK), May 5, 2015.

Meighan, Cate. "'Basketball Wives: LA' Star Gloria Govan Reportedly Admitted to Forging Husband Matt Barnes' Signature to Secure $150K Loan." *Music Times,* October 16, 2014.

Mittell, Jason. *Genre and Television*. New York: Routledge, 2004.

Mittell, Jason. *Television and American Culture*. New York: Oxford University Press, 2010.

Mohsin, Salma, and Katie Hunt. "Pakistan TV Show Hosted by Aamir Liaquat Hussain Gives Away Babies to Audience." CNN.com, July 31, 2013.

Morris, Pamela L., and Charissa K. Niedzwiecki. "Odd or Ordinary: Social Comparisons Between Real and Reality TV Families." In *Reality Television: Oddities of Culture*. Edited by Allison Slade, Amber Narro, and Burton P. Buchanan. New York: Lexington Books, 2014.

Morrissey, Tracie Egan. "VH1 Scrambles to Distance Itself from Reality Star, Murder Suspect." *Jezebel*, August 19, 2009.

Munson, Wayne. *All Talk: The Talk Show in Media Culture*. Philadelphia: Temple University Press, 1993.

Murray, Susan, and Laurie Ouellette. *Reality TV: Remaking Television Culture*. 2nd ed. New York: New York University Press, 2009.

Nededog, Jethro. "MTV's New Dating Show Proves You Shouldn't Social Everything." *The Wrap*, September 17, 2013.

Nededog, Jethro. "*Queer Eye*'s Jai Rodriquez Confesses 'I Was Not the Puerto Rican Emily Post.'" *The Wrap*, October 18, 2013.

Nelson, Steve. "'Sister Wives' Defeat Polygamy Law in Federal Court," *U.S. News & World Report,* December 16, 2013

Niklas, Rose. *Governing the Soul: The Shaping of the Private Self*. London: Free Association Books,1999.

O'Donnell, Virginia. *Television Criticism*. Los Angeles: Sage Publications, 2007.

Ogunnaike, Lola. "MTV's 'Super Sweet 16' Gives a Sour Pleasure." *New York Times*, April 27, 2006.

Orbuch, Terri. "How Real Is Reality TV's Love and Courtship? Reflections on *The Bachelorette*." *Huffington Post*, July 22, 2011.

Ouellette, Laurie, and Hay, James. *Better Living Through Reality TV: Television and Post-Welfare Citizenship*. West Sussex, England: Wiley Blackwell Publishing, 2008.

Parry, Wayne. "Poll: 'Jersey Shore' Not Hurting New Jersey Image." *USA Today*, July 18, 2011.

Perry, Pat. "The Dating Game." *The News Herald,* January 30, 2016.

Persad, Michelle. "Stacy London Can Tell You More Than Just What Not to Wear." *Huffington Post*, January 22, 2015.

Petersen, Anne Helen. "*Entertainment Tonight*: Tabloid News." In *How to Watch Television*. Edited by Ethan Thompson and Jason Mittell, 235–243. New York: New York University Press, 2013.

Pozner, Jennifer L. *Reality Bites Back: The Troubling Truth about Guilty Pleasure TV*. Berkeley, CA: Seal Press, 2010.

Pramaggiore, Maria, and Diane Negra. "Keeping Up with the Aspirations: Commercial Family Values and the Kardashian Brand." In *Reality Gendervision: Reality and Gender in Transatlantic Reality Television*. Edited by Brenda Weber, 76–96. Durham, NC: Duke University Press, 2014.

Quinlan, Christine. "The Double Life of Bravo's New Top Chef." *Food & Wine Magazine*, April 2010: 40, 42+.

Raftery, Brian. "Why *America's Funniest Home Videos* Won't Die." *Wired Magazine*, April 13, 2011.

Reed, T. V. *Digitized Lives*. New York: Routledge, 2014.

Rose, Deborah Byrd, and Richard Davis. *Dislocating the Frontier*. Canberra, Australia: ANU Press, 2006.

Rose, Niklas. *Governing the Soul*. London: Routledge, 1990.

Rosenberg Leah. "The Way We Were: Ritual, Memory and Television." In *Television and the Self: Knowledge, Identity, and Media Representation*. Edited by Kathleen Ryan and Deborah Macey, 11–26. Lanham, MD: Lexington Books, 2013.

Rothman, Michael. "Bill Rancic: How My Life Has Changed Since I Asked Giuliana to Marry Me." *ABC News*, December 15, 2014.

Roush, Wade. "Broadcast Your Life Online, 24–7." *MIT Technology Review*, May 25, 2007.

Sachs, Andrea. "Reality TV's *Cake Boss* Shows Off His Bakery and His Hometown, Hoboken, N.J." *The Washington Post*, March 14, 2010.

Schuld-Ergil, Andrea. "Playing with Hooks: Neo-Tribal Style, Commodification and Resistance." *How Real Is Reality TV?* Edited by David Escoffery, 167–179. Jefferson, NC: McFarland & Co. Inc., 2006.

Schulte, Stephanie. *Cached*. New York: New York University Press, 2013.

Sender, Katherine. *The Makeover*. New York: New York University Press, 2012.

Shifman, Limor. *Memes in Digital Culture*. Cambridge, MA: MIT Press, 2014.

Shorter, Edward. *Written in the Flesh: A History of Desire*. Toronto: Toronto University Press, 2005.

Sieczkowski, Cavan. "'Duck Dynasty' Star Phil Robertson Makes Anti-Gay Remarks, Says Being Gay Is a Sin." *Huffington Post*, February 2, 2016.

Sieczkowski, Cavan. "HGTV Drops Benham Brothers' 'Flip It Forward' after Anti-Gay Views Are Unearthed." *Huffington Post*, February 2, 2016.

Sieczkowski, Cavan. "Thousands Sign Petition to Cancel TLC's *19 Kids and Counting* over Stars' Anti-LGBT Sentiments." *Huffington Post*, November 19, 2014.

Slade, Allison F., Amber J. Narro, and Burton P. Buchanan. *Reality TV: Oddities of Culture*. Lanham, MD: Lexington Books, 2014.

Sobraske, Katherine Hanson, James S. Boster, and Steven J. Gaulin. "Mapping the Conceptual Space of Jealousy." *Ethos* 41, no. 3 (2013): 249–270.

Solomon, Benjamin. "A Complete History of MTV's Dating Game Shows." *The datereport.com*, Novemer 12, 2013.

Tannenbaum, Rob, and Craig Marks. *I Want My MTV*. New York: Penguin, 2011.

Taylor, Victoria. "MTV's '16 and Pregnant' and 'Teen Mom' Discouraging Teen Pregnancy: Study." *New York Daily News*, January 14, 2014.

Teachout, Terry. "Television/Radio Looking for Your 15 Minutes? All You Need Is Infidelity." *New York Times*, July 21, 2002.

Thielman, Sam. "Dragons, Nipples, and Technology: Why the Real Mad Men Are on the Run." *The Guardian,* May 15, 2015.

Thompson, Ethan, and Jason Mittell. *How to Watch Television*. New York: New York University Press, 2013.

Timmons, Heather. "In India, Reality TV Catches On, with Some Qualms." *The New York Times*, January 9, 2001.

Travers, Ben. "Are There Too Many TV Shows? With 350 Debuting This Year, Some Say, 'Yes.'" *Indiewire,* June 11, 2014.

Watts, Amber. "Melancholy, Merit, and Merchandise: The Postwar Audience Participation Show." In *Reality TV: Remaking Television Culture*. Edited by Susan Murray and Laurie Ouellette, 301–320. New York: New York University Press, 2008.

Weber, Brenda R. "From All-American Mom to Super Bitch from Hell: Kate Gosselin and the Classed and Gendered Politics of Reality Celebrity." In *Reality Television and Class*. Edited by Helen Wood and Beverly Skaggs, 156–168. London: Palgrave/Macmillan /BFI, 2011.

Weber, Kerry. "The Perfect Fit." *America,* June 17, 2013: 34.

Wellesley College. "New Study Finds MTV's '16 and Pregnant,' 'Teen Mom' Contributed to Record Decline in U.S. Teen Childbearing Rate." *Science Daily*, January 13, 2014.

Wilkins, Emily. "Texas A & M Student Pushing for Respect for Dwarfism Awareness Month." *The Eagle,* October 5, 2014.

Wissick, Joe. "End LGBTQ Fear Mongering by the Duggars." Change.org, n.d.

Wood, Helen, and Beverly Skaggs, eds. *Reality Television and Class*. London: Palgrave/ Macmillan/BFI, 2011.

Wood, Peter. "Television as Dream." In *Television as a Cultural Force*. Edited by Richard Adler and Douglas Cater. Santa Barbara, CA: 1976.

Yarrow, Allison. "*Here Comes Honey Boo Boo* Is a Fabulous Cultural Ambassador for America." *Atlantic Monthly*, May 22, 2013.

Index

Page numbers in **bold** indicate the location of main entries.

About the Author

Stuart Lenig, MFA, PhD, is a coordinator of humanities and full professor of media studies at Columbia State Community College, where he organizes and facilitates the humanities lecture series, sponsors a wide range of student activities, and develops new curriculum to provide new opportunities for students in the arts and humanities. Interests include global cultures, emerging media, and mobile aesthetic tech.

About the Contributor

Liz Hufford is the published author of poems, articles, essays, and short stories. She was one of four finalists for the 2017 Roswell Award for Short Science Fiction.